"Was deutsch und echt …": Richard Wagner and the Articulation of a German Opera, 1798–1876

National Cultivation of Culture

Edited by

Joep Leerssen (*University of Amsterdam*)

Editorial Board

John Breuilly – Katharine Ellis – Ina Ferris
Patrick J. Geary – Tom Shippey – Anne-Marie Thiesse

VOLUME 17

The titles published in this series are listed at *brill.com/ncc*

"Was deutsch und echt ..."

Richard Wagner and the Articulation of a German Opera, 1798–1876

By

Kasper van Kooten

BRILL

LEIDEN | BOSTON

Cover illustration: Ernst Benedikt Kietz, *Wagner Caricature*, 1840–1841, Paris. (© Richard-Wagner-Nationalarchiv und Richard-Wagner-Gedenkstätte, Bayreuth).

Library of Congress Cataloging-in-Publication Data

Names: Kooten, Kasper van, 1971- author.
Title: Was deutsch und echt... : Richard Wagner and the articulation of a
   German opera, 1798-1876 / by Kasper van Kooten.
Description: Leiden, The Netherlands : Brill, [2019] | Series: National
   cultivation of culture | Includes bibliographical references and index.
Identifiers: LCCN 2019003724 (print) | LCCN 2019004564 (ebook) | ISBN
   9789004245389 (ebook) | ISBN 9789004206816 (hardback : alk. paper)
Subjects: LCSH: Opera--Germany--19th century. | Wagner, Richard,
   1813-1883--Criticism and interpretation.
Classification: LCC ML1729.4 (ebook) | LCC ML1729.4 .K66 2019 (print) | DDC
   782.10943/09034--dc23
LC record available at https://lccn.loc.gov/2019003724

Typeface for the Latin, Greek, and Cyrillic scripts: "Brill". See and download: brill.com/brill-typeface.

ISSN 1876-5645
ISBN 978-90-04-20681-6 (hardback)
ISBN 978-90-04-24538-9 (e-book)

Contents

Acknowledgments

This book is the result of a PhD research project started in 2012 at the University of Amsterdam and finalized and defended in 2016. But the thread goes further back. It is also the result of my parents' stimulation to pursue my musical interests, and of the formative experience of playing the violin in a high school performance of Mozart's *Zauberflöte* that made me decide to study Musicology. I should thank all professors who fueled my enthusiasm and expanded my knowledge of music and culture throughout my studies, from the University of Amsterdam (Eddie Vetter, Sabine Lichtenstein, Jacques Boogaart, Rokus de Groot), and the Conservatory of Amsterdam (Michiel Schuijer, Willem Woestenburg, and Menno Dekker), to the Freie Universität Berlin (Bodo Bischoff and Jürgen Maehder). I must also express my gratitude to my supervisors, Joep Leerssen and Krisztina Lajosi, as well as the members of my assessment committee – Katharine Ellis, Kati Röttger, Barbara Titus, Anno Mungen, and Michael Wintle – for their valuable feedback from which this revised commercial edition has benefitted. It is sad that I am no longer able to personally express my gratitude to a great mentor, the late John Neubauer. I had the privilege to meet this authority on Romanticism, literature and music several times and I am grateful for his willingness to review parts of my dissertation. His gentle and acute spirit has found its way into this book, and I feel honored that it will be released in Brill's National Cultivation of Culture series, to which Mr. Neubauer has dedicated so much intellectual energy, including his last book, The *Persistence of Voice*.

I'd like to thank Wendel Scholma, Irene Jager and Kavya Natesan from Brill Publishers for their assistance in the coming together of this publication. Several other institutions and individuals should also be acknowledged, such as the *Royal Netherlands Academy of Arts and Sciences* that funded my research project, the Richard-Wagner-Nationalarchiv und Richard-Wagner-Gedenkstätte Bayreuth, and the Staatliche Museen zu Berlin for their permission to use illustrations, as well as Tobias de Haas for drafting the music examples. I would also like to thank several dear former University of Amsterdam colleagues, such as Wouter Capitain, Rutger Helmers, Julia Kursell, and Alexander Jackob. After having left the University in 2017, I feel blessed to have found a new place where quality, beauty and human beings still matter among my colleagues at the classical music label PENTATONE.

Outside my professional environment, I like to express my appreciation for the support offered by friends such as Djuro Leideritz and Vincent Dijkema, as well as my mother Edith van Eck and brother Boris van Kooten, and father- and mother-in-law Paul van Woerden and Rikie Oosterhuis. I cannot thank my better half Anneke enough for her patience and love, and for her ability to turn me into a more confident, steady and enjoyable human being. Together with our cats Flärke and Gonzo, she has made my life much brighter than it was before.

I dedicate this book – that feels like the summation of the passions and interests of my youth – to the loving memory of Hans Vroom, with whom I have shared so many meaningful musical and cultural experiences, but who unfortunately did not live to see its completion.

Figures

Abbreviations

AMZ   (Leipziger) Allgemeine musikalische Zeitung

BAMZ Berliner Allgemeine musikalische Zeitung

NZfM   Neue Zeitschrift für Musik

QMMR The Quarterly Musical Magazine & Review

WWSB Wagner, Werke, Schrifte und Briefe (Edited by Sven Friedrich, Berlin: Digitale Bibliothek, Directmedia Publishing GmbH, 2004)

Introduction

"Was deutsch und echt, wüsst' keiner mehr, / lebt's nicht in deutscher Meister Ehr,"[1] Hans Sachs sings in his notorious closing monologue of Richard Wagner's *Die Meistersinger von Nürnberg* (1868). Sachs's monologue is concerned with the danger of cultural alienation, and epitomizes the janus-faced nature of nineteenth-century German cultural nationalism. It can positively be interpreted as a plea for confidence, a belief in the values of one's own culture. At the same time, it signals a degree of cultural, if not ethnic xenophobia. Disregarding the slightly apocalyptic worldview in which Wagner's Sachs frames his plea for the glorification of German musical masters, the question "what is German and true" in music has been on the agenda of many nineteenth-century thinkers. Particularly in the discourse surrounding opera, the articulation of an opera congenial to a presupposed German national identity has been a concern to many, and resulted in a wide array of answers to the question what is German and true about German opera and how it could potentially become even more German and more truthful in the future. It is the wide array of answers and approaches to this question attended in German nineteenth-century music discourse that has inspired me to write this book.

By focusing on German nineteenth-century opera, this book aims to contribute to two scholarly fields: the comparative study of national opera in a transnational European context, as well as the investigation of the relation between German music culture and national identity formation in the 19th century. In both fields, attention for German opera has been limited. A more thorough understanding of German opera's entanglement with national identity formation requires both musical and contextual knowledge. This book, in providing both, highlights the importance of German opera for both musical and political history. It also enriches our understanding of national opera as a transnational, European phenomenon, and of the complex relationship between music and national thought in German nineteenth-century culture.

What makes German music special within the trans-European, nineteenth-century phenomenon of "musical nationalism"? Arguably its presupposed neutrality. In diverse manifestations of national music, German music – think of Beethoven's symphonies – often served as a norm, from which "national" composers at the margins of the European musical world deviated, for example by incorporating folkloric elements or by writing tone poems about national

---

1 "What is German and true no one would know, / if we would not honor our German Masters."

© KONINKLIJKE BRILL NV, LEIDEN, 2019 | DOI:10.1163/9789004245389_002

landscapes and heroes. In comparison, a Beethoven symphony calls up less "national" associations. We tend to perceive it as an abstract play of forms, and if Beethoven's music addresses a community, it must be all mankind: "Alle Menschen werden Brüder!"

Despite the universal appeal that is frequently associated with Beethoven and other German composers, music contributed considerably to the formation of a German national conscience. In fact, the universal significance that many nineteenth-century Germans attributed to music was actually an expression of chauvinism, based on the belief in an exclusive German capacity to address universal themes and compose universal music. This German perspective on music has proven persistent to this day, even beyond the German-speaking world.[2] A quick look at the common canon of classical music reveals the predominance of German composers; Bach, Mozart, and Beethoven constitute the holy trinity, while prominent places are occupied by artists like Haydn, Schubert, Mendelssohn, Brahms, and maybe Wagner and Mahler.

Another striking aspect of this list of canonic composers must be that these men chiefly made their mark in instrumental genres, such as symphonies, sonatas, and string quartets. This emphasizes another remarkable trait of a German musical identity: the idea that Germans excel in instrumental genres, and that the complexity and serious nature of these genres pertains to the German spirit. Church music composition equally conforms to the ideals of complexity and seriousness, but opera?

These general observations raise several questions, questions that are central to this book. How, for example, should we approach and value the hidden chauvinist agenda behind so many ideas about German music that we normally take for granted? What consequences does this covert ideology have for the way we see and study German nineteenth-century opera? And how did perceptions of German national identity and music affect opera makers during that period?

In scholarship, the persistence of nineteenth-century beliefs about the supremacy of German music up until the postwar period has been dealt with in at least three ways. From the 1980s onwards, American scholars such as Joseph Kerman, Philipp Gossett, James Hepokoski, and Richard Taruskin began challenging the chauvinist assumptions of a Germanocentric historiography that chiefly served, in Kerman's words, to vindicate "the overriding aesthetic value of the instrumental music of the great German tradition."[3] Their resistance to

---

2   Meirion Hughes and Robert Stradling, for example, argue that the domination of German music still forms "one of the most resilient hegemonic *blocs* of modern times – resembling, in broad anthropological terms, one of the great world religions." Hughes 2001: 156.

3   Kerman 1980: 313–314.

this historiography was fueled by the fact that it governed not only German musicology, but also their own traditions.[4] This critical first wave incited a second approach, as it spurred cultural historians such as Celia Applegate to recognize the potential of nineteenth-century music discourse as a way to interpret the complex nature of German nationalism in this period.[5]

In the 1990s, a third current in dealing with the entanglement of music and German national thought occurred, when German musicologists such as Sieghart Döhring, Sabine Henze-Döhring, Anselm Gerhard, and Anno Mungen attempted to come clean with the problematic ideology behind their domestic musicological traditions.[6] Their approach was twofold. On the one hand, they defended Carl Dahlhaus, the most prominent representative of post-war German musicology, against accusations of national bias formulated by Gossett and Hepokoski.[7] On the other, they strove to correct the chauvinist historiography of German opera. A first strategy was to rehabilitate cosmopolitan composers such as Meyerbeer and Spontini, who had been cold-shouldered by their German contemporaries and by German opera historiography in general. Besides, the formal regularity and innovative power of French and Italian opera and the significance of cultural transfers between these traditions were praised, countering negative conceptions of foreign opera that had previously dominated German musicology. In line with this embrace of foreign opera and internationalism, Döhring and Henze-Döhring characterize German opera between Mozart and Wagner as "unoriginal," a mere "cultural import," and conclude that "the traditional German conception of the historical development of opera is diametrically opposed to the contemporary music-theatrical situation."[8]

It appears that there is a double standard at work in this reproaching attitude towards nineteenth-century German opera production and its discourse,

---

4 See Kerman 1980, Gossett 1989, Hepokoski 1991, and Taruskin, Richard. Lemma 'National-ism' on *oxfordmusiconline.com*, consulted on 12 November 2015. The immense influence of nineteenth-century German music esthetics on post-WWII American music theory is partly caused by the many Jewish-German and -Austrian *emigré* musicians who fled the Third Reich, but disseminated the belief in the superiority of German instrumental music and its analytical methods through American music institutions. Chief examples are Arnold Schön-berg and Felix Salzer.

5 See Applegate 1992, but also Pederson 1994 and Rumph 1995.

6 See Gerhard 1992, Mungen 1995 and 1997, and Döhring 1997.

7 In the introduction to *Oper und Musikdrama im 19. Jahrhundert* (1997), Döhring and Hen-ze-Döhring brush aside Hepokoski's notion of Dahlhaus's "German-based musicological practice" as "nothing but a pipe dream [*Chimäre*]." Döhring 1997: 2.

8 Döhring 1997: 5. A similar attitude can be witnessed in the contributions of Eberhard Kremtz and Anno Mungen to the volume *Die Dresdener Oper im 19. Jahrhundert* (1995). See Kremtz 1995A , Kremtz 1995B, and Mungen 1995.

a standard arguably taken over from Dahlhaus. In *Propagating a National Genre* (2010), Kevin Robert Burke points out that Dahlhaus "attempts to separate the genre from the serious, intellectual German music tradition he admired," by putting opera in the music-as-event rather than the more elevated music-as-work category. As a result, "German opera [...] is conveniently absent in Dahlhaus's grand narrative of serious music."[9] From an ideological point of view, it seems as if German opera is castigated for the questionably chauvinist discourse that surrounded it, whereas instrumental music, for all that it used to be clothed in similar rhetoric, is spared such a treatment. This preferential treatment actually has a lot in common with traditional chauvinist glorifications of instrumental music of the great German tradition: a predilection for works that appear to transcend the milieu in which they originated, a dismissal of ideology as something that obfuscates a proper understanding of music history and does not really belong to it, and a rigid discrimination between good and bad works, based on an analytical method that was once developed to vindicate the former, and can therefore merely reaffirm this hierarchy.

In the case of Döhring and Henze-Döhring's *Oper im 19. Jahrhundert* (1997), we find something similar; the structural uniformity of French and Italian nineteenth-century opera grants these the status of a "tradition," whereas the eclecticism of German opera in this period renders it a haphazard bricolage. Moreover, somehow adopting the Hegelian, progress-oriented perspective that also governs Dahlhaus's general conception of music history, Döhring and Henze-Döhring scorn German early nineteenth-century opera for being style-historically insignificant, as German composers generally followed trends set elsewhere in Europe. Neither living up to the serious expectations of the "Great German tradition of instrumental music" nor complying with the formal regularity of Italian and French opera, German opera ends up in a limbo.

This impression of a limbo in which German opera resides is not restricted to music historiography in the German-speaking world. It is also noticeable, for example, in the culture-historical approach to German music culture and discourse of Applegate and like-minded scholars. These tend to focus on instrumental genres or the oratorio rather than opera.[10] Kevin Robert Burke also points out that whereas "musicological scholarship has addressed German music criticism at length over the past few decades [....], contemporary opera criticism is largely absent."[11] In many respects, German opera falls through

---

9   Burke 2010: 6.
10   See, for example, Rumph 1995, Dennis 1996, Beller-McKenna 2004, and Applegate 2005.
11   Burke 2010: 19–20. Burke lists Bonds 2006, Applegate 2005, Morrow 1997, and Pederson 1994 as examples of this phenomenon.

the cracks, a phenomenon that we will frequently revisit in this study, and which is related to what I would like to characterize as the *German Opera Problem*.[12]

1 The German Opera Problem

Although many historians have recently argued that national thought has a long history or pre-history,[13] there is relative consensus concerning the fact that nationalism as a mass movement, as potentially the most fundamental shaper of collective identity and political ideology, was chiefly a late-eighteenth-century invention that rose to prominence during the nineteenth century. Something similar applies to the phenomenon of national opera. Opera before 1800 can clearly be categorized in national styles, traditions, or schools, but the notion of a national opera as something that embodies the individual character of a nation, potentially increases a collective sense of nationality, and underlines a nation's sophistication – in short; something that all cultured nations should possess – is chiefly a nineteenth-century phenomenon. The widespread urge to establish a national opera spurred cultural transfers throughout Europe in this period, underlining the transnational nature of nationalism as a cultural phenomenon.[14]

It is particularly the element of sophistication that posed a problem to all nineteenth-century advocates of national opera, as it supposes that an artwork displays genuinely national traits while simultaneously showing a degree of cosmopolitan refinement which is inevitably derived from established foreign

---

12   This notion has been used in Carolyn Abbate and Roger Parker's *A History of Opera* (2012), where it serves as a title for the chapter on early nineteenth-century German opera. To Abbate and Parker, the "German opera problem" is related to the question "why German opera suddenly became so serious?" (Abbate 2012: 170) This issue of seriousness is certainly an element of my own definition of the *German Opera Problem*. Furthermore, it also has an academic ancestor in the form of Applegate's "German problem," which she defines as "the problem of whether one can or indeed ought to place music by Germans in a national context." (Applegate 1998: 276) Whereas Applegate's *German Problem* concerns the scholarly attitude towards nineteenth-century German music discourse, the *German Opera Problem* is itself actually one of the main concerns of this discourse, as I will demonstrate in this study.

13   Anthony D. Smith traces a long history of nationalism, whereas Leerssen discerns a prehistory of this phenomenon. See Smith 2004 and Leerssen 2006: 15.

14   This has become a topos of recent studies on cultural nationalism, formulated in the opening sentence of Anne-Marie Thiesse's *La creation des identités nationales* (1999): "There is nothing more international than the formation of national identities." Thiesse 1999: 11.

opera traditions.[15] The ideal of "cultivation"[16] so essential to nineteenth-century cultural nationalism often forced national opera creators[17] eventually to fall into the arms of those foreign models from which they had initially tried to distinguish themselves.

A comparatist perspective on the creation of and discourse surrounding national opera throughout Europe shows that there were many possible approaches to solve this problem. One could argue that in Central and Eastern Europe during the second half of the nineteenth century, arguably the heyday of national opera in those regions, the main hegemonic style from which to distinguish oneself was that of the "Great German tradition of instrumental music." Whereas in the regions under Habsburg reign, German culture was associated with an oppressive Viennese government, in Russia it was linked to the alleged "musical colonialism" of the German composer Anton Rubinstein and his German-inspired conservatory.[18] Taking the situation of Bohemia as an example, Philipp Ther argues that, generally speaking, two options were available. One could follow Wagner's model or that of a Verdian number opera.[19] That the first option was acceptable signals a fascinating late nineteenth-century ambivalence concerning Wagner's status as an opera composer, on the one hand considered a symbol of the post-1871 German triumphalism while on the other hand being too progressive and exciting to avoid.[20] The Verdian

---

15   A fascinating example of this is provided in Richard Taruskin's analysis of Glinka's *A Life for the Tsar* (1836) in the *Oxford History of Western Music* (2010), which will be discussed in Chapter 4.

16   See, for example, Joep Leerssen's *The Cultivation of Culture. Towards a Definition of Romantic Nationalism in Europe* (2005).

17   In scholarly debates concerning national opera, one of the matters in dispute is the question whether national operas are intentionally written according to a certain recipe, or whether operas merely become national through their reception (see Ther 2011, Dahlhaus 1980 and Konold 1992). When I speak of "national opera creators," I do not only mean people who write national operas (i.e. composers, librettists, etc.) but also those who, through their writing or through administrative activities, promote the rise of a native opera as a mental (tradition, a repertoire) or even concrete (a building) institution.

18   See Chapter 4.

19   Ther 2009: 104.

20   This attitude, which we also find with many French composers of that period, will be discussed in Chapter 5. With regard to composers in Central and Eastern Europe, Wagner's symbolic status as one of the torch-bearers of the ideal of program music may have mitigated his German descent. Unlike the idea of absolute music, which praises the detached, non-referential nature of instrumental music and therefore vindicates "classical" genres such as the sonata and the symphony, program music presupposes and therefore constitutes a relation between music and extra-musical phenomena, for example in a symphonic piece that expresses national themes and evokes national sentiment. Joep Leerssen also emphasizes that in many cases, "national music plays into a trend towards what became known as 'programmatic music'." (Leerssen 2014C: 616) The antagonism of

route was ideologically less ambivalent, his status as a composer of political liberation operas was arguably inspiring,[21] and his inclination towards a number opera esthetics moreover made the incorporation of demotic elements easier than with the through-composed structure of Wagner's music dramas. In sum, Central- and Eastern-European creators of national operas disposed of multiple options.

What options did German composers, librettists, and critics have when, around 1800, they launched their search for a genuinely German opera identity? In order to answer that question, traditional German attitudes towards opera should be addressed. Ever since its arrival in the German-speaking world in the course of the seventeenth century, opera faced severe criticism. John Warrack shows that as early as the late seventeenth century, the successful Hamburg opera company had been questioned by Lutheran authorities, because the obvious Italian – and therefore Catholic – character of the art form aroused suspicions of a Roman Catholic infection.[22] Gloria Flaherty mentions that Pietists went even a step further, linking the genre's name to the "work of the devil (*Teufelswerck/Opera Diabolica*)."[23] Less religiously-motivated, but similar in its rejection of opera was Johann Christoph Gottsched's dismissal of the genre as a hindrance to the development of a proper German dramatic art, as voiced in his *Versuch einer critischen Dichtkunst für die Deutschen* (1730).[24] Taken together, opera's inclination towards the lavish, the extravagant and the theatrical resulted in a frequently-attended attitude among German thinkers that can be described with Herbert Lindenberger's notion of the "antioperatic prejudice," a dismissal of the genre's theatricality and impurity.[25] The vehemence of this attitude was all the greater because this un-Protestant,

---

absolute music vs. the program music ideal of the *Neudeutsche Schule* (coinage of music historian Franz Brendel, 1859), the former often linked to Johannes Brahms, the latter to Franz Liszt, Richard Wagner, and others, has long been considered as one of the chief dynamics of nineteenth-century music. The association of the ideal of absolute music with the "Great German tradition of instrumental music," the fact that according to Pederson, "the absence of non-Germanic music in the realm of "absolute" music is hardly an accident, rather, this very concept was shaped by a new, exclusionary ideology directed at other nations," (Pederson 1994: 89) partly explains the partisanship for programmatic genres in many non-German musical cultures during the second half of the nineteenth century.

21 See, for example, Gossett 2012.
22 Warrack 2006: 43.
23 Flaherty 1981: 20–21.
24 On Gottsched's attitude towards opera see Markx 2016: 22–23, Warrack 2001: 72–75, and Flaherty 1978: 93–101.
25 See Lindenberger 1984: 197. Lindenberger takes his cue from Jonas Barish's *The Antitheatrical Prejudice* (1981), which discusses negative connotations of theatricality in Western culture. Although Barish does not restrict his analysis to German culture, Lindenberger

arguably un-German art form was highly popular, not only among the aristocracy, but also among the masses.[26]

The musicians and critics who dominated the formulation of a German national music discourse in the early nineteenth century were predominantly
middle class. These often associated opera with either a foreign, aristocratic
taste, or saw the art form as plebeian entertainment. A result of this general
inclination was that, when around 1800 "national self-searching in the realm
of music"[27] became a prominent theme in music histories, essays, and particularly in newly-founded music journals with a widespread readership,
German musical identity was often articulated as opposing the operatic. An
"ascetic"[28] esthetic was formulated, chiefly relating serious genres such as the
symphony, the sonata, the string quartet, and the oratorio to German virtues
such as "depth (*Tiefe*), hard work (*Arbeit*), thoroughness (*Gründlichkeit*), intellect (*Geist*), and inwardness (*Innerlichkeit*)."[29] Cheap sensuality and frivolity
served as the reprehensible antithesis to these ideals, and were mainly associated with Italian and, following the rise of *Grand Opéra* during the 1830s, also
increasingly with French opera.

Nineteenth-century proponents of German opera had to find their way
within this binary dynamic. In their search for a German opera identity, many
aimed for a genuinely individual opera genre, in which those ascetic German
virtues mentioned above were realized. In order to meet the demand of sophistication often deemed necessary to turn something native into something
national, many German opera makers strove for a genre that could live up to
the esthetic and moral dignity of instrumental music and the oratorio. But

---

clearly links the Antioperatic Prejudice to German attitudes towards opera, particularly
Wagner's esthetics of music drama.

26 Flaherty points out that "by the end of the seventeenth century, opera had become firmly
    established in all the German lands. It was being performed in permanent theaters, while
    spoken drama was still being presented either in makeshift structures by troupes of wan-
    dering players or in schools by young students." Flaherty 1981: 19.

27 I adopt this term from the subtitle of a collection of essays called *Deutsche Meister – böse
    Geister? Nationale Selbstfindung in der Musik* (2001), see Dannuser 2001.

28 Sanna Pederson uses this word in her discussion of Adolph Bernard Marx's musical
    esthetics. See Pederson 1994: 90.

29 This is an accumulation of labels listed in Sponheuer 2002: 40 and Hentschel 2006: 347,
    and can be revisited over and over in German nineteenth-century music discourse. Holly
    Watkins has traced the history of notions of seriousness and profoundness in German
    musical culture in *Metaphors of Depth in German Musical Thought* (2011). She shows "how
    the late eighteenth-century writings of Johann Gottfried Herder and Wilhelm Heinrich
    Wackenroder harnessed the vocabulary of depth and interiority circulating in German
    Pietism and the natural sciences in order to articulate an anti-French, anti-rationalist
    aesthetics of music" and explores "the transformation of this vocabulary" up until the
    writings of Arnold Schönberg. Watkins 2011: 16.

at the same time, they inevitably had to resort to structures and techniques derived from the well-established Italian and French opera traditions. This adoption could potentially mitigate an opera's national significance, and lead to accusations of sensuality, frivolity, triviality, or even *Ausländerei*; a neglect of one's German identity.

At the same time, in order to thrive onstage, an all too learned, or at least allegedly learned idiom could make German opera an extremely dull affair, as the young Richard Wagner concluded in *Die deutsche Oper* (1834). Yet his adolescent plea for cosmopolitanism in order to advance the cause of German opera would turn into a *Wehvolles Erbe*,[30] which he attempted to obscure later on in his career. Another potential problem was the operatic use of stories with an outspoken national-political subject. Whereas this type of stories of national crisis and heroes were a standard ingredient in the formation of many national operas elsewhere in Europe, it appears that their political nature was ill-suited to the non-political, transcendent self-identification of many German musicians and listeners. In this respect, German opera appears to present an anomaly within the Europe-wide phenomenon of nineteenth-century national opera. It is through scrutinizing this anomaly from a comparatist perspective that I simultaneously hope to contribute to a more thorough understanding of national opera as a European, transnational phenomenon.

All these considerations constitute the nucleus of the *German Opera Problem*: how to formulate a national opera identity in a music culture that in many cases was articulated in opposition to opera? This question forms a thread throughout this book, which chiefly investigates answers and solutions formulated by composers, librettists, and opera critics in a vast body of nineteenth-century music journals, as well as in the creation of operas themselves. Each of the five chapters focuses on a sub-aspect of the larger *German Opera Problem* and/or illuminates an important stage in the formulation of a German opera and its concrete realization in the form of operatic works.

2   Theory and Methodology

The study of nationalism has a long and rich history. In many cases, nationalism is chiefly approached as a political phenomenon or ideology, inextricably linked to state formation and/or consolidation.[31] Instead, this book builds on

---

30   A painful or problematic heritage, alluding to Grail King Amfortas's monologue in
     Wagner's *Parsifal* (1882).
31   Ernest Gellner is arguably the most important representative of political approaches to
     nationalism in recent scholarship. See Gellner 1983.

cultural approaches to nationalism, such as that of Joep Leerssen and Celia Applegate. Leerssen sees nationalism as a "cultural phenomenon," as "something
that emanates from the way people view and describe the world."[32] Applegate
is equally inclined to a cultural understanding of nationalism, pointing out
that "not all nationalisms are state-seeking, not all forms of nation-building
are state-building or state-centered," and proposing that "it makes better sense
of the evidence to look at nationalism as an emergent cognitive model for a
number of educated Europeans, a way of ordering experience, of looking at
the world and making sense of one's place and identity in it."[33] As a consequence, Applegate displays a certain reluctance to label people as "nationalist"
in her work on German national thought in the nineteenth century, because
"that word is simply too loaded with negative connotations to be useful in this
discussion."[34] The term "nationalism" indeed has such a political, and in the
case of German culture even diabolical undertone, that I also exercise a certain
restraint in using it in this book.

In comparison, I believe that national identity is a far more useful concept
for the subject under scrutiny. Less attached to the factual reality of, say, state
formation, Anne-Marie Thiesse defines national identity by definition as a
"postulate, an invention, a fiction that obtains reality only by a collective adhesion to its truth."[35] As Leerssen points out, from the mid-1970s onward the
idea has gained currency that "national identities are constructs, and that it is
the historian's task to analyse the process of their construction and the nature
of the constructedness."[36] In a similar vein, one could argue that Hobsbawm
and Ranger's notion of the *"Invention of Tradition* (1983)"[37] forms an integral
element of nineteenth-century culture, and not only an obfuscating force.
Ernest Renan's famous dictum in *Qu'est-ce qu'une nation? [What is a Nation]?*
(1882) that "forgetting, I would even say historical error, is an essential factor in
the creation of a nation"[38] shows that even a nineteenth-century thinker was
aware of this.

It is through the process of collective adhesion that operas can obtain significance as carriers of national identity, whereas the prominence of national
reasoning during the nineteenth century triggered opera makers and critics to
articulate a national opera identity. This opera identity complies with a more

---

32   Leerssen 2006: 14.
33   Applegate 1998: 280.
34   Ibid.: 288.
35   Thiesse 1999: 14.
36   Leerssen 2007: 23.
37   Hobsbawm 1983.
38   "L'oubli, et je dirai même l'erreur historique, sont un facteur essentiel de la création d'une
      nation." Renan 1992: 41.

general cultural self-image current in Germany while contrasting itself against the perceived opera identities of other nations. National stereotypes are the foundation for this articulation of opera identities.

What do I mean with articulation? In *National Thought in Europe* (2006), Leerssen uses it to describe the "process of self-silhouetting against an Outside."[39] Articulation is emphatically related to an act of distinction, a necessary activity in order to stand out, not to be overheard in a mass of several voices.[40] It applies to the attempts at conceptualization, institutionalization as well as canonization of German opera, three domains or consecutive stages that play a central role in this book. In order to launch a distinctive national opera genre, its formal shape must be conceptualized. In the case of German opera, this phase generally preceded the actual creation of operas. This points to a first step towards the articulation of a national opera identity, discussed in the first chapter. A second possible phase is the creation of operas that comply with the theoretical conceptualization, as well as the foundation of an institution where they can be performed. The most evident example of this is a theater, but the notion of a national tradition can equally serve as a useful institution.[41] Here articulation can be understood not only as a formulation of one's thoughts, but also with making one's voice be heard. As Brian Paltridge points out, "part of having a certain identity is that it is recognized by other people."[42] The third phase, canonization, is chiefly related to articulation as a means to silence those voices deemed inappropriate while making those works deemed suitable for canonization stand out. In the case of German opera, canonization also concerns the resistance against being silenced by a more powerful voice, that of the "great German tradition of instrumental music." In that sense, the canonization of German opera is not only concerned with standing out, but also with blending in.

I approach the articulation of a German opera identity by studying discourse, using methods derived from discourse analysis. With this, I mean that I am chiefly interested in recurrent ideas and expressions that, through their frequent use within a cultural sphere, constitute a discourse that contributes to the construction of outlooks on the world. A discourse-analytical approach is more interested in texts and ideas than in persons and authorial intent. Rather than questioning the validity of certain statements and correcting them, I am

---

39   Leerssen 2006: 17.
40   Articulation simultaneously points to a "modern awareness of the performative nature of identity," which Suzanne Aspden characterizes as "a particularly rich theoretical basis for the understanding of opera" in 'Opera and National Identity.' Aspden 2012: 283.
41   In *Building a National Literature* (1989), Peter Uwe Hohendahl approaches the formation of a German literary tradition between 1830 and 1870 as an institutionalization process.
42   Paltridge 2006: 38–39.

chiefly concerned with how these discourses came into being and how they shaped perceptions of German opera that, in many cases, have proven to be persistent until this very day. Technical knowledge of music-historical developments is necessary in order to understand the amount of construction in nineteenth-century chauvinist historiographies, but the scholarly task does not simply end by revealing the flawed nature of common conceptions. On the contrary, it forms a point of departure for a proper engagement with the ideological entanglements of nineteenth-century discourse on German opera, one that grants the genre its place in a European history of ideas.

What about the periodization of this book? Many studies on national music and opera in a German or European context choose political milestones, such as 1789, 1815, 1830, 1848, 1871, or 1914 as periodization markers, despite their alleged cultural approach. In that sense, my choice for the years 1798 and 1876 could be read as a polemic statement. At the same time, these dates are natural markers for the phenomenon I wish to discuss. 1798 is the year when the Leipzig-based *Allgemeine musikalische Zeitung* was founded, an authoritative and widely-read journal that helped to establish a public sphere of German music discourse with international appeal. As such, it contributed greatly to the articulation of a German opera identity. 1876 marks the opening of the Bayreuth Festival with the world premiere of Richard Wagner's *Der Ring des Nibelungen*. Wagner's Bayreuth project embodies many elements of the German opera identity as discussed in the previous eight decades. Moreover, one could argue that, in the public eye, Wagner's persona and his art have come to fully embody the stereotype of what a German opera identity entails. At the same time, the year 1876 makes it possible to situate the German opera campaign in the post-1871 Unification triumphalism, while the stretch of eight decades enables the reader to detect changes in the relation between opera and German national identity formation.

What, to conclude, is the geographical demarcation of the subject of this book? A first point to make is that, despite the fact that Germany did not form a nation-state in the majority of the period under scrutiny, to speak of Germany is not necessarily an anachronism. As many of the sources used in this book make clear, the term Germany already had currency, regardless of its vague geographical delineation. Applegate argues that, with regard to music, "Germany" included Austria just as much as the Northern regions that constitute Germany today.[43] This is certainly true in the field of instrumental music, where the Viennese Classics form the nucleus of a "great German tradition." For the articulation of a German opera identity, however, Austrian developments

---

43   "music always invoked a greater Germany, a *Grossdeutschland* as much centered on
      Vienna as Berlin – but essentially not centered at all." Applegate 1992: 30.

are arguably less significant. Even though Vienna's rich *Singspiel* tradition inspired early nineteenth-century opera composition in Northern parts of the German-speaking world, Viennese criticism was not as significant in the formation of an intellectual discourse on German opera. The phenomena under scrutiny in this book generally take place in Northern and Middle Germany, frequently in Saxony and Prussia, while occasionally ascending as deep south as Munich.

3   Structure of This Study

The first chapter discusses how a German opera identity was conceptualized through music journalism in the first quarter of the nineteenth century. The first 25 volumes of the *Allgemeine Musikalische Zeitung* provide the basic source material. After providing a survey of the various articulation strategies used to conceptualize the ideal shape of a German opera genre, it will be shown how reviews of individual works were used to consolidate a German opera identity. The works under scrutiny are Beethoven's *Fidelio* (1805/1814), E.T.A. Hoffmann's *Undine* (1816) and Carl Maria von Weber's *Der Freischütz* (1821). In the case of *Der Freischütz*, the work's perceived status as an emblem of Germanhood will be related to contemporary political developments.

The second and third chapter form a diptych, in which the intersection of Romantic opera and German national opera between 1800 and 1830 is discussed. Taking Novalis's notion of "Romanticization" as a point of departure, attempts to Romanticize German opera will be related to the ambition to elevate opera into a more sophisticated genre, a general concern of proponents of German national opera. Whereas the second chapter investigates attempts at Romanticization carried out while remaining *within* the *Singspiel* constellation of musical numbers alternated with spoken dialogues, the third chapter analyses attempts that move *beyond* this constellation.

The fourth chapter is concerned with the phenomenon of German-language opera companies outside the German-speaking world, mainly in the first half of the nineteenth century. The reception of German operas in other cultures broadens our scope on German nineteenth-century opera and our understanding of the articulation of a German opera identity. It illuminates transnational dynamics, not only in the cultural transfers that these German works sparked in the cultures where they were performed, but also in the sense that foreign reception of German operas shaped the domestic perception of a German national identity. The chapter consists of three case studies; Russia (St. Petersburg and Moscow), Paris, and London.

The fifth and final chapter deals with the relation between Wagner and the nineteenth-century German national opera tradition. Many studies of the relation between Wagner and German nationalism historically approach the subject backwards, taking the late nineteenth-century context and sometimes even the perversions of the Third Reich as a point of departure. This chapter aims to complement the scope by taking a different route, interpreting Wagner's esthetic project as a continuation of previous campaigns for the emancipation of German opera. It also takes Wagner's foreign experiences as stimuli to the articulation of *his* identity as composer of German opera into consideration. This contextualization of his esthetics will not only contribute to our understanding of Wagner, but also of the specific role that his operas have played in the development of German opera as a genre and as a cultural symbol.

As much as the average nineteenth-century German opera composer, within this book I have attempted to use all means necessary for the sake of the story. The five chapters discuss a wide range of phenomena from a wide range of methodological angles. I believe that this broad, interdisciplinary approach has enabled me to provide a rich image of nineteenth-century German opera identity and the many stages and shapes of its articulation.

CHAPTER 1

"Von der Oper, die der Deutsche will": The Conceptualization of German Opera during the First Quarter of the Nineteenth Century

Although German-language operas were already being composed before 1800 and achieved considerable success, – one may think of Mozart's much-acclaimed *Die Entführung aus dem Serail* (1782) and *Die Zauberflöte* (1791) – the conscious and widespread conceptualization of German opera as an urgent national need seems to be an early nineteenth-century phenomenon.[1] During the 1770s and 80s, cultivation of vernacular opera was generally still a top-down affair, spurred by a monarch, such as Joseph II, who provided patronage for German-language *Singspiele* in Vienna.[2] These top-down attempts were, however, inspired by a more widespread, bottom-up national theater movement that rose to prominence in the latter half of the eighteenth century. Playwrights such as Johann Elias Schlegel, Gotthold Ephraim Lessing and Friedrich Gottlob Klopstock strove for a higher prestige and qualitative improvement of German theater and combined this plea with notions of national identity. Ideally, the theater could fulfill the role of a meeting place for and mirror of the nation, reflecting on the German character.[3] In many ways, the early nineteenth-century campaign for German national opera was inspired by this movement.

One characteristic of this campaing is the fact that the conceptualization of a national opera style generally precedes and anticipates the actual composition of works. It involves a great amount of "wishful thinking," and composing national operas in its turn often forms an attempt to meet stylistic demands formulated beforehand in writings on music. Therefore, it seems that the best way to approach the advent of German opera in the early nineteenth century is by tracing its gradual conceptualization. Although a nationalist attitude towards music can also manifest itself within the realm of composition, for example in the employment of folk melodies and styles, I believe that

---

1   A rather isolated and little successful early attempt at national opera would be Ignaz Holzbauer (music) and Anton Klein's (libretto) *Günther von Schwarzburg*, premiered in Mannheim in 1777.

2   See for example Manning 1975.

3   See Höyng 2003: 145–176 for an elaborate discussion of the entanglement of the national theatre movement and the contemporary discourse on national identity.

© KONINKLIJKE BRILL NV, LEIDEN, 2019 | DOI:10.1163/9789004245389_003

nationalism in music is often primarily related to the way we think about music. National character or significance is a meaning we or others attribute to it. In that sense, it has a conceptual nature.

In this chapter, I will present a selection of early-nineteenth-century opinions and discussions on German national musical identity, and German opera in particular. First, I will address some early nineteenth-century German attitudes towards the difference between musical styles in general. Next, I will show how a German national opera was conceptualized in relation to established, Italian and French traditions. Lastly, I will demonstrate how the categories German and national were employed in the reception of three early nineteenth-century German operas.

1 The *Allgemeine musikalische Zeitung* as a Platform for the Articulation of a National Discourse on Music

Thinking about music in national terms and the use of German character as an esthetic criterion can be traced back into the eighteenth-century, but was enhanced by the increased dissemination of printed music journalism at the turn of the century. The most important and long-running magazine of these days was the *Allgemeine musikalische Zeitung*, founded by Friedrich Rochlitz in Leipzig in 1798. It is often considered to be the arch-father of nineteenth-century German music criticism.[4]

As both its adjective "Allgemeine" and the choice for "Zeitung" instead of "Zeitschrift" make clear, its target readership was not restricted to experts. The magazine aimed to be accessible for the middle classes, created a lively public sphere for discussing musical matters, and contributed substantially to the formation of a common public opinion concerning music in a region divided in several states. The infrastructure that the AMZ provided was necessary to turn an intellectual, esthetic discourse into a broadly based movement.

---

4 Imogen Fellinger characterized the journal accordingly: "the first music journal that had international appeal," (Fellinger 1962: 1041), whereas Sanna Pederson (1995:62), David Gramit (2002:6), and Celia Applegate recognize its role in the formation of an imagined German musical community. Applegate calls the foundation of the AMZ "the creation of a national music journal" and explains how it helped to shape an imagined German community: "Even reports from remote outposts emphasized their commitment to musical life, in effect affirming the community of musicians and music lovers throughout this Germany. The repeated use of the term *Deutschland* as a place with, for instance, few music schools or too many Italian operas on its stages or too little understanding of its own music history suggested that it was indeed a meaningful collectivity, a musico-cultural reality if not a political one." Applegate 2005: 86 + 93.

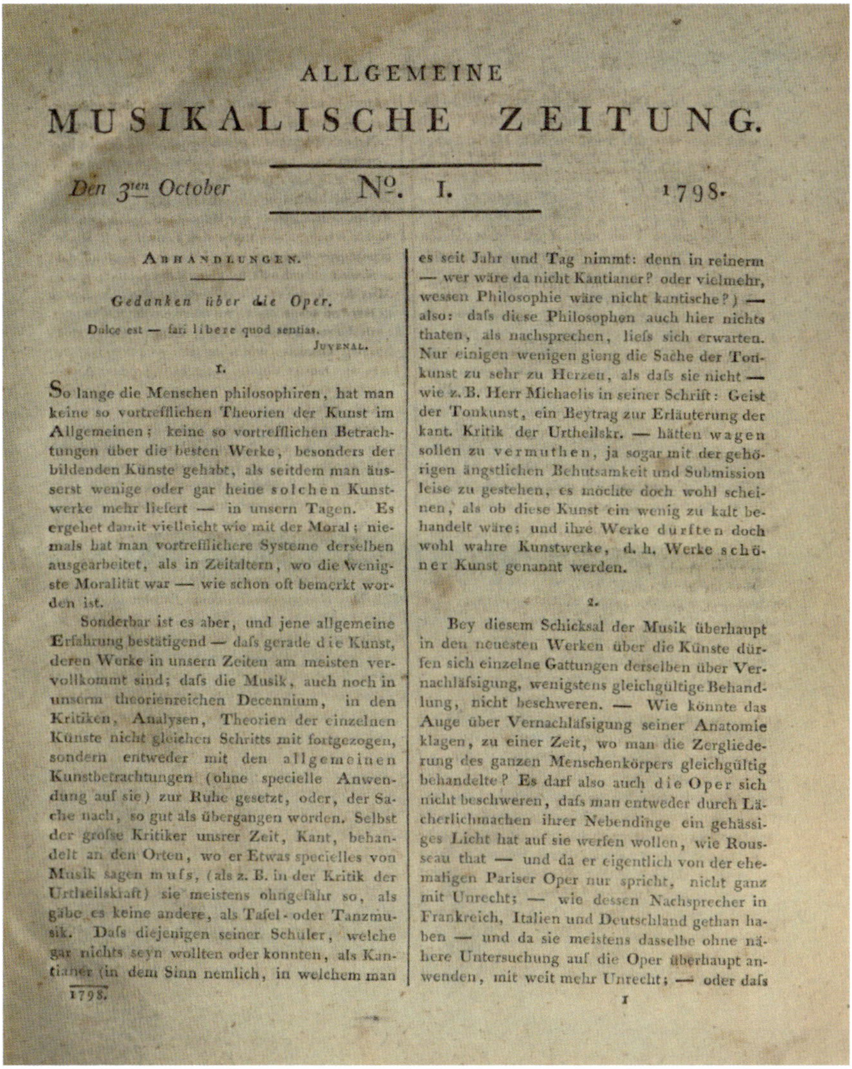

ALLGEMEINE

MUSIKALISCHE ZEITUNG.

Den 3ten October　　　　No. I.　　　　1798.

ABHANDLUNGEN.

Gedanken über die Oper.

Dulce est — fari libere quod sentias.
JUVENAL.

I.

So lange die Menschen philosophiren, hat man keine so vortrefflichen Theorien der Kunst im Allgemeinen; keine so vortrefflichen Betrachtungen über die besten Werke, besonders der bildenden Künste gehabt, als seitdem man äusserst wenige oder gar heine solchen Kunstwerke mehr liefert — in unsern Tagen. Es ergehet damit vielleicht wie mit der Moral; niemals hat man vortrefflichere Systeme derselben ausgearbeitet, als in Zeitaltern, wo die Wenigste Moralität war — wie schon oft bemerkt worden ist.

Sonderbar ist es aber, und jene allgemeine Erfahrung bestätigend — dafs gerade die Kunst, deren Werke in einzelnen Zeiten am meisten vervollkommt sind; dafs die Musik, auch noch in unserm theorienreichen Decennium, in den Kritiken, Analysen, Theorien der einzelnen Künste nicht gleichen Schritts mit fortgezogen, sondern entweder mit den allgemeinen Kunstbetrachtungen (ohne specielle Anwendung auf sie) zur Ruhe gesetzt, oder, der Sache nach, so gut als übergangen worden. Selbst der grofse Kritiker unsrer Zeit, Kant, behandelt an den Orten, wo er Etwas specielles von Musik sagen mufs, (als z. B. in der Kritik der Urtheilskraft) sie meistens ohngefähr so, als gäbe es keine andere, als Tafel- oder Tanzmusik. Dafs diejenigen seiner Schüler, welche gar nichts seyn wollten oder konnten, als Kantianer (in dem Sinn nemlich, in welchem man

1798.

es seit Jahr und Tag nimmt: denn in reinerm — wer wäre da nicht Kantianer? oder vielmehr, wessen Philosophie wäre nicht kantische?) — also: dafs diese Philosophen auch hier nichts thaten, als nachsprechen, liefs sich erwarten. Nur einigen wenigen gieng die Sache der Tonkunst zu sehr zu Herzen, als dafs sie nicht — wie z. B. Herr Michaelis in seiner Schrift: Geist der Tonkunst, ein Beytrag zur Erläuterung der kant. Kritik der Urtheilskr. — hätten wagen sollen zu vermuthen, ja sogar mit der gehörigen ängstlichen Behutsamkeit und Submission leise zu gestehen, es möchte doch wohl scheinen, als ob diese Kunst ein wenig zu kalt behandelt wäre; und ihre Werke dürften doch wohl wahre Kunstwerke, d. h. Werke schöner Kunst genannt werden.

2.

Bey diesem Schicksal der Musik überhaupt in den neuesten Werken über die Künste dürfen sich einzelne Gattungen derselben über Vernachläfsigung, wenigstens gleichgültige Behandlung, nicht beschweren. — Wie könnte das Auge über Vernachläfsigung seiner Anatomie klagen, zu einer Zeit, wo man die Zergliederung des ganzen Menschenkörpers gleichgültig behandelte? Es darf also auch die Oper sich nicht beschweren, dafs man entweder durch Lächerlichmachen ihrer Nebendinge ein gehässiges Licht auf sie haben werfen wollen, wie Rousseau that — und da er eigentlich von der ehemaligen Pariser Oper nur spricht, nicht ganz mit Unrecht; — wie dessen Nachsprecher in Frankreich, Italien und Deutschland gethan haben — und da sie meistens dasselbe ohne nähere Untersuchung auf die Oper überhaupt anwenden, mit weit mehr Unrecht; — oder dafs

I

FIGURE 1.1　First issue of the *Allgemeine Musikalische Zeitung*

Although not all my examples are derived from the *Allgemeine Musikalische Zeitung*, the first twenty-five volumes of this journal, comprising the years 1798 until 1822, provide significant information concerning the conceptualization of German opera. The reason for this is that reflection on the nature and future of German music in general, and opera in particular, formed an important impetus for the founding of the magazine.[5] In fact, the first article of the

---

5　Warrack points out that: "it is in the pages of the AMZ that one finds the most articulate, energetic and sustained campaign for German opera in these years." Warrack 1977–78: 84.

first issue was entitled 'Gedanken über die Oper' (see Figure 1.1), underlining the relevance of the genre. A second prominent player is Carl Maria von Weber, generally considered to be the most important early nineteenth-century advocate of German opera through his work as a composer, music director and critic. He sometimes wrote for the *AMZ*, but more often for local newspapers and journals in the cities where he worked. Taken together, the *AMZ* and Carl Maria von Weber's writings serve as a suitable means to trace the conceptualization of German opera in the first decades of the nineteenth century.

2 General Observations Concerning the Character and Development of German Music in Comparison to Italian and French Styles

From the start, the *Allgemeine Musikalische Zeitung* contained several publications on music and opera, discussing these subjects in national terms. Although the intellectual quality of these analyses differs, the national characterizations highly correspond to the point of creating a small but effective arsenal of commonplaces. This early nineteenth-century discourse on German musical identity is of course not a unique or isolated phenomenon, but a mode of thinking that employs deeply-rooted ethnic stereotypes – such as the difference between North and South, warm and cold climates, Catholicsm and Protestantism, and single nations – and is also interconnected with reflection on German national identity in other cultural domains. These ethnic stereotypes and modes of thought together form a framework that helps to situate and discern the different positions within music-critical discussions of this period. Three attitudes towards the foreign (generally either Italian or French) are particularly prominent.

The first is the German tendency to repudiate a hegemonic, central, aristocratic culture and its artificial art. In literary circles, this approach was mainly directed towards French literature, for example in the works of Gotthold Ephraim Lessing.[6] In German musical life, this status of malicious centre was attributed more to the Italian than to the French, particularly to the Italian court opera companies. This attitude is often combined with a second, more developmental thesis, namely that Italian culture and art may have

---

6 In *National Thought in Europe*, Joep Leerssen mentions how Lessing, in his *Hamburgische Dramaturgie* (1767–69): "resoundingly stated the need for German literature to abandon its formulaic classicism-by numbers and its slavish imitation of the high French style." Leerssen 2006: 96.

reached a high state of refinement in the past, but are now in a state of decay, whereas German culture, with its superior morals, will soon gain ascendancy. This theory can be considered as a revitalization of the cultural critique Tacitus voiced in *Germania* (98 A.D.).[7] We find it, for example, in Rochlitz's 'Gedanken über die Oper,' written in 1798, where the chief editor ascertains that Italian music's tendency to hold on to its traditions is now causing degeneration:

> In most recent, in our times, the Italians generally remained true to themselves: but the genius of their nation appeared to be exhausted – most of them became stale, and, as their usual melodies did no longer sort any effect, resorted to *bizarrerie*, to vocal and instrumental acrobatics.[8]

This historicist, developmental perspective on the demise of Italian music and its corollary, the future ascendancy of German music, was formulated in a more systematic way by G.L.P. Sievers in 1807. In his 'Charakteristik der deutschen Musik' he states:

> It appears as if German art still progresses towards a higher degree of perfection, whereas Italian art has stagnated. This can perhaps be explained by the fact that the cultivation of Italian culture has started far earlier than that of the Germans. As a consequence, it currently stands at a higher degree of luxury refinement, but this refinement necessarily leads to spiritual and physical demoralization, as Italians realize that their art has already reached its peak. A relapse into barbarism may not yet be on their doorstep, but it might not take centuries before it will occur.[9]

---

7 Leerssen observes how Tacitus functioned as a model for many theories addressing the superiority of northern peoples: "Tacitus' *Germania* denounces Roman decadence. As such, it was to effect the course of history repeatedly. [...] Anyone who believes that Northern Europeans are more trustworthy than Southern Europeans – is indebted to Tacitus." Ibid.: 41.

8 "In den neuesten, in unsern Zeiten, blieben die Italiener im Ganzen sich treu: aber der Genius der Nation schien sich hier selbst erschöpft zu haben – sie wurden meistens fad, und verfielen, weil ihre längst ausgesungenen Melodieen nichts mehr würken wollten, auf Bizarrerien, Seiltänzer- und Luftspringerkünste für Sänger und Instrumentisten." *AMZ* I/3, 17 October 1798: 37.

9 "Dass es das Ansehn hat, als ob die deutsche Kunst in der Vervollkommnung ihrer selbst da fortschreite, wo die italienische stehen geblieben wäre. Auch ist nicht zu läugnen, dass Italien, eben weil dessen Bildung früher, als die der deutschen begonnen hat, nunmehr schon auf einer so hohen luxuriöser Verfeinerung steht, welche Verfeinerung eine nothwendige geistige und körperliche Entnervung in ihrem Gefolge haben muss, dass dort kein höherer Gipfel der Kunst zu erreichen sein dürfte, und dass demnach ein Rückfall in die vorige Barbarey freylich noch nicht vor der Thür, aber doch keine viele hundert Jahre entfernt mehr seyn dürfte." *AMZ* IX/43, 22 July 1807: 686.

Sievers's adoption of the rhetorical scheme of Tacitus's *Germania* is stronger and more obvious than in Rochlitz's argumentation.[10] Furthermore, his argument is clothed in highly speculative theories about the rise and fall of civilizations, such as the idea that the perfection of *Kunstbildung* of a people takes four to six centuries (explaining the imminent demise of Italian culture) and the theory that civilization spreads gradually towards northern cultures. As a consequence of this thinking, German music is not a national achievement, but in fact a new stage in a universal development: "Because German music is not a national achievement and therefore neither has nor can have a national character, but is actually a pure, universal artefact that has been transplanted from Italy to Germany."[11] This second notion of a German mission in the perfection of cosmopolitan causes was widespread in music-critical writings in the first decades of the nineteenth century, and proved so successful that even until today, the universal claims are often being taken for granted and the hidden nationalist agenda behind such utterances is easily overlooked.[12]

The third assumption is less common, but nonetheless voiced, and comprises the idea that German and Italian art both have their unique, opposite character and merits, and can learn from one another. This approach could be characterized as the "Nazarene" attitude in painting. The Nazarenes, a collective of German painters living in Rome at the beginning of the nineteenth century, sought to reconcile both national traditions in their works. A painting that embodies the reconciliation between German and Italian culture and art as envisioned by the Nazarenes most strongly, and has become an icon of Italo-German sisterhood, is Friedrich Overbeck's *Germania und Italia* (1811–1820).

This Italophilia counterbalances the largely negative treatment of Italian culture and music in the first decades of the nineteenth century. In a 1808 anonymous contribution to the *AMZ*, entitled 'Bruchstücke aus den Briefen eines deutschen Tonkünstlers,' the author emphasizes the equal musical talents of both nations: "The Italian and German possess equal compositional talents,

---

10   Although Tacitus emphasizes the moral dimension in his comparison, the esthetic judgment of a nineteenth-century German like Sievers is not free of ethical considerations either, since the ethical dimension is never absent in the German art criticism of those days (think of the alliance between German art discourse and the critique of court culture around 1800 or a lecture such as Friedrich Schiller's *Die Schaubühne als eine moralische Anstalt betrachtet* (1784)).

11   "Da die deutsche Musik kein nationales Ereignis ist und also auch keinen nationellen Charakter hat, noch haben kann, sondern als reines, allgemeines Kunst-Produkt sich aus Italien verpfflanzt hat."*AMZ* IX/43, 22 July 1807: 689.

12   For a detailed analysis of this phenomenon, see Kerman 1980 and Applegate 1992 and 1998.

FIGURE 1.2   Friedrich Overbeck's *Germania und Italia*

[...] but highly different, opposed ones, according to their nature: In readiness and the capacity to please the ears, the Italian goes ahead, but through perseverance and diligence, the German catches up with him."[13] In another anonymous article of 1813, 'Schreiben eines in Italien reisenden Deutschen,' the Nazarene sentiment comes with a call to both musical traditions to end the battle over alleged supremacy and learn from one another instead:

> How nice would it be, if Italians would finally give up the dated prejudice that they *alone* have ownership of true opera music; and if Germans would accordingly give up the more recent conviction that there is hardly anything still to be learnt from Italians when it comes to composition, not even in the field of vocal and theatrical music.[14]

---

13   "Der Italiener und der Deutsche besitzen für die Tonkunst gleiche Talente, [...] aber äusserst verschiedene, ja entgegengesetzte, der Art nach; in Gewandheit des Geistes und in Geschicklichkeit des Ohrs, [...] gehet der Italiener dem Deutschen weit vor: durch Beharrlichkeit und Fleiss holet dieser jenen aber ein." *AMZ* XI/10, 7 December 1808: 153.

14   "Wie gut wäre es nun, wenn man in Italien das durch Verjährung eingewurzelte Vorurtheil, als sey die wahre Opernmusik ihnen *allein* eigen, endlich ganz aufgäbe; und in Deutschland die neuerdings aufgekommene, eben so unbegründete Ansicht, als könne

When a "Nazarene" perspective is adopted in music criticism, this treaty of friendship often goes hand in hand with a rejection of the rigid rules and un-musical nature of French music. This constellation is evident in one of Franz Horn's 'Musikalische Fragmente,' published in 1802:

> When it comes to French music, it is hard to deny that, generally, she neither appeals to the sentiment of the layman, nor to the taste of the expert, because in most compositions, we neither attend the profound sensitivity nor the refined judgment that we find in German and Italian masters. French compositions are either the result of a one-dimensional, sensualist esthetic, [...] or the product of a reasoning that is strictly confined to convenience.[15]

Interesting enough, this notion of Italo-German musical sisterhood at the expense of the French was also put forward in the *AMZ* by Giuseppe Cambini, an Italian composer living in Paris, who – regardless of his strong critique on French music – repeatedly refers to it as "our" music. The editorial board emphatically welcomed this friendly gesture by a foreigner and his accurate evaluation of German music in a footnote. In this 1804 essay with the explicit title 'Ueber den Charakter, den die italienische und deutsche Musik haben, und die französische haben sollte,' Cambini characterizes Italian and German music as follows: "The brisk sensuality of the Italian is realized in his melo-dy, whereas the slow, reflexive nature of the German finds expression in his harmony."[16] The ground for their difference in musical style and the legitima-cy of their co-existence lies in the fact that they both mirror their respective climate-related national character. On a vertical axis, Italy forms the first southern nation, whereas Germany is the first northern one. France floats somewhere in the middle, lacking a clear character.[17]

---

man von den Italienern in der Composition (auch für Gesang und Theater) gar nichts mehr lernen."*AMZ* XV/17, 28 April 1813: 279.

15   "Was die französische Musik betrifft, so ist es nicht zu leugnen, dass sie im Allgemein-en weder dem Gefühl des Laien, noch dem Geschmack des Kenners zusagen kann, weil bey den meisten Komponisten weder jene tiefe Empfindung, noch das geläuterte Urtheil anzutreffen seyn dürfte, welche wir bey deutschen und italienischen Meistern wahrnehmen. Entweder sind ihre Kompositionen Resultate einer einseitigen sensualen Aesthetik, [...] oder nur Resultat einer durch Konvenienz beschränkten Reflexion und Räsonnements."*AMZ* IV/50, 8 September 1802: 801.

16   "Die rasche, wollüstige Sinnlichkeit des Erstern gehet in seine Melodie; die langsame, ern-ste Reflexion des Zweyten in seine Harmonie über."*AMZ* VII/10, 5 December 1804: 152.

17   Ibid.: 151.

Paul Münch stresses that early nineteenth-century German writers on music often use ethnic stereotypes in an ambivalent way that can be instrumentalized both positively and negatively.[18] This is clearly the case in comparisons of German and Italian culture from a gender perspective. The sensual character and beauty of Italian culture is often perceived as feminine, whereas the rawer, but at the same time more thorough and reflexive nature of the German embodies the male principle. Ideally, a cross-fertilization takes place. However, often the feminine connotations go hand in hand with the suspicion of effeminacy. This train of thought was particularly influential in eighteenth-century music discourse, and reflected in the German condemnation of the castrato practice as unmanly and unnatural.[19] Although castrati nearly vanished from the opera stage after 1800, and the use of natural male voices increased, the contempt for alleged *Weichlichkeit* continued to dominate German outlooks on Italian music and opera.

3   The Definition of German National Opera through the Creation
        of Stereotypes

In early nineteenth-century debates on national style and character such as those mentioned above, the distinction between music in general and opera in particular is not always clear. Especially with regard to Italian and French national style, the terms music and opera are used almost interchangeably. However, in the German case, one must discern between instrumental music, often presented as a novel, German contribution to the development of music, and German opera, which has not yet reached such a state of perfection. It is the high state of instrumental music – realized in the works of Haydn, Mozart, and Beethoven – and the gained prestige of German literature – in the writings of Lessing, Goethe, and Schiller – that grant German musicians an amount of self-esteem and create the hope that something similar can be realized on the operatic plane.[20] Therefore, in discussing the nature and future of German opera, a different strategy is chosen. The emphasis lies not so much on the superiority or equality of German operas, but rather on the noble aspirations of German opera composers and the growth potential of the genre.

18   Ibid.: 22.
19   See Gruber 1982.
20   Aubrey S. Garlington Jr. also argues that "it appears that major concern with German opera as a German entity for German sensitivities came to the fore only after the language had reached the heights it attained in the hands of Schiller and Goethe." Garlington 1977A: 500.

The common discourse is generally as follows: Italian opera centralizes melody, euphony, the sensual and vocal virtuosity at the expense of the drama, whereas in French opera, the literary quality of the text is most important, leading to a neglect of the music, and correct declamation is more important than melody. This line of reasoning is employed, for example, by Carl Bernhard Wessely in his article 'Kritische Bemerkung über verschiedenen Theilen der Tonkunst' of 1 January 1800, when he writes:

> The Italians are used to perceive a libretto merely as a vehicle to realize the richest musical delight. [...] The French, on the contrary, see music in their operas as solely a means to give their lyrical drama a greater charm. [...] The worst opera subject can triumph in Italy, as long as the music is good. The most excellent music will not evoke a sensation in Paris if the opera[21] itself has no merits.[22]

German opera, as far as such a genre or style yet exists, is traditionally closer to its French sister, but ideally should incorporate the best of both worlds to create a coherent, unified work in which music and drama are perfectly balanced. We find this idea in 'Gedanken über die Oper,' where Rochlitz mentions "those current Germans who – with a calm spirit but profound knowledge, immaculate taste and not without originality – have attempted to unify the positive traits of the old and more recent music of Italy, France, and Germany."[23] Furthermore,

---

21   Wessely's usage of the term "opera" as referring to the libretto only is a relic of a past esthetics that started to wane after 1800.

22   "Die Italiäner sind gewöhnt, ein zur Komposition bestimmtes dramatisches Gedicht blos als Vehikel zu betrachten, durch welches man ihnen einen desto reichhaltigern musikalischen Genuss verschafft. [...] Die Franzosen hingegen betrachten bey ihren Opern die Musik blos als Hülfsmittel, ihrem lyrischen Drama höhern Reiz zu geben. [...] Das schlechteste Opernsujet kann in Italien Glück machen, sobald die Musik schön ist. Die vortrefflichste Musik wird in Paris keine Sensation erwecken, sobald die Oper an und für sich nichts taugt."*AMZ* II/14, 1 January 1800: 242–243.

23   "jetzigen Deutschen, welche mit ruhigerm Geiste, aber reichen Kenntnissen, reinem Geschmack und nicht ohne Eigenthümlichkeit das Gute der ältern und neuern Musik Italiens, Frankreichs und Deutschlands zu vereinigen gesucht haben."*AMZ* II/3, 17 October 1798: 38. This line of reasoning, which we will frequently revisit during the nineteenth century, can be traced back at least to Johann Joachim Quantz's 1752 *Versuch einer Anweisung die flute traversiere zu spielen*: "By selecting the most tasteful music from several nations, one will arrive at a mixed taste, which, without transgressing the confines of modesty, could very well be called *the German taste*." ("Wenn man aus verschiedener Völker ihrem Geschmacke in der Musik, mit gehöriger Beurtheilung, das Beste zu wählen weiss; so fließt daraus ein vermischter Geschmack, welchen man, ohne die Gränzen der Bescheidenheit zu überschreiten, nunmehr sehr wohl: *den deutschen*

musically the German composer distinguishes himself through the attention he pays to harmony and orchestral accompaniment, thereby creating a middle ground – sometimes referred to as "symphonic"[24] – between the melodicist Italian style and the submissive role music plays in French opera.

Carl Maria von Weber adopted a great deal of this familiar argumentation in his writings. In his 1817 article 'An die kunstliebenden Bewohner Dresdens,' in which he presented himself as the new music director of the newly founded German opera department, he stated:

> The art forms of other nations have expressed their selves more exact than German ones. In a certain respect, however. The Italian and French-man created an opera form, in which they complacently move back and forth. The German is different. His characteristic ambition and desire is to adopt and internalize foreign influences, and take them to a next level. But he is more profound ["er greift alles tiefer"]. Whereas the others aim mostly at the sensual and sensational, he wants a closed artwork, in which all parts unite to form a beautiful whole.[25]

This statement combines a set of ideal-typical characterizations of German opera composition, which we find in many other sources as well. The first is the idea that a German opera composer adopts foreign influences to perfect

---

Geschmack nennen könnte.") (Quantz 1752: 332) The belief in a cosmopolitan mission of German culture is not restricted to music alone. One also finds it, for example, in August Wilhelm Schegel's discussion of theater in his *Vorlesungen über dramatische Kunst und Literatur, Band I*: "Our mission as Germans is, I believe, to search for a perfect form that excludes the merely local or temporary traits of other forms, but combines all their truly poetic features. In this process, however, the German nationality should certainly predominate." ("Unsere Aufgabe ist, wie mich dünkt, eine Form, welche das wahrhaft Poetische aller jener Formen, mit Ausschließung des auf herkömmliche Übereinkunft Gegründeten in sich enthalte; im Gehalte aber soll deutsche Nationalität vorwalten.") Schlegel 1923: 21.

24   The French musicologist Etienne Choron (1771–1834) refers to Mozart as the champion of contemporary German "Anhänger der sinfonistischen Oper," as a translation of his work, published in the *AMZ* in February 1813, shows. *AMZ* XV/5, 3 February 1813: 78.

25   "Die Kunstformen aller übrigen Nationen haben sich von jeher bestimmter ausgesprochen als die der Deutschen. In gewisser Hinsicht nämlich. – Der Italiener und Franzose haben sich eine Operngestalt geformt, in der sie sich befriedigt hin und her bewegen. Nicht so der Deutsche. Ihm ist es rein eigentümlich, das Vorzügliche aller übrigen wißbegierig und nach stetem Weiterschreiten verlangend an sich zu ziehen: aber er greift alles tiefer. Wo bei den andern es meist auf die Sinnenlust einzelner Momente abgesehen ist, will er ein in sich abgeschlossenes Kunstwerk, wo alle Teile sich zum schönen Ganzen runden und einen." Kaiser 1908: 276–277.

them (as Rochlitz stated in 1798) and take them to a next level. A second thesis is the emphasis on thematic, formal coherence associated with German opera composition. A third, less prominent but somehow related postulate is the ideal of multimedial coherence, referring to a meaningful integration and collaboration of the individual arts within an opera.[26] This general ideal of organic unity is arguably derived from contemporary German discourse on instrumental music, and was also employed to vindicate, for example, Bach's fugues and the "classical" compositions of the Viennese School (Haydn, Mozart, Beethoven). As Kerman argues in 'How We Got into Analysis and How to Get Out' (1980), "organicism can be seen not only as a historical force which played into the great German tradition but also as the principle which seemed essential to validate that tradition."[27] We can trace this train of thought already in the famous Bach biography of Johann Nikolaus Forkel of 1802, in which the author praises Bach's "elimination of all superfluous notes that do not necessarily contribute to the unity of the whole."[28]

A concrete example – the edition and reception history of Peter von Winter's opera *Das unterbrochene Opferfest* (1798) – may serve to demonstrate the importance of the notion of organic unity in early nineteenth-century discourse on opera. The divergent versions in which the work was performed reflect the advent of this ideal of coherence, unity and economy as a typical characteristic of German opera. Initially a *Singspiel* with spoken dialogues, the work was translated into Italian (*Il sacrifizio interrotto*) with the dialogues transformed into recitatives. As Stephen C. Meyer shows: "roughly a decade after its premiere (1811), the opera was again produced in Dresden in its original language, but in a revised version, purged of its comic characters, [...] adumbrating in many ways the 'new German opera' that composers such as Weber hoped to create."[29]

Both Weber and E.T.A. Hoffman greeted this alteration as an improvement, not only due to the serious character that the piece obtained in its new form, but especially because it gained in coherence and unity. In 1811, Weber wrote: "That the opera was presented as an entirely serious work [...] delighted the critic, because even if one loses a few neat musical numbers, the whole does

---

26   This ideal is touched upon lightly by some eighteenth and early nineteenth-century commentators, but most thoroughly by Weber, as we will see in the analysis of his 1817 review of E.T.A. Hoffmann's *Undine*. Around 1850, Richard Wagner based his idea of the *Gesamtkunstwerk* on similar ideas.

27   Kerman 1980: 315.

28   "Entfernung jeder willkürlichen, nicht zum Ganzen notwendig gehörigen Note." Forkel 1900: 66.

29   Meyer 2003: 35.

gain in character and unity."[30] E.T.A. Hoffman made a similar point when he wrote about the eliminated comic character Pedrillo: "This jester runs in circles around the opera, panting, without ever finding an appropriate entry to find a proper place in the work; even if he has some charming music, we gladly relinquish those pieces, and enjoy the increased roundedness of the opera."[31]

Of course, all propositions of this ideal conceptualization of German opera composition involved – as I stated earlier – a great amount of "wishful thinking." Weber was very aware that this ideal, rounded artwork was anything but realized in his days. He sketched the painful reality in *Tonkünstlers Leben*, a fragmentary novel he wrote between 1809 and 1820 (the passage concerned was drafted in 1810). The novel contains an anecdote in which a *Hanswurst* subsequently brings the Italian, French, and German opera – in anthropomorphic shape – onto the stage to present themselves. The author typifies the Italian opera as:

A long, rawboned, transparant figure with a characterless face, that stays the same regardless of whether it is supposed to depict a hero, an Adonis, or a barbarian, and always radiates the same sweetness. It wore a thin dress with train, with a color that could actually not be called a proper color, covered with small, glittering diamonds that drew the audience's attention.[32]

The transparency and colorless dress serve as an allegory for the lack of character of Italian opera, whereas the little diamonds are the arias that detract attention from this shortcoming. In a subtle way, the fragment also employs issues of gender. Although Italian opera is portrayed as feminine, the hero, Adonis and barbarian she portrays are all male characters. This underlines the

---

30   "Daß die Oper ganz als ernsthafte Oper gegeben wurde [...] war Ref. eine angenehme Erscheinung, denn obwohl man einige sehr niedliche Musikstücke verliert, gewinnt das Ganze dadurch doch an Haltung und Einheit." Kaiser 1908: 119.

31   "Dieser Spaßmacher läuft keuchend neben der Oper her, ohne auch nur ein einziges mal hineinkommen zu können; freilich ist mit ihm manches anmutige Musikstück ausgeschieden, indessen wollen wir das alles gern vermissen und dafür uns an der gewonnenen Ründe des Stückes erfreuen." Quoted after Geyer-Kiefl 1987: 148.

32   "Eine, lange, hagere, durchsichtige Figur, charakterloses Gesicht, das als Held, Seladon und Barbar sich immer gleich blieb und nur eine ungemeine Süßlichkeit über sich verbreitet hatte. Sie trug ein dünnes Schleppkleid, dessen Farbe eigentlich keine Farbe zu nennen war, und auf dem hin und wieder kleine blitzende Steinchen saßen, die die Augen des Publikums auf sich zogen." Kaiser 1908: 479–480.

previously-mentioned idea that Italian opera is effeminate. After her exit, the French opera walks onto the stage:

> A wellborn *Parisienne*; she enters on a Soccus[33] and moves graciously in her inconveniently tight Greek garment. She is permanently surrounded by the *Corps de ballet*; several Gods lurk in the background. The action takes place between 12 AM and afternoon.[34]

This description makes fun of the stifling dramatic prescriptions of French opera, its close imitation of Greek tragedy and its superficial elegance.

Eventually the German opera appears, albeit after a long time and hesitantly:

> A break occurred. The audience gradually became more restless. Tumult increased. The German opera would still not appear. [...] Finally *Hanswurst* walked onto the stage, exhausted and covered in sweat, and said: "[...] Please wait, wait a little longer, it seems appropriate to tell you why you have to wait so long. To be honest, the German opera isn't doing well. She suffers from cramps and is fully incapable of getting back on her feet. [...] In vain, the tailors try to dress her with a French, then with an Italian garb, in order to adorn her, but it simply doesn't fit her. [...] Now, finally some Romantic tailors have conceived the idea to pick a national material, and weave anything into it that other nations have previously come up with."[35]

The fragment is both striking for its vivid, entertaining use of familiar esthetic judgements as for the way in which Weber makes fun of an artistic project so

---

33   Greek slippers that were generally worn by ladies in ancient Rome.

34   "eine wohlgeborene Pariserin; geht auf dem Soccus einher und bewegt sich sehr höflich in dem sie etwas unbequem beengenden griechischen Gewande. Das Corps de Ballet umgibt sie beständig; verschiedene Götter lauern im Hintergrunde. Die Handlung spielt zwischen 12Uhr und Mittag." Ibid.: 482–483.

35   "Es entstand eine Pause. Das Publikum fing an, nach und nach unruhig zu werden. Wiederholte Pause. Neuer, verstärkter Tumult. Die deutsche Oper wollte noch immer nicht zum Vorschein kommen. [...] Endlich erschien Hanswurst, ganz erschöpft und in Schweiß und sprach: '[...] Nun, warte, warte nur noch ein wenig, es ist fast billig, dir auch zu sagen warum du warten sollst! Es geht ehrlich gesagt, der deutschen Oper sehr übel. Sie leidet an Krämpfen und ist durchaus nicht [fest] auf die Beine zu bringen. [...] Vergebens ziehen die Herren Verarbeiter bald der französischen, bald der italienischen einen Rock aus, um sie damit zu schmücken, das paßt alles hinten und vorn nicht. [...] Nun endlich sind einige romantische Schneider auf die glückliche Idee gefallen, einen vaterländischen Stoff zu wählen, und in diesem womöglich alles zu verweben, was Ahnung, Glaube, Kontraste und Gefühle je bei andern Nationen wirkten und wirbelten." Ibid.: 484–485.

dear to him, the creation of a German national opera. It does, however, have an important characteristic in common with his more serious statement in 'An die kunstliebenden Bewohner Dresdens.' In both analyses, Weber frames the individual national genres into a historical narrative. This is most clear in *Tonkünstlers Leben*, where the consecutive appearances of the national genres correspond to the historical development of opera, and the hesitant entry of German opera underscores its troubled coming of age. Even though it is still in an early stage, there is ample room for artistic development, as the German is a diligent student, eager to learn.[36]

In contrast, the Italian and French tradition are more static and move complacently back and forth in their respective opera forms. Their complacency and fixed tradition lead to stagnation, as the anecdote underlines. Italian opera is monotonous, uncharacteristic and colorless, whereas French music theatre is constrained by the rigid dramatic prescripts that govern it. German opera may still be a vulnerable or even ridiculous creature, but it is better to be under construction than to be over the hill.

4   *German* and *National* as Esthetic Criteria in Early Nineteenth-Century Opera Criticism

All these common propositions and ethno-typical descriptions not only found their way to theoretical and fictive writings, but were also applied to music criticism, as the early nineteenth-century reception of three operas by German composers reveals. The employment of the adjectives German and national in reviews of Beethoven's *Fidelio*, E.T.A. Hoffmann's *Undine* and Weber's *Der Freischütz* reveal how music criticism played a decisive role in shaping the conceptualization of German opera.

4.1   *Ludwig van Beethoven's* Fidelio
Although Beethoven's *Fidelio* (1805–1814) deviated from common German opera in its subject matter and stylistic orientation, and does not have a clear status within narratives concerning the development of German opera, the work could function as a means for distinguishing German opera composition from foreign examples. Paradoxically, this was particularly due to its close affiliation to French and Italian models. At the same time, Beethoven had a symbolic function as Germany's most acclaimed composer of instrumental music putting effort into vernacular opera. The piece had obvious affinities with the French rescue opera type, developed by composers such as

---

36   "wißbegierig und nach stetem Weiterschreiten verlangend."

Grétry, Dalayrac, Méhul and Cherubini, and evoked the spirit of the French Revolution. Beethoven's librettists[37] based their story on *Léonore, ou l'amour conjugal*, an opera with a text by Jean-Nicolas Brouilly set by Pierre Gaveaux in 1798. This French original was later rendered in Italian in operas by Ferdinando Paer (*Leonora, ossia l'amore conjugale*, 1804, libretto by Giovanni Schmidt) and Simon Mayr (*L'amor coniugale*,1805, libretto by Gaetano Rossi).

In an extensive article in the *AMZ* of 1815, entitled 'Gedanken über die neuere Tonkunst,' Amadeus Wendt, a Leipzig professor of philosophy, evaluated the quality of Beethoven's opera through a comparison with Paer's *Leonora, ossia l'amore conjugale*. The article does not only serve to vindicate the greatness of Beethoven's work, but also to demonstrate the superiority of German music over its Italian sister. Before delving into the work, Wendt states: "As the more elevated instrumental works have become so dominant and are so intimately related to the German character, it hardly needs mention that Italian music is no longer to be feared as a potential hindrance to the tremendous rise of German music."[38] The author regards the German as someone not settling for pleasurable musical forms, but instead desiring to penetrate into the essence and meaning of things, a familiar national stereotype.[39] This attitude expresses itself in the new prominence of the orchestra, and has consequences for the shape and function of singing within opera. He mentions a:

> Tendency not to simply enjoy pleasant forms, but rather to penetrate deeply into the true meaning of things, searching for their inner essence, thereby even taking the risk of creating something formless [...]. That

---

37   The text of the 1805 version was drafted by Joseph von Sonnleithner, in 1806 Stephan von Breuning revised it, and the final libretto of 1814 was adapted by Georg Friedrich Treitschke.

38   "Kaum bedürfte es hier der Worte, da die Werke der reichern Instrumentalcomposition schon eine solche Herrschaft gewonnen haben, und dem Charakter der Deutschen so verwandt sind, dass kaum zu befürchten steht, die italienische Musik werde, besonders in ihrem *jetzigen* Zustande, den gewaltigen Flug der deutschen Musik noch aufhalten können."*AMZ* XVII/22, 31 May 1815: 367.

39   Wendt adopts the common image that the German prefers ideas over appearance, an archetypal observation that had also been formulated two years earlier by Madame de Staël in her *De l'Allemagne* (1813): "It is reasonable to say that the French and the German present two extremely contrasting mentalities; whereas the former chiefly considers the exterior objects, the latter approaches the world from the viewpoint of ideas." ("On pourrait dire avec raison que les Français et les Allemands sont aux deux extrémités de la chaîne morale, puisque les unes considèrent les objets extérieurs comme le mobile de toutes les idées, et les autres, les idées comme mobile de toutes les impressions.") Staël 1853: 10.

explains why German music has recently acquired such a profound and elevated character, which now and then may have harmed singing and harmony.[40]

In this case, the orchestra is not regarded as the material surface or exterior of the music,[41] but its instrumental music is rather seen as representing the inner essence of reality within opera, an idea intimately tied to nineteenth-century German thinking on opera.[42] Wendt goes on to advocate this new relationship between voice and orchestra, and particularly praises the vocal style that comes with it:

Here we believe that the true virtue of contemporary German music lies, in the fact that we do not necessarily need Italian singing anymore [...]. The character of Beethoven's opera, for example, is far too grand and all-encompassing to allow Italian singing a dominant place in it. Nonetheless, only the biased would dare to argue that the parts of this opera lack in song.[43]

In his review of Florestan's scene and its prelude, ('Gott! welch dunkel hier' in Beethoven's rendition) he distinguishes Paer's Italian and Beethoven's German setting in their ability to grasp the character and atmosphere of the scene,

---

40 "Neigung, sich weniger an der angenehmen Form zu vergnügen, als selbst auf die Gefahr ins Formlose zu verfallen, den Sinn und die Bedeutung der Dinge zu ergründen, und in ihr tiefstes Innere forschend einzudringen [...]. So ist es klar, warum die deutsche Musik in der neuern Zeit jenen tiefsinnigen und erhabnen Charakter angenommen hat, durch welchen zuletzt der Gesang wohl gelitten und von der Harmonie zuweilen unterdrückt worden seyn mag."*AMZ* XVII/22, 31 May 1815: 369.

41 In a negative sense, this exterior quality makes orchestration a secondary aspect of music, it is merely the medium through which the musical substance is communicated, and too much attention paid to orchestration is often considered to be a compensation for lack of "real" musical ideas on the part of the composer. Tobias Janz, for example, states that "to say that a music has been orchestrated well has until today generally carried a pejorative undertone." Janz 2006: 13.

42 In *Die Idee der absoluten Musik* (1978), Dahlhaus touches on this peculiar paradox of nineteenth-century German musical esthetics, namely that "absolute music" could in fact blossom within opera as the "essence of things" Dahlhaus 1994: 16.

43 "Darin dünkt uns also liegt ein Vorzug der neuern deutschen Musik, dass wir des italienischen Gesangs nicht unbedingt mehr bedürfen. [...] Der Charakter der genannten *Beethovenschen* Oper zum Beyspiel ist viel zu gross und umfassend, als dass der *ital.* Gesang darin herrschen könnte; demohngeachtet wird nur der *Eingenommene* behaupten, dass es den Partieen dieser Oper am *Gesange* fehle." *AMZ* XVII/22, 31 May 1815: 372.

and emphatically relates this difference to their nationality. He points out that Beethoven:

> masterly evokes the horrible scene. For the same situation, Paer created a decent concert aria, that nevertheless fails to grasp the atmosphere the way Beethoven's composition does. In the *German* rendition, the religious elevation and patience, springing from Florestan's pure conscience and the wistful memory of his wife, is emphatically highlighted.[44]

It is not surprising that Wendt lifts out this fragment as a fine example of German opera composition. Although the aria's form is quite conventional, the dark-hued orchestration and chromatic harmony of the prelude, evoking the atmosphere of the sinister, subterranean dungeon, form a typical example of the musical depiction of the supernatural, evil and mysterious realm in many future German operas. In a comparable way to Mozart in the Commendatore scene of *Don Giovanni*, Beethoven realized this with the most advanced symphonic means, especially when we regard the fact that he wrote the majority of the prelude already in 1805. Even if the famous *Wolfsschluchtszene* in Weber's *Der Freischütz* of 1821 is more transgressive and its melodramatic design pervades the structure of the opera in a more radical way, the orchestral introduction of Florestan's scene may be considered as an early progenitor.

4.2   *E.T.A. Hoffmann's* Undine

Another work that not only in its musical design, but especially in its subject matter would prove to be formative within the development of German opera, was E.T.A. Hoffman's *Undine*. Friedrich de la Motte-Fouqué, who had already published a novel based on this fairy-tale about the love between a human and a water nymph in 1811, wrote the libretto. It is often considered to be the first opera of its era to set a text of real literary merit.[45] The work was premiered in Berlin in 1816. Although E.T.A. Hoffmann nowadays is primarily known as a writer, just as Weber he was also active as a composer, music director and critic. Hoffmann's music journalism, such as his interpretation of Mozart's *Don*

---

44   "Der dritte Akt, der Beethoven als Meister im ungeheueren und schrecklichen zeigt [...]. Paer hat zu derselben Situation eine Arie – mit *concertirenden Violine* und *Bratsche* geschrieben, eine recht brave Concertarie, die aber [...] bey weitem nicht so tief in die Situation eingreift, als Beethovens Composition. [...] In der *deutschen* [Wendt's emphasis] Bearbeitung ist der Zug der religiösen Erhebung und Geduld, die aus dem reinen Bewusstseyn hervorgeht, neben der wehmüthigen Erinnerung an die Gattin, mit Bedeutung hervorgehoben." *AMZ* XVII/26, 28 June 1815: 429.

45   For example in Warrack 1976: 224.

Giovanni and his dialogue *Der Dichter und der Komponist* (both published in the AMZ in 1813), contributed considerably to German early nineteenth-century discourse on opera.

In many respects, his outlooks are congenial to Weber's, but Hoffmann is less inclined to discuss opera in national terms than Weber is.[46] For Hoffmann, the primary requirement of an opera is that it triggers a Romantic conscience, and transcends everyday life. Although the Romantic opera he envisioned would come to be understood as the first genuinely German contribution to opera history, Hoffmann's reasoning is less overtly nationalist, and his later public support of Spontini's *Olympia* during the high days of *Freischütz* fever in 1821 has often even been interpreted as a betrayal to the German cause.[47]

Despite Hoffmann's anything but outspoken partisanship for the national cause in opera, *Undine* was nonetheless framed into a national perspective from its earliest reception. This is partly the result of the performance context and the stage designs by Karl Friedrich Schinkel. Francien Markx points out that "the première did take place on the King's birthday" and was "preceded by an address penned by Friedrich Förster, [alluding] to the loyalty among Germans and to the King during the Wars of Liberation."[48] On top of that, Markx signals an unprecedented prominence of Gothic architecture in Schinkel's design, increasingly associated with German national identity at the time.[49]

---

46 Only incidentally, for example in his review of Paer's *Sofonisbe* (1811), does Hoffmann adopt national stereotypes. In that case, he writes: "As is widely-known, the more recent Italian music flatters the ear with pleasant melodies, and provides room for the singer, to display his abilities in all splendor: but the truly dramatic, the expression of the story, the situation, this she all neglects as much as German composers make it their prime goal, which often results in a neglect of the singer and his technique." ("Die neuere italienische Musik schmeichelt bekanntlich dem Ohre durch angenehme Melodien, und gibt dem Sänger Gelegenheit, seine Kunstfertigkeit im höchsten Glanze zu zeigen: aber das eigentlich Dramatische, den Ausdruck der Handlung, der Situation, vernachlässigt sie in dem Grade, als es die deutschen Komponisten zur Hauptsache machen, und freilich oft darüber das Individuum des Sängers, und was in seinem Kehle liegen mag, vergessen.") The last sentence, criticizing German composers' ability to write for voices, however softens his praise of German opera composition. AMZ XIII/11, 13 March 1811.

47 Norbert Miller writes "that E.T.A. Hoffman's betrayal of the Romantic opera, his abandonment of his loyal friend Carl Maria von Weber, and his partisanry for the Roman court composer Gasparo Spontini in Berlin, have always annoyed German cultural historiography." Miller 1985: 369. Miller marks the Weber biography written by Max Maria von Weber – the composer's son – in 1864 as a clear marker of this sentiment.

48 Markx 2016: 255.

49 "The emphasis on Gothic architecture in Schinkel's design is found neither in the tale nor in the libretto, although Hoffmann had expressed his hope to Fouqué that Schinkel would build a 'Gothic tomb' for him. It is unclear, however, whether he was referring specifically to this scene. Schinkel hardly needed Hoffmann's encouragement in this direction,

FIGURE 1.3   Schinkel's stage design for Act II, scene I of *Undine*. The fountain and cathedrals
in the back are all in Gothic style.

In his 1817 *AMZ* review, Carl Maria von Weber contributed to the national
framing of *Undine*. At the beginning of his interpretation, he formulates
the criterion to which the work will be measured. He explains his ideal by
writing:

though, for he had a lively interest in Gothic – or as it was also called 'old German' –
architecture and he had carefully studied this style. [...] Goethe had earlier celebrated
the ingenious builder of the Strasbourg Cathedral, Erwin von Steinbach, in his essay 'Von
deutscher Baukunst' (1773), and had hailed Gothic architecture as 'deutsche Baukunst,
unsre Baukunst, da der Italiener sich keiner eignen rühmen darf, vielweniger der Fran-
zos.' [...] During the French occupation, Gothic architecture had gained importance as a
reminder of a glorious German past and of German unity, especially after the fall of the
Holy Roman Empire of the German Nation in 1806." (Markx 2016: 246–247) The visual
splendor of the premiere performance may have considerably affected the opera's success, as some early reviews emphasized (See Ibid.: 258–260). This may also explain the
lack of success outside Berlin. On 29 July 1817, after the fourteenth performance of *Undine*,
the Royal National Theater burnt down, and the lavish premiere sets were demolished.
Ripped of Schinkel's exceptional designs, *Undine* never truly managed to equal its initial
success in Berlin, and failed to gain a foothold in the German opera repertoire, despite
the relative merit of Hoffmann's music, the literary quality of Fouqué's text, and the theoretical relevance of *Undine* as a model for German Romantic opera. More on *Undine* in
Section 2.2.

It goes without saying that I speak of the opera that the German wants: a closed artwork, in which all individual contributions of the single arts are molded together, finally to dissolve and create a new world.[50]

In a way, Weber here explicitly relates the ideal of coherence to multimedial integration, a concept that had been on the German opera agenda in some way already from its humble, late eighteenth-century beginnings, and that Wagner later also employed with his theory of the *Gesamtkunstwerk*.[51] Weber sees the ideal of fusion, leading to a transformation and sublimation of the individual constituents, not only on a multimedial level, but also reflected in the relation between the individual musical numbers and the work as a whole, when he writes:

---

50   "Es versteht sich von selbst, daß ich von der Oper rede, die der Deutsche will: ein in sich abgeschlossenes Kunstwerk, wo alle Theile und Beyträge der verwandten und benutzten Künste ineinanderschmelzend verschwinden, und auf gewisse Weise untergehend – eine neue Welt bilden."*AMZ* XIX/12, 19 March 1817: 203. The attentive reader may have noted that Weber had used the same phrase about the German's predilection for a "closed artwork" in his 'An die kunstliebenden Bewohner Dresdens (1817)' (see above). Intriguingly, Weber re-used the same sentence even a third time, in a fragment from *Tonkünstlers Leben* also written in 1817, now adding a significant detail. In *Tonkünstlers Leben* Weber lets the composer Felix use the same description to refer not only to the type of opera that the German, but also the Frenchman wants (see Kaiser 1908: 469). Indeed, Weber generally regarded his French fellow composers as allies in the battle against the trivial and undramatic nature of Italian opera. At the same time, it is clear that the greater part of the French opera world hardly cared as much for this type of a transformative higher unity. In France, clearly-delineated forms and conventions were far more important than Weber's Romantic notion of a proto-*Gesamtkunstwerk*. That Weber's esthetic was indeed fully different from French opera practice we can witness in his struggles against the way in which his operas were performed in Paris, struggles which will be discussed in Chapter 4. Moreover, one rarely finds esthetic judgments with a comparable tenor to Weber's in contemporary French discourse on music, whereas the ideal of a "closed artwork" proved to be an ongoing trope, if not cliché, of German nineteenth-century thought on opera. In the context of *Undine*, Weber was not the only to attribute the work the merit of multimedial coherence. In fact, Ludwig Friedrich Catel had reached a similar conclusion in his *Vossische Zeitung* review of 8 August 1816: "What a close alliance is realized between the Romantic poetry of Undine, the marvelous music and the magic stage design; an inseparable unity of the arts!" ("In welch innigem Bunde tritt hier die romantische Dichtung Undines mit dem Wunderbaren der Tonsetzung und dem Zauber der Bühnendarstellung, in ein ganzes der Kunsteinheit zusammen!") Quoted after Markx 2016: 256.

51   John J. Daverio writes that Weber "was not so much foreshadowing Wagner's fully developed *Gesamtkunstwerk* theory as he was repeating what had become an obligatory formula," also proclaimed by Herder, Novalis and August Wilhelm Schlegel. (Daverio 1986/87: 63) Daverio refers to Alfred R. Neumann's 1951 dissertation *The Evolution of the Concept of the Gesamtkunstwerk in German Romanticism* (Neumann: 1951).

Generally, a few outstanding musical pieces decide the success of the whole. Only rarely do these individual pieces eventually dissolve in the overall sense of unity, as it should. Every individual piece appears as an independent, organic, closed being. But it should become a part of the entire structure and dissolve in the experience of this overarching structure.[52]

After this preliminary delineation, Weber delves into Hoffmann's opera itself, and does indeed recognize the ideal of a rounded, coherent form in it when he describes the final moments of the opera as:

Overture and final chorus eventually shake hands, enclosing the work. The former evokes and discloses the world of the wondrous, [...] without truly closing, as the overture music immediately flows on into the action, whereas the latter has a fully calming and satisfying effect. The entire work is one of the most brilliant operas of recent times.[53]

Weber also recognizes Hoffmann's ability to preserve the musical and dramatic balance of the whole without trying to please his audience with individual numbers (as opposed to, for example, Italian opera). He describes the opera as: "truly *a flow*, and after many hearings, the author can think of no moment that disrupted the magic circle of images that the composer evoked in his soul."[54]

With regard to the music, Weber praises the composer's use of instrumental effects and his knowledge of harmony, familiar elements associated with German opera composition. To balance his praise, he makes minor remarks concerning excessive use of violoncellos, violas and diminished seventh chords; elements that were in fact all principal traits of Weber's own musical style, techniques that he would use perhaps no less abundantly in *Der Freischütz*. Ultimately, Weber's praise clearly outweighs his criticism, as he concludes by

---

52   "Meistens entscheiden einzeln hervorstechende Musikstücke den Beyfall fürs Ganze. Selten verschwinden diese [...] im grossen Allgefühl am Schlusse, wie es eigentlich seyn sollte. [...] Jedes Musikstück erscheint durch den ihm zukommenden Bau, als ein selbstständig-organisches, in sich abgeschlossnes Wesen. Doch soll es als Theil des Gebäudes verschwinden in der Anschauung desselben." *AMZ* XIX/12, 19 March 1817: 203.

53   "Ouvertüre und Schlusschor geben sich hier, das Werk umschliessend, die Hände. Erstere erregt und eröffnet die Wunderwelt, [...] ohne gänzlich abzuschliessen, in die Handlung eingreifend; letztere beruhigt und befriedigt vollkommen. Das ganze Werk ist eines der geistvollsten, das uns die neuere Zeit geschenkt hat." Ibid.: 206.

54   "Wirklich *ein Guss*, und Ref. erinnert sich bey oftmaligem Anhören keiner einzigen Stelle, die ihn nur einen Augenblick dem magischen Bilderkreise, den der Tondichter in seiner Seele hervorrief, entrückt hatte." Ibid.: 205.

voicing the wish that Hoffmann will soon give the world a new opera of similar quality. Yet the composer's untimely death in 1822 frustrated this desire.[55]

4.3 Carl Maria von Weber's Der Freischütz

In the end, it turned out that Weber himself would compose "the opera that the German wanted" with his *Freischütz*. The national significance attributed to the work is partly related to its subject matter,[56] but also to Weber's affiliation with the contemporary nationalist movement in Germany. He had set the song cycle *Leyer und Schwert* on texts by the fallen poet Theodor Körner (1791–1813) to music in 1814, and the premiere of *Der Freischütz* in Berlin took place on the 18th of June 1821, the six-year anniversary of Waterloo.

The libretto, written by Friedrich Kind, was derived from August Apel and Friedrich Laun's *Gespensterbuch* (1811). In its depiction of rural life in a hunter's society, its Faustian struggle between good and evil and the encounter between humans and spirits, it corresponded considerably to images of German nationhood and to the fascinations of contemporary German opera. In composing the work, Weber achieved a symbiosis between catchy folksongs such as the hunters' chorus and the *Jungfernkranz*, and a more elevated "symphonic" style. This facilitated the work's approval both by the public at large and among connoisseurs. Yet the enormous success did also raise some critical voices.

Although the premiere took place in June 1821, it took until the beginning of 1822 until an unprecedented storm of reports on *Der Freischütz* reached the *AMZ*. An anonymous report from Vienna of January 1822 celebrates the opera in an ecstatic way, stating:

> Wonder of wonders! In our time of sham art, at a moment, at which only musical acrobatics and stale tinkling tirades appear to gain public acclaim, Weber's *Freischütz* has scored an eminent victory, and evoked an enthusiasm that [...] has given German composers the prospect that they simply have to offer truly decent operas in order to stir the national conscience of their compatriots – who have for quite some time been lulled into sleep by Italian sweets – and may awaken the unspoiled sense for the truthful and beautiful out of its lethargic slumber.[57]

---

55 In fact, his compositional activity had already nearly ceased in 1813, after completing *Undine*. In the following years, he dedicated most of his creative powers to writing, and only influenced opera developments as a commentator from the sidelines. See Garlington 1979: 24.

56 National traits of *Der Freischütz* will be discussed in detail in most of the following chapters. Within this chapter, focus lies on its national reception in contemporary journalism.

57 "Wunder über Wunder! In unserer mit Recht verrufenen Afterkunst-Periode, in einem Zeitpunkte, wo nur musikalische Seiltänzerey, sinnloses Tongewirre und abgedroschene

Although the critic praises the individual numbers, and concedes that these songs particularly caused the popularity of the opera by the people at large, he simultaneously emphasizes the quality of the whole, thereby employing the ideology of structural coherence and organic unity: "Admittedly, the masses were attracted to some of the popular melodies in the work, but thanks to these favorites, the rest of this magnificent whole also gained well-deserved recognition."[58] The author concludes with a poetic statement, in which he both underlines the specific German character of Weber's music and the way in which *Der Freischütz* quenched the thirst of the fatherland at a moment of utmost urgency:

> All voices unite to praise this thinking, original, truly brilliant composer who has provided the fatherland, at this particular moment of dire necessity, this priceless spiritual rebirth, in which harmony and melody fraternally branch out, and the exquisite craft of a German instrumentalist unfolds in splendid magnificence.[59]

In this statement, many common traits of German opera composition are touched on. The composer is a thinker ("er greift alles tiefer"); harmony and melody branch together, underlining the ideal of symbiosis; and the association of German opera with the craft of instrumental composition is stressed. Furthermore, it is noteworthy that this Viennese critic published his review in the Saxon *AMZ*, instead of in an Austrian newspaper. As Wolfgang Michael Wagner concludes from a source study on Austrian reports concerning the Vienna performances of *Der Freischütz* at the end of 1821, explicit statements concerning the German quality of the work were usually avoided.[60]

Klingklangs-Tiraden auf Beyfall rechnen zu können schienen, hat Webers *Freyschütze* einen eminenten Sieg davon getragen, und einen Enthusiasmus hervorgebracht, der [...] Deutschlands Tonsetzern dadurch das erfreulichste Prognostikon stellt, dass sie nur etwas rechtlich gediegenes zu liefern brauchen, um in ihren Landsleuten das durch italienische Leckerey eingelullte bessere Selbstgefühl, wenn auch etwas gewaltsam, aufzurütteln, und den unverdorbenen Sinn für das einzig Wahre und Schöne aus seinem lethargischen Schlummer zu erwecken." *AMZ* XXIV/1, 2 January 1822: 12–13.

58 "freylich waren es besonders einige populäre Melodieen, [...] wodurch die Menge sich angezogen fühlte; aber diese erklärten Favoritstücke verschaften auch allmählig den übrigen Theilen des herrlichen Ganzen gerechte Anerkennung." Ibid.: 13.

59 "Alle Stimmen vereinen sich zum Lob und Preise des denkenden, originellen, wahrhaft genialen Componisten, der das Vaterland gerade in dem Momente des dringendsten Bedarfes mit dieser köstlichen Geistesgeburt beschenkte, worin sich Harmonie und Melodie brüderlich verzweigen, und die ganze Kraft eines kunstgerechten deutschen Instrumentalisten in glänzender Herrlichkeit sich entfaltet." Ibid.: 13.

60 Wagner 1994: 158. At the same time, Wagner hardly adresses the question whether this phenomenon is motivated by deviating loyalties or by fear for the harsh censorship of

Even if it is often impossible to evaluate the political undertone of artistic judgments, it is nonetheless clear that these Austrian reports covertly adhere to esthetic reasoning that asserts notions of German musical nationhood. A reporter from the *Wiener Zeitschrift für Kunst,* for example, praised the work for its: "correspondance and unification of all parts into a ravishing, craftful total effect, an all-embracing unity."[61] A critic from the *Wiener Allgemeine Musikalische Zeitung* in his turn stated: "The profundity of this excellent composer impresses incredibly at a time, in which composition is mostly executed and judged in a factory-made way."[62] It is remarkable that Viennese critics called *Der Freischütz* an organic unity, whereas the censorship was so far-reaching that the formal shape of the music and the logic of the story was deeply affected, to Weber's huge disappointment.[63] Apparently, the ideal of

---

Metternich's restoration politics. Thanks to a detailed study by Joachim Reiber, we do, however, know which alterations were made in *Der Freischütz* as it was performed in Vienna in 1821, and can estimate their ideological motivations. Most censorship measures were taken from a religious point of view, as both the hermit and the diabolical spirit Samiel had to be omitted. But there was also a national-political dimension. Originally, the opera takes place in Bohemia in the years after the Thirty Years War (1618–1648). In the Viennese version, the opera was transplanted to the politically-neutral, imaginary *Weidenhorst,* and some lines referring to the Thirty Years War were left out. (See Reiber 1990: 112–118) This appears to have been motivated by the fact that the Thirty Years War had been an uproar of Bohemian subjects against Habsburg reign, and the Austrian government clearly did not want to stir anti-Habsburg national sentiments among its population. Reiber argues that the dissociation of historical moments and geographical locations was a standard procedure in Viennese theater in those days, based on what Jakob Zeidler has called "das Gesetz der idealen Ferne." This law was enforced even more meticulously when the story concerned Habsburg history and its territorial relations. (See Ibid.: 123 and Zeidler 1898: 307) That Bohemia here serves as a picturesque emblem of German folk culture changed the matter only slightly. During the 1820s, Habsburg attitudes towards the vindication of German culture and language were less negative than they were towards non-German minorities, as long as it did not advocate political disintegration of the multi-ethnic empire. (See, for example, Bruckmüller 1984: 136–143) However, the fact that, in a climate of severe censorship, the former may function as a veiled form of the latter does complicate the matter.

61   "Übereinstimmung und Vereinigung aller Theile zu einem entzückenden, kunstgemäßen Totaleffekt, [und] im ganzen herrschende Einheit." Derived from Wagner 1994: 158.

62   "die Tiefe dieses trefflichen Tonsetzers [...] imponiert in der Zeit, in der die Tonsetzkunst von manchen ganz fabrikmäßig betrieben und von vielen ebenso fabrikmäßig beurtheilt wird, ganz wunderbar." Derived from Ibid.: 159.

63   This becomes evident in a private letter he wrote to his wife Caroline: "For the sake of politics, I must look as if I'm pleased, but I can hardly understand that the opera was a success in this form. I beg you not to be annoyed, and particularly not to reveal to others my dissatisfaction. One must be careful, and in the end, everyone did what he could. And above all, the enthusiasm for the opera is really outstanding." ("Dazu mußte ich nun aus Politik gute Miene machen, und alles schön finden. Ich begreiffe nicht, daß die Oper gefallen konnte. – Ich bitte dich erstlich dich nicht zu ärgern, und dann auch nicht von

organic unity was simply a given where it concerned an opera of a serious German composer such as Weber, regardless of the question whether or not the piece made an organic impression in its performed appearance.

If we take a look at other reports in the *AMZ* concerning performances of *Der Freischütz* in other cities, we revisit familiar reasoning. A review by an anonymous reporter from Prague of April 1822 also praises Weber as a counterweight to the dominance of Italian opera:

> When it comes to the composition, one can hardly praise Mr. von Weber enough for the fact that he, as a veritable German artist, has created a true counter-example to the *Rossiniades* of these days, and has proven that, beside all that mellifluous sensuality, there is still a road to salvation in the realm of music.[64]

A Vienna critic, writing in May 1822, goes as far as to characterize a performance of *Der Freischütz* conducted by Weber as: "a true national ceremony [ein wahres Nationalfest]."[65] A more critical perspective is heard in June from a Munich reporter, who rejects the poor libretto and argues that Weber "has established a brilliant tone-painting, but not a classical structure that is timeless and worth following."[66] The lack of unity within the work is mainly caused by the inconsistencies and poor quality of the libretto, which Weber's music cannot compensate sufficiently:

> A folk tale, [...] without dramatic art, devoid of poetic disposition, this is simply not enough to promise the work a lasting merit. The power of the music alone simply does not suffice to develop this work, to mold it into a unified, beautiful whole, it forms a succession of shattered, atomized, isolated figures that remain unrelated.[67]

---

meiner Unzufriedenheit zu sprechen. Man muß vorsichtig sein, und am Ende haben doch alle gethan was sie konnten. Und der Enthusiasmus für die Oper ist wirklich gränzenlos."). (http://www.weber-gesamtausgabe.de/de/A002068/Korrespondenz/A041911).

64   "Was nun die Composition betrifft, so ist Herr v. W. schon deshalb nicht genug zu loben, dass er, als wahrer deutscher Künstler, [...] ein wahres Widerspiel zu den Rossiniaden unserer Tage bildete, [und zeigt] dass es ausser jenem Gebiete lieblicher Sinnlichkeit auch noch ein Heil in der Tonkunst gebe." *AMZ* XXIV/15, 20 April 1822: 243.

65   "Ein genialisches Tongemälde hat Hr. von Weber aufgestellt; aber ein klassisches Kunstgebilde, das auf Dauer und Nacheiferung Anspruch zu machen hätte, ist damit noch nicht gewonnen."*AMZ* XXIV/19, 8 May 1822: 303.

66   *AMZ* XXIV/23, 5 June 1822: 370.

67   "Ein Volksmärchen, [...] ohne dramatische Kunst, ohne poetische Haltung, all dieses ist wohl nicht geeignet, dem Werke ein bleibendes Verdienst zu versprechen. Denn die der

The reporter concludes by denying the work the national significance that many of his contemporaries attribute to it: "The rifleman may have hit the mark of a folk opera, but fully missed the target of creating a national opera, or even a proper opera at all, arguably even causing a regression of this national enterprise."[68] Thereby he employs the crucial difference between *Volk* and *Nation*, the first referring to the common folk, the second to the cultured community.[69] In the eyes of this critic, a "national" artwork must elevate the masses, and may therefore not descend to popular taste by incorporating demotic songs. The character of *Der Freischütz*'s music showcases the "dilemma of the popular" that David Gramit recognizes in German music discourse between 1780 and 1840, the situation in which "the concept of popularity implicit in the *Volkston* proved difficult to contain in the context of the developing culture of serious music."[70]

Regardless of such esthetic issues, the eminent success of *Der Freischütz* and its function as a celebration of nationhood immediately after its premiere reflect a significant shift in the status of German opera. Where the national foil initially functioned primarily as a tool to promote the work of native composers formerly considered inferior, in the case of Weber's work, a German opera could actually perform the role of national symbol. Of course this is partly due to the political situation of the time. The "urgent moment (Momente des dringendsten Bedarfes)" to which the first Vienna reviewer refers is obviously the situation after the liberation from Napoleonic reign, when an impaired self-esteem was craving for an artwork to be proud of. This created fertile soil for the national appropriation of *Der Freischütz*. But the fact that a German opera could actually fulfill this national desire firmly underlines the eventual success of the genre's advocates.

Tonkunst eigene Kraft konnte eben desswegen nicht aus sich selbst sich entwickeln, [...] sie musste zersplittert und in vereinzelte, unter sich getrennt dargestellte Figuren zersetzt werden, welche weder in einander greifen, noch zu Einem schönen Ganzen sich vereinen." Ibid.: 370.

68   "Die Scheibe einer Volksoper hat der Schütze wohl getroffen, das Ziel einer National-überhaupt einer ächten Oper aber gänzlich verrückt, oder doch viele Stadien weiter hinausgesetzt." Ibid.: 370.

69   Wolfgang Michael Wagner elaborates this distinction in relation to the reception of Weber's works quite extensively in Wagner 1994: 32–38.

70   Gramit 2002: 65.

"Romanticizing the *Singspiel*": The Intersection of Romantic Opera and German National Opera between 1800 and 1821

> Nun hörten sie eine rührende Waldmusik von durcheinander spielenden Hörnern aus der Ferne; sie standen still und horchten, ob es Einbildung oder Wirklichkeit sei: aber ein melodischer Gesang quoll durch die Bäume ihnen wie ein rieselnder Bach entgegen, und Franz glaubte, die Geisterwelt habe sich wohl plötzlich aufgeschlossen, weil sie vielleicht, ohne es zu wissen, das große, zaubernde Wort gefunden hätten.
>
> LUDWIG TIECK, *Franz Sternbalds Wanderungen* (1798)[1]

These words, derived from Ludwig Tieck's characteristic *Künstlerroman*, very much epitomize the contemporary ideal of a perfectly Romantic opera, as it was put forward by German composers, poets, and critics during the first decades of the nineteenth century. The distant sound of hunting horns, the signifying power of music as a messenger of the miraculous, the merging of imagination and reality, the opening up of a spirit world and, most importantly, the frenetic search for a key to unlock this world of fantasy and rapture, all this was crucial to German Romantic opera esthetics at the start of the nineteenth-century. Whereas Franz and his companion Rudolph's spiritual forest experience is presented through the medium of literature, a similar or even more tangible sensation could be created by bringing the forest and all its charms onto the opera stage, with music supplying the appropriate otherworldly aura. The question how to evoke this experience in the most convincing way was nearly as prominent in those days as the pressing question how to found a native opera tradition. But was not the forest experience written down by Tieck quintessentially German, and could not the opening up of a Romantically transfigured world of hunting horns, enchanted forests and supernatural creatures simultaneously be the key to this desired creation of an elevated, distinctively German opera?

---

1 "Now from afar they heard a moving forest music of horns playing together; they stood still and listened, to decide whether this was imagination or reality: but a melodic chant swelled out towards them through the trees like a rippling brook, and Franz believed that the spirit world might suddenly have opened up, because perhaps, without knowing, they had discovered the great, magic spell."

© KONINKLIJKE BRILL NV, LEIDEN, 2019 | DOI:10.1163/9789004245389_004

This chapter investigates the intersection of Romantic opera and German national opera between 1800 and 1821, not only from the viewpoint of their respective development, but also by scrutinizing contemporary reflection on both ideals in music periodicals. The chapter opens with a discussion of Romanticism in general and Romantic opera in particular, with special attention to the question of their respective German cultural anchorage. In this section, Novalis's notion of "Romanticization" will be proposed as a suitable metaphor for approaching developments within German Romantic opera, as it revolves around the distinction between and interplay of trivial and elevated Romanticism. This theoretical is followed by a discussion of early nineteenth-century German operas, to see how different composers and librettists sought to Romanticize the genre with various strategies and varying success. The analysis runs from the allegedly trivial Romanticism of Kauer and Hensler's *Donauweibchen* (1798) to the more ambitious attempts to Romanticize the *Singspiel* by E.T.A. Hoffmann and Carl Maria von Weber. This chapter on Romanticization *within* the *Singspiel* has been designed as part of a larger argument that also involves the next chapter, which discusses Louis Spohr and Carl Maria von Weber's experiments that went *beyond* the *Singspiel* constellation by substituting a sung-througout structure for spoken dialogue, and will evaluate whether this move facilitated the desired Romanticization and elevation of German opera more than could be done within the stylistic confines of *Singspiel*.

The argument of Chapter 2 and 3 centers around the term "Romantic," which is, as Stephen C. Meyer observes, a "notoriously slippery adjective."[2] But while acknowledging its unsettledness, it is nonetheless useful to discuss the meaning of the word, particularly the meaning that historical sources attribute to it when using it. Therefore, the meaning of Romanticism and its relation to opera and German nationhood in the early nineteenth century must be scrutinized.

1   Theoretical Concerns

1.1   *Romantic Opera, a German Invention?*
The aspirations for an elevated, German national opera in the first decades of the nineteenth century cannot be seen in isolation from the desire to found a Romantic opera. The conceptualization of German and Romantic opera take place in the same period,[3] the esthetic demands and characterizations

---

2 Meyer 2003: 116.
3 Ludwig Schiedermair entitles the chapter dedicated to the period in his *Die deutsche Oper* as "Die romantische Nationaloper." Schiedermair 1940: 206–234. Aubrey Garlington Jr. speaks

of both genres highly correspond, and discussion of them revolves around similar exemplary works (as we will see, E.T.A. Hoffman's *Undine* and Weber's *Der Freischütz* form key points of reference in both cases). Whereas *Grand opéra* has come to be understood as the principal French opera genre during the first half of the nineteenth century, and *Belcanto* delineates the general style of contemporary Italian opera, Romantic opera is often considered to be the German early nineteenth-century contribution to this genre-stylistic palette. Furthermore, within German opera historiography, it is often presented as the first significant, genuinely German contribution to opera history, and therefore marks the coming of age of German national opera.[4]

In *Propagating a National Genre, German Writers on German Opera, 1798–1830* (2010), Kevin Robert Burke questions the term "German Romantic Opera," because he considers it "a modern phrase that did not develop until the twentieth century," often used for "constructing a teleological narrative that leads inexorably to Wagner's music dramas."[5] His main problem with the dominance of this notion is that it obscures other, less Romantically-inclined currents in early nineteenth-century German opera. Burke therefore suggests "Early Nineteenth-Century German Opera" as a neutral, and therefore more useful alternative.[6] This study is less concerned with providing an ontology of German opera, a new terminology or a revision of music history. The frequent association of German opera with Romanticism shows that a Romantic label was probably one of the most effective means to articulate a distinct German opera identity. That historiography filters out many events in order to foreground those developments that later generations find most relevant is a given, as well as its tendency to shape narratives that are clear and easy to remember. At the same time, I believe that many of the nineteenth-century sources discussed in this study suggest that the association of German opera

---

of "an intrinsically Romantic opera, synonymous with German opera, if only for the German composer." Garlington 1979: 32.

4   Hermann Kretzschmar writes in his *Geschichte der Oper* (1919): "The Romantic direction in opera [...] joins into the mainstream again and aims for the vacant position of former Renaissance opera, and intends to take the lead in high-style music drama. With *Der Freischütz* Germany takes the decisive step into opera history, it accelerates a movement that ends with Richard Wagner and the ascendancy of German spirit in the international music drama." ("Die romantische Richtung in der Oper [...] lenkt wieder in den Hauptweg ein und strebt nach dem frei gewordenen Platz der ehemaligen Renaissancoper [sic.], sie macht Anstalt die Führung im Musikdrama höheren Stils zu übernehmen. Mit dem ‚Freischütz' tut Deutschland den entscheidenden Schritt in der Geschichte der Oper; es beginnt eine Bewegung, die mit Richard Wagner und mit der Vorherrschaft deutschen Geistes im internationalen Musikdrama endet.") Kretzschmar 1919: 255.

5   Burke 2010: 2–4.

6   Ibid.: 178.

with Romanticism was a familiar trope from the outset, and not a twentieth-century invention.

Besides the tendency to associate the term "Romantic opera" with German early nineteenth-century opera, sometimes it is also used to describe a broader, international current in the first half of the nineteenth century. An example of this is Edward J. Dent's acclaimed study *The Rise of Romantic Opera* (1976), which deals with Romanticism not only in German, but also particularly in French and Italian opera. The twofold usage of the term Romantic opera reflects a tension between conflicting notions of Romanticism on a more general, cultural-historical level. To clarify the position taken in this study, it is useful to reflect on these divergent viewpoints.[7]

For many German scholars, the anchorage of Romanticism and German culture seems self-evident and undisputable. The title of Rüdiger Safranski's recent history of Romanticism – *Romantik, eine deutsche Affäre* (2009) – forms a clear example of this attitude. In his introduction, Safranski underlines his point when he writes that Romanticism "isn't a strictly German phenomenon, but it experienced such a marked character in Germany, to the extent that, even outside Germany, German culture is occasionally identified with Romanticism and the Romantic."[8] In *Romantik. Geschichte und Begriff* (1996), Gerhard Schulze also assumes that the German identity of Romanticism is internationally accepted:

> For Europe, Romanticism formed a primarily German affair, defined and established by Germans. Only gradually did the word obtain a theoretically determined cultural-historical meaning, signifying literary tendencies beyond the German borders.[9]

The international acceptance of this view is, however, less widespread than Safranski and Schulze want us to believe. In the introduction to *The Rise of Romantic Opera*, Edward J. Dent argues that "the ordinary educated person's general conceptions of the Romantic Movement" depends heavily upon "that ordinary educated person's nationality." According to Dent, an Englishman would perhaps mention Wordsworth and Byron, "his first associations with Romanticism will be literary." A Frenchman will think of Hugo, and refer particularly to theatre and painting, whereas a German would probably

---

7 I have chosen to present a few recent perspectives on Romanticism, and do not at all pretend to provide an all-encompassing, adequate picture of the existing literature on this phenomenon. A bibliography of Romanticism is as infinite as the longing of its practitioners.

8 Safranski 2009: 12.

9 Schulze 1996: 43.

state that "the Romantic art of Germany is music, and [...] the characteristic of Romantic literature in Germany is its close association with music."[10]
Commonplaces though they are, they do show that each culture has its own
canon, its own favored arts and artists, and therefore, its own conception of
Romanticism.[11] In a 1998 article called 'Romantik. Ein typisch deutsches Phänomen?,' the French cultural historian Michael Werner also defines Romanticism as an international rather than German phenomenon, disseminated
through cultural transfers beyond nations.[12]

Although there is a plethora of reasons to problematize the idea of Romanticism as a specifically, nearly exclusively German phenomenon, a more
general, neutral and international usage of the term has its shortcomings too.[13]
Especially in the case of opera, using the adjective "Romantic" for nearly all
operas between 1800 and 1850 with slight Romantic traits, or using it simply as
a label for a relatively long historical period,[14] damages the analytical focus and
denoting potential of the term.

To situate discussions concerning Romantic opera somewhere between literary Romanticism and Romantic music esthetics in general, Hans Heinrich
Eggebrecht's notion of a *Zwei-Welten-Modell* can be of use. He bases this idea
on the writings of several Romantic artists and thinkers, among them Wilhelm
Wackenroder, E.T.A. Hoffmann, Arthur Schopenhauer and Richard Wagner.
Eggebrecht developed this model in *Musik im Abendland* (1991) and revisited his
theory in a 1997 article entitled 'Romantik, was ist das?' In the latter, he writes:

> Romantic yearning [...] is based on a fully negative perception of the rela-
> tion between self and actual reality. [...] The antithesis of reality defines
> the Romantic direction. I call this the other world, and I recognize a dual-
> ity of two worlds: reality – other world.[15]

---

10   Dent 1976: 1.
11   Dent's reasoning is clearly in line with Arthur Oncken Lovejoy's use of "Romanticisms"
     in plural in *On the discrimination of Romanticisms* (1924). There, Lovejoy states that "the
     'Romanticism' of one country may have little in common with that of another, that there
     is, in fact, a plurality of Romanticisms, of possibly quite distinct thought-complexes."
     Lovejoy 1948: 235.
12   Werner 1998: 190.
13   This is not the case in Werner's analysis, in which a framework of supranational charac-
     teristics is formed, which then serves as a tool to distinguish particularly German features
     of Romanticism. See Ibid.: 197–199.
14   For example, in *Die Deutsche romantische Oper*, Siegfried Goslich uses it to mark the
     period between 1813 and 1850, and indiscriminately addresses nearly the entire German
     opera production of this era, with little reference to the specific character and qualities of
     Romantic opera. See Goslich 1975: 9.
15   Eggebrecht 1997: 23.

In Eggebrecht's interpretation of Romanticism, this "other world" can be either represented by art or approached through the contemplation of art, as he explains in *Musik im Abendland*: "The real world *generates the desire for the art world, the world of music* that provides *redemption* from the real world. The reception of healing, the redemption through art affects the attitude toward the negative real world."[16]

This idea of a co-existence of two worlds, one real and one otherworldly, and the belief that art – particularly music – can realize traffic between these realms figures prominently in early nineteenth-century theory on Romantic opera. It is central to Dahlhaus's definition of Romantic opera as governed by a characteristic dramaturgy of opposing spheres. While several definitions of Romantic opera can be and have been formulated, this description still seems to be the most adequate way to define it. Dahlhaus writes that "Romantic opera is based on a dramaturgical antagonism of the otherworldly and the earthly that is centered around one single moment, the appearance of the miraculous."[17]

This description has a few merits. To begin with, it distinguishes between operas in which this basic dramaturgical principle forms the inner core of the work and pieces that obtain a Romantic *couleur locale* at the outside, but diverge from Romantic principles in their inner dramatic structure.[18] Furthermore, the thesis of opposed spheres and miracle – the breakthrough of the one sphere into the other – as the key moment of the drama applies to many German operas considered Romantic. It is traceable in the closing scenes of E.T.A. Hoffmann's *Undine* (1816) and Weber's *Der Freischütz* (1821), as well as in the arrival of the swan knight in the first act of Wagner's *Lohengrin* (1848).

16　Eggebrecht 2008: 595–596.
17　Dahlhaus 2007: 288.
18　One may think, for example, of Rossini's *La donna del lago* (1819), which is based on Walter Scott's *The Lady of the Lake*, but regardless of its sixteenth-century Scottish milieu and Romantic *couleur locale* lacks the contrast between an earthly and supernatural sphere so central to most German "Romantic" operas. Wolfgang Michael Wagner offers a detailed comparison to distinguish German, "genuinely" Romantic opera from the quasi-Romantic Italian and French operas *La Cenerentola* (Rossini, 1817) and *La dame blanche* (Boieldieu, 1825). Wagner recognizes a remarkable fascination for metaphysics and superstition and a strongly developed idealism and religious attitude, which sets German Romanticism apart from its French and Italian counterparts. (see Wagner 1994: 80–86) In a similar vein, Everist argues that supernatural elements can indeed also be found in non-German operas, for example in *La dame blanche*, but points out that "when French audiences experienced the supernatural, it was as part of a deception," whereas "the German supernatural tended to depict genuine inhabitants of other worlds on stage." (Everist 1994: 243).

1.2   Opera and the Process of Romanticization

After discussing a few perspectives on Romanticism, opera, and German nationhood from recent secondary literature, it is useful to take a look at some
historical sources, in order to trace the most prominent notions of Romanticism in German culture around 1800 and to examine how and to what purpose
the adjective 'Romantic' is employed in German discussions concerning the
development of opera. One famous literary statement on the essence of Romanticism seems crucial to understand what German opera could gain from
Romanticism. This statement was written down by Novalis (a pseudonym of
Georg Friedrich Philip Freiherr von Hardenberg) in a fragment in 1798:

> The world must be Romanticized. [...] To Romanticize means nothing
> but a qualitative potentiation ["Potenzierung"]. [...] In that I grant the
> common a higher significance, the ordinary a mysterious appearance,
> the known the dignity of the unknown, the finite an infinite aura, thereby
> I Romanticize it. For the higher, the unknown, the mystical and the in-
> finite, it works the other way around, [...] they are expressed in a more
> familiar way.[19]

Novalis presents the idea of Romanticizing as a mental process, an act that
can be executed by an individual. His notion of Romanticizing relates to several key aspects of German Romanticism as it developed in literature and
philosophy around 1800.[20] On the one hand, it points to a state of mind in
which everyday reality transcends into a higher, more meaningful consciousness through the imagination (an expression of the Romantic notion of *Universalpoesie* as practiced by the *Frühromantiker* in Jena).[21] In line with this is
the tendency to approach nature as a symbolical, mystical realm, which we

---

19   "Die Welt muss romantisiert werden. [...] Romantisieren ist nichts als eine qualit[ative]
      Potenzierung. [...] Indem ich dem Gemeinen einen hohen Sinn, dem Gewöhnlichen ein
      geheimnisvolles Ansehn, dem Bekannten die Würde des Unbekannten, dem Endlichen
      einen unendlichen Schein gebe so romantisiere ich es – Umgekehrt ist die Operation für
      das Höhere, Unbekannte, Mystische, Unendliche [...] – es bekommt einen geläufigen
      Ausdruck." Mähl 1978: 334.
20   Safranski calls it "the best definition of the Romantic [die beste Definition des Roman-
      tischen.]" Safranski 2009: 13.
21   Johann Gottlieb Fichte, the brothers Friedrich and August Wilhelm Schlegel, Novalis,
      Friedrich Schelling, Ludwig Tieck and others formed an intellectual community at Jena
      between 1794 and 1799, which is generally considered to be the first, "early" Romantic
      movement on German soil. The term 'Universalpoesie' was coined by Friedrich Schlegel
      in Fragment 116 of *Athenäum*, written in 1798: "Romantic poetry is a progressive, univer-
      sal poetry. [...] It aims to make life and society poetic." ("Die romantische Poesie ist eine

find for example in the landscape paintings of Caspar David Friedrich. On the other, the elevation of the common as something meaningful and non-trivial is in line with the rise of interest in folk poetry and fairy-tales we witness in Heidelberg Romanticism.[22]

At the same time, Novalis's ideal of elevating the common also applies to opera, in the sense that the desire for a more elevated, sophisticated opera formed the main ambition of many early nineteenth-century German writers on the genre. In Chapter one, we have seen how this desire formed an important impetus to the conceptualization of German opera. One way to achieve this "qualitative potentiation" of the genre was by means of "Romanticizing," adding a Romantic layer to the common plot of early nineteenth-century German operas.[23] This could be done either on the level of story line, or by incorporating more ambitious music.

Instrumental music, which was quickly gaining prominence in the first decades of the nineteenth century,[24] formed a model for this ambitious music that could grant the *Singspiel* a new, Romantic profundity. Comparisons of music with the supernatural and mystical formed an important part of the Romantic canon, and were made by authors such as Johann Gottfried Herder and Ludwig Tieck.[25] E.T.A. Hoffmann emphatically interpreted the alleged metaphysical character of music as Romantic in his review of Beethoven's *Fifth Symphony*, published in the AMZ in 1810:

> It [music] is the most Romantic of arts, – one could nearly say, exclusively truly Romantic. [...] Music leads man into an unknown realm, a world

---

progressive Universalpoesie. [...] Sie will [...] das Leben und die Gesellschaft poetisch machen.") Behler 1967: 182.

22   Heidelberg formed a second meeting point for Romantic thinkers after the early gathering at Jena. Between 1804 and 1809, philologists collecting and editing folk culture, such as Clemens von Brentano and Achim von Arnim (who compiled the folksong collection *Des Knaben Wunderhorn*, 1805–1808) and Joseph Görres (editor of *Die Teutschen Volksbücher*, 1807), resided in Heidelberg. See for more information Schlechter 2007.

23   Stephen C. Meyer also argues that "the idea of a *romantische Oper* intersected with this idea of 'genre elevation'." Meyer 2003: 117.

24   See for more information considering this phenomenon Dahlhaus 1994 and Neubauer 1986 and Neubauer 2017.

25   Concerning the power of music, Johann Gottfried Herder wrote in his *Kalligone* (1800): "What man cannot perceive, the invisible world, can be mediated only through her" ("Was anschaulich dem Menschen nicht werden kann, wird ihm in ihrer Weise, in ihrer Weise allein, mittheilbar, die Welt des Unsichtbaren.") (Herder 1955: 152), whereas Ludwig Tieck called music "the last secret of faith, the mysticism, religion fully revealed" ("Das letzte Geheimnis des Glaubens, die Mystik, die durchaus geoffenbarte Religion.") in his *Phantasien über die Kunst* (1799). Wackenroder 2005: 107.

that has nothing in common with the external, phenomenal world that surrounds him. In this realm, man leaves behind all verbally expressible feelings, to dedicate himself to the ineffable.[26]

Hoffmann's famous interpretation of Beethoven's symphony – often considered to be the cornerstone of Romantic music esthetics – features a striking contradiction. In order to advocate the absolute, metaphysical qualities of Beethoven's music, Hoffmann employs a highly speculative narrative, in which he illustrates how the symphony irresistibly carries the listener into "the wondrous spirit realm of the infinite":

> Deep inside his mind, Beethoven carries the Romanticism of music. The critic never experienced this so vividly as in the present symphony. In an ongoing, ever-increasing climax up until the end, it unfolds Beethoven's Romanticism in an unprecedented way, and irresistibly carries the listener into the wondrous spirit realm of the infinite.[27]

From the perspective of Novalis's definition of Romanticizing, this narrative can be understood as an attempt to give "the higher (instrumental music) a more familiar expression (a concrete story)." In fact, the storyline of an opera can provide a similar narrative, in which the abstract art of music is combined with a phenomenal level, on which its metaphysical character and wondrous workings can be made visible.[28] The late nineteenth-century apotheosis of this line of thinking forms Wagner's definition of his stageworks as "musical deeds made visible [Ersichtlich gewordene Thaten der Musik]" in *Über die Benennung*

---

26   "Sie [Die Musik] ist die romantischste aller Künste, – fast möchte man sagen, allein *rein* romantisch. [...] Die Musik schliesst dem Menschen ein unbekanntes Reich auf; eine Welt, die nichts gemein hat mit der äussern Sinnenwelt, die ihn umgibt, und in der er alle durch Begriffe bestimmbaren Gefühle zurücklässt, um sich den Unaussprechlichen hinzugeben." *AMZ* XII/40, 4 July 1810: 631.

27   "Tief im Gemüthe trägt Beethoven die Romantik der Musik [...]. Lebhafter hat Rec. dies nie gefühlt, als bey der vorliegenden Symphonie, die in einem bis zum Ende fortsteigenden Climax jene Romantik Beethovens mehr, als irgend ein anderes seiner Werke entfaltet, und den Zuhörer unwiderstehlich fortreisst in das wundervolle Geisterreich des Unendlichen." Ibid.: 634.

28   One could argue that the desire to present the miraculous power of music was the most important motivation for the invention of opera around 1600. This is evident from the prominence of Orpheus in the earliest operas. The artist who – through his singing and lyre-playing – could move the Gods and descend into the underworld to bring Eurydice back to life exemplifies this interest in the wondrous workings of music. For more information, see for example Marchenkov 2009.

"Musikdrama" (1872).[29] Although Wagner's idea, which Dahlhaus connects to a paradoxical "triumph of the idea of absolute music within the doctrine of music drama,"[30] represents a later stage in opera esthetics, it is clearly modeled on the Romantic ideas of E.T.A. Hoffmann and his contemporaries.

1.3   *"Trivial" versus "Elevated" Romanticism and Foreign Impulses*

An interpretation of early-nineteenth-century German discourse on Romantic opera is complicated by, again, the loose use of the adjective Romantic. Dahlhaus tries to categorize two types of Romanticism in relation to German opera by following Sénancour's distinction between "romanesque" and "Romantic," introduced in his epistolary novel *Obermann* (1804). In Dahlhaus's eyes, "the romanesque is bound to magic fairy-tales and *Schauergeschichten* (the German equivalent of 'Gothic' novels)," whereas "the Romantic is a product of an elevated, metaphysically-directed imagination."[31] Although this distinction is useful, the alternative "romanesque" plays no role in the German music periodicals under scrutiny. In fact, the adjective "Romantic" is used both to refer to intellectual, "elevated" Romanticism and to its more fashionable, allegedly "trivial" counterpart. To complicate the matter even further, many operas of the time that are considered to be Romantic display serious or elevated Romantic traits while simultaneously containing elements that tend towards the more trivial, fanciful side.

Another crucial distinction can be made between "elevated" Romanticism and works in which Romantic elements function as mysterious charms within an essentially Enlightened framework. In the field of literature, Safranski points to the vogue of the *Geisterseher-* and *Bundesroman* in the last two decades of the eighteenth century, in which the mysterious is ultimately explained.[32] In "elevated" Romanticism, fascination shifts from explanation towards the unexplainable, irrational qualities of the miraculous: "The mystery is cherished not only to highlight the power of Enlightenment, but rather because it defies rational clarification."[33] Many works deemed "romanesque" are characterized by this former, Enlightened attitude towards the mysterious. But again, this

---

29   *WWSB*. Sämtliche Schriften, Band 9: 306.
30   Dahlhaus 1994: 16.
31   Dahlhaus 2007: 280.
32   Müller-Dyes signals the same phenomenon in trivial literature of this period, when he writes: "[eventually], the imagined magic landscape turns out to be of cardboard. A look behind the scene – which the authors visibly enjoy to share with us – is enough to detect the machines that created the illusion." Müller-Dyes 1965: 82.
33   Safranksi 2009: 57.

attitude also figures in some serious or elevated Romantic operas,[34] making it increasingly difficult to draw clear distinctions.

The essays that E.T.A. Hoffmann's wrote about Romantic opera around 1810 generally grant him the status of being the first important theorist of the genre, but his outlooks were actually anticipated by other critics. For example, Franz Horn's contribution to this discussion is generally overlooked.[35] Franz Horn was a writer and literary scholar who studied in Jena and Leipzig between 1799 and 1803, and spent most of his life in Berlin. Both in Jena and Berlin, he lived close to Romantic circles, although his artistic viewpoints were diverse, and it seems questionable to label him an arch-Romantic. Horn gravitated towards a rather conservative Romanticism, contributed to patriotic literature during the Liberation Wars, and had a short-lived success with his handbook *Poesie und Beredsamkeit der Deutschen von Luthers Zeit bis zur Gegenwart* (1822–1829).[36]

Despite his conservative image, Horn was quite ahead of his times in applying the adjective Romantic in its serious and elevated sense in relation to German opera already in 1802. In a contribution to the *AMZ*, Horn listed the recipe for a successful German opera libretto, summing up the greatest clichés of the *Singspiel* tradition:

> Pick a young man and girl who represent the innocence of country life, in other words, that have fallen in love in an upright way. Season this innocence and love with some rudeness, virtue, [...] some coarse jokes and hot-tempered lustiness to all sides. Then, furthermore, look for a noble lord, [...] that wants to make half of the world happy, and kill the other half [...]. Then make sure you'll find a spurned lover, a real villain, who threatens to cause upheaval to the entire community, and [...] sets all thinkable traps to everyone. The girl rejects all this with great contempt and praises the sincere and enduring love [...] of her youngling. Mercilessly she makes fun of the city, and wants to know nothing of its delights, balls and operas, even though she is a principal in one herself. The inveterate villain won't be led off, but now really carries out his [...] plan. If

---

34   One may think of Ännchen's Romanze Nr. 13 in *Der Freischütz*, a *Schauergeschichte* in which a frightening ghost eventually turns out to be the watchdog Nero. Within the opera it is counterbalanced, however, by Agathe's more genuinely Romantic belief in providence.

35   A positive exception is Christoph E. Hänggi, who in *G.P.L. Sievers (1775–1830) und seine Schriften* (1993) observes a group of so-called 'early Hoffmanns (die frühen 'Hoffmanns)' who, during the first decade of the nineteenth century, anticipated many of Hoffmann's' later ideas on music, Romanticism and opera, and lists Horn among them. See Hänggi 1993: 113 + 139–145.

36   See Heinemann 1972: 627.

yet one includes a few oneliners of delicate sweetness, food and drinks, sugar-sweet homeliness, quarrel and love, despair, anger and enjoyment, one only has to join these together, and the majority of the public will most probably not remain unaffected.[37]

This description particularly refers to the tradition of sentimental German opera, initiated by composer Johann Adam Hiller and his librettist Christian Felix Weisse in operas such as *Lottchen am Hofe* (1767), *Die Liebe auf dem Lande* (1768), and *Die Jagd* (1770), but it applies to many later works as well. In fact, the template also pretty much fits *Der Freischütz*, premiered only in 1821, although this sentimental, idyllic side is counter-balanced by the work's more radically Romantic aspects.

Instead of this "most common, torn out of the common,"[38] Horn looks for more elevated subject matter. In the same essay, he proposes "the voluptuously blooming and fantastic that, for example, Carlo Gozzi presents" as another source of inspiration.[39] He characterizes the true opera as "Romantic throughout. It presents the most blooming, harmonic life with voluptuous élan [...], and – elevated by the euphony of delicate music – the most beautiful moments of life speak to us with more clarity than a mere drama could ever achieve."[40]

---

37   "Suche dir einen jungen Mann und ein junges Mädchen aus, die die ländliche Unschuld repräsentiren, dass heisst, die sich wacker in einander verliebt haben, würze diese Unschuld und Liebe mit etwas Grobheit, Tugend, [...] ein wenig derbem Spass und hitziger Rüstigkeit nach allen Seiten hin. Dann siehe dich um nach einem edlen Gutsherrn, [...] der die halbe Welt glücklich machen und die andere umbringen will [....]. Dann bemühe dich ferner nach einem verschmähten Liebhaber, einem reellen Bösewicht, der der ganzen Wirthschaft den Umsturz droht, und [...] alle nur ersinnliche Fallen legt. Das Mädchen weist alles mit grossartiger Verachtung zurück und lobt sich das wackere Gemüth, und die dauerhafte Liebe [...] ihres Jünglings. Auch persifflirt sie die Stadt ganz unbarmherzig, und fragt nichts nach ihren Vergnügungen, Bällen und Opern, ob sei gleich selbst in einer die Hauptrolle spielt. Der eingefleischte Bösewicht lässt sich natürlich nicht irre machen, sondern legt nun erst recht seinen Plan [...] an. [...] Fügt man nun noch eine Menge Sprüchlein hinzu von feinpulverisierter Zärtlichkeit, Essen und Trinken, zukkersüsser Häuslichkeit, Prügel und Liebe, Verzweiflung, Reize, Bosheit und Spass, so braucht man nur das alles sich freundlich und feindlich durcheinander zu bewegen und an einander schlagen zu lassen, und ein grosser Theil des Publikums wird gewiss nicht unberührt bleiben." *AMZ* IV/28, 7 April 1802: 450–451.
38   "Das Gewöhnlichste aus dem Gewöhnlichen herausgerissen." Ibid.: 450.
39   "das üppig blühende und fantastische, das uns etwa Carlo Gozzi darstellt." Ibid.: 450.
40   "Die wahre Oper ist durchaus romantisch. Sie lässt das blühendste, harmonische Leben im üppigen Schwunge [...] vorbeygleiten und von dem Wohllaut zarter Musik gehoben, sprechen uns die schönsten Momente jenes Lebens mit höherer Klarheit an, als je in einem blossen Drama wird geschehen können." Ibid.: 452.

In 1813, eleven years later, E.T.A. Hoffmann would voice a similar, albeit intensified opinion in his dialogue *Der Dichter und der Komponist*:

> Ludwig [the composer]: isn't music the mysterious language of a distant spirit realm, whose miraculous accents resound in our inner self, and awaken a higher, intensive life? [...] This is the ineffable effect of instrumental music. But now, music should tread completely into life, she should [...] refer to specific emotions and actions. [...] But is music capable of communicating anything else than the miracles of that realm, from where she sends her sounds towards us? – The poet must prepare himself for the adventurous flight into the distant realm of Romanticism; there he will find the miraculous that he should bring into life.
>
> Friedrich [the poet]: So you exclusively approve of the Romantic opera with her fairies, ghosts, miracles and transformations?
>
> Ludwig: Indeed, I consider the Romantic opera the only veritable, because music is only at home in the realm of Romanticism.[41]

Just as Horn did eleven years earlier, the fictive composer proposes Gozzi's work as a model for Romantic libretto writing: "In his dramatic fairy-tales, he realized exactly what I expect from an opera poet, and it is unbelievable that this rich source of excellent opera subjects has not been used more until today."[42]

In fact, there had been some Gozzi-based operas in Germany. Hoffmann himself had set to music a libretto in the spirit of Gozzi: Clemens von Brentano's *Die lustigen Musikanten* in 1805. But in this opera, emphasis lies on the comic side through Brentano's adoption of commedia dell'arte characters, and "Romantic" qualities are less prominent. A noteworthy exception to Hoffmann's observation of the relative neglect of Gozzi by Romantic poets and composers

---

41   Ludwig: "Ist nicht die Musik die geheimnisvolle Sprache eines fernen Geisterreichs, deren wunderbare Accente in unserm Innern widerklingen, und ein höheres, intensives Leben erwecken? [...] Dies ist die unnennbare Wirkung der Instrumentalmusik. Aber nun soll die Musik ganz ins Leben treten, sie soll [...] von bestimmten Leidenschaften und Handlungen sprechen. [...] Kann denn die Musik etwas anderes verkünden, als die Wunder jenes Landes, von dem sie zu uns herübertönt? – Der Dichter rüste sich zum kühnen Fluge in das Ferne Reich der Romantik; dort findet er das Wundervolle, das er in das Leben tragen soll. Friedrich: Du nimmst also ausschliesslich die romantische Oper mit ihren Feen, Geistern, Wundern und Verwandlungen in Schutz?"
      Ludwig: "Allerdings halte ich die romantische Oper für die einzig wahrhafte, denn nur im Reich der Romantik ist die Musik zu Hause." *AMZ* XV/49, 8 September 1813: 800–801.

42   "In seinen dramatischen Märchen hat er das ganz erfüllt, was ich von dem Opern-Dichter verlange, und es ist unbegreiflich, wie diese reiche Fundgrube vortrefflicher Opernsujets bis jetzt nicht mehr benutzt worden ist." Ibid.: 802.

was Friedrich Himmel's *Zauberoper* called *Die Sylphen*, which premiered in Berlin in 1806. Ludwig Robert's libretto was based on Gozzi's *Zobeide* (1763).[43]

It is remarkable that a departure from the stagnated *Singspiel* tradition, once a reaction to Italian *opera seria*, was undertaken through the adoption of an Italian playwright's esthetic. However, this cosmopolitan move was necessary to facilitate a form of music theater in which "Romantic" instrumental music in the German spirit of Mozart and Beethoven could be implemented. Another foreign impulse into German Romantic opera was the theater of Shakespeare, particularly *The Tempest*, in which supernatural creatures and magic play a prominent role.[44] The play was transformed into several operas, all named *Die Geisterinsel*, composed by Johann Friedrich Anton Fleischmann (Weimar 1798), Johann Friedrich Reichardt (Berlin, 1798) and Johann Rudolf Zumsteeg (Dresden, 1805). Reichardt's version was the most successful, and was frequently revived in Berlin until roughly 1825. Norbert Miller argues that it was Ludwig Tieck who steered Reichardt's attention towards foreign "proto-Romantic" models, in order to create a new music-theatrical genre: "a comedy of the miraculous, based on Shakespeare, Calderón and Gozzi,[45] in which a German *Nationaloper* became conceivable."[46]

As mentioned earlier, supernatural creatures did not exclusively inhabit the "elevated" Romantic opera, but already figured prominently in operatic

---

43   For a discussion of the work, see Garlington 1977B: 260.

44   The topos that Shakespeare somehow belongs to the Germans is a recurrent figure throughout the nineteenth-century, reinforced by influential thinkers such as Heinrich Heine and Friedrich Theodor Vischer. It was mainly introduced by August Wilhelm Schlegel in a 1796 article in the journal *Die Horen*: "One may dauntlessly state that, besides the English, Shakespeare properly belongs to the German people, as his work is read, studied, and loved so much, as well as perceptively studied. To us, this is not a passing vogue, it is incomparable to the way we have submitted ourselves to foreign modes of thought and manners: we do not have to abandon our character in order to call him ours." ("Man darf kühnlich behaupten, daß er nächst den Engländer keinem Volke so eigenthümlich angehört, wie den Deutschen, weil er von keinem im Original und in der Kopie so viel gelesen, so tief studirt, so warm geliebt, und so eisichtsvoll bewundert wird. Und dieß ist nicht etwa eine vorübergehende Mode; es ist nicht, daß wir uns auch einmal zu dieser Form dramatischer Poesie bequemt hätten, wie wir immer vor andern Nazionen geneigt und fertig sind, uns in fremde Denkarten und Sitten zu fügen. Nein er ist uns nicht fremd: wir brauchen keinen Schritt aus unserm Charakter herauszugehn, um ihn ganz unser nennen zu dürfen.") Quoted after Eke 2014: 47.

45   Reichardt arguably inspired Hoffmann's fascination for Gozzi, since Hoffmann took composition classes from Reichardt as from 1798, and later frequently returned to Reichardt during Berlin sojourns. For more information concerning Hoffmann's apprenticeship with Reichardt, see Streitenberg 1989: 39–54.

46   Miller 2007: 87.

Schauerromantik (the German equivalent of Gothic art) of the more trivial sort. Hoffmann's fictive composer in *Der Dichter und der Komponist* does, however, distinguish the Romantic opera he envisions from those "poor products, in which silly, spiritless spirits appear, and miracles are piled up with neither a cause nor any effect, solely to enthrall the eye of the futile plebs."[47] Instead, "an inspired librettist of genius brings the miraculous apparitions of the spirit realm over the abyss that normally separates it from daily life, transports us to this magical domain, and makes us feel at home in this foreign land."[48] This oscillation between natural and supernatural, the real and the wondrous creates a Romantic atmosphere, in which language and action are elevated by the otherworldly quality of music to mesmerizing effect: "in the opera, a Romantic being opens up in front of our eyes, in which language is potentiated [höher potenzirt], i.e. becomes music-song, where even action and situation, floating in mighty tones and sounds, capture and enrapture us."[49]

1.4   *Romantic Opera as a Combination of Enchantment and Dramatic Focus*

In many respects, Hoffmann's opera theory seems governed by a predilection for boundlessness often associated with Romanticism in general. It may be tempting to recognize in certain passages of *Der Dichter und der Komponist* a plea for excess. Aubrey S. Garlington jr., for example, reads it in this way, when he argues that Hoffmann's ideas concerning the integration of arts within Romantic opera could have been influenced by August Wilhelm von Schlegel and his *Vorlesungen über dramatische Kunst und Literatur* (1808–09). He mentions a diary note of Hoffmann, written down in January 1812, in which the composer acknowledges his fascination after reading Schlegel's *Vorlesungen*.[50] Schlegel considers the relation between Greek tragedy and current opera as utterly contrasting, especially from the viewpoint of poetry, as he writes:

---

47   "diesen armseligen Producte, in denen läppische, geistlose Geister erscheinen, und ohne Ursache und Wirkung Wunder auf Wunder gehäuft werden, nur um das Auge des müssigen Pöbels zu ergötzen." *AMZ* xv/49, 8 September 1813: 801.

48   "Der geniale, begeisterte Dichter führt die wunderbaren Erscheinungen des Geisterreichs ins Leben; auf seinem Fittig schwingen wir uns über die Kluft, die uns sonst davon trennte, einheimisch geworden in dem fremden Lande." Ibid.: 801.

49   "In der Oper soll [...] vor unsern Augen sich ein romantisches Seyn erschliessen, in dem auch die Sprache höher potenzirt, [...] d.h. Musik-Gesang ist, ja wo selbst Handlung und Situation in mächtigen Tönen und Klängen schwebend, uns gewaltig ergreift und hinreisst."Ibid.: 801.

50   Garlington 1977B: 506.

In Greek tragedy, poetry was the primary object: other elements served in strict subordination. On the contrary, in opera poetry is merely of minor importance, a means to connect the other arts, she is nearly drowned in their presence. The best prescription for an opera text is therefore to provide a poetic sketch, later to be filled in and colored by the other arts. This anarchy of arts, in which music, dance and decoration try to outdo each other through lavishing their sumptuous charms mutually, this is the proper essence of opera. [...] In the voluptuous rivalry of forms of presentation, in the entanglement of opulence lies the fantastic enchantment of opera. A rapprochement towards the austerity of Antique taste would in a way hamper this.[51]

The lineage that Garlington establishes between Schlegel's views and later theories of German Romantic opera is indeed plausible. For example, in early nineteenth-century German discourse on opera, we do often meet the idea that a libretto should be merely sketch-like, and leave room for the other arts – particularly music – to fill in the gaps. This is also the case in E.T.A. Hoffmann's *Der Dichter und der Komponist*, where the composer Ludwig writes that "the librettist should, like the stage designer, jot down the entire picture in strong, powerful contours, and music will put the whole into the right light and perspective, [...] it will unite the seemingly random strokes and bring forth complete shapes."[52] There is also a strong affinity between Hoffmann's thinking and Schlegel's Romantic reading of form as "organic, that is, determined by the substance of the artwork," a form that he recognizes in the works of

---

51 "In der Tragödie war die Poesie die Hauptsache: alles übrige war nur dazu da, ihr, und zwar in der strengsten Unterordnung zu dienen. In der Oper hingegen ist die Poesie nur Nebensache, Mittel das übrige anzuknüpfen; sie wird unter ihren Umgebungen fast ertränkt. Die beste Vorschrift für einen Operntext ist daher, eine poetische Scizze zu liefern, deren Umrisse nachher durch die übrigen Künste ausgefüllt und gefärbt werden. Diese Anarchie der Künste, da Musik, Tanz und Decoration durch Verschwendung ihrer üppigsten Reize sich gegenseitig zu überbieten suchen, ist das eigentliche Wesen der Oper. [...] In dem schwelgerischen Wetteifer der Darstellungsmittel, in der Verwirrung des Ueberflusses liegt gerade der fantastische Zauber. Dieser würde durch Annäherung an die Strenge des antiken Geschmacks in irgend einem Punkte [...] gestört werden." Schlegel 1923A: 49.

52 "Der Operndichter müsse, dem Decorations-Maler gleich, das ganze Gemälde nach richtiger Zeichnung in starken, kräftigen Zügen hinwerfen, und es ist die Musik, die nun das Ganze so in richtiges Licht und gehörige Perspective stellt, [...] dass [...] sich einzelne, willkürlich scheinende Pinselstriche zu kühn herausschreitenden Gestalten vereinen." *AMZ* XV/50, 15 December 1813: 813.

Shakespeare and Calderón.[53] In his review of Beethoven's *Fifth*, Hoffmann writes something similar:

> Esthetic geometricians used to complain about a complete lack of true unity and inner coherence in Shakespeare, whereas only a profound look provides insight into the way in which buds, leafs, blossoms and fruits of a beautiful tree all grow from the same germ: in the case of Beethoven, a profound involvement into the inner structure is also necessary to lay bare the master's deliberate design.[54]

Yet in another fundamental respect, I challenge Garlington's assertion. Notions such as "sumptuousness," "opulence" and "lavishness" seem rather alien to most early nineteenth-century German opera critics, and "austerity" appears to be a crucial element to the opera reform that Weber and Hoffmann envisioned indeed.[55] This becomes particularly clear from a later statement in Ludwig and Ferdinand's imaginary discussion. Ludwig here emphasizes the importance of the "economy of the whole" and continues that "no dramatic poem needs clarity as much as an opera, because music easily seduces the listener into other regions, and can only be curbed through steering attention constantly towards the dramatic focal point."[56]

---

53   "Auch in der schönen Kunst wie im Gebiete der Natur, der höchsten Künstlerin, sind alle ächten Formen organisch, d.h. durch den Gehalt des Kunstwerkes bestimmt." Schlegel 1923B: 112.

54   "Wie ästhetische Messkünstler im Shakespeare oft über gänzliche Mängel wahrer Einheit und inneren Zusammenhang geklagt haben, und nur dem tiefern Blick ein schöner Baum, Knospen und Blätter, Blüthen und Früchten aus einem Keim treibend, erwächst: so entfaltet auch nur ein ganz tiefes Eingehen in die innere Structur Beethovens die hohe Besonnenheit des Meisters." *AMZ* XII/40, 4 July 1810: 634.

55   Francien Markx also concludes that "Ludwig [...] clearly argued against allegations of 'anarchy' among the participating arts." Markx 2016: 183. Whether or not Ludwig's opinions equal Hoffmann's personal outlooks has been a matter of debate, particularly among literature historians. Hartmut Steinecke calls the traditional identification of Ludwig with Hoffmann not only "one-sided," but even "faulty." (Steinecke 1998: 238) Francien Markx counters this thesis by pointing out that "as many of the views voiced in the dialogue return in Hoffmann's opera reviews, Steinecke's standpoint seems equally one-sided." (Markx 2016: 170). Within the context of this study, which is concerned with discourse rather than personal beliefs, the difference is nearly irrelevant. Regardless of the question whether or not Hoffmann fully endorsed Ludwig's opinions, *Der Dichter und der Komponist* turned out to be one of the most influential early nineteenth-century texts on German Romantic opera theory.

56   "Der Operndichter [muss] die Oekonomie des Ganzen [...] treu bleiben. [...] Kein dramatisches Gedicht hat diese Deutlichkeit so im höchsten Grade nöthig als die Oper, da [...] die Musik gar leicht den Zuhörer in andere Regionen entführt, und nur durch das

In this statement, we encounter a combination of two requirements; music and action's vicinity to the wondrous workings of the spirit realm must enrapture us, but simultaneously, a focus, a coherent narrative must be retained. We find exactly the same thing in Hoffmann's review of Beethoven's *Fifth Symphony*. The critic states that this composition carries us into "the wondrous spirit realm of the infinite," but argues that the composer realizes this effect through his deliberate formal coherence and monothematic design.[57] In his review, Hoffmann interprets the symphony as an organically growing elaboration of a single musical idea (the famous four-note motif – ta-ta-ta-taaa – at the start of the first movement): "it is above all the inner affinity of the single themes which creates that type of unity that keeps the listener's mind in the same mood."[58]

In the end, it is this formal awareness and organic unity, and particularly the underlying dramatic idea or narrative that governs the piece, which contributes to its "elevated" Romantic character. In contemporary thinking on Romantic opera, we find something similar. Although the "wondrous spirit realm" must overwhelm the spectator, it must not remain merely fanciful. "Spirits remain spiritless and silly" without a clear dramatic necessity, if the opera lacks a sense of direction, a narrative focus. Ultimately, in the early nineteenth-century concept of "elevated" German Romantic opera, a voluptuous magic goes hand in hand with a certain austerity and coherence of plot, which serves to distinguish it from its trivial or "romanesque" ancestors. At the same time, this aspect shows the close relation between Romantic opera theory and contemporary discourse on German national opera, epitomized by Weber's earlier mentioned notion of "a closed artwork, in which all parts unite to form a beautiful, rounded whole."[59]

After presenting and discussing these early-nineteenth-century viewpoints on the character and ambitions of Romantic opera, in the rest of this chapter we will shift attention to the analysis of a selection of operas. These works provide

---

beständige Hinlenken auf den Punkt, in dem sich der dramatische Effect konzentrieren soll, gezügelt werden kann." *AMZ* XV/50, 15 December 1813: 813–814.

57   Michael Tilmouth defines "monothematic" as "a term used to describe a piece of music constructed on a single theme, either in one movement or in several, throughout which that theme is used; any incidental material that appears is of little structural importance. [...] Monothematicism is perhaps a more remarkable feature in music conceived in forms normally exhibiting thematic plurality, such as the sonata or rondo." Oxfordmusiconline. com, lemma "monothematic," consulted on 7 February 2013.

58   "ist es vorzüglich die innige Verwandtschaft der einzelnen Themas untereinander, welche jene Einheit erzeugt, die des Zuhörers Gemut in einer Stimmung hält." *AMZ* XII/41, 11 July 1810: 658.

59   Kaiser 1908: 77. For full quotation, see Chapter 3.

insight into the way German composers sought to "Romanticize" opera –
to varying success – while remaining within the *Singspiel* constellation.

2 E.T.A. Hofmann's Romantic Operas: From Romanticized Classicism to a Transfigured Folk Style

2.1 Der Trank der Unsterblichkeit

How, then, and to what extent did E.T.A. Hoffmann manage to realize all these
theoretical ambitions in his operas? The first time he used the classification
Romantische oper to describe a music-theatrical work of his own was with *Der
Trank der Unsterblichkeit* in 1808.[60] The title of this work, composed as an aptitude test for his appointment as music director in Bamberg, creates certain
Romantic expectations. Such a potion appeals both to the Romantic desire
for the infinite and signals an aspiration towards the immortal nature of supernatural creatures. Nonetheless, the libretto that Bamberg theatre director
Count Julius von Soden wrote roots in the "romanesque" tradition. The story is
situated in an Oriental, Persian setting, and the elixir turns out to be a placebo,
which is typical of a late eighteenth-century form of early Romanticism[61] in
which the enjoyment of the miraculous is always counterbalanced by an eventual rational, Enlightened explanation.[62] In the end, key character Naramand
realizes that his desire for immortality is pointless, and learns to cherish the
treasures of his mortal life.

The amount of spoken dialogue in *Der Trank der Unsterblichkeit* is vast
in comparison to the sparse and moreover conventional musical insertions.
This is far removed from Hoffmann's ideal of a drama in which language is
potentiated through music. One particular scene would lend itself for a truly
Romantic music-dramatic design as a flight into the spirit realm: the dream in
which Naramand envisions the consequences of his immortality. In this vision,
his loved ones have all died, and the Shah has incarcerated him, regarding
him as a potential threat to state security. Since Hoffmann faced serious time
pressure – the commissioned work had to be delivered within little more than a
month – he had little room for experiments and remained within a traditional,
late eighteenth-century stylistic framework.

---

60   The work was never performed during Hoffmann's lifetime and was premiered only
     recently, in Erfurt in 2012.
61   To discern between these forms of trivial "early" Romanticism and the *Frühromantik* of
     the Jena School, the latter type is translated as Early Romanticism with a capital e.
62   See my earlier remarks on this phenomenon in Section 2.1.3.

2.2   Aurora

Hoffmann classified his next work, *Aurora* (1812)[63] – a collaboration with librettist Franz von Holbein – as a *Große romantische Oper*. This designation
emphasizes his ambition to elevate the Romantic *Singspiel* tradition through a
cosmopolitan fusion with both Italian opera seria and French grand opera[64] in
the spirit of Gluck and his followers. That Hoffmann sought to innovate German
opera through a conscious adoption of these foreign influences reinforces the
view that he had limited appreciation for the German but trivial character of
the *Singspiel*.

The idea that Gluck's *Reformoper* had its merits as a model for German Romantic opera may not come as a surprise, but his works long suffered from
a relative negligence on German soil. Until 1807, it was rather usual to consider Gluck chiefly as a composer of French opera for a French audience, as
an anonymous critic does in an 1802 contribution to the *AMZ* entitled 'Was ist
charakteristisch an deutscher Opernmusik.'[65] After 1807 his status gradually
changed. For example, an anonymous *AMZ* critic praises the inclusion of his
works in the Berlin *Nationaltheater* repertory in 1807.[66] It seems that Gluck's
oeuvre enjoyed an enthusiastic rediscovery and reappraisal around that time.
The French musicologist Alexandre-Etienne Choron recognized a sudden
Gluckian revolution in Germany around 1810, as a translation of his work in
the *Allgemeine Musikalische Zeitung* in 1813 shows. At the same time, he did,
however, perceive a strong opposition to this trend by those who privileged the
"symphonic" opera style of Mozart over the "dramatic" Gluck.[67]

As with the Gozzi fever discussed earlier in this chapter, Hoffmann played
a pivotal role in the Gluck revival. He published a fantastic short story, *Ritter
Gluck* in the *AMZ* in 1809, in which a fictive meeting takes place in Berlin with

---

63   This opera also remained unperformed during Hoffmann's lifetime.
64   This term points not to the post-1828 grand opera genre with its very specific stylistic
      requirements, but rather more generally to an all-sung opera with a grand subject matter.
65   "That the artist Gluck should be regarded as a Frenchman, since he composed in the spirit
      of this nation and found his true audience in the French." ("Dass Glucks deutsche Ab-
      stammung nicht hindert, ihn, den Künstler, als Franken anzusehen, da er ganz im Geiste
      dieser Nation schrieb und unter ihr sein eigentliches Publikum fand und findet.") *AMZ*
      IV/45, 4 August 1802: 723.
66   The critic praises "the efforts of Kapellmeister [Bernhard Anselm] Weber to perfect the
      German opera, a cause which he serves already a great deal by including Gluck's music to
      the repertory." ("[wir erwarten] von der Thätigkeit und dem Eifer des Kapellmeisters We-
      ber möglichste Vervollkommnung der Oper, wozu er allerdings schon sehr vieles durch
      die sorgsame Aufstellung Gluckscher Musik thut.") *AMZ* X/11, 9 December 1807: 175.
67   *AMZ* XV/5, 3 February 1813: 77–78.

an extravagant, apparently mentally disturbed man who claims to be Gluck.[68] By adding the madness of Gluck's *Doppelgänger* – perhaps a sign of Romantic genius – to the conventional image of a balanced and restrained, (neo-)classical eighteenth-century master, we may witness a certain attempt to Romanticize both his character and his musical legacy. This facilitated the adoption of Gluck's style of musical tragedy in Hoffmann's grand Romantic opera *Aurora*.

Hoffmann's review of the vocal score of Gluck's *Iphigénie en Aulide*, published in the *AMZ* in 1810, adds a dimension to our understanding of the technical side of Hoffmann's Gluck reception and the fusion of opera styles in *Aurora*. In the opening lines of this article, he blames the recent advent of operas with spoken dialogue as the reason for Gluck's relative absence from the repertory: "the recently introduced, in fact reprehensible form of opera in which spoken dialogues interrupt the singing is the main reason why Gluck's works, which cannot be cramped into this structure, are – with the exception of large theaters such as Munich and Berlin – hardly performed in Germany."[69] Here Hoffmann's disapproval of spoken dialogue hints at a desire to move away from it. This ambition is partly realized in his future works through a more dynamic alternation of spoken dialogue and sung numbers, and through the prominence of recitatives and through-composed ensembles and finales, in which music and dramatic development go hand in hand. He continues his review by expressing his disappointment with the recent disregard for true opera seria, when he writes the following:

> Modern-day composers fully disregard the true *opera seria*. Through this neglect, the highest attainable fusion of poetry and music for the stage is on the brink of extinction. [...] Nowadays one searches in vain for works if only slightly in this spirit, carrying this genuinely tragic pathos that was expressed by works of past masters, even of those who lacked the greatness of Gluck. It is foremost the style, in which the artwork forms a unified and rounded whole that vividly expresses the character of its

---

68   In *Ritter Gluck's "Unglück": The Crisis of Creativity in the Age of the Epigone*, John Fetzer characterizes this Gluck double as either a "revenant," a "psychotic," or a "schizophrenic." He interprets the fate of Ritter Gluck as an allegory for Hoffmann's own struggles as an epigone of older musical styles in a cultural climate that is hostile to his artistic beliefs. Fetzer 1971: 317.

69   "Die in neuerer Zeit eingeführte, eigentlich verwerfliche Form der Oper, nach welcher der Dialog den Gesang unterbricht, [...] mag wol mit die vorzüglichste [Ursache] seyn, warum man, wenige unserer grossen Theater in Deutschland (Wien, Berlin etc.) ausgenommen, Glucks Meisterwerke, die sich in jene Form nicht einengen lassen, auf der Bühne fast niemals sieht." *AMZ* XII/48, 29 August 1810: 770.

subject, which is absent in most recent works, whereas within Gluck's dramas, this style can be found in a rarely superb way.[70]

Three aspects of this quote are noteworthy. Firstly, it is significant that Hoffmann does not distinguish between the French *tragédie musicale* and Italian *opera seria*. This also implies that, contrary to most of his contemporaries, he considered Italian *opera seria*, at least some of its elements, as a viable model for his own works.[71] Secondly, the conservatism of his statement is striking, as he clearly privileges old masters over modern-day composers. For a "Romantic" artist, this embrace of eighteenth-century Classicism is remarkable. The link between this Classicist stance and his contribution to German Romantic opera lies in the third aspect. This is Hoffmann's appreciation of the unified and rounded quality of Gluck's dramas, which acknowledges the ideal of the "closed artwork," the common denominator of German national opera and Romantic opera discernible both in *Der Dichter und der Komponist* and in Weber's ideal-typical definition of German opera.

The same ideal can be found in a subsequent statement, when Hoffmann links Gluck's work to the ideal of music-dramatic economy and permanent concentration on the dramatic focal point which, as we saw, would form an important aspect of his later theory of Romantic opera as well:

Gluck's opera is the truly musical drama, in which action develops without interruption. Anything that hinders this development, everything that weakens the listener's concentration and draws attention to peripheral matters, – one could say, from content to ornament [von der Gestalt auf den Schmuck] – is carefully avoided.[72]

70　"[Dass] die Componisten der neuesten Zeit [...] die wahre *Opera seria* ganz vernachlässigen, und dass auf diese Weise bald das Höchste, was die Dichtkunst mit der Musik verbunden für die Bühne leisten kann, ganz verschwinden wird. [...] Sucht man jetzt vergebens Werke, die nur im mindesten in jenem Geist, in jenem wahrhaft tragischen Pathos geschrieben sind, den die Opern früherer, selbst gegen den Riesen Gluck klein erscheinender Geister aussprechen. [...] Es ist vorzüglich der Styl, der das Ganze zu einem, den Charakter des Stoffes lebhaft aussprechenden Kunstwerk eint und ründet, welcher den mehrsten neuen Opern mangelt, und herrlicher möchte er nicht leicht anzutreffen seyn, als eben in den Gluckschen Dramen." Ibid.: 771–772.

71　Hoffmann's *Iphigénie* review does, however, contain a condemnation of operas in which "scenes are strung together only to provide virtuosic singers a possibility to display their skills" ("Componisten, die [...] Scenen an Scenen reihen, die nur dazu dienen, den Sänger das ausführen zu lassen, was glänzt und imponirt."), which is in line with anti-Italian sentiments in contemporary German opera criticism. Ibid.: 771.

72　"so ist die Glucksche Oper das wahre musikalische Drama, in welchem die Handlung unaufhaltsam von Moment zu Moment fortschreitet. Alles was diesem Fortschreiten hinderlich ist, alles was des Zuhörers Spannung schwächen und seine Aufmerksamkeit

In the conclusion of his review, Hoffmann advises young composers with ambitions in the field of tragic opera to study Gluck's classic masterworks, instead of pursuing the high Romanticism of Mozart.[73] A look into Hoffmann's ambitious, tragic opera *Aurora* shows that this study of Gluck's masterpieces informs his music-dramatic style as well. Stylistically, Hermann Dechant recognizes a Gluckian influence in the prominence of the choir within the work.[74] Another affinity with Gluck lies in the continuous music-dramatic development, which Hoffmann reaches through the design of large, through-composed sections and extended finales. This technique is not only inspired by Gluck, but also clearly derived from modern composers of French opera who continued his operatic legacy, such as Cherubini and Méhul.[75]

The influence of Italian *opera seria* shows most firmly from the decision to turn the character of Cephalus – in fact the principle role – into a *Hosenrolle*, sung by a mezzo-soprano. A probable model for this procedure was the part of Sesto in Mozart's *La clemenza di Tito*, which Hoffmann held in high esteem.[76] Cephalus presents a significant exception within early nineteenth-century German opera, because *Hosenrollen* were nearly completely eliminated from serious German opera, in opposition to the situation in Italy and France.[77] In those countries, remnants of the seventeenth- and eighteenth-century queer approach to gender in opera could more easily be found, whereas one of the characteristic traits of early nineteenth-century German opera was its emphasis on heterosexual, binary gender stereotypes.

It is clear that Hoffmann hoped to realize the "grand" quality of his *Große romantische Oper* through a deliberate use of elements from Gluck and the

---

auf Nebendinge – man möchte sagen, von der Gestalt auf den Schmuck – lenken kann, ist auf das sorgfältigste vermieden." *AMZ* XII/49, 5 September 1810: 784–785.

73 "so glaubt er das Wichtigste berührt zu haben, weshalb die Gluckschen Opern classische Meisterwerke sind und bleiben, die jeder jungen Tonsetzer, der sich an ernste, tragische Dramen wagen will, nicht genug studiren kann. [...] Schon einen gewissen Styl wird er sich aneignen, der dem Zuhörer wohlthut. Eben deshalb hält der Rez. es für gerathener, ältere, energische Werke zu studiren, als ohne dieses Studium der hohen Romantik Mozarts nachzujagen." Ibid.: 786–787.

74 Dechant 1975: 178.

75 Ibid.: 276–278.

76 In February 1813, Hoffmann writes in his diary that "he received a new impulse from a performance of *La clemenza di Tito*" ("Neue Anregung durch den 'Titus' erfahren, dessen Aufführung ich beygewohnt.") Hoffmann 1971: 113.

77 Famous nineteenth-century Italian and French *Hosenrollen* are Oscar in Verdi's *Un ballo in Maschera* (1859) and Siebel in Gounod's *Faust* (1859). The only key male character played by a female singer within nineteenth-century German opera is the part of Adriano in Wagner's *Rienzi* (1842), but this work was originally conceived as a grand opera, which Wagner hoped to see performed for a French audience in Paris.

"true *opera seria*," but what about the second adjective of his genre definition? Can a spirit of "elevated" Romanticism be found in *Aurora*, or do we witness Romantic aspects of the trivial sort? The most obvious moment in which a Romantic spirit can be detected is the opening of the second act. Cephalus has been sentenced to death by the king and is abandoned at the beachside where Aurora's sanctuary is built. He begs the goddess for protection and mercy. Dawn breaks, the sun creates a red glow, and the pillars of the temple start to resonate. Aurora appears out of the ocean, albeit invisible to the overwhelmed Cephalus. She is carried by a divine horse, and her radiance covers the entire surroundings in a rosy light. She immediately falls in love with the young shepherd, who begs her to help him regain his beloved Procris. Instead of helping him, she deceives him and abducts him into her submarine castle.

This spectacular magic imagery of a goddess rising out of the sea seems rooted in late-eighteenth-century traditions such as the *Zauberoper* and the French *comédie féerie*.[78] Her invisibility does, however, not only make Aurora's appearance more practical from a theatrical point of view, but also reveals a significant shift from visual spectacle towards the atmospheric evocation of nature and mood, which is congenial to a Romantic esthetic.[79] Miller also points out that this scene (nr. 8 in the score) is usually considered to have a "Romantic" character that distinguishes it from the rest of the work.[80] He goes on to argue that the entry of Aurora in fact functioned as a showcase for and adumbration of Hoffmann's image of a "miraculous apparition of the spirit realm"[81] Miller believes that "this entry of the goddess Aurora occurred to Hoffmann as the most perfect realization of his demand that music, when it steps out into the real world, can only herald the miracles of its own spirit realm."[82]

The otherworldly quality of Aurora's appearance is supported by music that bears Romantic traits, albeit in a premature form. After Cephalus's arioso, in which he begs the goddess for support, Aurora's appearance is evoked

---

78   As Dechant argues, see Dechant 1975: 178.

79   Dechant writes that "the inclusion of nature and natural phenomena [indicates] an altered sensibility for the environment, for example at the beginning of the second act. Here it is that Hoffmann is inspired and strikes out on new pathways." Ibid.: 14.

80   "The instrumental introduction to the second act that returns in Cephalus's prayer and the appearance of the goddess is regularly considered to be Hoffmann's proper contribution to musical Romanticism, albeit as a kind of special case within the score." Miller 2007: 231.

81   The core idea of *Der Dichter und der Komponist* which has been treated earlier in this chapter.

82   Ibid.: 232. Miller thereby refers to Hoffmann's rhetorical question, posed in *Der Dichter und der Komponist*, whether music is "capable of communicating anything else than the miracles of that realm, from where she sends her sounds towards us?"

musically by a passage in the highly unusual key of A-flat minor.[83] A melody in the double basses and celli over a string accompaniment in the middle register creates a descending chromatic bass line, and sets in motion a modulation towards the more familiar key of D-major. This key serves as a dominant preparation for a passage in G minor. This section, during which dawn breaks and enlightens the highest pillars of the temple, is often referred to as the *Säulenmusik*.[84] A sharp coloristic contrast is created through a scoring for three flutes and clarinet in a high register. Hoffmann's creation of musical contrasts at the service of the drama, both in terms of tonality and timbre, might be seen as an early attempt at Romantic opera, although the mesmerizing effect the composer probably aimed at is not realized yet. The "Romantic being" evaporates as soon as it is established; after the arrival of Aurora, she and Cephalus engage in a rather conventional duet. Nevertheless, this scene within *Aurora* forms an example for similar breakthroughs from the spirit realm that would become key moments in the dramaturgy of his next opera, *Undine*.

2.3   Das Donauweibchen (*Kauer/Hensler*)

Before moving on to Hoffmann's most ambitious and arguably most Romantic opera, it seems expedient to make a small digression to discuss its less elevated, but extremely popular forerunner, *Das Donauweibchen*. This *romantisch-komisches Volksmärchen*, designed as two full evening entertainments, was composed by Friedrich Kauer on a text by Karl Friedrich Hensler, and premiered in 1798 in Vienna. To call it an opera is an exaggeration, since the piece was basically a spoken play with inserted songs. The *Singspiel's* success was not restricted to Vienna, but spread through Northern German regions, and even other parts of Europe as well. It also reached Bamberg, where E.T.A. Hoffmann conducted the piece five times in 1809. Whereas two characters in Carl Maria von Weber's novel *Tonkünstlers Leben* criticize the success of the work as detrimental to public taste in 1811,[85] it is probable that the trivial rendition of the

---

83   In eighteenth- and nineteenth-century theories of key characteristics, keys with many flats (such as A-flat minor, which has no less than seven flats) are often related to the abnormal, the otherworldly, the spiritual etc. This partly explains "Romantic" composers' fondness of keys with flats. See for more information concerning this phenomenon Van Kooten 2013.

84   For example Dechant 1975: 109–110.

85   In a fragment written down in 1811, Weber presents a discussion between the composer Felix and his friend Diehl. The latter states: "The commoners hit the bottle and stuff themselves with food before the performance, and only want entertainment. They see a *Donauweibchen*, nearly die of laughing, applaud, hail, and see, the thing makes a splash." Felix fully agrees: "The noble plebs hears of its success, wants to see it too, scolds it, but nevertheless attends it again, and through this, taste perishes" ("Das gemeine Pack säuft

water nymph story did trigger Hoffmann's artistic imagination in the light of his own, more exalted *Undine* project.

Hensler's rendering of the love between a mortal man and a female water creature[86] was based on Christian August Vulpius's novel *Die Saalnixe. Eine Sage der Vorzeit* (1795, initially published anonymously). According to Schläder, *Das Donauweibchen* formed the beginning of a new type of *Singspiel*, the *romantisch-komisches Volksmärchen*.[87] This genre fits in the "romanesque" sphere, in the sense that miraculous and horrifying passages are counterbalanced with disenchanting comic relief: "The fascinating world of the elementary and wondrous, the incomprehensible phenomenon of a magic force is contrasted and compensated by comedy. Magic and comedy are all the more dramaturgically intertwined as they result from one another."[88] We find this for example in the comic action between the old spinster Salome and Käsperle, whose love the former tries to claim. This comic action mirrors the more serious story of the *Donauweibchen* Hulda's attempts to demand love from the knight Albrecht. This mirrored proceeding of a serious and a comic pair reminds us of the character constellation in Mozart's *Zauberflöte* (1791), with the princely pair Tamino-Pamina and the common pair Papageno-Papagena. In this, and in many other respects as well, Mozart's opera is a significant forerunner rooted in this Viennese tradition of comic *Zauberoper*.[89]

Whereas E.T.A. Hoffmann did not conceal his indebtedness to the popular Viennese *Singspiel* by characterizing his *Undine* as *eine romantische Zauberoper*,[90] most serious Northern German composers distanced

---

und frißt vorher gut und will nur unterhalten sein, sieht ein Donauweibchen, lacht sich halb tot, klatscht, ruft ein Paar heraus, und siehe, das Ding macht furore." Felix: "Der noble Pöbel hört dann davon, will es auch sehen, schimpft, geht aber wieder hin, und so verdirbt sich der Geschmack"). Kaiser 1908: 491.

86   A motive which we find in many fairy-tales, for example in the French Melusine, the German Undine, the Slavonic Rusalka and Andersen's *Little Mermaid*. For a detailed account of these narrative traditions, see the second chapter of Jürgen Schläder's *Undine auf dem Musiktheater*. Schläder 1979: 39–98.

87   Ibid.: 84–85.

88   Ibid.: 26.

89   In his lemma on *Zauberoper* on *Oxford Music Online*, Peter Branscombe emphasizes the Viennese descent of this opera type, which was, in opposition to the *romantisch-komisch Volksmärchen* not a term regularly used by contemporaries, but rather by later scholars. Oxfordmusiconline.com, Lemma "Zauberoper," consulted on 14 March 2013.

90   Beate Heinel argues that E.T.A. Hoffmann was probably the first composer who explicitly defined his work as a *Zauberoper*, but did not coin this term, which was already applied to refer to a Viennese tradition of comic *Singspiel* in which magic played a prominent role. The author presents a letter by Johann Wolfgang von Goethe to E.G. von Voigt of 1808 as a first literary trace of the term. Heinel 1994: 15–16.

themselves from this "vulgar" tradition. This shows the increasing prominence of a "theory of unity," discernible in Northern German music discourse, starting with Reichardt's 1774 treatise *Über die deutsche comische Oper*, which, according to Walter Salmen, "clearly distinguished his conceptualization of the Northern German *Singspiel* from the Viennese *Singspiel*, marked by variation of diverse materials."[91] Although Northern-German composers regarded the Viennese *Singspiel* problematic in this respect, it is hard to overlook the significance of this genre for the foundation of German opera.[92] The question whether this gradual elimination of the comical and the emphasis on a unifying, overarching, often exalted character in Northern German opera formed a blessing or a curse from an esthetic point of view remains to be answered. It will be addressed in relation to *Undine*, and will return at other points within this book.

Another important aspect of *Das Donauweibchen*, also perceivable in later Romantic operas, is the tendency to "nationalize" or "regionalize" a fairy-tale by transporting it to domestic territory, in this case to the Danube shores.[93] In this, we can recognize a tendency to present archetypal narratives – which until 1800 were mostly tied to an ancient Greek, Roman or perhaps Biblical setting – in a medieval environment, closer to home both in time and space. This geographical fixation often involves an adaptation to local (music-)theatrical traditions as well. In the case of *Donauweibchen*, this is the Viennese comedy, evolving around Käsperle. The character of Käsperle, a late eighteenth-century Viennese Hanswurst, was created by the famous actor Johann Laroche, who was the absolute star of the Leopoldstädter Theater. Many comedies and *Singspiele* were designed particularly to highlight his abilities, similar to the prima donna practice in Italian opera. Of course, this centralization of comedy affected the Romantic character of *Das Donauweibchen*. Nonetheless, the work prefigures many Romantic fascinations, especially in its depiction of the title heroine, in which the trivially frivolous as well as the numinous are present.

The common love triangle of a knight torn between his love for a supernatural water nymph and a socially more acceptable mortal noblewoman, characteristic of all water creature fairy-tales, governs *Das Donauweibchen*. In the first part of the diptych, Hulda demands Albrecht to remain loyal and to spend at

---

91 Salmen 1974: Nachwort (unnumbered). Regarding the prominence of comical side-action in *Das Donauweibchen*, Schläder speaks of Hensler's adherence to the principle of contrast respectively of variation, see Schläder 1979: 148.

92 Otto Beer, for example, states "that the history of the Viennese *Singspiel* of the Mozart era is perhaps the most decisive chapter within the history of origins of German opera." Fragment of Otto Beer's dissertation *Mozart und das Wiener Singspiel* (Beer 1932: 3), quoted after Schläder 1979: 222.

93 In the case of Vulpius to the Thuringian shores of the Saale river.

least three nights a year in her company. He is not willing to commit this infidelity towards Bertha, his mortal wife to be, regardless of his sexual attraction to the water nymph. Through masquerades, the use of their love baby Lili and all kinds of magic, Hulda sends bad omen for the wedding to come, which she eventually disturbs as a wicked fairy. The curtain falls with Hulda and Albrecht descending into earth and a wedding chorus sung by the water nymphs, praising their union. This tragic ending of the first part is counterbalanced by the ultimate happy outcome of the second. In this part, Albrecht wanders the world to escape the ennui of his life with Bertha at his castle. He is forced to return when a rival knight threatens to take over his castle. He liberates Bertha from this siege, but soon goes to Hulda again, who forbids him ever to inform his wife about their encounters. When he returns to his land, he falls victim to pestilence.[94] On his deathbed, he confesses his infidelity to his wife. Hulda appears, and instead of punishing him, she breaks her spell and forgives the sinner, heals him and grants him and his wife a happy life and a large offspring.

Both the ending of the first and that of the second part contain genuinely Romantic traits. In the case of the first, tragic conclusion, Albrecht cannot escape the numinous web in which he finds himself. There is no *deus ex machina* to bring about a happy end, and the magic which Hulda employs is not dismantled by a rational explanation. The outcome of the second part appears to be reassuringly *Biedermeier*. The numinous power is overcome, the human married couple reconciled, and they live happily ever after. Nevertheless, the motives of reconciliation and redemption will turn out to be crucial aspects of Romantic opera to come.

It is noteworthy that Albrecht is freed from his curse not through an intervention of an overpowering Christian authority, but rather by the pagan, numinous force itself. Most Romantic renditions of the water nymph story present the desired union between a pagan, supernatural creature and a Christian knight as doomed to fail and as a one-way ticket to eventual destruction. In *Das Donauweibchen*, a solution of the conflict is possible at the moment that Hulda gives up her demands, although this reconciles the human pair and not the relationship between the knight and the nymph, who withdraws empty-handed.[95] To understand the sudden peripeteia of the title-heroine, the water nymph's name and the assumed identity of the goddesses Frau Holda and Venus, common to

---

94 Infertility and disease are common punishments for the moral decadence of a leader in many fairy-tales and mythologies. One may think in this regard of the tainted prosperity of the Grail realm as a result of its king Amfortas's moral sin in Richard Wagner's *Parsifal* (1882).

95 She does get to keep her and Albrecht's second love baby, Huldebert (we may foresee a new Oedipal conflict between a demanding mother and a son trying to extricate himself from her sultry claims coming up, but there is no *Donauweibchen dritter Teil*).

Romantic philology and confirmed by Jacob Grimm in his *Deutsche Mythologie* in 1835, are noteworthy.[96] Whereas Hulda acts as a sensual Venus throughout most of the two parts of *Donauweibchen*, at the final close she (re)turns to the role of guardian of family life that the Nordic goddess fulfils.

2.4 Undine (*Fouqué/Hoffmann*)

The immense success of *Das Donauweibchen* in the theater was followed up by the literary success of Friedrich de la Motte Fouqué's short story *Undine* (1811). The book appealed to E.T.A. Hoffmann, who found in it a foil in which many of his ideals concerning Romantic opera could perhaps be realized. He hoped to find the desired Romantic librettist, one of the main concerns of *Der Dichter und der Komponist*, in Fouqué,[97] and asked him to rework his narration into an opera text, a challenge that the latter accepted. At the same time, the artistic collaboration was clearly dominated by Hoffmann, who sent his colleague a(n) (unfortunately lost) detailed scheme of the action and the musical realization he envisioned.[98] That the literary-gifted writer-composer turned to Fouqué for a libretto is often explained as caused by his awareness that he was not a great poet himself.[99]

Hoffmann was very pleased with Fouqué's libretto, which he called "an exquisite masterpiece [höchst vortreffliches Meisterwerk]" in a diary entry of

---

96   In *Daß wissend würde die Welt. Religion und Philosophie in Richard Wagners Musikdramen* (2005), Ulrike Kienzle writes the following about Jacob Grimm's reading of Holda: "Holda provides rain and snow, the harvest, domestic order. [...] To Jacob Grimm, Holda and Venus are certainly the same goddess. What became of Holda, this miraculous maternal goddess? At the one hand Venus, [...] a horrifying witch and demon, but at the other side – the difference could not have been greater – Maria." Kienzle 2005: 92.

97   Norbert Miller writes that "[to Hoffmann], Fouqué appeared to have squared the circle successfully [found the appropriate adaptation of his story into a libretto], a proper combination of the popular enchantment modeled after *Das Donauweibchen* and simultaneously the truly Romantic opera, that only an inspired poet of genius could create. In Fouqué's stage version of his fairy-tale, he saw all his observations in *Der Dichter und der Komponist* realized." Miller 2007: 269.

98   Hartmut Steinecke, who investigated the genesis of the libretto, mentions a letter of Fouqué written in 1817, a year after the first performance, emphasizing that any possible alteration for a future performance should be discussed with Hoffmann, whose intellectual property the *Undine* libretto is: "Hoffmann's share in the dramatic poem is so great, that I could not even change one sentence without consulting him, it would be a blatant unjustice if I did." Quoted after Steinecke 1998: 239.

99   In July 1812, one month before he sends Fouqué his dramatic scheme, Hoffmann writes two letters to his friend Hitzig, in which he states that "Undine is a magnificent subject for an opera," but later acknowledges that he is "not so familiar with versification." ("die Undine soll mir einen herrlichen Stoff zu einer Oper geben. [...] Sie wissen, daß mir das Versifizieren nicht geläufig ist.") Quoted after Kohlhase 1998: 247.

14 August 1812.[100] Not all contemporaries agreed with this judgment. For example, reviews of *Undine* in the *Allgemeine Musikalische Zeitung* criticized the logic of Fouqué's libretto. In 1816, an anonymous critic wrote that "the story of this opera is known from the lovely poem of the famous librettist, and rather incomprehensible if one's not familiar with it, which hinders the impression the opera makes with the public at large."[101] Carl Maria von Weber voiced a similar opinion, while challenging the idea that the plot was fully incomprehensible, in his 1817 *AMZ* review:

> the adaptation appears to me as a dramatized fairy-tale, in which much of the inner coherence could have been expressed more clearly and precisely. Mr. Fouqué knew the fairy-tale all too well, and often then the risk of self-deception occurs, which presupposes that others are equally well informed. Nevertheless, the plot is far from incomprehensible, as some have argued.[102]

Although Fouqué's original short story is sometimes dismissed as trivial literature or ready-to-wear Romanticism,[103] a shift from the frivolous to a more austere, elevated rendition of the story can be detected between *Das Donauweibchen* and *Undine*. For example, the earthly union between man and supernatural creature turns out to be irreconcilably doomed, with a fatal outcome. At the same time, the moral dimension, embodied by the Christian authority Pater Heilmann, obtains more emphasis than in the Viennese comedy. This Christian authority is counterbalanced by the pagan force Kühleborn, Undine's uncle who foresees Huldbrand's eventual betrayal and pours out his wrath upon the knight. When finally equipped with a soul, Undine succumbs

---

100 Quoted after Ibid.: 247.
101 "Der Inhalt dieser Oper ist aus dem lieblichen Märchen des berühmten Dichters bekannt, und ohne dasselbe auch nicht ganz verständlich, was den Eindruck auf die Menge schmälert." *AMZ* XVIII/38, 18 September 1816: 655.
102 "Die Bearbeitung scheint Ref. als ein dramatisirtes Märchen, in dem wol manch innere Zusammenhang bestimmter und klarer hätte verdeutlicht werden können. Herr v. Fouqué kannte das Märchen gar zu gut, und da ist denn oft eine Art von Selbsttäuschung möglich, die auch die Andern wissend glaubt." *AMZ* XIX/12, 19 March 1817: 204–205.
103 The fiercest advocate of this opinion is the early twentieth-century literary historian Richard Benz, who repudiates De la Motte Fouqué: "He was the writer that prepared 'Romanticism' for a hungry, common readership [...]. This could only be achieved by a complete renunciation of its inner being. Fouqué only has the external appearance of Romanticism, an empty dress [...]. The miraculous, which from a more elevated poetic standpoint is the chief aim of all Romantic theory, he uses, but only as ornamental Medievalism, to evoke a vulgar shiver in a similar way to that of Apel and Laun." Benz 1908: 131–132.

to the expected contemporary ideal of a submissive wife, and leaves her Hulda-like trickery behind. Although we might consider Hulda's fate as tragic and her demands legitimate, her tragedy is far less moving than that of Undine, who, as a result of her husband Huldbrand's[104] infidelity, is forced to impose her numinous powers on him and devastate him, regardless of her incessant love.

When asked on which sources his story was based, Fouqué mentioned only the *Liber de nymphis, sylphis, pygmaeis et salamandris et de caeteris spiritibus* (published 1590) by the sixteenth-century occult philosopher Paracelsus, claiming all other aspects of the fairy-tale to be his own invention.[105] But Paracelsus was certainly not the only influence, as the book contains several significant correspondences to *Das Donauweibchen*. There is, for example, a remarkable similarity between Hulda's attendance at the wedding as a singer, singing a ballad with an inconvenient allusion to Albrecht's questionable amorous behavior, and Undine's ballad during Bertalda's saint's day – the only part of Fouqué's story that is explicitly sung –, in which she reveals the inconvenient simple descent of her friend and rival in love, who had always supposed that she was of noble birth.

In fact, in the libretto Fouqué wrote for E.T.A. Hoffmann, traces of the plotline of the successful *Singspiel* are all the more obvious. One may think, for example, of the appearance of Undine, followed by a group of other water creatures, disturbing the wedding ceremony of Huldbrand and Berthalda[106] in the closing scene of the opera. This action departs from Fouqué's story,[107] but closely resembles the conclusion of the first *Donauweibchen* part, albeit in a sublimated form. In both works, the stage suddenly transforms into a transparent cave full of water creatures. Norbert Miller argues that Hoffmann – therein departing from Kauer and Hensler – tried to evoke the water spirit realm through subtle suggestion rather than the trivial (often poorly executed) magic of machinery, since the technically-demanding scene change could have a grotesque, ridiculous effect, damaging the opera's Romantic aura.[108] Furthermore,

---

104   The name of Huldbrand could probably be an allusion to Hulda's son Huldebert in *Das Donauweibchen*, emphasizing the continuity with its popular precursor. That Huldbrand's scolding of Undine and her race takes place during a sailing trip down the Danube is another intertextual wink to the location where the action of *Das Donauweibchen* takes place.

105   See de la Motte Fouqué's description in *Die Musen. Eine norddeutsche Zeitschrift* of 1812, quoted after Max 2003: 420.

106   In the opera, Bertalda's name is spelled as Berthalda.

107   In the short story, Undine's ascent from the spring to kill Huldbrand takes place during the desolate wedding night, and not during the festivities.

108   "E.T.A. Hoffmann was reluctant to evoke the miraculous and Romantic in an overly plastic way, both as a composer and a writer of ghost stories and fairy-tales. He believed that a

FIGURE 2.1   Stage design by Karl Friedrich Schinkel of the finale scene of *Undine* for the premiere performance at the *Königliches Schauspielhaus* in 1816. Through smoke, this vague vision should appear of Undine holding the deceased Huldbrand in her arms, accompanied by other water creatures with a giant water spirit Kühleborn in the back, transforming the wedding hall into a final image of the spirit realm.

in Fouqué's libretto, the emergence of the water world does not function as a diabolic disturbance of the ceremony, but rather as the final reconciliation of Undine and Huldbrand – of nature and man – in their '*Liebestod*,' endorsed by the Christian authority Pater Heilmann.[109]

Scenes like the finale of *Undine* clearly reflect Hoffmann's ideal of a sudden breakthrough of a supernatural Romantic realm into our everyday life, which he addressed in *Der Dichter und der Komponist*, a text he wrote while composing the opera. If Hoffmann actually succeeded in realizing this ideal is a different question. His score and music-theatrical design are certainly original, and one should at least acknowledge the pains he took to transcend the common trivial Romanticism of his age. It is, therefore, important to judge *Undine* on its own terms, against the framework of its time. Judging the convincing and

---

subject like *Undine* could easily loose its lightness and subtlety in the reality of stage practice. Therefore, he took pains to scenically present the realm of Kühleborn as uncertain, oscillating between transparent vision and delusion." Miller 2007: 279.

109   In the final moment of the opera, Heilmann sings: "O stille, des Himmels milder Wille hat ihn zum reinen Liebestod erkoren (Oh, silence, the merciful will of heaven has chosen him for a pure love-death)." This statement is followed by the final chorus, closing with the words: "Gute Nacht aller Erdensorg und Pracht (Good night to all trouble and world's splendor)."

mesmerizing effect of his *Undine* in comparison to later works will perhaps make this opera appear rather pale.

The same counts for Hoffmann's musical depiction of supernatural evil – one of the key elements of Romantic opera – in the music he granted Kühleborn.[110] Kühleborn's stage presence is largely restricted to the second act,[111] in which he has two remarkable appearances. In the first (No. 8 within the score), he climbs out of a spring to tell Undine about Berthalda's humble origin, and frightens the latter with his alien appearance. His second entry is a grand aria with chorus (No. 12), in which he summons other water spirits to join him in his fight for vengeance and justice. In the first case, Hoffmann creates a small-scale melodrama in which he tone-paints Kühleborn's appearance from the spring by a gradually ascending melody in the low strings and woodwinds (See Figure 2.2). Schläder labels this passage as "one of the most impressive scenes within the entire opera. Through tone painting and use of characteristic intervals, Hoffmann builds an acoustic-atmospheric frame for the entry of the miraculous into earthly reality."[112] Miller, on the contrary, describes this moment as "Kühleborn's grotesque appearance,"[113] which seems to be a more appropriate characterization. The music may arrive unexpectedly after the mellifluous, conventional duet of Undine and Berthalda. Nevertheless, the literal and therefore trivial tone painting, the regular walking bass and the use of bassoon create a rather silly impression, most probably for contemporary listeners as well.[114]

---

110   Whereas in the short story, Kühleborn initially welcomes Undine's marriage to Huldbrand and the soul she gains by this, and only gradually turns against the knight when he foresees his future betrayal, in the opera Kühleborn is evil throughout, and repudiates all contact between humans and spirits. Schläder writes that "the Kühleborn of the opera libretto is the big antagonist, with a fundamental desire to take revenge on mankind. This vengeance is elementary motivated [since he is a water spirit], and not morally." Schläder considers this constant, unconditional hatred of Kühleborn to have brought about a "highly significant loss of action within the opera [...], a gravitational shift from a dramatic action to a static conflict." Schläder 1979: 240–242.

111   His musical appearance is more extended, since he is the only character within *Undine* to which musical motifs are clearly tied, an early example of a leitmotivic procedure in Hoffmann's art.

112   Ibid.: 267.

113   Miller 2007: 273–274.

114   The bassoon is traditionally linked to the grotesque and silly. This is also brought forward by Hector Berlioz in his famous *Grand traité de l'instrumentation* (1843): "its timbre, totally lacking in *éclat* and nobility, has a propensity for the grotesque which must be borne in mind when giving it prominence" ("Sa sonorité n'est pas très forte, et son timbre, absolutement dépourvu d'éclat et de noblesse, a une propension au grotesque, don't il faut toujours tenir compte quand on le met en évidence."). Berlioz 1843: 128.

FIGURE 2.2 Kühleborn's ascent from the spring, Act II, no. 8

Kühleborn's second prominent appearance, the grand aria with chorus 'Ihr Freund' aus Seen und Quellen' (No. 12), is certainly more impressive. The broken chords of the brass ensemble, the expansive harmony[115] and the large intervals (often octaves) in the vocal line give Kühleborn a powerful, menacing character. Miller mentions "how, already at the premiere, this number was celebrated as the first completely successful Romanticization of a form derived from grand opera,"[116] and uses Weber's review in the *AMZ* as a reference.[117] At the same time, the "mesmerizing" effect of Kühleborn's aria is attenuated by the frequent repetitions, the undramatic one-dimensional message and the considerable length of the number: characteristics that retard the action.[118]

---

115   Within this aria, Hoffmann rarely uses the diabolical sonority of the diminished seventh-chord, but frequent dominant seventh-chords do create a harmonic expansion that fits the large gesture of Kühleborn's message.

116   Miller 2007: 274.

117   Weber signals "how powerfully Kühleborn appears, through the consistent choice of melody and instrumentation that emphasizes his uncanny vicinity" ("Am Mächtigsten springt Kühleborn hervor, [...] durch Melodienwahl und Instrumentation, die, ihm stets treu bleibend, seine unheimliche Nähe verkundet"). *AMZ* XIX/12, 19 March 1817: 205.

118   In a review for the *Dramaturgisches Wochenblatt*, Johann Philipp Schmidt also praises the scene while pointing out that the extensive length decreases its effect onstage: "In this number, the apparition of the water spirits is [...] successfully realized. The length of the scene, however, does not have a positive effect on the scenic impression" ("In dieser [Nummer] ist die Erscheinung der Wassergeister [...] gelungen durchgeführt. [...] Uebrigens scheint uns diese ziemlich lange Scene, so wie sie gestellt ist, nicht von ganz günstiger Wirkung auf die Bühne"). *Dramaturgisches Wochenblatt in nächster Beziehung auf die königlichen Schauspiele zu Berlin* III/21, 23 November 1816: 167.

Not only in the case of the diabolic Kühleborn does musical characterization play an important role in *Undine*. Hoffmann granted Berthalda, the
fisher's daughter who supposes to be of noble birth, a rather Italian vocal idiom, with many coloraturas, adopting the topos of virtuosity and artificiality.
Although Hoffmann's dismissal of Italian vocal virtuosity is not as unequivocal
as Weber's, and less motivated by nationalist reasoning,[119] it is hard to overlook the conscious, dramatically meaningful use of an Italian style for the vain,
artificial Berthalda. Through this stylistic differentiation, Hoffmann appeals to
the contemporary nationalist aversion to Italian singing and the artificiality
of court life. This element is already latently present in Fouqué's short story:
it is hard to overlook the symbolical nationalist significance of the portrayal
of Bert(h)alda, a supposed aristocrat who clings to her false noble identity instead of accepting and embracing her true, more humble roots. Even when,
as Schläder argues, the exposition of Berthalda's vanity and court manners is
absent in the libretto,[120] her character is lifted out in the opera through her
style of singing.[121]

Berthalda's vocal style is all the more noticeable since it clearly deviates
from the dominating musical character of the work. If we consider the musical
style that governs the vocal contributions of Undine and her foster parents –
the fisherman and -wife – we find a *verklärte Volkstümlichkeit* (a transfigured/
elevated folk style), as Miller calls it, in line with the "naïve-intimate" tone of
Fouqué's narration.[122] Here Hoffmann created the musical equivalent of the
contemporary *Kunstmärchen*,[123] in the sense that he wrote it in a style that
is actually invented, but apparently demotic, which presents the low-class
characters with a certain natural, Romantic dignity. Through this, Hoffmann

---

119   On the one hand, Hoffmann's review of Paer's *Sofonisbe* shows his dismissal of Italian
      vocal virtuosity, whereas Dechant argues that "Hoffmann does not reject coloraturas per
      se, but insists that they should be inserted at appropriate moments and sparsely, to avoid
      deviation of the listener's attention." Dechant 1975: 183.

120   Schläder 1979: 243.

121   This is a clear example of Hoffmann's conviction as voiced in a letter of July 1812 to his
      friend Hitzig, namely that "when many events are eliminated, because the drama leaves
      no room for them, and several nuances seem to be lost, music can make up for this absence" ("wenn manche Begebenheiten wegfallen, weil der Raum des Dramas sie nicht
      aufnehmen kann, und dadurch manche Nüanzirung verlohren zu gehen scheint, die
      Musik [...] alles wieder zu ersetzen im Stande ist"). Müller 1967: 347.

122   Miller 2007: 267.

123   In contrast to the anonymous and orally-communicated *Volksmärchen*, a *Kunstmärchen*
      is created by an individual. The latter is modelled after folk tales, but deviates from this
      tradition in its formal and narrative complexity.

avoided the "abundant banality"[124] he associated with common *Singspiel*. A clear example of this simple but simultaneously complex style is the Fisher's romance 'Wir weinten still' in the first act (No. 2), which passes over into the first appearance of the water spirit world. As Schläder writes, "this song has all elements of a typical inserted number [...], but the relation between the single motifs and the harmonic disposition betray its exceptional compositional quality and its particular function within the dramatic exposition."[125] The transgression of a *Singspiel* esthetic is established even further by the fact that this apparently inserted song, normally a closed form extraneous to the main action, turns out to be a vehicle towards the subsequent scene. With his invented *verklärte Volkstümlichkeit*, Hoffmann ended the common stylistic dichotomy of simple strophic songs for low-class characters and an Italian idiom for noblemen, adding an alternative, non-trivial folk style to the stylistic palette of German Romantic opera: a serious, genuinely German alternative.

Of course, this solemnity was gained at the expense of something else, namely comedy. In *A History of Opera* (2012), Carolyn Abbate and Roger Parker entitled their chapter on early nineteenth-century German opera 'The German Problem,' and ask "why, in short, did opera in German quite suddenly become so *serious*?"[126] The most straightforward answer to this question must be that German opera composers desired to elevate the genre and find an operatic niche that fitted their notions of German nationhood.

No one has analyzed the consequences of this divorce of the Romantic and the comic – which eventually took refuge in the less prestigious genre of *Spieloper* – more eloquently than Jürgen Schläder in his interpretation of *Undine*. He points out that "the one-sided musical-Romantic poetry has its flaws from a music-dramatic point of view, flaws that hinder the general impression of an opera like *Undine*. But at the same time, the work is invaluable in its sublimation of expressive musical means."[127] Nevertheless, he remains critical about the price paid for this sublimation:

> eliminating comic elements from magic- and fairy-tale operas implies depriving them of their theatrical lifeblood. The complementary and contrasting function of comedy is highly significant, if magic is perceived

---

124   In a 1795 letter to his friend Hippel, Hoffmann complained about a performance of Wenzel Müller's *Sonnenfest der Brahmanen*, in which "the music was abundantly banal" ("Die Musik war bis zum Ueberdruß alltäglich"). Müller 1967: 73. We have witnessed many other examples of Hoffmann's problems with common *Singspiel* earlier in this chapter.

125   Schläder 1979: 315.

126   Abbate 2012: 170.

127   Schläder 1979: 238.

as poetically real in a Romantic sense. This is the dramaturgical defect of the *Undine* libretto.[128]

The lack of comic relief is not only harmful to the dramaturgy of *Undine*, but also contrary to the ideal image of the Romantic as a realm "in which the comic and tragic smoothly blend together into a total impression, marvelously gripping the spectator" that Ferdinand advocates in *Der Dichter und der Komponist*.[129] Perhaps this is what Hoffmann had in mind when he spoke of "the high Romanticism of Mozart," but the sublime alternation of the comic and tragic we find in *Don Giovanni* – Hoffmann's "opera of operas"[130] – is hard to find in *Undine*. In the end, it seems that early nineteenth-century German opera was burdened by its own Romantic ambitions. One might argue that the evocation of a Romantic world only became realizable a few decades later, when, for example, Richard Wagner had more appropriate music-dramatic means at his disposal. At the same time, most of Wagner's operas also show a considerable lack of comic relief. The move away from the common variation principle of opera was a daring one, but it turned German opera into a tenacious, to some even unbearably heavy affair.

3   The Elevation of *Singspiel* in Carl Maria von Weber's *Silvana* and *Der Freischütz*

At first sight, Weber's music-theatrical works are less defined by an overarching tendency to facilitate the breakthrough of a Romantic world than Hoffmann's *Undine*. Moreover, it seems that even in Weber's more mature works, such as *Silvana* (1810) and *Der Freischütz* (1821), the ground structure of the *romantisch-komisches Volksmärchen* is retained to a certain extent, thereby deviating from Hoffmann's more genuinely Romantic approach in *Undine*. As a consequence, it is increasingly hard to discern between "trivial" and "elevated" Romanticism in Weber's operas. But due to this complexity, his opera oeuvre is more problematic, and therefore perhaps more representative of its age. An analysis of *Silvana* and *Der Freischütz* can help to clarify the diffuse nature of German Romantic opera in the first quarter of the nineteenth century.

---

128   Ibid.: 256.
129   "Nur im wahrhaft Romantischen mischt sich das komische mit dem Tragischen so gefügig, daß beides zum Totaleffekt in eins verschmilzt, und das Gemüt des Zuhörers auf eine eigene, wunderbare Weise ergreift." *AMZ* XV/49, 8 September 1813:805.
130   In his 1813 short story *Don Juan*, Hoffmann refers to Mozart's *Don Giovanni* as "Oper aller Opern." *AMZ* XV/13, 31 March 1813: 220.

3.1   Silvana

Weber composed *Silvana* between 1808 and 1810 in Stuttgart on a libretto of Franz Carl Hiemer.[131] It was premiered in Frankfurt in 1810 and revived in a slightly altered version in Berlin in 1812. Weber and Hiemer modeled it after *Das Waldmädchen* (1800), the first performed opera by Weber, completed when the composer was only thirteen years old. Unfortunately, most of the score of *Das Waldmädchen* is lost. What we do know is that it was a *romantisch-komisches Volksmärchen* on a libretto by Karl von Steinsberg in the style of *Das Donau-weibchen*. Small wonder, as it was based on *Das Waldweibchen* (1800), a spin-off from the famous Viennese *Singspiel*, also written by Hensler. Similar to *Das Donauweibchen*, the action of Weber's opera revolves around the love between a knight and a female nature creature he finds in the woods. In many respects, the opera follows formulas derived from Viennese *Singspiel* and particularly from Hensler and Kauer's famous piece. In *Silvana*, composed ten years later, we still find many remnants of this model. For example, the opening scene of *Silvana* seems to be closely modeled after *Das Donauweibchen*: it starts with a hunter's chorus and involves the chase of a bear, after which a strange but beautiful nature girl is found.

The story revolves around the arranged marriage between Count Rudolph von Helfenstein and Mechtilde, daughter of Count Adelhart. Mechthilde refuses to marry, since she is in love with Albert von Cleeburg, the son of her father's arch-enemy. Her father is enraged over this disobedience, whereas the more upright Rudolph is hesitant to wed a woman who loves someone else. When Rudolph meets a dumb nature girl in the woods and falls in love with her, he is no longer willing to fulfill his duty and marry Mechthilde. He has, however, given Adelhart his word, and his supposed father-in-law insists on the marriage.

A tournament takes place at Adelhart's court, in which Albert – unrecognizable because he wears a helmet – turns out to be the winner and asks for Mechtilde's hand.[132] The enraged Adelhart threatens to incarcerate him, but Rudolph prevents this and Albert and his men flee the castle. Adelhart's rage is now directed at the mute girl, brought to the castle by Rudolph and evidently the cause of his altered attitude. All bystanders try to convince Adelhart not to kill the girl. He is only convinced when Silvana's (the mute girl) foster father enters and announces that the girl is actually Adelhart's

---

131   Jähns mentions another librettist, Referendar Toll, who changed a few lines in the arias nr. 4 and 10 for the Berlin performances in 1812, but the majority of the libretto has been created by Hiemer. Jähns 1871: 107.

132   In Hensler's *Waldweibchen*, the hand of Agnes (the part of Mechthilde in *Silvana*) is explicitly at stake in the tournament. The occasion of the competition within *Silvana* is less clearly motivated.

second daughter Ottilie, who had been abandoned in the woods because she resembled his archenemy, Albert's father. Albert, who has re-entered the castle, proves Silvana/Ottilie's descent by disposing a characteristic mole on her arm (it remains unclear how he has obtained this knowledge). Adelhart's retrieval of his daughter effects the ultimate peripeteia: he allows his children to marry their loved ones, and Silvana can suddenly speak. It turns out that she was not dumb after all, but only obeyed her foster father's prohibition to speak. After a final chorus and several dances, the curtain closes.

The biggest weakness of the story of *Silvana* is perhaps that it lacks conflicts and tragic dilemmas. As soon as Rudolph finds Silvana, he gives up his desire for Mechthilde, and the only real opponent to the two pairs of young lovers is the one-dimensional, outrageous Adelhart. Just as flat are the heroic figures, whose spotless behavior simultaneously makes them rather characterless. In the 1812 version, Mechthilde's attitude is one-sided as well. She is determined to marry Albert from the start, regardless of her father's threats, and the dilemma of choosing between the love for her father and her friend – present in the 1810 version (particularly in the original version of Mechthilde's aria nr. 10) – is lacking. Since the characters do not really come to life, the story does not lift off either.

Silvana has received several genre characterizations from Weber and Hiemer, varying from a *romantische* to a *heroische* or *heroisch-komische Oper*. Müller shows that the first designation can be found in the Frankfurt premiere score of 1810, whereas the second was chosen for the 1812 vocal score, and the last for an edited copy for Dresden performances in 1818.[133] These altered characterizations may point to an interesting development in Weber's thinking. It seems that over the years, it became clearer to Weber that his "Romantic" opera was perhaps not so Romantic after all, and could better be typified by genre designations that emphasize its descent from trivial turn-of-the-century forms of music theater.

The adjective *"heroisch-komisch"* is not far removed from the label *"romantisch-komisch."* In *Die heroisch-komische Oper* (1987), Helen Geyer-Kiefl shows that this subgenre was, similar to the *romantisch-komisches Volksmärchen* and the *Zauberoper*, a light-versed Viennese form of music theatre, dominated by Hensler.[134] The label "heroic-comic" that *Silvana* eventually obtained points to its combination of chivalry and comedy, as opposed to the *romantisch-komisch*

---

133   Müller 1996: 43.
134   Geyer-Kiefl 1987: 26–27.

mixture of a magical ghost story and comic relief.[135] At the same time, Miller states that Weber had good reasons for labeling *Silvana* as a *Romantische Oper*: "Weber's *Silvana* may count as the first German *Singspiel* that – through its invocation of nature, its treatment of the mystery of fate and its depiction of the soul – breathes the spirit of Early Romanticism."[136] This would imply that *Silvana*'s Romanticism is intellectual and elevated indeed.

At first sight, *Silvana* mainly displays forms of trivial Romanticism. The most peculiar aspect of the story, Silvana's muteness, eventually turns out not to be related to her non-human descent, but simply to be the result of a prohibition to speak. Although the rational explanation of the title heroine's mysterious silence makes *Silvana* in a certain respect perhaps even less Romantic than *Das Donauweibchen*, the way in which Silvana communicates through instrumental music[137] does resonate with Romantic notions of music as language of the ineffable. Another Romantic aspect of *Silvana* is the atmospheric depiction of nature and forest life, from the opening hunter's chorus of the first to the storm at the start of the third act.[138] Although nature still occupies a pictoresque rather than transcendental significance in *Silvana*, the orchestral means Weber uses in order to evoke it point to a certain elevation, and foreshadow the significance of nature music in *Der Freischütz*. Both Silvana's music and the orchestral depiction of nature reflect a tendency towards musical Romanticism, but the story somewhat lags behind.[139]

This conviction is enforced by those who saw the first performances, since Hiemer's libretto did not enjoy a favorable response in contemporary criticism. After the Berlin performance of 1812, an anonymous critic from the *Berlinische Nachrichten von Staats- und gelehrten Sachen* characterized the text as "utterly

---

135 The only evidence that the young Weber was inclined to ghost stories is his unfinished opera fragment *Rübezahl* (1804), a Bluebeard-like story about a subterranean spirit who abducts a maid. Weber wrote some music for this libretto by Johann Gottlieb Rhode, based on a tale from Johann Karl August Musäus's *Volksmärchen der Deutschen*. According to Joachim Veit, a 1811 letter suggests that Hiemer and Weber planned to rework *Rübezahl*, similar to the way they turned *Das Waldmädchen* into *Silvana*. However, this plan never materialized. Veit 1990: 358.

136 Miller 2007: 338.

137 The most prominent example of this technique is Rudolph's aria nr. 7 "Willst du nicht diesen Aufenthalt," in which Rudolph's lines alternate with passages for solo cello, which express Silvana's responses.

138 "As soon as the characters find themselves in the open air, new invention breathes into them," according to Warrack. Warrack 1976: 82.

139 Concerning Hoffmann's *Undine*, one might argue the contrary. Here nature is Romantically transfigured within the story, but the music lacks the proper aura to evoke this sensation.

commonplace [sehr gewöhnlich],"[140] whereas Friedrich Wilhelm Gubitz – a future advocate of *Der Freischütz* – wrote the following in the *Morgenblatt für gebildete Stände*:

> The subject and the text display a sample card of all possible theatrical effects, but regardless of the bear hunt, the forest cave, the tournament and serious battles, thunder and dance of torches, regardless of the initially apparently wild, Gurli-like[141] dumb maid and the Armide-like scenes, the whole did not elevate itself.[142]

The listed sample card calls Franz Horn's earlier mentioned recipe for a common German opera to mind, although Hiemer's text employs clichés of knight's plays rather than the stereotypes of rural, sentimental-comical plays to which Horn refers.

For a heroic-comic opera, comedy plays a limited and, moreover, uneven role in *Silvana*. The biggest comic role is that of Krips, squire of Count Rudolph von Helfenstein, the male Romantic lead. Krips was initially the most popular part in *Silvana*, and his simple, strophic songs enjoyed popularity far beyond the opera stage, for example as drinking songs. He is not only modeled after clownish characters such as Hanswurst and Käsperle, but has a lot in common with Mozart's Papageno as well. The way he unrightfully boasts about killing the bear and the subsequent signs of his cowardice during the first act conform to Papageno's behavior, and his comic songs on the subject of love share the spirit of Mozart's *Der Vogelfänger bin ich ja* and *Ein Mädchen oder Weibchen*.

From a dramaturgical point of view, Krips is intimately tied to his lord Rudolph, since every Romantic aria by the latter is followed up by a light-versed rendering of the same theme by his servant. This strong alliance between Romantic and comic action is typical for the *romantisch-komisches Volksmärchen*, but the prominence of Krips is mainly restricted to the first act and diminishes afterwards: the third act lacks a comical element altogether. Although

---

140   Quoted after Huck 1999: 159.

141   This refers to a character in August von Kotzebue's 'Lustspiel' *Die Indianer in England* (1790). Gurli is an Indian girl with a naïve charm. Kotzebue's storyline contains some elements we also find in *Silvana*: tension between love and duty, arranged marriages and the retrieval of lost family members.

142   "Das Sujet und der Text sind eine Musterkarte von allen möglichen Theatereffekten, aber trotz der Bärenhetze, der Waldhöhle, dem Turniere und ernstem Gefechte, dem Ungewitter und dem Fackeltanze, trotz dem erst wild scheinenden gurlihaften stummbleibenden Mägdlein und der armidenartigen Szenen hob sich das Ganze nicht." Quoted after Huck 1999: 159.

the second act contains a number in which the comical and Romantic-heroic action are mirrored – the quartet of Mechthilde and Albert and their servants Klärchen and Kurt – the comical action gradually loses its dramaturgical function as commentary on the serious action. In the eyes of Huck, this gives the opera a character somewhere in between the Viennese *Singspiel* and Romantic opera, which damages the strength of the whole.[143] Although Huck's judgment seems adequate, one may object that the elimination of comedy does speed up the dramatic pace towards the end, lending the work a clearer direction and stronger focus.

The elimination of the comic – albeit less radical than Hoffmann's, but still clearly conceivable – creates room for the heroic element as the most important sphere within the drama. Unlike *Das Donauweibchen*, in which the aristocrats are all given spoken roles, the musical weight shifts to the "heroic" noblemen in *Silvana*. To find a heroic musical idiom for his main characters, Weber could hardly rely on German opera models. A possible exception was Mozart's *Zauberflöte*, and we find some parallels in Weber's depiction of heroic characters in *Silvana*. The accompagnato recitative of Rudolph's aria (nr. 4) 'So soll denn dieses Herz nie Liebe finden,' for example has some striking similarities to Tamino's 'Dies Bildnis ist bezaubernd schön.' Both numbers present the Romantic tenor hero, and follow up on a scene in which a wild animal is killed, and the comic side role unrightfully claims to have defeated it. Musical parallels can also be traced: both numbers start in E-flat major in a slow tempo, and both opening melodies are directed towards a high g and a high a-flat, reached by jumps from b-flat. Furthermore, Mozart and Weber both intersperse the vocal line with short orchestral gestures in primary colors, played by either strings, woodwinds, or horns.[144]

At the same time, some noteworthy differences can be observed. Whereas Tamino's aria is in a slow tempo throughout and employs a lyrical but nonetheless restrained, syllabic vocal style, Weber writes the second part of Rudolph's aria (from "Nein, von dannen will ich eilen") in a florid, melismatic style, full of giant leaps and coloraturas. By including this stretto coda,[145] Weber depicts his

---

143 "[Within the conception of *Silvana*,] some fundamental conditions are altered, in the sense that the genre limits between Viennese *Singspiel* and Romantic opera are transgressed, causing the former form to lose its sustainability." Ibid.: 159.

144 This analysis discusses the 1812 version of this scene.

145 The passage has many characteristics of a cabaletta, but only a few years later this specific form was first established. The cabaletta was the most important technique in Italian opera from Rossini until roughly middle-Verdi. It concerns the second, faster part of an aria, filled with ornamentation and coloraturas, chiefly "designed to stimulate applause" in the eyes of Julian Budden (Oxfordmusiconline.com, Lemma "Cabaletta," consulted on 12 Juny

hero in an overtly Italian vocal style. Thereby, he models Rudolph after *opera seria* conventions, departing from the common use in serious German opera that coloraturas mostly serve to underline evil, or at least enraged characters. We find this, for example, in Mozart's famous arias for the Queen of the Night, but also in the scenes Weber would later write for the villains Caspar (*Freischütz*) and Lysiart/Eglantine (*Euryanthe*).[146] The virtuosity of the final section takes down the noble image of Rudolph that the music had created in the previous sections of this number. To contemporaries, another objection lay in the inappropriate relation between coloratura music and the underlying text, as an 1813 anonymous review of the vocal score in the AMZ shows:

> The critic believes that v. Weber pays too much homage to a fashion that entails giving coloraturas to words that, due to their meaning, do not call for ornamentation; for example in Nr. 4, where Rudolph searches for peace and rest on the battlefield (which means: in death); on the word "Rast." [...] The vowel a is [...] in itself not at all sufficient to justify the passages that Weber has written.[147]

In the end, the mixed quality of *Silvana* reflects the situation of German opera with Romantic ambitions around 1810. It was Weber's first considerable opera success and enjoyed quite some revivals before *Der Freischütz* eclipsed it in 1821, but several remarks by Weber show that the composer regarded the work mainly as a valuable learning experience. In a diary entry of May 1812, he commented on a discussion about *Silvana* with fellow composer Friedrich von Drieberg: "He told me that my opera would do fine, and made a few

---

2013). Sieghart Döhring and Sabine Henze-Döhring emphasize that the true cabaletta came into existence in the years after 1813. (Döhring 1997: 21) The final part of Weber's aria forms a typical example of a proto-cabaletta.

146 Stephen C. Meyer exemplifies the dramatic use of vocal style in German opera around 1800 by a comparison of evil and comic characters in Peter von Winter's *Das unterbrochene Opferfest* (in its original 1798 version): "The contrast between the vocal style of the evil and the comic characters is even more striking. Pedrillo and his cohorts combine square-cut *Volkstümlichkeit* with the *zärtliche* ('tender') style, whereas the idiom of the evil characters is the exact opposite, a combination of what German critics might call the *läufige* and *kraftvolle* styles, characterized by large leaps and spectacular passages." Meyer 2003: 37–38.

147 "Fürs erste findet Rec., dass Hr. v. W. dadurch einer gewissen Mode zu sehr gehuldigt, dass er einigemal Passagen und Coloraturen auf solche Worte gesetzt hat, zu deren Bedeutung keine dergleichen glänzende Verzierungen passen; nämlich S. 9 [Nr. 4, T. 134ff.] wo Rudolph Ruhe und Rast auf dem Schlachtfelde (also im Tode) sucht, auf das Wort: 'Rast' [...] Der Vocal a ist [...] noch bey weitem nicht hinreichend, um die dort angebrachten Passagen zu rechtfertigen." AMZ XV/14, 7 April 1813: 241.

observations: I strain for effects, the instrumental element is the most brilliant aspect, but the vocal parts are treated less well, [...] and the whole is characterized by a certain monotony. The first remark is absolutely true, [....] the last one made me very sad."[148] Two months later, Weber emphasized the learning effect of his experiences performing *Silvana* in Berlin in a letter to Rochlitz, saying: "Again I have learnt quite a lot through this performance, some altered arias and little cuts have aided the opera, and taught me a great deal about effect and proportion."[149] Weber put the lessons he had learned into practice in *Der Freischütz*, and it is hard to overlook his progress in compositional skill. But did this also lead to a more genuinely Romantic opera?

3.2 Der Freischütz

In the famous 1864 biography on his father, Max Maria von Weber writes the following about a 1814 Berlin revival of *Silvana*:

> *Sylvana* was given on 5 September in a packed house, but seems to have been coldly received by the audience, because neither a newspaper nor Weber himself in the letters to his wife Caroline have mentioned a notable acclaim. This lack of engagement on behalf of the audience is understandable if we consider that the spirit of the times was moving away from the sentimental hyper-Romanticism of the *Sylvana* story, with all its artificial emotions and unnatural situations that did not evoke a sympathetic response from a people recently made powerfully sensitive by events on the world stage.[150]

---

148 "Er sagte mir, dass alles mit meiner Oper gut gehen würde, und machte mir verschiedene Bemerkungen: ich hasche nach Effecten, das Instrumentale sei die brillianteste Seite, die Singstimmen zuweilen vernachlässigt, und [behauptete dass] eine gewisse Eintönigkeit sich über das Ganze verbreite. An der ersten Bemerkung finde ich viel Wahres, [...] Die letzte Bemerkung machte mich sehr traurig." Quoted after Huck 1999: 147.

149 "Ich habe bey dieser Aufführung wieder vieles gelernt, ein Paar neue Arien die ich an die Stelle der Alten schrieb, und ein paar kleine Schnitte haben der Oper sehr aufgeholfen, und mich wieder über Effekt und Zuschnitt neu belehrt." Quoted after Ibid.: 148.

150 "*Sylvana* ging am 5., bei brechend vollem Hause, in Scene, scheint aber das Publikum sehr kühl gelassen zu haben, da weder ein Journal noch Weber selbst in den Briefen an Caroline irgend erheblichen Beifalls Erwähnung thun. Diese Theilnahmloßigkeit des Publikums erklärt sich sehr natürlich aus der Zeitströmung der Geister, die, mit ihrem großen, kräftigen, sonoren Wellenschläge, weitab von der sentimentalen Hyperromantik des Sujets der "Sylvana" lenkte; das mit all seinem Apparat von pappenen Rüstungen, gemachten Empfindungen, unnatürlichen Situationen in dem von Weltereignissen bewegten, kräftig-fühlenden Volke keine sympathischen Empfindungen wecken konnte." Weber 1864: 462.

In 1821, the Berlin premiere of *Der Freischütz* created quite the contrary; an incredible hype. Whereas *Silvana* had seemed irrelevant to its audience at a decisive moment within the Liberation Wars, the idyll of *Der Freischütz* – employing many similar ingredients, such as hunting choruses, glorification of forest life and open air festivities – fully appealed to the spirit of 1821 and its euphoria over regained independence. The Romanticism in the work was no longer old-fashioned, but obtained a remarkable national significance, became a political expression exactly due to its seemingly apolitical, idyllic character.[151] Obviously one cannot detach the success of *Der Freischütz* as a national opera from the reputation Weber had gained through his works on patriotic texts. But the secret of its triumph may also lie in the fact that Kind and Weber succeeded to instrumentalize elements of Romantic opera, which can also be found in operas like *Silvana*, in a nationalist context. Within *Der Freischütz*, the cosmos of Romantic opera is expanded by adding the notion of community to High-Romantic elements such as Max's *Weltschmerz* and the desire for reconciliation between man and nature. In this triangular relation between individual, nature and community, a balance that needs to be restored, Romanticism and nationalist thinking find a union within *Der Freischutz*.

The following analysis of Weber's *Freischütz* is restricted to four aspects:

1) Romantic elements with nationalist significance within the work,
2) the ideal of organic unity in Weber's musical design,
3) the *Wolfsschluchtszene* in which the "appearance of the miraculous" – the decisive moment of Romantic opera – takes place,
4) and ultimately a few important critical responses to *Der Freischütz*, and to the *Wolfsschluchtszene* in particular.

---

151 The number of (music-)theatrical renditions of Apel and Laun's 1810 *Freischütz* story after the defeat of Napoleon is remarkable, and shows to what extent the narration appealed to post-war audiences. Already in 1812, Franz Xaver von Casper wrote an opera designated to be composed by Carl Neuner, whereas in 1816, two Viennese *Freischütz Singspiele* saw the light (one by Ferdinand Rosau and the other by Joseph Alois Gleich and Franz de Paula Roser). In the same year Louis Spohr turned down an offer to write a *Freischütz* opera, not wanting to compete with Weber, and in August 1821, two months after the premiere of Weber's opera, a five-act tragedy by Franz Graf von Riesch with the same subject matter was produced in Würzburg. See Schreiter 2007: 110–112. The situation surrounding the *Freischütz* story forms a clear example of what Joep Leerssen refers to as "the past as gold rush." Regardless of the abundance of discovered sources, early nineteenth-century German scholars and artists all clung to the same sources for editions and artistic renditions, creating a severe competition and the impression of scarcity, whereas, in fact, sources "were surfacing in great number all over Europe." Leerssen 2010: 67–68. In the case of the *Freischütz* story, it is obvious that Weber left with all the gold.

As mentioned, it is striking that a few elements that *Silvana* shares with *Der Freischütz* sorted a completely different effect in the latter work. Both operas feature a hunting chorus glorifying forest life. The musical design of these choruses is quite similar: a homophonous four-part male chorus with prominent horns in the orchestral accompaniment. Michael C. Tusa points out that "the choral singing and hunting imagery [...] evoke the singing of patriotic songs within the Burschenschafte and gymnastics movements of the decade, the widespread urban male chorus societies of the period, and the more rural shooting clubs."[152] Furthermore, Susan Youens maintains that "at this fraught juncture in European history [around 1815], the German *Jäger* becomes a na-tionalistic emblem, a masculine-heroic model of irresistible bravery and sexu-al appeal."[153] In that sense, there might already have been a latent nationalist connotation to the hunting chorus in *Silvana*. But whereas that number merely serves to establish a certain locale, in *Der Freischütz* the societal significance receives more emphasis. Here the chorus epitomizes the way of life of an entire community. The central issue of the opera is Max's crucial trial shot, neces-sary for his initiation into this community. This homogenous forest society can clearby be read as a utopian, small-scale version of the German nation, and its vicissitudes seem to reflect national concerns.

The main character Max does, however, not fully conform to Youens's image of a masculine-heroic model of irresistible bravery and sexual appeal. The fact that his shooting skills desert him at the moment when he needs them the most points to an impotence with covert, but nonetheless conceivable sexual undertones. As Max's insecurity is possibly related to traumatic experiences during the Thirty Years War (1618–1648),[154] it may not present the highest na-tional virtue, but it does reflect an urgent national concern.

Max also embodies a certain Romantic *Weltschmerz* that is more funda-mental, and transcends the specific circumstances of a historical moment. His ponderous nature and dramatic development within *Der Freischütz* equal that of the Faust myth, as he sells his soul to the devil (Caspar/Samiel) in exchange

---

152   Tusa 2006: 500–501.
153   Youens 1997: 43.
154   Modern-day stage directors often interpret the work from this point of view, linking the historical context of the *Freischütz* story not only to that of 1821, but also to the situation in Germany after 1945. Henderson mentions the 1973 Kassel production by Nicholas Sulz-berger as a prime example of this, and writes: "More recent existential scenarios have put greater emphasis upon the personal plight of Max and Agathe. These productions, which began to multiply in the 1970s, suggest that despite the return of social stability and rise of prosperity [...], internal scars from the war had not yet healed." Henderson 2011: 165.

for magic bullets,[155] in order to pursue worldly joy. Similar to Goethe's Faust,[156] Max is eventually saved and redeemed of his curse by an overpowering Christian authority, the hermit. By alluding to the Faust story, Kind and Weber referred to a cultural icon that had already acquired both an elevated Romantic and national significance.[157]

This intertwining of Romanticism and national thinking pervades *Der Freischütz* on various levels. In his seminal study *Biedermeierzeit* (1971), Friedrich Sengle shows how "Romantic," anti-Enlightened sentiments clearly had a nationalist, anti-French undertone in the years after 1815: "Enlightenment, Satan and France – forming the mighty triumvirate of the past epoch – all appeared to be defeated once for all in the bliss of Christian-German victory."[158] In that sense, the Romantic struggles of Max – a Faustian hunter – underline to what extent Romanticism could help articulate a firmly Christian German national identity.

It has already been pointed out that Romantic and German national music esthetics shared an idealization of organic unity. Moreover, it is clear that Weber played an active part in the dissemination and anchorage of this ideal,

---

155 Interestingly, in the earliest German Faust tales, Faust is said to have held nocturnal sabbaths in the woods (In *Historia von Doktor Johann Fausten* (1587), comparable to the *Wolfsschlucht* rite, and used his magic for excellent shooting during a tournament in Strasbourg (*Fliegendes Blatt aus Köln*). These aspects both reinforce the analogy of Faust and Weber's Max. See Völker 1975: 30 + 25.

156 Goethe's work on the *Faust* myth stretches a period of sixty years, from 1772 (start of the *Urfaust*) until 1832 (publication of the second part of the *Faust* tragedy). A milestone within this process was the publication of the first part of the tragedy in 1808.

157 Already in 1802 did Schelling write in his *Philosophie der Kunst* that "Dr. Faust is a spitting image of the German character and its ground physiognomy (Doktor Faust [ist] recht aus der Mitte des deutschen Charakters und seiner Grundphysiognomie wie geschnitten)." (Quoted after Wagner 1994: 87) With a characteristic touch of irony, Heinrich Heine wrote the following in a 1846 comment on his *Doktor Faustus. Ein Tanzpoem*: "Our Doctor Faustus is such an honest, truthful, profoundly naive nature who aims to penetrate into the essence of things, and even in sensuality is so learned that he can only be a fiction or a German (Unser Doktor Johannes Faustus ist eine so grundehrliche, wahrheitliche, tiefsinnig naive, nach dem Wesen der Dinge lechzende und selbst in der Sinnlichkeit so gelehrte Natur, daß er nur eine Fabel oder ein Deutscher seyn konnte.)." (Heine 1851: 60) The further "nationalization" of Faust mainly took place after the German unification in 1871. Herfried Münkler argues that "without Goethe's version, the *Faust* story could never have turned into a national myth." Münkler mentions Heinrich Treitschke's 1879 statement that Goethe's *Faust* appeared "as a symbolical image of our native history (wie ein symbolisches Bild der vaterländischen Geschichte)" and Franz Dingelstedt's 1876 characterization of Goethe's *Faust* as "second bible of our nation (zweite Bibel unserer Nation)." Münkler 2010: 110.

158 Sengle 1971: 138.

for example in his 1817 review of Hoffmann's *Undine*. Later generations have glorified the formal awareness of Weber as a sign of German greatness, presenting him as an important forerunner to the complex structures of Wagner's music dramas. Although organic unity obviously is an ideological-esthetic construction often imposed upon a musical piece, it is nonetheless useful to understand in which fields Weber strove for unity, in order to gain a better understanding of the opera's reception.

The popularity of *Der Freischütz* with the public at large was chiefly based on the catchiness and charm of folk tunes such as the *Jungfernkranz* (Nr. 14) and the hunters' chorus (Nr. 15). To Weber, the quality of an opera should, however, not be measured by the effect of single numbers, but rather by the way these single parts constitute a coherent whole.[159] Within *Der Freischütz*, Weber uses three techniques to establish musical structure beyond the level of single numbers: 1) recurring musical motifs, 2) the creation of a tonal web with symbolical implications, and 3) a dramaturgical use of characteristic instrumentation. The effect of these methods is further enforced by the way they are interrelated: motifs recur in similar keys and with similar instrumentation, heightening the recognition, and thereby the dramatic potency of these musical ideas. Although the first technique has traditionally been highlighted as a novel music-dramatic procedure anticipating Wagner's leitmotif, in fact, the other two were far more innovative, and deserve attention.[160]

Even if Weber never expressed his working procedure concerning tonal planning within *Der Freischütz*,[161] the majority of the music adheres to a strict tonal design with symbolical implications. The tonal centers of *Der Freischütz* are derived from the diminished seventh chord f♯ – a – c – e♭. Together they

---

159　Weber emphasizes this idea in a passage within his 1817 *Undine* review, which has already been quoted in the previous chapter: "every musical piece appears – due to its structure – to be an independent, organic, closed being. When contemplating the whole work, each piece should nevertheless vanish as a constituent part of the total construction." AMZ XIX/12, 19 March 1817: 203.

160　Reminiscence motifs already played a prominent part in French opera around 1800.

161　An insightful analysis of his own masterpiece in a fictive conversation with Johann Christian Lobe (published 1855/1869) has often been misunderstood as a faithful recollection of a meeting that actually took place, but Lobe clearly stylized the exchange of ideas in a similar way to Hoffmann's fantastical stories. Finscher argues that "Weber's analysis of his own opera is literally too good to be true: granted that the composer was in his time an outstanding music critic – what he tells us here is singular in the whole nineteenth century. We know of no other composer analyzing his own work in this way, with such a wealth of detailed information, and such lucidly stated principles of opera (or rather dramatic) composition. The *Freischütz* analysis is the work of a brilliant music critic and writer from the middle of the century, but not the work of Weber." Finscher 1983: 89.

form the *Leitklang* of the demonic Samiel and his dark powers. Moreover, the tonal structure of the *Wolfsschluchtszene*, centerpiece of the work, is fully based on these tones: it opens and ends in F-sharp minor, and its middle part is dominated by C minor, alternated by short stretches in A minor and E-flat major. Within the tonal complex, C minor and F-sharp minor represent the dark powers whose attraction Max tries to withstand ("mich umgarnen finst're Mächte," sings Max in his extended first act scene and aria (nr. 3)). They derive their evil significance from being a negation of the victorious C major, the key in which both the overture and the opera in its entirety open and conclude.[162] C minor negates C major as being the parallel minor, whereas f-sharp is a tritone – the interval traditionally typified as *diabolus in musica* – removed from c, and at a 180-degrees distance from it within the circle of fifths.

E-flat major is related to Providence and Christian faith, as it is the key in which the hermit sings during the final scene. Stephen C. Meyer argues that, regardless of the fact that the referential meanings of E-flat major are "less obvious," the key is "associated with Agathe and the hope of redemption that she represents," both in Max's aria and in the overture.[163] With this, Meyer points to an important carrier of unity and coherence within *Der Freischütz*, namely the referential network of keys which governs and connects different musical numbers over a large time span within the drama. The most obvious interrelations can be found among the overture, Max's scene and aria, and the *Wolfsschluchtszene*, which all represent pieces in which the battle between good and evil over Max's soul is fought out. Although other numbers are more autonomous and closed, at least from a musical point of view, the crucial scenes are held together by this tonal design.

---

162   The association of C major as a victory of light over darkness is perhaps the most common key character of all within eighteenth- and nineteenth-century theories on *Tonartencharakteristik*. Two prominent examples of this association are Haydn's sudden blazing C major chord in *Die Schöpfung* after the words 'Und es ward Licht,' and E.T.A. Hoffmann's similar interpretation of Beethoven's return to C major in the famous review of the *Fifth Symphony*: "The full orchestra enters with the beautiful, jubilant theme of the final movement – like a radiant, dazzling ray of sunlight, that suddenly illuminates the night (Mit dem prächtigen, jauchzenden Themas des Schlusssatzes, C dur, fällt das ganze Orchester [...] ein – wie ein strahlendes, blendendes Sonnenlicht, das plötzlich die tiefe Nacht erleuchtet)." AMZ XII/41, 1810: 655. In *Der Freischütz*, the unisono opening melody of the overture hints at C major, but lacks the common optimistic character that the key later obtains. The second musical idea within the overture, the cantilena for four horns and string accompaniment, does, however, invoke the positive, idyllic character of this key. For more information on the phenomenon of key characteristics in the eighteenth and nineteenth century, see Auhagen 1983 and Steblin 2002.

163   Meyer 2003: 93.

Ingenious though this tonal planning is, it concerns a structuring device on a deeper level, not immediately perceivable to the average listener. The character of Weber's music is to a greater extent defined by his remarkable use of orchestration. Jürgen Maehder recognizes a *Dramaturgie der Klangfarben*[164] in Weber's operas, and this dramaturgy arguably is most prominent and effective in *Der Freischütz*.

The two most important dramatic spheres within the work, the "natural" hunters' environment and the supernatural realm of Samiel, are characterized by contrasting orchestral colors, and introduced in the opening measures of the overture.[165] The hunters are surrounded by the sound of horns, which is highly atmospheric and effective, but simultaneously rather conventional. The diminished seventh chord on f-sharp, *Leitklang* of Samiel and the dark powers he wields, is lifted out by means of a remarkable, synthetic orchestration. At its first appearance in m. 26 of the overture, the single tones of the chord are played in highly unusual instrumental combinations and uses of registers: the upper $C4$ by tremolo violins and bassoon, $E\flat3$ and $F\sharp3$ by violas and clarinets in a peculiarly low register, whereas the $A2$ is provided by pizzicato double basses and timpani. Later in the work, for example in the *Wolfsschluchtszene*, even more instruments are added to this cluster of instrumental colors, to deepen its diffuse sound quality.

These techniques, which are regularly employed within the score of *Der Freischütz* and omnipresent in the *Wolfsschluchtszene,* fall in an esthetic category often referred to as "characteristic *(Das Charakteristische)*." A characteristic esthetic departs from a classical, balanced and euphonious one, and favors the attraction of remarkable moments over balanced melodic lines and a transparent structure. This category could be used both in an appreciative way as a sign of the progressive nature of modern music, and in a condemning way, signaling decay in the form of a betrayal of beauty or a cheap resort to sensationalism.[166] The non-classical ethos of the early nineteenth-century

---

164   Maehder 1988: 163.

165   In contrast to the masculine hunter's music, we can discern a third, feminine sound sphere surrounding Agathe, who is regularly accompanied by clarinets, bassoons and horns. In her third act cavatina 'Und ob die Wolke sie verhülle,' solo passages of the cello and clarinet – conventional markers of female tenderness within Romantic opera – add to this intimate, feminine impression. The contrast between a male and female society is also clearly perceivable in the alternation of scenes within the opera. Whereas public life, dominated by men, takes place in the open, the scenes evolving around Agathe all take place inside the forester's house.

166   Dahlhaus demonstrates how, for example, Friedrich Schlegel, a prominent theorist of the "characteristic," used the term in 1797 in a pejorative sense, whereas a year later he reinterpreted it as a positive sign of a future Romantic era (Dahlhaus 1988: 225) John Daverio

characteristic musical style made it a marker of musical Romanticism, and the Romantic significance that is often attributed to *Der Freischütz* is closely related to Weber's exploration of this style.

Apart from the synthetic orchestration mentioned before, the characteristic nature of the music of *Der Freischutz* is elaborated even further in the *Wolfsschluchtszene*, for example in the "shrieky" high woodwinds that accompany the outcries of the female chorus of spirits. Through his "alienating instrumentation" and deliberate "deformed euphony," as Maehder calls it,[167] Weber suddenly found himself among the avant-garde of early nineteenth-century music. Particularly the sounds of the *Wolfsschluchtszene* formed a rich source of inspiration for later orchestral experimenters, such as Berlioz and Wagner. Regardless of the fact that *Der Freischütz* was chiefly a blend of conventions derived from *Singspiel* and the French *opéra comique*, its audacious orchestration clearly put German Romantic opera – for the first time in its modest history – in the limelight as an innovative force within the international music scene.

The modernity of the chromatic harmony and characteristic orchestration within *Der Freischütz* certainly contributed to the work's Romantic aura, but the opera contains many elements that undermine this impression. Carl Dahlhaus, for example, maintains that "the librettos of *Der Freischütz*, *Euryanthe*, and *Oberon* would definitely be considered not to be Romantic in Friedrich Schlegel's sense of the term, but rather belonging to a tradition of eighteenth-century trivial Romanticism, if one could separate music from text."[168] Moreover, he argues that "the characteristic" may be a useful category to distinguish Romantic musical works from their Classical forerunners, but is incapable to discern elevated from trivial Romanticism, as it figures in both types.[169]

It takes a closer look to decide to which side of Romanticism *Der Freischütz* gravitates, and possibly, both manifestations will eventually turn out to be too indissolubly entangled to decide. A close examination of the *Wolfsschluchtszene* may help out, since it reveals the way in which Weber and his librettist Friedrich Kind tried to bring about the "appearance of the miraculous" – arguably the decisive moment of Romantic opera. Do Samiel and the apparitions that take place during the cast of bullets merely remain – from

argues that Schlegel's ambivalent attitude towards "characteristic" modern art "suggests that some of the seemingly negative moments in the present offer the most promise for the future." Daverio 1993: 13–14. For more information on Schlegel's notions of the characteristic and interesting in art, see Behler 1978: 38–40. A more general perspective on the "esthetics of the characteristic" among German thinkers around 1800 can be found in Kanz 2008.

167 Maehder 1980: 103.
168 Dahlhaus 2007: 482.
169 Ibid.: 482.

the viewpoint of Hoffmann's fictive composer Ludwig – "silly, spiritless spirits," or do they indeed "open up a Romantic being that enraptures us?" And if the latter is the case, is it solely effectuated by the quality of the music? The following analysis of the scene might provide an answer to these questions.

As an adaptation of a story taken from August Apel and Friedrich Laun's *Gespensterbuch* (1811), Friedrich Kind's libretto is firmly rooted in a tradition of trivial *Schauerromantik*. Notwithstanding the initial, relatively warm reception, it has come to be commonly considered to be a poor opera text, which is a slight exaggeration, as it has proven to be quite effective.[170] The depreciation of Kind's contribution to *Der Freischütz* is partly a consequence of Weber's glorification as a national composer. As the latter's music was idealized, Kind was increasingly blamed for the possible flaws of this national masterpiece.[171] Furthermore, he faced the accusation of plagiarism due to the similarities between his libretto and an earlier *Freischütz* text by the Munich librettist Franz Xaver von Caspar.[172] The impression of an uneven collaboration between a Romantic composer and a trivial, unoriginal playwright keen on popular acclaim is, however, clearly in need of revision. The suggestion of an innovative musician and a backward, *Biedermeier* poet is also incorrect, since even in his most daring *Wolfsschlucht* music, Weber employs techniques derived from older *Schaueroper* of the trivial sort.

170　Dahlhaus, for example, has ascertained that the collaboration was a lucky one in the sense that Kind's text suited Weber's music-dramatic techniques and covered his compositional shortcomings. See Ibid.: 486.

171　In 1843 Kind published a *Freischütz-Buch*, containing information on the genesis of the libretto and the opera in general. According to Wolfgang Michael Wagner, his main objective was to emphasize his contribution to Weber's success, and to counter the load of repeated criticism directed at his allegedly "childish/kindisch" libretto, making fun of the writer's name (Wagner 1994: 213) Exactly the same happened to the librettist of Weber's next opera, *Euryanthe* (1823), which will be rendered later within this chapter. Considering its reception, Meyer writes that "the failure of what was supposed to be the prototype of a new German operatic genre caused serious problems for those critics and scholars who were anxious to chronicle the triumph of German art. [...] That Helmine von Chézy was a little-known female poet made her a convenient scapegoat for those who would explain *Euryanthe*'s lack of success. [...] Attacks on the libretto of *Euryanthe* became so intense that Chézy felt compelled to defend herself in an article in the *Neue Zeitschrift für Musik* (1840)." Meyer 2003: 153–154.

172　Most important common elements are the happy ending – which deviates from Apel and Laun's original – the *Wolfsschlucht*-like Satanic cult in the fourth act, the presence of a Hermit and the redeeming love of the heroine. Gottfried Mayerhofer published the text of the 1812 *Freischütz* in 1959, and is fully convinced that Kind used Caspar's original and denied this in later correspondences with the original author (see Mayerhofer 1959: 3–11). Wagner challenges this view, arguing that the specific characteristics of Caspar's libretto were not idiosyncratic, but rather general traits of the contemporary *Schicksalsdrama*. Wagner 1994: 75.

The most interesting model for the *Wolfsschluchtszene* is a passage from *Das wütende Heer*, a 1781 *Singspiel* composed by Johann André on a text by Christoph Friedrich Bretzner. Within this opera, a magic castle guarded by a supernatural army of wild huntsmen is visited at midnight. The huntsmen sing a monotone line containing e-flat in hollow octaves, and are accompanied by a diminished seventh chord containing exactly the same tonal material as Weber's *Samiel-Leitklang*. The opening spirit chorus of the *Wolfsschluchtszene* also takes over the monotonous melodic line, albeit on f-sharp instead of e-flat. Considering the shocking sensation that these effects sorted in Weber's 1821 opera, it is not hard to imagine how André's audience responded to it in 1781 at its Berlin premiere; *Das wütende Heer* played to an empty house already by its fifth performance. Thomas Baumann argues that this was partly the result of a general oversaturation with André's works, which had dominated the Berlin stage for years, but was also related to the audience's dissatisfaction with the all too characteristic quality of the music. Reviews repudiated the screaming chorus as unserious and incompetent, whereas André had in fact explicitly demanded to sing "in a fearsome, cavernous voice."[173]

Weber and Kind certainly did a better job in captivating the audience in the *Wolfsschluchtszene*, but by no means convinced all critics. What to think of the way in which supernatural spiritis were evoked and depicted in this scene? The question how to do this was crucial to early nineteenth-century discussions concerning the genuinely Romantic quality of an opera. Although written down two decades before the creation of *Der Freischütz*, an essay in the AMZ on the proper treatment of spirits in opera by Friedrich Rochlitz (1799) provides an impression of the common practice concerning this element in opera at the beginning of the nineteenth century. It is possible that Weber and Kind were familiar with this text, considering the fact that both had frequent contact with Rochlitz during the genesis of the work (1817–1821).

In his first letter of the 1799 'Bruchstücke aus Briefen an einen jungen Tonsetzer,' concerning 'Die Behandlung von Geistern von einigen neuern Komponisten,' Rochlitz first complains about the all too often deplorable way in which spirits occur in recent operas, and then lists three promising ways in which they can be musically evoked. The first is exemplified by Mozart's *Don Giovanni* (1787), in which the Stone Guest sings in unusual, large intervals, with long notes in a solemn tempo, and to a harmonically rich, "shivering" orchestral accompaniment. A second possibility is to let the spirit sing a vocal line that recites only one tone, surrounded by a harmonically dynamic accompaniment, which Rochlitz finds in Reichardt's rendition of Goethe's *Erlkönig* (1794).

---

173   Baumann 1985: 184–188.

A third option is a melodramatic design, with the spirit speaking against the background of a softly playing orchestra. Rochlitz exemplifies this procedure by Karl August Freiherr von Lichtenstein's opera *Die steinerne Braut* (1799).[174] Whereas Hoffmann, for example, chiefly used the first, melodic procedure to evoke Kühleborn in *Undine*, Weber privileges the monotonous technique for the spirit choirs and a melodramatic approach to the exclamations of Samiel and the majority of Max and Caspar's vocal contributions within the *Wolfsschluchtszene*.

Notwithstanding the menacing effect of parts of the music, there is a peculiar clumsiness to the *Wolfsschluchtszene*, described by Theodor W. Adorno as a "*Höllenvision aus Biedermeierminiaturen* [an infernal vision of *Biedermeier* miniatures]" in his article *Bilderwelt des Freischütz* (1962).[175] This judgment – certainly not meant in a derisive way – is particularly directed at the succession of apparitions that concludes the largely melodramatic scene. Kind decided to have any individual cast of one of the seven bullets accompanied by a new, ghostly image. Consecutively, the surrounding is covered by a dark cloud (1), forest birds hop around the campfire (2), a wild boar runs across the scene (3), a storm blows up and the flames rise (4), remains of a carriage are heard, and burning wheels roll over the stage (5), nebulous hunters and dogs cross the scene, chasing deer (6) and finally the sky turns pitch-dark and thunder strikes, with flames coming out of the earth (7). Meyer interprets these "*Biedermeier* miniatures" as an "evil inversion" of the "normal world":

> Perhaps the most striking thing about these images is the extent to which they partake of the same mythology of the hunt that informs so much of the "normal world" in *Der Freischütz*. The images of the black boar trampling through the forest, the galloping horses, the "wilde Heer," and above all the figure of the Black Huntsman himself form a kind of evil inversion of the joys of the hunt celebrated in the third-act "Jägerchor."[176]

Weber composed this finale as a programmatic miniature polyptich, consisting of short sections with a musical idea depicting the stage events or the psychological state of the cult's participants. Tension is created by the gradual crescendo and intensification of the individual pieces towards the final

---

174   See *AMZ* II/1, 2 October 1799: 1–5. During the creation of *Der Freischütz*, Weber was probably aware of Lichtenstein's work, since the former produced the latter's *historisch-komische* opera *Die Waldburg* (1811) in Dresden in 1822.

175   Adorno 2003: 40.

176   Meyer 2003: 103.

FIGURE 2.3 Sixth apparition of the *Wolfsschluchtszene*

climax. The most impressive and interesting apparition is the sixth, that of the hunters, since it is the clearest "evil inversion of the joys of the hunt," to use Meyer's phrase. The dramaturgical device of evil inversion is matched on the musical level by the fact that the nebulous hunters sing monotonously in A-flat major,[177] a tritone removed from the "innocent" hunters' tonality of D major. Moreover, the prominence of the tone d within the passage in A-flat major and the "alienated euphony" of the brass chorus that accompanies the "normal" hunters' choruses further underline the downside of the "innocent" hunters' sphere.

The menacing hunters' chorus underlines that not only nature, but also the apparently idyllic society of *Der Freischütz* can turn evil, something that can be witnessed already in the first act *Spottchor* (mocking chorus). This, of course, compromises the glorification of German country life and hinders a one-dimensional ideological reading, which made *Der Freischütz* all the more suitable for critical readings of German nationalism following the catastrophe of the Second World War. Adorno, for example, in 1962 considered the opera to have a certain innocent German character, unburdened by overt nationalist ideology, in

---

177   If we consider the entire passage, A-flat major functions in fact as a sixth degree in C minor, but the governing sonority of this piece is really built upon the resounding A-flat major chords.

contrast to the highly-infected works of Wagner.[178] Quoting Elias Canetti's *Masse und Macht* (1960), Adorno stresses the identity of forest and army in the German imagination, relating this identity to the reception of *Der Freischütz*:

> The mass symbol of the Germans was the army. But the army was more than just the army: it was the marching forest. In no other modern country has forest experience remained so vital as in Germany. The rigidity and parallelness of the upright trees, their density and number fills the German heart with a profound, mysterious joy.[179]

It is exactly in the realization that apparently innocent ideals have dark motivations that the power of Adorno's analysis and the potential of *Der Freischütz* as a critical perspective on German nationalism and societal dynamics lies.

In 'Ludwig Tiecks Konzeption des Wunderbaren und Webers "Freischütz" (1985), Hartmut Wecker also recognizes an identity of forest and society and a covert critique on societal dynamics in *Der Freischütz*, arguing that the *Wolfsschluchtszene* must be seen as an emanation of the demonic as an allegory of social coercion". He writes that, "as the scenery of the *Wolfsschlucht* subtly refers to everyday reality, it simultaneously casts this life in the twilight of obscure deception. Its real essence becomes evident."[180] Wecker recognizes an affinity with the writings of Ludwig Tieck,[181] in which "the experience of everyday life, empirical reality, is relativized and presented as ambiguous, creating a more profound understanding of the world. Whereas the miraculous gains normality, the common world becomes – in a reversal of state – alien and unreal."[182]

If *Der Freischütz* is basically about the relation between a normal and a miraculous world, privileging the latter, and if its main theme is the struggle of an intellectual individual against a flawed society rather than his initiation into an idyllic community, the opera might actually be a Romantic rather than a nationalist work. The presupposed triangular relation between individual, nature and society established earlier on in this chapter may not be so solid after all. One must, however, concede that this ambivalent or critical reading was not

---

178   Adorno opens his 'Bilderwelt des Freischütz' with the following statement: "Der Freischütz has more right to be considered as the German national opera than Die Meistersinger, because the German element appears in a different light, without compromising itself by a nationalist disposition." Adorno 2003: 36.

179   Quoted after Ibid.: 36.

180   Wecker also argues that the orchestral accompaniment of Max's phrase 'Rothgraue, narb'ge Bäume strecken nach mir die Riesenfaust' echoes the remarkable "mocking" motive of the first act *Spottchor*. Wecker 1985: 40–41.

181   Particularly *Der blonde Eckbert* (1797), *Der Runenberg* (1804), and *Die Elfen* (1811).

182   Ibid.: 31.

picked up during its nineteenth-century reception in Germany. Furthermore, as with many recent reinterpretations of works with clear ideological connotations, we do not know whether ambiguous signs in an artwork are the result of a deliberate strategy of the composer and librettist.[183] And ultimately, does not Wecker's interpretation, tempting as it is, display a typical post-WWII anxiety towards manifestations of German nationalism in Romantic, nineteenth-century art? The fact that Weber and Kind's work is arguably less picturesque and societally-affirmative certainly enriches its Romanticism, but does not necessarily mitigate its significance as an emblem of German national identity.

The question remains whether Weber's contemporaries considered his and Kind's opera, and particularly the *Wolfsschluchtszene*, to be genuinely Romantic in an elevated sense. And who could better be consulted than the man who proposed the fundamentals of Romantic opera theory, E.T.A. Hoffmann himself. There has been much debate concerning Hoffmann's *Freischütz* judgment. Hoffmann attended the premiere and had promised Weber to write a review after the 1821 premiere, a friendly service he owed his colleague after Weber's highly positive *AMZ* article on *Undine*. Scholars have long dedicated an influential anonymous, moderately enthusiastic review in the *Vossische Zeitung* to E.T.A. Hoffmann. In this article, the critic praises the music, but classifies the libretto as belonging to the trivial vogue of "vampirism," and typifies the visually excessive *Wolfsschlucht* as the culmination of "Romantic" opera, written down in ironic quotation marks.[184] Thanks to the work of Wolfgang Kron, we now know that Hoffmann did not write this review.[185]

---

183   One might think of current academic discussions concerning the question whether Wagner's Siegfried is actually glorified or rather covertly ridiculed by its creator. See for example Žižek 2005, Janz 2011, and Kitcher 2005 (especially Chapter 20 with the illustrative title "Siegfried and Other Problems").

184   "Dieser Vampyrismus ist es denn, der in der Poesie des Augenblicks (und nicht nur in Deutschland) allmächtig spukt. Man will nicht ergriffen, nicht gerührt, man will gepackt, geschüttelt werden, es soll sich das Haar sträuben, der Odem stocken – und die Poesie hat ihre Wirkung gethan. Es schien nötig, diesen Augenblicklichen Zustand kurz anzudeuten, wenn von der neuen Oper die Rede sein soll, die soeben die Berliner Freunde beschäftigt, denn es ist dieselbe so ganz ein Kind des Augenblicks, daß man mit der Schilderung ihrer Abstammung sie selbst schon charakterisiert hat. [...]Nun folgt der Kulminationspunkt der "romantischen" Oper [Die Wolfsschluchtszene], für welchen vor allen den Dekorateurs und Maschinisten der gefühltesten Dank gezollt werden muß, worin alle weichen Seelen einstimmen. Aber eben weil das Auge hier so übermäßig beschäftigt ist, hat das Ohr kaum Kraft, ihm zu folgen, was doch bei den düster-wilden Musikstücken dieses Finals wohl not täte." Derived from Istel 1907: 301–304 (In 1907, the article was still presumed to be Hoffmann's, and was therefore included in his collected musical writings, compiled by Edgar Istel).

185   See Kron 1957. Norbert Miller interprets Hoffmann's response to *Der Freischütz* in Miller 1985.

In the article 'Für und wider den Wolfsschlucht' (1985), Norbert Miller has speculated on Hoffmann's possible response to *Der Freischütz*. According to him, Hoffmann must have mainly objected to the sensational and all too literal images of the *Wolfsschlucht*,[186] a frequently-heard complaint in reviews of the premiere performance that Graf Karl von Brühl directed. In fact, August Apel, the archfather of *Der Freischütz* who had written the *Gespensterbuch*, had already warned for this danger in his article 'Ueber die Behandlung musikalischer Geister,' published in the *AMZ* in 1805:

> Esthetic veracity demands that the apparition is indefinite and ambivalent. The contradicting symbols of the two worlds of being and nonbeing, life and death, power and impotence to which the spirit belongs, these symbols immediately appear as alien to our everyday world and arouse a shivering horror in the spectator's sensation through this inner and insoluble contradiction. But exactly due to this does the apparition fully achieve its aim; then to what goal does art use apparitions, if not to evoke the sensation of the sublime and horrific through its representation. This sensation is realized perfectly exactly by means of the indeterminate and contradicting.[187]

Friedrich Kind voiced a similar opinion, and was highly disappointed after seeing the first Dresden performance, modeled after the Berlin premiere. In an article for the *Dresdner Abend-Zeitung* of 23 February 1822, he wrote: "The poem gives no occasion for such a phantasmagoria. In order not to be rightfully accused of having created merely an opera spectacle, a grotesque ghost story, poetry and scenery must present these unknown forces in the most indeterminate outlines, they must never appear in the forefront nor in a bright light."[188]

---

186 See Miller 1985.
187 "Die ästhetische Wahrheit fordert von der Geistererscheinung das Unbestimmte und Zweydeutige, die widersprechenden Symbole der zwey Welten des Seyns und Nichtseyns, des Lebens und des Todes, der Kraft und der Ohnmacht, welchen der Geist angehört, und welche ihn in dem ersten Momente der Anschauung, durch diesen innern und unauflöslichen Widerspruch, als einen Fremden in dieser Welt ankündigen und die sinnliche Natur des Menschen in ein schauerndes Schrecken versetzten. Aber eben hierdurch erreicht die Erscheinung ihren Zweck vollkommen; denn zu welchem Ende bedient sich die Kunst der Erscheinungen, als um durch diese Darstellung die Empfindung des schauerlich Erhabenen und Grausenden im höchsten Grade zu erregen? Diese Empfindung wird nun eben am vollkommensten erregt durch jenes Unbestimmte und Widersprechende." *AMZ* VIII/8, 20 November 1805: 121–122.
188 "Zu einer Phantasmagorie dieser Art [...] ist nirgend in der Dichtung Veranlassung gegeben. [...]um nicht mit Recht den Vorwurf eines bloßen Opern-Spektakels, eines fratzenhaften Spuks auf sich zu laden [...] muß die Dichtung und Bühnenkunst jene

DER FREISCHÜTZ.
IIᵗᵉ Aufz. 6ᵗᵉ Auftr.
Caspar. Fünf! Wehe! Das wilde Heer!

FIGURE 2.4   Illustration of the apparition of "Das wilde Heer" in the *Wolfsschluchtszene*,
            made by painter and satirist Johann Heinrich Ramberg (year of creation unclear,
            between 1822 and 1840). The image emphasizes the sensationalist esthetic of the
            opera's staging.

Of course one must admit that criticism concerning the visual design concerns the stage director rather than the composer, as Miller acknowledges.[189] Huck also speaks in defense of Weber, arguing that his revolutionary transgression of musical conventions releases him from the conviction of cheap sensationalism.[190] But the fact that Weber innovated the musical language of the early nineteenth-century does, however, not fully discharge him from the accusation of sensationalism, which was frequently heard in the first years after the premiere. One might argue that his "characteristic" musical esthetics used a similar technique as Brühl's staging, in highlighting specific elements at the cost of the overall development and atmosphere. One of the most eloquent writers criticizing the sensational nature of the music was Wilhelm Christian Müller, who wrote the following concerning the *Wolfsschluchtszene* in his *Aesthetisch-historische Einleitungen in die Wissenschaft der Tonkunst* (1830): "It is truly an infernal music, in which everything rolls and runs around in a wild, hideous cacaphony. But this exaggerated dissonant noise arouses laughter instead of horror. [...] The devil and hell turn into a comedy, something which neither the poet nor the composer intended to achieve."[191]

One indication of *Der Freischütz*'s immediate popularity is the number of parodies created in the years following the premiere,[192] but from judgments such as Müller's, one might conclude that the *Wolfsschluchtszene* was actually already a parody of itself. The scene never fully transcends the level of triviality, the "opening up of a Romantic being" – to borrow Hoffmann's phrase – is compromised by clumsy, overly determinate effects that distort the illusion. If this renowned scene underlines one important observation about German Romantic opera, this must be that it is nearly impossible to distinguish between elevated and trivial forms of Romanticism. But perhaps it is this curious coexistence of the high and low, of the audacious and the conventional, which makes *Der Freischütz* the quintessential Romantic opera, and has secured the sympathy of audiences long after the historical moment of its premiere.

---

unbekannten Gewalten in möglichst unbestimmten Umrissen zeigen, sie müssen nie ganz im Vorgrunde und in hellem Lichte auftreten." Quoted after Huck 1999: 330–331.

189   Miller 1985: 376.
190   Huck 1999: 332.
191   "Es ist eine wahre Höllenmusik – wo Alles ins Wilde und Grässliche durch einander läuft und braust. Dieser übertriebene Dissonanzlärm erregt aber Lachen, statt Schauergefühle. [...] Teufel und Hölle werden komisch, welches doch weder des Dichters, noch des Tonsetzers Absicht war." Quoted after Finscher 1983: 87.
192   A famous example was Franz Grillparzer's *Wolfsschlucht-Parodie* (1822).

CHAPTER 3

"Die Oper erheben zu größerer Einheit": Romantic Opera and the Move beyond Spoken Dialogue in the 1820s

In many of the *Freischütz* reviews discussed in the first chapter, one finds the conviction that this opera would form the decisive breakthrough of German opera, and lead the way towards new national works. But to many colleagues of Weber, *Der Freischütz* formed a conclusion of an era rather than a point of departure. Whereas many German operas had aimed at a further Romanticization of the genre, these attempts had always remained within the confines of *Singspiel* with its characteristic alternation of sung numbers and spoken dialogue. Some scholars consider the *Singspiel* structure to have compromised *Der Freischütz*'s Romantic potential, for example Eberhard Kremtz in his interpretation of Hoffmann's glorification of Spontini: "It is very probable that Hoffmann had realized that *Der Freischütz* actually led away from the goal of a Romantic opera, and was only forward-looking in some single respects, whereas the work as a whole actually formed the conclusion and apotheosis of a different development, that of the German *Singspiel*."[1]

Kremtz seems to imply that the true goal of Romantic opera after 1821, at least for Hoffmann, was to develop into an all-sung genre in the spirit of Gluck, his French followers, and particularly the contemporary example of Spontini. But how did this affect the initial core of Romantic opera theory, the co-existence and interdependence of a normal and a supernatural world? Had the *Singspiel*, with its alternation of music and spoken dialogue, not been the perfect vehicle for depicting the oscillation between these worlds? Was the apparent triviality of the *Singspiel* style not actually facilitating Romanticization, as Dent saw Romantic opera as "derived from comic opera and not from *opera seria*," and considered "the glorification of the trivial" to be "one of the most curious aspects of Romanticism"?[2] Had not the elimination of "trivial" comic action in Hoffmann's *Undine* in fact deprived this *Singspiel* of its theatrical lifeblood, as Schläder stated?[3] And to conclude, did not the *Singspiel* perfectly embody the intersection of German and Romantic opera, because the spoken

---

1 Kremtz 1995B: 115.
2 Dent 1976: 15–16.
3 See Section 2.2.4.

dialogue defined the character of German opera to a far greater extent than that of France, where *opéras comiques* co-existed with a considerable tradition of operas with recitatives? This chapter is concerned with the question what was left of the Romantic opera ideal once German opera composers decided to move beyond spoken dialogue.

The first composer who propagated a move towards the "grand" style of Spontini was E.T.A. Hoffmann, in his extensive series of articles on the opera *Olympie*,[4] published in the *Zeitung für Theater und Musik zur Unterhaltung gebildeter, unbefangener Leser* between June and September 1821. Already during his work on *Aurora*, Hoffmann's aversion to spoken dialogue was retrievable from his writings, as well as his desire to realize a fusion of *opera seria*, French opera and Romantic opera in a "*große romantische Oper*." Whereas he saw his ideal chiefly realized in works of the past, especially those of Gluck, he was pessimistic with regard to current grand opera of Spontini and others.

By 1821, however, Hoffmann had come to believe that "the operas prior to *Olympia* – *La Vestale* and *Fernand Cortez* – had convincingly shown that Spontini's compositions aim at nothing less than dramatic expression in its highest strength and perfection."[5] Hoffmann voiced his expectation that Spontini would create convincing works for the German audience: "Spontini is now in Germany, is here in Berlin, and we cannot only hope, we may indeed expect that he will compose operas for us, operas that belong to the invisible church that is built on nothing less than the truthful in its purest integrity."[6] The reference to an invisible church seems to grant Spontini's music the metaphysical depth so crucial to Romantic music esthetics and, to quote Miller, to "incorporate the composer into the canon of immortal greats of music, that of Gluck, Haydn, Mozart, and Beethoven."[7]

Although in 1821, Spontini was certainly the most famous opera composer working on German soil, he was not the only artist who wrote German-language

---

4 A work that Spontini had composed for Paris (1819) and that was performed in Berlin in 1821 to introduce the newly appointed *Generalmusikdirektor* to a Prussian audience. E.T.A. Hoffmann translated the French original verses into German.

5 "Die der Olympia vorhergegangenen Opern, die Vestalin und Cortez, haben schon auf das überzeugendste dargethan, daß Spontinis Kompositionen nichts wollen, nichts beabsichtigen als den dramatischen Ausdruck in seiner höchsten Stärke und Vollendung." Istel 1907: 283.

6 "Spontini ist jetzt in Deutschland, ist jetzt hier in Berlin, [...] und nicht die Hoffnung, nein, die gewisse Erwartung können wir aus dem Wesen der drei Meisterwerke, die den Reihen eröffnet, schöpfen, daß er für uns Opern komponieren wird, die zugleich der unsichtbaren Kirche angehören werden, deren Glieder, von dem himmlischen Feuer der Kunst durchglüht, nichts wollen als das Wahrhaftige in der reinsten Integrität." Ibid.: 296.

7 Miller 1980: 454.

grand operas for German audiences. In Munich, Johann Nepomuk Freiherr von Poißl had achieved a considerable success with *Athalia* (1814) and *Der Wettkampf zu Olympia* (1815). Although the former work was based on a tragedy by Racine and the latter was an adaptation of a libretto by Metastasio, both these "classical" works fared well on the German stage in the years after their premiere, and Poißl's style was considered to have a distinct German character. A 1814 review of *Athalia* in the *Münchner Theater-Journal* praised the way in which Poißl "had striven to give us, in the way that the Italians and the French have their own national opera, emphatically *German* grand opera music."[8] By using the first scene of the opera as an example, Warrack shows in which field this German quality of the music could be found: "It is the arioso music which dominates; recitative is always instrumentally accompanied, and essentially melodic rather than after the Italian *secco* model; and there is a complete absence of display coloratura."[9] But after some successful performances, Poißl's works –lacking Romantic traits – lost their attraction, and the experiment of sung-throughout German opera remained overshadowed by the more popular *Singspiel.*[10]

1   Louis Spohr's *Aufruf an deutschen Komponisten* and *Jessonda* (1823)

A greater impulse to German composers to develop an opera style without spoken dialogue came from Louis Spohr's (1784–1859) 'Aufruf an deutschen Komponisten,' published in the AMZ in 1823. Spohr had already contributed considerably to the Romantic *Singspiel,* and enjoyed his first small opera success with *Faust,* premiered in Prague in 1816 under the baton of Carl Maria von Weber. The name *Faust* may create expectations of Goethean profundity, but one should see this work, full of magic frivolities, in the tradition of Viennese *Zauberoper* rather than in the intellectual sphere that the name of the title-hero suggests.[11] Nevertheless, the opera's music is convincing, a

---

8   "Er hat gestrebt, uns – wie Italiener und Franzosen ihre nationale Oper haben – auch eine in bestimmten Charakter hervorgehobene *deutsche* große Opernmusik zu geben." *Münchner Theater-Journal* 1/7 (1814), 187.

9   Warrack 2001: 291.

10   Ludwig F. Schiedermair writes in *Deutsche Oper in München* (1992) that these "serious works on antique themes, in a new guise of a classicist, Gluckian style, were highly successful, but soon vanished from the stage. The new world of Romanticism, with which Poißl saw himself confronted after Weber's *Freischütz,* was never his habitat." Scheidermair 1992: 63.

11   This claim is also made by Sieghart Döhring and Sabine Henze-Döring. Döhring 1997: 98–99.

blend of nearly-Mozartian melodic charm combined with harmonic audacity, and governed by an intricate web of recurrent motifs.[12] After *Faust*, Spohr considered an opera on the *Freischütz* story, but dropped the project when he discovered that Weber was already composing one. Instead, he decided to write *Zemire und Azor* (1819), substituting the German Romantic milieu of *Der Freischütz* for a late eighteenth-century French oriental fairy-tale.

The lyrical charm and colorful orchestration of *Zemire und Azor* made it a highly popular opera among nineteenth-century German audiences, and concerning the success of Weber's *Freischütz* Spohr later stated: "I have not regretted that I abandoned the materials of Apel's story, for with my music, which is not adapted to please the multitude and excite popular enthusiasm, I should never have met with the success that *Der Freischütz* obtained."[13] On the one hand, this remark underlines Spohr's practical awareness, but on the other, it involves a critical note as well. In his *Aufruf*, Spohr acknowledged that an opera must obviously appeal to the common folk in order to be successful, but simultaneously argued that a popular libretto must be accompanied by elevated, sophisticated music:

> First one must look for a libretto which appeals to the masses, because they decide whether an opera stays in the repertoire. If one succumbs to common taste with the choice of a libretto, one must set it to sophisticated music. If one senses the talent to write folk melodies, the insertion of these may enhance the effect on the audience at large, and it will perhaps be enjoyable to hear one's own melodies revived in parades, church masses and by hand organs. But the music's dignity will suffer from it.[14]

---

12   In his announcement of the work's premiere, Weber stated that "a few melodies, felicitously and aptly devised, weave like delicate threads through the whole, and hold it together spiritually (Glücklich und richtig berechnet gehen einige Melodien wie leise Fäden durch das Ganze und halten es geistig zusammen)." Kaiser 1908: 275.

13   "Indessen habe ich es nie bereut, den Apelschen Stoff aufgegeben zu haben; denn mit meiner Musik, die nicht geeignet ist, ins Volk zu dringen und den großen Haufen zu enthusiasmieren, würde ich nie den beispiellosen Erfolg gehabt haben, den 'der Freischütz' fand." Spohr 1968: 50.

14   "Zuerst suche man also, ein Buch zu bekommen, dass den grossen Haufen anspricht, denn dieser entscheidet, ob die Oper auf dem Repertoire bleiben soll. [...] Hat man aber so den Geschmacke der Menge das Buch geopfert, so schreibe man eine gediegene Musik dazu. [...] Fühlt man in sich Talent, Volksmelodien zu erfinden, so kann man auch durch Einmischung solcher auf die Menge einwirken und vielleicht die Freude haben, sich auf Paraden und Kirchmessen zu hören und in den Drehorgeln fortzuleben. Die Würde der Musik muss aber nothwendig darunter leiden." *AMZ* XXV/29, 16 July 1823: 462.

Although the person Spohr refers to remains anonymous, there is little doubt that Weber's popular approach to the music of *Der Freischütz* is addressed, and in a footnote, Spohr actually reflects on his colleague's opera success. In a somewhat cryptic passage, he states that "it is a felicity for the re-animation of German opera and its credit that the successful and sophisticated parts of *Der Freischütz* make it deserve the acclaim that it has gained for its popular melodies."[15] The crucial question of Spohr's *Aufruf* is how the sophistication of German opera music can be brought about. Spohr recognizes the transformation of dialogue into recitative as the most important step to take:

> It is an altogether different question, whether we Germans should not finally elevate the opera to a state of greater unity [endlich die Oper als Kunstwerk zu grösserer Einheit [...] erheben sollten] by transforming spoken dialogue into recitatives. If estheticians dismiss the opera as a monstrous artwork, this opinion is justified by the alternation of song and speech. It is only bearable because we have grown accustomed to it. But I will surely not demand that dialogues concerning trivial, common subject matter, which are still so prominent in our operas, should be composed, because one could just as well set political newspaper articles to music. No; an opera in which everything is sung 1) must have a poetical content from beginning to end, 2) should have a simple story which is comprehensible also when one cannot understand the text properly, 3) should have a cast of no more than five or six singers, because pronunciation is generally poorly developed among singers, let alone the

---

15   "Bey dem Wiedererwachen der deutschen Oper und für den Credit derselben ist es ein Glück, dass der Freyschütz durch gelungene und gediegene Musikstücke den grossen Beyfall verdient, den ihm die in's Volk gegangenen Melodien verschafft haben." Ibid.: 462. Clive Brown argues that "Spohr's relationship with Weber [...] seems to have been a decidedly one-sided affair; for while Weber clearly recognised Spohr's deep musicality, Spohr was never quite able to dissociate Weber's flair for writing popular music from charlatanry." Brown 1984: 47. Weber's loyalty to his colleague is further underlined by the fact that in 1821 he recommended Spohr to become *Hofkapellmeister* in Kassel, where the latter would be highly successful as composer and conductor. Evidence also suggests that Weber did his best to make up with Spohr for having forestalled him with *Der Freischütz*. When invited to write a German Romantic opera for London in 1824, he chose *Oberon* instead of the other proposed subject of *Faust*, probably anxious to overshadow Spohr once again. See Warrack 1976: 312. In a French letter sent 7 October 1824 to Covent Garden director Charles Kemble, Weber writes: "I prefer the poem of Oberon over Faust, for several reasons (La chose principale est, de m'envoyer sitôt que possible, le Poême de l'Oberon; que je prefère par quantites de raisons a celui du Faust)." http://www.weber-gesamtausgabe.de/de/A002068/Korrespondenz/A042354.

capacity to sing recitative. If a libretto does not meet these demands, it is better to stick to spoken dialogue.[16]

If Spohr's practical considerations underline one thing in particular, it must be that opera with spoken dialogue is a clear sign of backwardness and triviality. With this, he not only criticizes Weber's *Freischütz*, but also other early nineteenth-century German works and his own previous opera output. The relation between chauvinism and his attitude towards foreign opera is, however, complex, as the opening lines of his article reveal:

> The time seems to have come that our German audience, tired of the sweet and dull recent Italian music, yearns for something more substantial. [...] The moment thus appears to have come at which German art will make itself felt also in the theater, and the aim of these lines is: to summon German composers to occupy the opera repertoire by great and effective activity and to gradually dispel everything foreign/alien [*fremde*] (meaning anything that lacks substance) from it.[17]

On the one hand, Spohr's appeal is emphatically directed at German composers, and his article opens with a general dismissal of "foreign" opera, whereby foreign points to a lack of content more likely to be found in Italian than in German works. On the other, his dismissal of spoken dialogue and advocacy of

---

16   "Eine andere Frage ist aber, ob wir Deutsche nicht auch endlich die Oper als Kunstwerk zu grösserer Einheit dadurch erheben sollten, dass wir die Dialoge in Recitative verwandeln. Wenn die Aesthetiker die Oper als Kunstwerk verwerfen und monströs nennen, so ist es hauptsächlich der Wechsel von Rede und Gesang, der sie dazu berechtigt. Auch ist es wirklich nur die Macht der Gewohnheit, die ihn ertragen lässt. Doch bin ich weit entfernt, zu verlangen, dass man Dialoge über triviale, aus dem gemeinen Leben genommene Gegenstände, wie unsere Opern noch so viele enthalten, komponiren solle, denn eben so gut könnte man auch einen politischen Zeitungsartikel in Musik setzen. Nein; eine Oper in der alles gesungen werden soll, muss 1) eine, vom Anfang bis zu Ende poetischen Inhalt haben, 2) eine so einfache, dass der Zuschauer durch was geschieht, auch ohne den Text zu verstehen, den Inhalt errathen kann, und 3) zur Besetzung nur wenige Personen, höchstens fünf bis sechs verlangen: das zweyte weil unseren meiste Sänger den Text undeutlich aussprechen, und das letzte, weil noch wenigere von ihnen Recitativ zu singen verstehen. Entspricht ein Opernbuch diesen Anforderungen nicht, so behalte man lieber den Dialog bey." *AMZ* XXV/29, 16 July 1823: 463–464.

17   "Es scheint also nun der Zeitpunkt da zu seyn, wo sich deutsche Kunst auch im Theater wird geltend machen können, und der Zweck dieser Zeilen ist: die deutschen Komponisten aufzufordern, sich durch grosse und zweckmässige Thätigkeit in Besitz des Opern-Repertoires zu setzen und alles Fremde (wenn es nämlich gehaltlos ist) nach und nach davon zu verdrängen." Ibid.: 457.

recitatives as well as the demand that the story must even be comprehensible when the words are not literally understood points to an esthetic that takes the experience of foreign-language operas as its starting point. Still Spohr does reveal a nationalist attitude as he appears to desire that the good reputation of German composers in genres other than opera will finally be met with corresponding success on the opera stage.[18] These other genres are obviously related to the dominant ideology of unity and coherence, an ideal which Spohr hoped to attain by creating a continuous musical fabric. Spohr, therefore, adopts the foreign model of French grand opera[19] with sung recitatives to elevate German opera.

The work in which Spohr tried to realize his theory was his *"große Oper" Jessonda*, premiered in Kassel in 1823. Spohr's use of foreign models, mainly that of French opera and Spontini's works in particular, is evident. To begin with, he and his librettist Eduard Gehe based it on Antoine Lemierre's *La veuve de Malabar* (1770), a French story on the encounter of Indians and Portuguese in Goa. Spohr had become acquainted with the story during a visit to Paris in 1820–1821. Although he resented the Parisians' lack of interest in his serious, German music and wrote in a *Brief aus Paris* published in the AMZ that "one does not need to stay long in Paris to affirm the common opinion that the French are an unmusical nation,"[20] this sojourn nevertheless left his mark

---

18 "Mein Aufruf gilt hauptsächlich einigen ausgezeichneten, allgemein geachteten Komponisten, die, abgeschreckt durch einen oder ein Paar misslungene Versuche, der Theaterkomposition ganz entsagt zu haben scheinen und sich in neuerer Zeit nur auf Concert- und Kirchenkomposition beschränken." Ibid.: 458.

19 A certain confusion of tongues is at work concerning the term "grand opera." As a genre with specific stylistic requirements, it only came into being after Auber's *La muette de Portici* (1828). In an 1820 article, Weber typifies "grand opera/große Oper" as a style in which musical pieces are continually connected by instrumental recitatives (orchestral accompagnati and not the common secco recitatives of opera seria) with stories with a "grand or grandiose (großartig)" character. The composer praises Gluck's operas as the highest achievements in this genre. (Kaiser 1908: 310–311). Weber's characterization is in line with older French definitions, for example that of Pierre Nougaret, stating in 1768 that *grand opéras* refer to "all-sung operas [and] to works characterized by 'marvels, variety, theatrical splendor,' including ballets." (Quoted after Charlton 2003: 3) Looking at the historical situation around 1820, this ideal of the through-composed and grand – or rather grandiose – opera was realized most prominently in the *tragédies lyriques* of Gasparo Spontini, which may be seen as the most important predecessor of the later, spectacular grand opera genre of Auber, Meyerbeer and others.

20 "Man braucht nicht lange hier zu seyn, um der schon öfter ausgesprochenen Meynung beyzutreten, dass die Franzosen ein unmusikalisches Volk sind." AMZ XXIII/10, 7 March 1821: 158. In the *Aufruf*, he also argues that French opera can no longer compete with its German counterpart: "the previously dangerous competition from the French has now ceased as well, because their most excellent composers are partly dead, partly no longer

on his views on opera. The prominence of choruses and ballets, as well as the impressive tableaus within *Jessonda* call Spontini's *tragédies lyriques*, and especially his conquest opera *Fernand Cortez* (1809), to mind.

Jessonda was a huge success in Germany and it clearly highlights Spohr's compositional craft. But notwithstanding the musical sophistication, on the story level both the Romantic and the German national character are hard to discern. At the same time, one must admit that Romanticism was never an artistic aim in its own right for Spohr – the word does not occur in his *Aufruf* at all – and far less important than the "re-animation of German opera" that he proposes. Moreover, by 1820 perhaps the time had indeed come for composers to move beyond Romanticism in opera, something that is also perceivable in the field of literature. But by giving up Romanticism, the German fairy-tale-like setting of his *Faust* as well as the esthetics of *Singspiel*, Spohr simultaneously lost three decisive markers of German opera identity. One may ask whether he adequately compensated this loss by his sophistication of music's role within *Jessonda*. In the long term, it did not come to be seen as the big next step towards a fully-fledged German opera that Spohr had envisioned it to be in his *Aufruf*.

2   Weber's *Euryanthe* (1823)

Despite the incredible success of *Der Freischütz*, Weber must also have felt that the time had come to move in new directions. In that sense, he was probably susceptible to Hoffmann's praise of Spontini, and secretly endorsed Spohr's critique on writing popular melodies for the masses. With his new project, *Euryanthe*, he aimed to write not necessarily the most popular German opera music, but rather the most elevated and sophisticated. Just as Spohr had done, Weber sought that elevation primarily in the replacement of spoken dialogue by sung recitatives and the creation of a continuous musical flow. More than in the case of *Jessonda*, in which the melodic flow maintains its primacy, Weber centralized the accompagnato recitative, in which the music is full of inflections that express every detail of the text.[21] In the eyes of many of his

---

composing for the theater, whereas those remaining are moderate at best, and not to be feared (Die früher sehr gefährliche Concurrenz der Franzosen hat nun auch aufgehört, da die vorzüglichsten ihrer Komponisten theils todt sind, theils nicht mehr für's Theater schreiben, und die noch übrigen, als unter dem Mittelmässigen, nicht zu fürchten sind)." AMZ XXV/29, 16 July 1823: 458.

21   Dahlhaus provides an illuminating analysis of Weber's formal procedure in *Euryanthe*, arguing that it combines an attention for microscopic detail with a large-scale scenic

contemporaries, this procedure resulted in a work often considered to be too learned, lacking the freshness and immediate appeal of *Der Freischütz*.[22] *Euryanthe* was indeed burdened by Weber's deliberate artistic ambitions,[23] and its problematic aspects complement those of *Der Freischütz*, as both works reflect the troubled state of German Romantic opera around 1820 in a different way.

It has long been thought that Weber chose to move beyond the *Singspiel* style chiefly to counter the criticism that *Der Freischütz* had met,[24] but based on personal letters of Weber, Tusa argues that the "pressure to attempt a more ambitious type of opera" came "from within," rather than "from without."[25] Meyer paraphrases Weber's self-imposed intention with *Euryanthe* as follows:

> The music of *Euryanthe*, Weber seems to be suggesting, should be heard in a different way than that of *Freischütz*. If the "serious" music of *Freischütz* (to use Hoffmann's words again) "served to bring before our eyes the wonderful apparitions of the spirit-realm," the work nevertheless was "pulled back to earth" by the traditions of the *Singspiel*. The music of *Euryanthe*, by contrast, would be thoroughly transcendental, sublime, and "Romantic," purged of the earthly dross that had "weighed down" his earlier work.[26]

Unlike Spohr, who typified his *Jessonda* as a *"große Oper,"* *Euryanthe* is generally referred to as a *"große romantische Oper,"*[27] a designation already used

---

architecture at the expense of its middle ground, the classical schemes of set piece forms which the majority of his audience expected. See Dahlhaus 2007: 748.

22   The most famous and ferocious criticism of Weber's *Euryanthe* after its Viennese premiere came from Franz Grillparzer, who had also parodied the *Wolfsschluchtszene*. Grillparzer wrote in his diaries that "there is no trace of melody, not only in the sense of a pleasing melody, but of melody in general. Fragmented thoughts, held together by the text and without internal musical consistency. [...] This music is disgusting (Keine Spur von Melodie, nicht etwa bloß von gefälliger, sondern von Melodie überhaupt. Abgerissene Gedanken, bloß durch den Text zusammengehalten und ohne innere Konsequenz. [...] Diese Musik ist scheußlich)." Frank 1964: 888–889. For more nuanced variations on this dismissal by Weber's contemporaries, see Tusa 1991: 63–66.

23   Tusa argues that "many of the criticisms brought to bear against the music of *Euryanthe* cover precisely those points where Weber seems most closely to have approximated his ideals of operatic dramaturgy." Ibid.: 66.

24   This idea was introduced by Max Maria von Weber in the biography of his father, but is not supported by any source evidence. See Weber 1864: 352.

25   Tusa 1991: 12–13.

26   Meyer 2003: 116–117.

27   As was also the case with *Silvana*, several designations are found in various editions and sources. Regardless of this diversity, all characterizations circle around the decisive

by Hoffmann for *Aurora*. In *Euryanthe*'s case, this points to an ambition to retain Romantic traits while simultaneously moving beyond the *Singspiel* constellation. In an 1820 introductory note on Poißl's *Der Wettkampf zu Olympia*, Weber had still expressed his conviction that German grand opera did not really have a future since the spirit of the age seemed so much inclined to Romanticism.[28] But soon afterwards, Weber started to reconsider the possibility of "a commixture of two genres, 'grand opera' and 'Romantic opera,' that for the most part had previously been kept apart because of their particular stylistic and structural idiosyncracies," as Tusa writes.[29] Although from a strictly technical point of view, Tusa's genre-based comparison conflicts with Dahlhaus's thesis that "Romantic opera was an idea rather than a genre and could be attached to any genre for scenic-musical realization,"[30] it is hard to deny that up until 1820, Romantic opera was firmly rooted in the stylistic milieu of *Singspiel*. In that sense, the conception of *Euryanthe* entailed a clash of genres indeed.

Whereas the grand Romantic character of Hoffmann's *Aurora* lay chiefly in transporting the Romantic "breakthrough of the spirit realm" to ancient Greece, the *Euryanthe* libretto which Helmina von Chézy wrote aimed to portray a Romantic medieval environment in a grand manner. Chézy based her story on a French 13th-century romance, Gerbert de Montreuil's *Roman de la violette*,[31] collected and adapted by Comte Louis de Tressan in 1780. In his *Sammlung romantischer Dichtungen des Mittelalters* (1804), Friedrich Schlegel had presented it – along with a translation of the French story of Merlin

---

combination of "Romantic" and "grand." Tusa writes: "Certain sources, notably two librettos associated with the first Viennese production – the first printed libretto and a manuscript libretto proofed by Weber himself – call the work a 'romantische Oper,' while several of the draft librettos [...] describe it as a 'große historisch-romantische Oper.' Weber's autograph score lacks any designation at all, and in his correspondence he informally referred to the work simply as a 'große Oper ('grand opera'). However, 'official' sources that are demonstrably close to the composer, including the Steiner piano-vocal score prepared by Weber himself and manuscript copies of the score prepared in Dresden under his supervision for distribution to other German theatres, designate the opera 'eine große romantische Oper,' that is, a 'grand Romantic opera.' It is the last designation that best reflects [...] the fundamental novelties of the work." Tusa 1991: 50.

28   "Wir haben in Deutschland nicht sehr viele dieser Klasse [der großen Oper] angehörige Originalwerke, und der, besonders jetzt, zum Romantischen sich neigende Zeitgeist wird ihrer Vermehrung immer bedeutender in den Weg treten." Kaiser 1908: 311.

29   Tusa 1991: 50.

30   Dahlhaus 2007: 286.

31   This romance is also known under the name *L'histoire du très-noble et chevalereux prince Gérard, comte de Nevers, et de la très-virtueuse et très chaste princesse Euriant de Savoye, sa mye*, and inspired Bocaccio's *Decamerone* (1353) and Shakespeare's *Cymbeline* (1611).

the magician – to a German audience. For this interesting French-German Romantic cultural transfer, Schegel invited Chézy, a German poet married to a Frenchman and at that time living in Paris, to translate Montreuil's *Roman*,[32] and her adaptation would serve as the source for the libretto of Weber's opera two decades later.

Miller argues that Weber was attracted to the romance of Euryanthe mainly because it was an authentic, medieval literary work, transcending the milieu of rural folk tales so prominent in *Der Freischütz*, and therefore appropriate for the genre elevation he desired.[33]

Dahlhaus suggests that Weber must have been "misled by the picturesque charm of the subject, thereby overlooking the fragility of the story,"[34] whereas Miller states that "he wanted to penetrate into the core of Romanticism. Therefore, he wanted no sidestep to regional, not even to national subject matter or the folksiness of *Singspiel*. But how is this intention reconcilable with the choice of the Euryanthe story that, even in Chézy's version, retained its faltering (*Schwankhaft*) character."[35] Indeed it is a common conception that the chief problem of Weber's *Euryanthe* was the flawed libretto, which will be briefly summarized.

Both the medieval romance and the opera revolve around the lovers' vows of Euryanthe and her betrothed (Gérard in the romance, Adolar in the opera) and a wager between this betrothed and the wicked count Lysiart, who questions the fidelity of Euryanthe. By means of trickery, Lysiart and his female accomplice (the old Gondrée in the romance, the young Eglantine[36]

---

32   Although Schlegel did little more than supervising the project, he never mentioned the
      names of the actual translators, Von Chézy and his wife Dorothea, in the publication.
      Von Chézy was clearly offended by this neglect (See Dieckmann 1980: VIII), and her later
      quarrels with Weber about the lack of acknowledgment and financial reward for her con-
      tribution to *Euryanthe* may be seen as another attempt at emancipation in an artistic
      world still dominated by men. Whereas musicologists chiefly know Von Chézy as the
      writer of the "flawed" *Euryanthe* libretto and the play *Rosamunde* with stage music by
      Franz Schubert, her literary activities still enjoy some favorable attention within feminist
      academic circles. See for example Baumgartner 2011.
33   "Different from the folk tales and *Sagen der Vorzeit* on which the Viennese *romantisch-
      komische Zaubermärchen*, and to some degree also his *Freischütz* was based, the vicinity
      of these poems to great masters such as Chrétien de Troyes, Gottfried von Straßburg and
      Wolfram von Eschenbach gave them an elevated aura. When the music drama should be
      established as the highest genre, should not this be done by setting a subject derived from
      the highest medieval literary circles?" Miller 2007: 546–547.
34   Dahlhaus 2007: 746.
35   Miller 2007: 544.
36   This dramatic character was derived from the side figure Eglantine in the medieval origi-
      nal, a beautiful woman who, during Gérard's quest to retrieve his beloved, inflames love in

in the opera) obtain an objective sign that suggests that Euryanthe has been unfaithful, whereas she is actually innocent. By winning the bet, Lysiart dispossesses Gérard/Adolar of his land, and the apparently deceived lover drags his Euryanthe to the forest, planning to kill her. When a snake appears, Euryanthe offers her body to spare Adolar's life. He, however, attacks and kills the snake, and thereupon decides to abandon Euryanthe in the wild instead of killing her, leaving her to God's will. Eventually the scheme is revealed and Euryanthe's fidelity proven, after which Lysiart and his partner in crime are punished – in the opera, Lysiart is sentenced to death after having murdered Eglantine, who, haunted by visions of a deceased wandering spirit, has confessed their crime – and the good pair lives happily ever after.

Within this dramatic constellation, the objective sign of Euryanthe's apparent infidelity is crucial. In the medieval story and Chézy's translation, it was Lysiart's knowledge of a secret spot on Euryanthe's breast in the form of a violet – hence the name *Roman de la violette* – which he had gained by secretly spying on her while she was taking a bath. As this voyeuristic element was deemed inappropriate in an elevated Romantic narration, Weber found another solution to this dramaturgical problem. In the opera, Euryanthe breaks an oath of allegiance to Adolar by revealing a secret to Eglantine. It concerns the fact that Euryanthe has seen the ghost of Emma, Adolar's sister, who has committed suicide after having lost her beloved Udo in battle, and cannot find peace. The ghost has told Euryanthe that she can only be redeemed when the ring that contained the deadly venom is washed clean by the tears of an innocent woman who is willing to sacrifice her own life. Eglantine passes the secret, including the ring, on to Lysiart, who uses these to disclose Euryanthe's alleged treason. Weber wrote impressive music for the wandering ghost of Emma, combining a characteristic timbre consisting of flute, high muted divisi violins and tremoli in the violas with a peculiar chromatic harmony. It is introduced during the overture (mm. 129–143), resounds during Euryanthe's narration to Eglantine and the latter's confession of her betrayal and reoccurs in a consonant variation at the end of the opera, on Adolar's words "Ich ahne Emma, selig ist sie jetzt."

Although musically this procedure represents an impressive example of proto-Wagnerian leitmotific development towards a so-called *Erlösungsschluss*,[37] dramatically the Emma motif was poorly exposed and somewhat

---

his heart with the use of a magic potion, but is ultimately overcome by a magic bird who reminds him of his fidelity to Euryanthe.

37   The term *Erlösungsschluss* refers to a plagal cadence that is used at the conclusion of all Wagner's operas and music dramas from *Der fliegende Holländer* (1843) onward, signalling

extraneous to the action, and Von Chézy did not approve of it. Miller is more appreciative of Weber's invention, which, according to him, "effaced the randomness of the plot and clothed the internal and external confusions of the action with the aura of a second spirit world, dominated by divine and demonic powers."[38] Moreover, this switch granted the story, which is generally an intrigue opera,[39] the dramaturgical antagonism of the otherworldly and the earthly that defines Romantic opera, thereby safe-guarding a continuation of the constellation that governs *Undine, Der Freischütz* and other Romantic works. At the same time, Miller acknowledges that creating this otherworldly dimension also compromised the elevated nature of *Euryanthe*, "since curse and redemption were the standard recipe of the contemporary *Schauerroman* and silly *Schicksalsdramatik*."[40]

But even if the dramatic Emma motive tied the loose ends of the narrative together, its ineffective exposition remained a problem. This shortcoming, as well as other problematic aspects of the libretto were brought forward in a highly perceptive analysis by an anonymous critic, published in *Die Wiener Zeitschrift für Kunst, Literatur, Theater und Mode* on 8 November 1823, two weeks after the premiere:

> That which is especially lacking in the dramatic action is the necessary clarity, whose deficiency is most painfully sensed in the principal motive, in the very point on which the drama really turns. This is Euryanthe's narration about the appearance of Emma, the sister of her betrothed, and of the fabulous poison-ring, from which the departed once drank her death, but which in future, rinsed by the tears of innocence [...] is to become the sign of reconciliation. This circumstance, which is stated only a single time in recitative, has in addition to the obscurity that surrounds it yet other faults, and the substitution with the circumstance mentioned in the

---

the dramatic catharsis and redemption at the end of the work. Often this *Erlösungsschluss* forms the resolution of a chromatic harmonic tension or complex, for example the famous *Tristan* chord which is resolved only in the final bars of *Tristan und Isolde*. The "resolution" of Emma's harmony prefigures this procedure. As you can read in Chapter 5, Wagner used the consonant resolution of Emma's music as a metaphor for Weber's spiritual homecoming in the music he wrote for Weber's reburial ceremony in Dresden in 1846. Weber had initially been buried in London, the place where he died in 1826. See for more information on the dramaturgy of the *Erlösungsschluss*, Van Kooten 2013: 7.

38   Miller 2007: 548.
39   Meyer establishes that "*Euryanthe* returns to the more familiar plot tropes of serious opera, in which the path to Romantic fulfilment is blocked not by supernatural powers but by human villains motivated by jealousy and greed." Meyer 2003: 118.
40   Miller 2007: 549.

romance, however necessary it might have been, cannot be considered successful. In the first place the marvellous appears as a highly foreign component in an action that otherwise makes no use of it. Second, [...] Euryanthe ought but to have said a single word, just confess [...] and the betrayal would thus be discovered. The danger is more significant in the romance, where the unfortunate girl does not know how it has happened and can only assert her innocence without having the means to prove it. The jealousy of the treacherous Eglantine is an equally unfortunate invention, since she could hope to win Adolar's hand after the separation of the lovers is brought about, and consequently should not give her hand to Lysiart so hastily. [...] Lysiart is most successfully drawn, even if he at times does sigh too much and then again rages too violently. [...] Leaving aside these faults, the piece still distinguishes itself from many others, both through its Romantic character and its noble bearing.[41]

The noble bearing of the piece was not agreed upon by all of Weber's contemporaries. Stephan Schütze wrote a devastating critique of the *Euryanthe* libretto in *Caecilia* in 1825, not only ridiculing the poem's quality but particularly repudiating the moral side of the story and the wager in particular: "Is such a piece of roguery – scandalous for both parties –, a bet concerning the innocence of

---

41   "Was außerdem der dramatischen Handlung abgeht, ist ganz besonders die nöthige Klarheit, deren Mangel in dem Hauptmotiv, in demjenigen Punct, um welchen das Drama eigentlich sich dreht, am schmerzlichsten empfunden wird. Dies ist die Erzählung Euryanthe's von der Erscheinung Emma's, der Schwester ihres Verlobten, und dem fabelhaften Giftring, aus welchem einst die hingeschiedene den Tod sog, der aber künftig, von den Thränen der Unschuld benetzt [...] das Pfand der Versöhnung werden soll. Dieser Umstand, der nur ein einziges Mal im recitirenden Ton vorgetragen wird, hat außer jener Dunkelheit, die ihn umhüllt, noch andere Mängel, und die Verwechslung mit dem in der Geschichte angegebnen, so nöthig sie auch war, kann nicht gelunen heißen. Erstlich erscheint das Wunderbare als ein höchst fremdartiger Bestandtheil in einer Handlung, die sonst dessen überall entbehrt. Dann ist das Geständnis im Betreff dieser Erscheinung auch kein zureichender Grund zum schimpflichsten Verdacht. Euryanthe dürfte nur ein Wort verlauten lassen, nur gestehen, wozu ihr ohnehin Zeit und Gelegenheit genug verbleibt, so würde der Verrath entdeckt. Bedeutender ist die Gefahr in der Erzählung, wo die Unglückliche nicht weiß, wie ihr geschehen, und nur auf ihre Unschuld sich berufen kann, ohne Gründe bey der Hand zu haben. Die Eifersücht der verrätherischen Eglantine ist eben so wenig eine glückliche Erfindung, da sie hoffen darf, nach bewirkter Trennung der Liebenden, Adolar's Hand zu gewinnen, folglich dem Lysiart die ihrige nicht so eilig geben wird [...]. Am glücklichsten ist Lysiart gezeichnet; wenn er gleich hier ein Mal zu viel seufzt, dann wieder etwas zu heftig tobt. [...] Dieser Mängel ungeachtet, zeichnet sich das Stück vor vielen andern sowohl durch den romantischen Charakter, als die edle Haltung, noch bedeutend aus." *Wiener Zeitschrift für Kunst, Literatur, Theater und Mode* XIII/134, 8 November 1823: 1102–1103.

a girl, is this a dignified, artistically acceptable, in short, a beautiful dramatic subject? And even if it could be: how can a poetess present such an obscene intrigue to an audience that also contains female spectators?"[42] Schütze has a more specific problem with the fact that the story is essentially an intrigue, since its main ingredient, deception, does not fit the nature of music: "It is sad that the core of the action is an intrigue. Such a thing is ill-suited to music, because it shuns emotion as well as veracity. How should music express cunning and guile, pretended grief and feigned emotion?"[43] However, what the conservative critic conspicuously overlooks is the fact that music is actually fully capable of this, and that one of Weber's greatest achievement in *Euryanthe* laid in the depiction of the treacherous friendship and love of the villainous characters.

The scene between Euryanthe and Eglantine in the first act (Nr. 5–8) is an impressive essay in deceptive style. Immediately following Euryanthe's idyllic cavatina 'Glöcklein im Thale,' Eglantine's wicked character is introduced through a "snake-like" motif consisting of descending sixteenth notes and articulating a "diabolic" diminished seventh chord. This motif is transformed into an "innocent" major variant during Eglantine's conversation with Euryanthe. After this charm offensive, Eglantine sings a small aria in E minor to win Euryanthe's compassion. She convinces Euryanthe to disclose her secret, and when Euryanthe, after having narrated the story of Emma's ghost, bursts out of regret after having broken her oath to Adolar, Eglantine pulls the grieving A minor music ('Unter ist mein Stern gegangen') back towards A major,[44]

---

42   "Ist eine solche, von beiden Seiten schändliche Büberei, ist eine Wette um die Unschuld eines Mädchens, ein würdiger, ein künstlerisch zulässiger, kurz ein schöner Gegenstand des dramatischen Interesse's, - und wenn er es, an sich betrachtet, auch allenfalls sein könnte: wie mag eine Dichterin einem, doch auch aus weiblich verschämten Zuschauern bestehenden Publicum eine so obscöne Intrigue vorführen?" *Caecilia* 1825 (2): 53. To an early nineteenth-century German audience, a skeptic attitude towards amorous fidelity was unacceptable, hence the limited popularity of Mozart's *Cosi fan tutte* in those days.

43   "Es ist an sich schon schlimm, dass der Hauptbestandtheil in einer Intrigue besteht. Eine solche eignet sich wenig für Musik, [...] weil sie der Empfindung und der Wahrhaftigkeit ausweicht. Wie soll die Musik List und Verstellung, vorgeblichen Schmerz und geheucheltes Gefühl ausdrücken?" Ibid.: 43.

44   Although it is impossible to state objectively that Eglantine effects the shift to A major, it is clear that she introduces major elements into Euryanthe's minor elegy. For example, Eglantine's words "Kannst du sagen" are sung on the chord of B-flat major, and realize a temporarily shift to F major. The deceptive nature of this B-flat major harmony is underlined by the fact that the first words of Euryanthe's elegy are sung to the same harmony, but in that context function as a Neapolitan sixth chord – a symbol of grief – within A minor. Even if one must admit that we cannot know whether Weber deliberately used the harmony of B-flat major for this particular "deceptive" goal, there is no question that the score of *Euryanthe* contains many of these subtleties on the micro level of word-tone relations.

comforting her "friend." When Euryanthe has left, Eglantine sings an extensive recitative and aria in which she voices her true feelings: contempt of the naïve Euryanthe, grief over her own vain love for Adolar, and finally an outcry for revenge with coloraturas. Within the entire scene, musical antagonisms such as diatonic vs. chromatic, major vs. minor and a plain, lyrical vs. an acrobatic vocal style reveal Eglantine's hidden agenda and the way she realizes her goals. Dahlhaus also recognizes a dramaturgy of deception in Von Chézy's use of "tragic irony," in the sense that idyllic moments are immediately doomed by a disenchanting subsequent event.[45] By adding extra layers to the drama, these musical and dramatic forms of commentary on the action sophisticatedly reveal the deception to the spectator. This creates a level of complexity in word-tone relations that had hitherto been rarely found in opera, and certainly adds to the sophisticated nature of the work.

In narrating the story, Weber used distinctions in vocal style that can be more or less pinned down to national stereotypes. To depict the treacherous nature of Lysiart and Eglantine, Weber chose an Italian vocal idiom, with coloraturas highlighting their artificial behavior and rage. Moreover, since rapid changes of mood are a crucial element of Italian opera dramaturgy, Italian musical forms are very suitable for depicting the ambivalent character of these love-driven villains. The slow movement of Lysiart's aria Nr. 10, for example, emphasizes his tender feelings for Euryanthe, whereas the rapid cabaletta shows his evil side. In the third act, the Lady Macbeth-like deterioration of Eglantine's guilt-burdened soul is evoked by fractured melodic gestures during her confession and a furious, hysterically triumphant vocal virtuosity after hearing the deceptive message that Euryanthe has deceased.

For the far from malicious, but nevertheless unsteady and undetermined character of Adolar, Weber embraced an equally foreign idiom. In contrast to the similarly wavering character of Max in *Der Freischütz*, Adolar has a far less ponderous and all the more impulsive nature, and is therefore closer to the Italian than to the German conventional opera hero. But from a vocal point of view, Miller particularly recognizes a French prototype in Adolar's agile, heroic part with high tessitura.[46] His elaborate vocal lines clearly deviate from the German ideal of simplicity, but even if Adolar's vocal lines sometimes tend to the artificial side, this is not to display his moral vices, but rather to highlight him as a representative of a formal courtly lifestyle.[47]

---

45   Dahlhaus 2007: 746–747.

46   Miller 2007: 564.

47   Tusa argues that "the artificiality of language throughout the libretto seems calculated to strengthen the impression of an extremely formal and courtly age. And to a certain extent, Weber seems also to have subtly aimed at a musical style that would correspond to this fanciful image of life at court. Thus in comparison to the examples in *Der Freischütz*

The most genuinely German vocal idiom is reserved for Euryanthe, obviously the most virtuous character within the opera. Her lines are lyrical but restrained, devoid of coloratura, and in that sense very similar to those of Agathe in *Der Freischütz*. Her vocal contributions lack the swift hovering between emotional states and the musical contrasts we find in the villains' music. Anger and rage are entirely absent in her character, and her prayer-like arias generally depict only one affect, instead of the common two or three contrasting ones. Meyer argues that:

> If Euryanthe's music manifests some of the aesthetic ideals of early-nineteenth-century criticism, so does her personality manifest some of the most important aspects of its ideology. In this context, Euryanthe's piety and inwardness make her a kind of ideal woman. [...] When Adolar and Lysiart bet all of their lands on Euryanthe's faithfulness, they are enacting what for early-nineteenth-century Germany was a self-evident truth: that women's purity and chastity was essential not only for a marriage, but for the life of a community.[48]

Whereas the courtly world of the opera is governed by external matters; land, honor and objective signs of betrayal, Euryanthe's *Innigkeit* makes her a complete outsider. This certainly enhanced her identification as a woman of German virtue in this French, aristocratic milieu, but compromised her dramatic liveliness. As Meyer points out: "if Euryanthe's absolute passivity is an ideological necessity, it also tends to undermine the drama of the opera. Euryanthe's spotless virtue and inability to act robs her of her operatic nature."[49]

The analysis above reveals the complex nature of this German opera on a French medieval subject, in which different national styles are employed to articulate the piece's dramaturgy. How to value the Romanticism and genuinely German character of Weber's *Euryanthe*, and – perhaps more interestingly – how did Weber's contemporaries value these? In Wolfgang Michael Wagner's eyes, the German identification of *Euryanthe* to Weber's audience was already hindered by the fact that the opera was based on a French original, and was therefore

---

and the norms for genres like the Lied and *romance*, the strophic pieces in *Euryanthe* [such as Adolar's *Romanze* 'Unter blüh'nden Mandelbäumen'] are rather self-consciously complicated compositions filled with harmonic and rhythmic artifices and 'unusual' turns perhaps to suggest the refinement of courtly life." Tusa 1991: 76.

48   Meyer 2003: 146. Meyer bases his thesis on contemporary literature on *Geslechtsverhält-nisse*, for example on a lexicon article by Theodor Welcker in his and Carl von Rotteck's *Staats-Lexicon* (1834–1843).

49   Ibid.: 150.

built around supposedly French characteristics such as "burlesque piquancy," "frivolity," "playful insobriety" and "rational motivations."[50] Dahlhaus, on the other hand, argues that the French origin of the story and aristocratic nature of its main characters did not thwart its national and Romantic significance, since early nineteenth-century German bourgeois audiences strongly identified medieval chivalry with these ideals.[51] Nonetheless, it is hard to deny that the French artificial, courtly milieu in which *Euryanthe* takes place is more difficult to reconcile with German national ideals than that of *Der Freischütz*. It seems that the "un-German" environment in which Euryanthe finds herself is deliberately created and serves to lift out her German virtue, but this results in a drama in which it is hard to sympathize with most of the characters, to a certain extent even with the protagonist Adolar.

In the depiction of characters of flesh and blood that are driven by good as well as evil, Weber and Von Chézy moved away from a German Romantic idealism towards a more characteristic and realistic esthetic. The way Weber's music articulated the contrasts between single characters and between diverging emotional states and tried to express nuances of the drama as detailed as possible further contributed to its allegedly un-Romantic nature, as Tusa argues that "from the Romantic point of view the opera's music failed in its mission as music precisely because its close alliance to specific characters and situations diminished the autonomy from concrete ideas that made music the perfect vehicle for the expression of the ideal and transcendant."[52] To Weber, the close affiliation between music and text in *Euryanthe* realized one of his main ideals of German opera, that of multimedial coherence. To his earliest audiences, the apparent lack of musical unity created the impression of a deficient coherence. *Euryanthe* is perhaps the first work in German music history that created such a lively and at times heated discussion between adherents of an absolute and those of a more poetic attitude towards music.[53]

---

50   Wagner 1994: 177–178.

51   Dahlhaus 2007: 743–744.

52   Tusa 1991: 68.

53   For someone like Franz Grillparzer, strictly musical principles and the ideal of Italian opera, in which music always had primacy, governed his dismissal of *Euryanthe*. To Weber, it was obvious that his music served a dramatic function and could only be adequately appreciated within the context of a stage performance. For example, in a letter of 20 December 1824 to the Akademische Musikverein of the University of Breslau, he forbade a concert performance of the work, arguing that "*Euryanthe* is a purely dramatic essay, building its hopes only on the united collaboration of all of the sister arts, and surely ineffective if robbed of their assistance (*Euryanthe* ist ein rein dramatischer Versuch, seine Wirkung nur von dem vereinigten Zusammenwirken der Künste

That *Euryanthe*'s premiere would fall victim to a mixed reception is partly the result of elements within the work itself, but also of the fact that Weber had misjudged the expectations of his Viennese audience. To Weber, Vienna represented the most prestigious center of serious German music – the city of Haydn, Mozart, and Beethoven – and therefore seemed the perfect stage for his serious German opera. But in fact, in Vienna Weber saw himself confronted with three dominant parties. Firstly, Vienna experienced the height of Rossini fever in 1823, and considering the fierce Rossini-Weber antagonism of those days, many Viennese opera-goers were hostile to Weber's art. Secondly, being the cradle of the *Singspiel*, as well as the second city where *Der Freischütz* triumphed after its Berlin success, Vienna expected something similarly appealing and comparably structured as *Euryanthe*'s predecessor.[54] In short, it expected a *Singspiel* with folk songs and other demotic elements. If this part of the audience cheered at the first performance, this was probably chiefly motivated by their renewed acquaintance with the cherished *Freischütz* composer, but the enthusiasm faded away after a few performances. Thirdly, with the elevated forms of *Euryanthe*, Weber had hoped to find a warm welcome from admirers of serious German genres, such as the sonata, the string quartet and the symphony, but the un-classical and audacious nature of his music frustrated this acknowledgment.

Rumors of the moderate success of Weber's new opera soon spread to other German regions, and Tusa states that "the authority that Vienna had earlier attained as a great musical center was still strong enough to influence opinions in other German cities."[55] But to some, the Viennese rejection of *Euryanthe* confirmed the superiority of Northern German esthetic values and the questionable quality of Austrian criticism, thereby strengthening the ties between Weber's work and (Northern) German national identity. Adolph Bernard Marx, for example, wrote the following in the *Berliner allgemeine musikalische Zeitung* concerning the upcoming 1826 Berlin performances:

> In Berlin, the work will be judged for the first time on the overarching idea of the whole. In current Vienna, one may not expect this. That the

---

hoffend, [sonst] sicher wirkungslos ihrer Hülfe beraubt)" www.Weber-Gesamtausgabe. de/Korrespondenzen/A042377.

54   To Weber, this expectation was a curse, as he wrote in a letter of 22 December 1822 to his friend Thaddäus Susan that "the excessive applause that *Der Freischütz* has received is a dangerous enemy to all of my future operas (Der übergroße Beyfall, den der Freyschütze erhalten, ist ein gefährlicher Feind aller meiner nachfolgenden Opern)." www.Weber-Gesamtausgabe.de/Korrespondenzen/A041997.

55   Tusa 1991: 58.

Viennese worship Rossini and jubilate their ghost farces, that they have not taken the effort to make *Euryanthe* their own, and that they see their opera theaters deteriorate: this is all connected. If one must speak of a misconception on the part of Weber and the librettist, it is that they had their opera first performed in Vienna, where no attempt was made to illuminate his ideas and intentions – where people have been satisfied with shallow reviews that either praise or insult.[56]

But regardless of the questionable qualities of Viennese criticism, even Marx could not deny the shortcomings of *Euryanthe*, which he saw in its incapacity to make the spectator believe in and sympathize with the characters, an incapacity that – taken together with the elevated nature of the drama and the delightful music – creates a discrepancy.[57] In the eyes of Marx, the true merit of the opera lies in its *couleur locale*, in its ability to depict the time and place of courtly medieval southern France.[58] Comparing *Euryanthe* to Goethe's *Pandora* and Mozart's *Figaro* and *Don Juan*, Marx expresses his belief that this initially poor-received artwork will enjoy a higher appreciation in the – hopefully nearby – future.[59]

---

56 "In Berlin wird man – ganz abgesehen von dem Enthusiasmus für den Komponist Einzelheiten seines Werkes – zuerst auf die Idee des Ganzen allgemein eingehen. Im heutigen Wien ist dies nicht zu erwarten gewesen. Daß die Wiener Rossini anbeten und in ihren Geisterpossen jubeln, dass sie aufgegeben haben, Euryanthe sich anzueignen, und dass sie ihre Operntheater zugrunde gehen sehen: das hängt ganz eng zusammen. Wenn von einem Misgriffe Webers und der Librettistin die Rede sein soll, so ist es der, daß sie die Oper zuerst in Wien habe aufführen lassen, wo nicht einmal versucht worden ist, über das Werk sich zu verständigen, über seine Idee und Tendenz aufzuklären, - wo man sich an leeren preisenden oder verunglimpfenden Korrespondenzen befriedigt hat." *Berliner Allgemeine Musikalische Zeitung* (*BAMZ*) III/1, 4 January 1826: 5.

57 "Allein die Bühne stellt den Menschen körperlich vor uns hin und hält uns drei Stunden lang nur an ihm fest. Ist es da nicht gelungen, uns an ihn glauben, mit ihm leben, ihn uns werth und theuer zu machen, so fühlen wir uns unbefriedigt; und jenes kann mit Sicherheit nur da erreicht werden, wo der Mensch in seiner Würde – das heißt selbstständig handelnd – und statt jenes Undings, Zufall, der Gott im Menschen erscheint. [...] Die Fabel der Euryanthe hat ihre Anwendung nicht zugelassen, während der Ernst und die Gewichtigkeit des Inhalts, durch den Nachdruck der herrlichen Musik noch erhöht, sie dringend verlangte." Ibid.: 7.

58 "Hiermit hat aber der Unterzeichnete angedeutet, was ihm an der neuen Oper das Werthvollste, dasjenige zu sein scheint, was sie von allen bisherigen Opern karakteristisch unterscheidet; das ist die getreue Auffassung der Zeit und des Orts, in denen sich die Begebenheit ereignet. Das südlichere Frankreich in der Blüte der Ritterzeit – das ist der Inhalt der Musik, wie des Gedichts." *BAMZ* III/2, 11 January 1826: 10.

59 "Es hat sich aber schon oft ereignet, daß ein dem Künstler natürliches und nothwendiges Werk, während es in den Augen derer, die ihn verstehen, seinen Werth erhöht, der

Euryanthe would indeed find a more favorable reception in the future. After attending a performance in 1847, Robert Schumann wrote in his *Theater-büchlein* that "this music is far too unknown and underappreciated. Weber has invested all his passion and nobility in it, [creating] a chain of gleaming jewels from beginning to end."[60] And in *Oper und Drama* (1851), Richard Wagner, who was more ambivalent concerning the quality of *Euryanthe*, nevertheless pointed out that "criticism has not given *Euryanthe* the degree of attention that it deserves on account of its uncommonly instructive content."[61] Both these eminent composers of a new German generation not only praised *Euryanthe*, but actually used it as a model for two operas with a similar plot line and many other striking similarities, *Lohengrin* and *Genoveva* (both premiered in 1850). In that sense, the work could veritably guide future developments in German Romantic opera.[62]

In the nearby future, however, *Euryanthe* and the principle of German sung-throughout opera would not really make school. Although Spohr continued his experiment in his moderately successful *Berggeist* (1824), Weber returned to the principle of spoken dialogue and an oriental, "romanesque" setting in *Oberon* (1826), which is closer to Mozart's *Zauberflöte* than to *Euryanthe*. And even if Heinrich Marschner, the most important German composer of the second half of the 1820's, displayed a tendency towards a more through-composed opera, he nevertheless stuck to spoken dialogue in his Romantic operas *Der Vampyr* (1827) and *Hans Heiling* (1833).[63] In Miller's eyes, the persistence of dialogue opera in Germany was motivated by an increasing "arrogance and xenophobia" in German music criticism, and led to a "degeneration of German culture into provincial culture," a situation "in which composers could either

Mehrzahl der Zeitgenossen noch verschlossen bleibt, ja wol gar mißfällig erscheint. Eines der größten Werke Göthes, seine Pandora, ist noch jetzt, während ganz Europa dem Dichterfürsten huldigt, unbekannt. Mozarts Figaro und Don Juan gingen so weit über die Vorstellungen der Zeit hinaus, daß man sie schwerfällig, überladen, unmelodisch nannte. Auch Euryanthe scheint dem Ref. mehr der Zukunft und hoffentlich einer nahen, zuzugehören, als der Gegenwart." *BAMZ* III/1, 4 January 1826: 5.

60   "die Musik ist noch viel zu wenig erkannt und anerkannt. Es ist herzblut, sein Edelstes was er hatte; [...] eine Kette glänzender Juwelen von Anfang bis zum Schluß." Simon, Band IV. 1888: 164.

61   "Die »Euryanthe« ist von der Kritik nicht in dem Maaße beachtet worden, als sie es ihres ungemein lehrreichen Inhaltes wegen verdient." *WWSB*. Sämtliche Schriften, Band 3: 292.

62   The model function of *Euryanthe* for two esteemed German composers obviously strengthened the idea of a clear direction within German opera history for nineteenth- and early-twentieth century music historians.

63   Marschner called *Der Templer und die Jüdin* (1829) a *große romantische Oper*, but apart from an incidental Berlin performance with recitatives in 1831, the work was generally played in its original form, with spoken dialogue.

fail by following the fashion of *Der Freischütz* or emigrate to France or Italy."[64] The voyage of discovery that Spohr and Weber had embarked on eventually led to a retreat to the safe confines of German opera's still brittle traditions.

Looking back at the last two chapters, one sees how during the first quarter of the nineteenth century composers tried to transform German opera from a marginal, intranational *Singspiel* tradition into a genre of international allure while simultaneously retaining a distinguishably German character. For two reasons, Romanticism seemed an ideal vehicle to realize this goal. Not only does the core of Romanticism appear to lie in the process of elevating the common and trivial – think of Novalis's process of Romanticization – but the Romantic worldview and esthetics were also strongly identified with German nationhood, particularly in the field of opera.

As the writings of Franz Horn and E.T.A. Hoffmann make clear, the distinction between high and low forms of Romanticism – for example that between "silly spirits" and "miraculous apparitions of the spirit realm" (Hoffmann) – was a crucial aspect of early nineteenth-century German opera theory. Furthermore, in these writings we find a clear desire to elevate contemporary (German) opera into a truly Romantic, elevated art form. However, in many cases, it is difficult or even impossible to discern between trivial and elevated manifestations of Romanticism in German opera. No oeuvre highlights the dual nature of Romantic opera better than that of Carl Maria von Weber, who, up until *Der Freischütz*, preserved elements of the popular Viennese *romantisch-komische Volksmärchen*, while simultaneously innovating the musical language of German opera with unprecedented audacity.

Although Hoffmann's music in *Undine* is far less bold, it nevertheless offers novelty in what Miller has called *Verklärte Volkstümlichkeit*, an idiom that is apparently demotic but nonetheless elevated and ingenious. Nowhere in German opera do we find such a deliberate attempt to divorce high Romanticism from its trivial counterpart as in *Undine*, but the work's exalted tone and complete elimination of comedy eventually risks to "deprive it of its theatrical lifeblood (Schläder)." Apart from the exceptional character and particular merits of Hoffmann's *Undine*, the work underlines the fact that early-nineteenth-century German opera was in many cases burdened by its own Romantic ambitions.

To German opera composers such as Spohr and Weber, attempts to move beyond spoken dialogue went hand in hand with an ambition to elevate the genre and to leave behind the apparent marginality of a *Singspiel* esthetics. These attempts generally materialized in a form akin to the French model of grand opera. Along with the all-sung nature of this genre came a shift from

---

64   Miller 1980: 468.

ideal to realistic characters, a move from a cosmic drama to an intrigue and from simple plots to a grandiose action entailing ballets and massive crowd scenes. Not only did this grand opera esthetics lead away from assumed German virtues such as simplicity, naturalness and *Innigkeit*, it also proved difficult to retain the dramaturgical antagonism of the otherworldly and the earthly that had defined Romantic opera up until then. Works such as *Euryanthe* or Heinrich Marschner's *Der Templer und die Jüdin* (1829) can still be characterized as Romantic in a more general sense, but this defining marker of German operatic Romanticism is poorly developed or entirely absent in these operas.

From the point of musical style, the move towards grand, all-sung opera also compromised the German identification of these works.[65] Tusa, for example, argues that "the very heterogeneity of genre and style" could serve to identify an opera as German, "since to a greater or lesser extent *all* German operas of the late eighteenth and early nineteenth century were characterized by their appropriation of genres, styles, and techniques of French and Italian opera."[66] But at the same time, the *Singspiel* constellation had offered an overarching structure in which these various styles and techniques could be implemented, a structure that was, moreover, closely associated with German character, since German opera without spoken dialogue was rare.[67] By entering the cosmopolitan opera world after 1821, German opera left its infancy behind, but simultaneously gave up its most distinctive feature.

The status of *Der Freischütz* as a beacon of "innocence in a disenchanted world," as Henderson calls it,[68] which gives the work a timeless relevance in German history,[69] also holds true on a more stylistic level. Its *Singspiel*

---

65   The exemplary function of *Der Freischütz* as a national opera was certainly partly responsible for this. Miller, for example, writes "that the worldwide success of the *Freischütz* made its form obligatory for German operas in the following twenty years. [...] This explains why experiments with grand operatic form remained marginal in most operas of that time." Miller 1992: 77.

66   Tusa 1991: 55.

67   With regard to the limited success of sung-throughout German opera in the 1830s, Klaus Pietschmann for example argues that "neither were German singers trained for it, nor were German audiences willing to accept the 'unnatural' character of sung conversation." See Pietschmann 2014: 17.

68   Henderson 2011: 165.

69   In many respects, *Der Freischütz*, but also early nineteenth-century *Singspiel* in general, can be compared to the *Heimatfilm*, which has also proven to be of ongoing relevance as an emblem of German national identity in diverse chapters of German history. In *When was Romantic Nationalism; The Onset, the Long Tail, the Banal* (2014), Joep Leerssen writes the following about the *Heimatfilm*, which equally applies to *Der Freischütz* and to the Romantic *Singspiel*: "That genre, offering an idyllic escape from the here and now, effortlessly survived the transition from the Third Reich to Adenauer Germany. [...] As a whole,

structure and folk nature stirred nostalgia among German audiences far into the second half of the nineteenth century, when through-composed opera had become an extremely successful form in the hands of Richard Wagner. To twentieth- and twenty-first-century commentators – think of Adorno's earlier mentioned characterization – *Der Freischütz* is surrounded by an aura of innocence exactly because of the fact that it is unburdened by the overt nationalist ideology that rose to prominence in the second half of the nineteenth century and which is often associated with the immensely influential work of Richard Wagner. Paradoxically, what once started as a cosmopolitan move beyond the stylistic and thematic confines of German opera became an ideologically problematic heritage in the hands of Wagner, the greatest composer of German through-composed opera. Although *Singspiel* may have been a dead end within the development towards a more elevated German opera, it has remained one of the most popular and harmless manifestations of German culture on the opera stage, because it clearly embodies notions of Romanticism and German nationhood worth to be treasured.

---

the process shows how Romantic-National rusticism can become National-Socialist, postwar-nostalgic and postmodern-regionalist, and cycle from low-prestige popular art to totalitarian propaganda to no-prestige commodity, and thence back again to prestigious art-form. And throughout all these changes, the genre invokes a national relevance, articulates a German-national self-image, and presents its return to rustic-familial roots as a way of engaging with a collective German identity." Leerssen 2014B: 26.

CHAPTER 4

"Blondes et rêveuses primedonnes" and "Allies from Abroad": German-Language Opera Companies Touring Abroad during the First Half of the Nineteenth Century

After having discussed the conceptualization and creation of German opera in the first decades of the nineteenth century, this chapter is concerned with its institutionalization. The "coming of age" of German opera is intimately tied not only to the success of Weber's *Der Freischütz*, but also to the composer's creation of a German opera department which could compete with its Italian counterpart in Dresden between 1817 and 1826. The fact that Weber received the same salary as his Italian colleague Francesco Morlacchi and eventually obtained the same title of *königlicher Kapellmeister* points to a rise in status of German opera in general.[1] Just as significant was the move to a new performance location for German operas; from the suburban *Theater am Linkeschen Bade*, where travelling troupes used to perform, to the prestigious court theater downtown. And thanks to the dedicated support of the intendant Count Heinrich von Vitzthum and the financial protection of King Friedrich August I, Weber could put some of his esthetic ideals concerning German opera into practice, or at least test their viability.

In the light of Weber's reception as the German national opera composer par excellence, it hardly surprises that his period at the Dresden opera is surrounded by myth-making and exaggeration. Up until the Second World War, scholars instrumentalized Weber's service at the Dresden opera as a first strike within a history of gradual German victory over foreign operatic oppression, employing the militant metaphors of the Liberation Wars against Napoleonic reign. We find this attitude, for example, in Ludwig Schiedermair's *Die deutsche Oper* (1940), where the author writes:

> The returning front troops received *Der Freischütz* jubilantly, the younger generation sensed in it the final, devastating stroke at Italian opera. Indeed, the opera had to be followed up by other works with a nationalist

---

1   See Kremtz 1995A: 109–111.

leaning and national artistic force, before the Italian bulwarks in Berlin (1825/1841), Munich (1825), Dresden (1832) and Vienna (1848) collapsed.[2]

In his *Beiträge zur Geschichte der deutschen romantischen Oper* (1937), Goslich argues in a similar vein: "Indeed already in the 1820s the majority of leading positions were occupied by Germans: Weber triumphed over the Italian opera with his German department in Dresden, Spohr was appointed at Kassel in 1822 and Marschner at Hannover in 1831."[3] In both cases, the patriotic fervor of these scholars was arguably increased by the historical context in which they published their works, but adopting the trope of political liberation on the esthetic plane is as old as the Liberation Wars themselves.[4]

After 1945, we find a tentative tendency towards a less overtly nationalistic perspective on Weber's directorship in Dresden. In *Die deutsche Oper in Dresden unter der Leitung von Carl Maria von Weber 1817–1826* (1962), the most elaborate scholarly account of Weber's work as a *Kapellmeister* in the Saxon capital, Wolfgang Becker provided a more nuanced picture of this project, partly based on quantitative evidence.[5] Although Becker had already mitigated the overtly nationalist image of Weber's Dresden project, Anno Mungen went one step further in the article 'Morlacchi, Weber und die Dresdner Oper' (1995). He generally characterizes the traditional discourse on the subject as "stylizing a tentative initiative, lacking a clear concept, into the birth of German national opera as an institution."[6] To Mungen, the lack of conceptual focus is already

---

2 Schiedermair 1940: 207–208.
3 Goslich 1937: 14–15.
4 See for example the reception of *Der Freischütz* in the years after its premiere in Chapter 1. A middle phase between the enthusiasm of 1821 and the ideological stance of scholars working in the Third Reich can be found in the era of German unification, for example in Jähns's *Carl Maria von Weber in seinen Werken* (1871), in which the author writes about the *Freischütz* premiere that "just as Germany on this very day (18 June 1815) liberated itself from the yoke of foreign domination, exactly six years later did German music liberate itself from the domination of foreign artistic elements; with the simple German Weber opposing the armor-clad Spontini [...]. In this victorious battle Weber helped the German people to gain [...] consciousness about their own position in musico-dramatic art ("Wie Deutschland einst an diesem Tage [18. Juni 1815] sich vom Joche der Fremdherrschaft befreite, so entwand sich an ihm, 6 Jahre später, die deutsche Musik, der gerade in diesem Momente besonders einflussreichen Herrschaft fremdländerischer Kunstelemente; stand dem schlichten deutschen W. doch der geharnischte Spontini unmittelbar gegenüber. [...] In dem durch W. siegreich bestandenen Kampfe wurde dem deutschen Volke [...] das Bewusstsein gewonnen, auch in der musikalisch dramatischen Kunst seine eigne Stelle einzunehmen")." Jähns 1871: 311.
5 See Becker 1962.
6 Mungen 1995: 101. In the same volume, the altered approach towards the significance of Weber's years in Dresden for the establishment of a German national opera is underscored by

evident from the fact that Weber made his debut with a performance of the French composer Méhul's *Joseph*, albeit in German translation. Meyer, however, argues:

> It was to be through these performances of foreign operas that Weber was able to firmly establish his new institution, preparing the way, he hoped, for a truly national operatic genre. Although Weber did not speak of *opéra comique* in precisely those terms, it is clear from an analysis of his repertoire that the realistic drama of the French operas made them a natural "stepping stone" between the *Singspiel* and the "new German opera."[7]

Concerning the above-mentioned data that induced Goslich to proclaim the victory of German over Italian opera, Mungen opposes the following:

> These data appear to provide the cornerstones of an independent German opera culture, whereas in fact, until the rise of Wagner it lacked the international prestige of French and Italian opera. Throughout the first half of the nineteenth century, German opera remained – apart from exceptions – a national, if not a regional phenomenon.[8]

If we compare the widespread European dissemination of Italian and French works during this period, German opera was indeed an intra- rather than international affair. But, nonetheless, there have been German operas that achieved success abroad. Moreover, when reading nineteenth-century music periodicals, one encounters several attempts to create German-language opera institutions in foreign countries.

This chapter traces this appearance of German operas and companies outside the German territory, a history that has been largely forgotten in the extensive musicological literature on nineteenth-century opera. It is a story that has fallen through the cracks of many nationally-orientated music historiographies. In the countries where these experiments took place, they often escaped scholarly attention, whereas in German historiography, these often short-lived, trial-and-error enterprises did not really fit into the discourse of a victorious march of German opera. This feeling of cultural superiority could only be maintained by mythologizing the situation within Germany while

---

Eberhard Kremtz in the title of his contribution, putting "Deutsches Department" between quotation marks. See Kremtz 1995A: 107.

7   Meyer 2003: 57.

8   Mungen 1995: 87.

closing one's eyes for the still marginal status of German opera in, for example, France and Italy.

With this chapter, I expand the scope on the institutionalization and popularization of German opera in the first half of the nineteenth century by focusing on the cultural transfers brought about by these initiatives abroad. Sieghart Döhring and Sabine Henze-Döhring present German opera in this period as merely a result of "cultural import," unlike the intensive "cultural exchange" that took place between the Italian and French opera scene.[9] Philipp Ther does recognize cultural transfers from German opera, functioning as a source of inspiration, to other "national" genres, but situates these towards the end of the 19th century, following the success of *Der Ring des Nibelungen* (1876).[10] But on a more modest scale, similar transfers can be observed in the first decades of the century as well. Both the international success of Wagner's works after 1850 and the exemplary function his oeuvre obtained for the foundation of national operas elsewhere in Europe were facilitated by the intermediary work of a previous generation.

This chapter entails a comparative journey from Russia, where the first loosely institutionalized German opera companies can be found, through the cultural metropolises and opera centers of Paris and London. Although these selected countries have divergent cultural and political identities, they share not having any form of German government, and the companies producing German-language opera worked bottom up rather than top down. In Eastern European regions under Habsburg reign, on the contrary, German-language opera institutions – such as the German theater in Prague were Weber worked from 1813 to 1817 – were part of a top-down promotion of German culture. Of course, these "Habsburg" German-language opera companies affected opera activity in these areas – oscillating between adoption and what Jim Samson describes as "hostile imitation"[11]– but I have chosen case studies in which German culture is less evidently representing a center, and certainly not a center from a political point of view.

The analysis focuses on matters concerning repertoire and audiences – for example the popularity of these companies as well as the question of whether

9   Döhring 1997: 5.
10   Ther 2009: 101.
11   Samson takes over this term from Ernest Gellner in his *Music in the Balkans* (2013), pointing to a conscious attempt to distance one's own culture from a central, hegemonic cultural sphere: "The fact that humanism, cosmopolitanism and modernism were understood as essentially European or western categories not only by those at the centre but by those who were marginalised [...], produced an experience of liminality, an awareness of the minority vantage-point, that promoted (in art music at least) a culture that might be characterised by way of Gellner's category 'hostile imitation'." Samson 2013: 114.

these performances mainly attracted German immigrants or natives as well – but also local responses to German opera performances, either critical or artistic. At the same time, the foreign reception of German works had repercussions for the way German musicians and critics perceived their own opera tradition. Since the existing literature on the phenomenon of German opera abroad in the first half of the nineteenth century is rather limited – apart from some scholarly accounts of the situation in Russia – I rely heavily upon accounts in nineteenth-century music periodicals. Although this is not a history of triumph, it is certainly a history worth writing, which adds to our understanding of German opera's development by expanding our focus beyond the national level.

1   German Opera in Russia (St. Petersburg and Moscow)

After centuries of relative isolation, the first steps towards cultural exchange with Western Europe in Russian history are often attributed to the government of Peter the Great (1682–1725), who founded St. Petersburg as a potential "window to the West." In his campaign to modernize Russia, Western culture served as a tool to arouse enthusiasm among his people, or, as the Russian historian S.M. Solovieff put it in 1962: "watches, sculptures, coaches and theater performances should seduce the Russians towards reform, like toys that entice a child into learning."[12] Peter's policy also lead to the invitation of a German theater company in 1702, housed on the Red Square in Moscow. Despite the fact that the upper classes of Russian society took an increasing interest in Western art, the German performances of those days do not seem to have really appealed to them.[13]

A considerably more successful and enduring enterprise was the Italian opera that Tsarina Anna Ioannovna installed in 1734.[14] During the reign of Catherine the Great (1762–1796), many famous composers, such as Traetta, Paisiello, Sarti, Cimarosa and Martín y Soler, were invited to St. Petersburg to compose and perform their works.[15] But Catherine aimed at more than just the continuation of the Italian court opera and its repertoire. In September 1762, only two months after her coronation, she signed a decree to form a French troupe performing *opéras comiques*,[16] which reflects the gradual gravitational shift towards comic works as the center of operatic attention during the

---

12   Quoted after Lomtev 2003: 11.
13   See Ibid.: 11 + 26.
14   Amburger 1982: 202.
15   Taruskin 2010: 235.
16   Lomtev 2003: 11–12.

second half of the eighteenth century. The German *Singspiel* also profited from the growing appreciation for comic operas with spoken dialogues, and a German troupe led by Karl Knipper flourished in St. Petersburg between 1775 and 1779. Although the audience mainly consisted of the by now considerably large German enclave in St. Petersburg, performances were also attended by members of the Russian nobility, and even by Catherine herself.[17]

In the last two decades of the eighteenth century, other German troupes were active in St. Petersburg, but could not match the success of Knipper's company. The legal status of these companies changed rapidly, from free traveling troupes to state institutions. Although the status of a state institution might appear a considerable gain in prestige, this was in fact not always the case. For example, in 1783 the German theater troupe fell under supervision of the state theater administration, but this was nothing more than a rescue attempt for an enterprise that was no longer profitable.[18] In 1806, similar circumstances persuaded the government to take over the German company, when a fire had destroyed its theater.[19] Moreover, a state theater company was easier to monitor for the censors.

Despite the relative lack of success of German (music) theater companies in Russia between 1780 and 1800, German music remained *en vogue* within the higher circles of Russian society, partly thanks to the Russian diplomat Rasumovsky,[20] who worked mainly in Vienna and promoted the instrumental "Viennese Classics" of Haydn, Mozart and Beethoven.[21] Moreover, this instrumental music was far more accessible to Russian audiences than the German-language opera performances, and to a certain extent incited an interest in German opera regardless of language barriers.

After 1800, the German theater also imported many works from Vienna, mainly popular genres such as the *Zauberoper* and the *romantisch-komisches Volksmärchen*.[22] As in the German-speaking world, Kauer's *Donauweibchen* (1798), premiered in St. Petersburg in 1802,[23] proved to be the most popular

---

17   Ibid.: 34.
18   Ibid.: 31.
19   Gubkina 1999: 99.
20   Rasumovsky is chiefly remembered for the three string quartets op. 59 he commissioned from Beethoven in 1806.
21   Amburger 1982: 204.
22   Gubkina points out that the share of music theater within the repertoire of the German company expanded after the appointment of the skillful music director Anton Kalliwoda in 1800. Gubkina 1999: 98.
23   Gubkina dates its St Petersburg premiere in 1802, as well as Mel'nikova, who argues that a German comedy attended by the royal family on 6 December 1802, unspecified in state annals, was in fact Kauer's *Donauweibchen*, whereas Taruskin argues that the German *Singspiel* was first performed in 1803. It is probable, however, that Taruskin refers to the

and frequently performed work. It was arguably through Kauer's *Singspiel* that some interesting cultural transfers between German and Russian art were set in motion. Although the German company's audience mainly consisted of the lower and middle classes of the German St. Petersburg community,[24] a small group of Russian intellectuals and artists attended the performances as well, taking the German performances as a source of inspiration for the foundation of a Russian Romantic nationalism.[25]

In the case of *Das Donauweibchen*, a gradual Russification can be witnessed; the text was translated into Russian by N.S. Krasnopol'sky[26] and the action was transplanted from the Danube to the Dnepr.[27] This move was supported by six supplementary numbers by the Russian composer Stepan Ivanovich Davïdov, "added for the sake of local color to facilitate the transplanting of the action" according to Taruskin.[28] This version was followed up by a new rendition, *Lesta, ili Dneprovskaya rusalka* (*Lesta, or the Dnepr Water Nymph*, 1805), in which new music by Davïdov fully supplanted Kauer's score.

Besides *Das Donauweibchen*, which kept the stage at the German theater, Davïdov's *Lesta* also remained highly popular in St. Petersburg and Moscow during the first decades of the nineteenth century. The work inspired the famous poet Alexander Pushkin to create an unfinished dramatic poem about a water nymph, which would be set to music by Dargomïzhsky in the opera *Rusalka* (1856). Moreover, the heritage of Kauer's *Donauweibchen* found its way into Pushkin's most famous work, *Eugene Onegin* (1833). Section 2/XII of this poem ends with the sentence "Come to my golden palace, dear," an allusion to

---

first Russian-language performance. See Ibid.: 104–105, Melnikova 1996: 534, and Taruskin, lemma "Lesta, ili Dneprovskaya rusalka" from oxfordmusiconline.com, consulted on 19 February 2014.

24   Gubkina quotes the governer Vigel, who argued that "the higher German circles with a distinguished taste avoided this theater. It was the evening entertainment of the German working class and merchants." Gubkina 1999: 113.

25   For instance, the student Stěpan Petrovič Žicharev, who attended many performances, spent much time behind the stage of the German theater and wrote memoirs which form a rich source of information on the company. See Mel'nikova 1996: 523.

26   In spelling the Russian names of persons and works mentioned in this chapter, I have followed the most common orthography among musicologists, the one that is observed in the *New Grove*. I must express my gratitude to Rutger Helmers for his advice in this matter.

27   We already observed this "tendency to 'nationalize' or 'regionalize' a fairy-tale by transporting it to domestic territory" in the previous chapter. The international character of this nationalization procedure is further underscored by the fact that we find the same on Czech soil; there *Das Donauweibchen* was translated into Czech and moved to the shores of the Moldova in *Vodní žínka z Vltavy* (*The Water Sprite from the Moldova*, 1804). See Tyrrell 1988: 152.

28   See Taruskin, lemma "Lesta, ili Dneprovskaya rusalka" from oxfordmusiconline.com, consulted on 19 February 2014.

Krasnapol'sky's translation of Hensler's text "In meinem Schlößchen ist's gar fein. Komm, Ritter! Kehre bei mir ein."[29] Albeit a tiny transfer, it marks the reception of German *Singspiel* in Russian high culture, facilitated by the performances of the German St. Petersburg company.

Another interesting German-Russian transfer involving a work of Pushkin took place with the ballet *Ruslan i Lyudmila* (*Ruslan and Lyudmila*, 1821), a collaboration of the Russian choreographer Glushkovsky and the German composer Friedrich Scholtz. The piece was based on Pushkin's famous epic fairy-tale of the same name, first published in 1820 and revised in 1828. The binational collaboration not only points to an increasing integration of German musicians in Russian cultural life,[30] but also to the considerable influence that German musical Romanticism was to have on the creation of a Russian national opera tradition. Scholtz's ballet featured a magical sphere, full of transfigurations, flights and fantasy creatures, evoked by a contrasting, chromatic harmonic idiom. Mikhail Glinka, who was probably familiar with Scholtz's ballet,[31] would adopt the same technique in his famous *Ruslan i Ljudmila* of 1842, which has come to be understood as the quintessential Russian Romantic opera.[32]

Concerning this aspect in Glinka's *Ruslan*, Taruskin writes that "sorcery of a harmonic kind was perhaps the opera's most enduring legacy. Glinka established a convention that lasted at least to the time of *Firebird* and *Petrushka*, whereby human characters are represented by diatonic music and supernatural ones by chromatic."[33] Taruskin has a point in ascertaining the significance of Glinka's harmonic procedure within the history of Russian music, and the

---

29   See for example Nabokov 1975: 246–247 and Naroditskaya 2006: 220.

30   Lomtev describes this situation as follows: "Among these German composers, gradually the tendency arose to use Russian texts or Russian folk melodies for their works. [...] The new generation of 'Russian Germans' created composers that were either born in Russia and/or had lived the majority of their life in this country. To say the least, they all received their musical education in Russia. Retaining their native tongue stimulated their ethnic identification with German culture, but did not erase Russian traits in their mentality. The result was an inseparable alliance of Russian and German traditions." Lomtev 2003: 14–15.

31   Lomtev writes that many musical similarities between both works suggest that Glinka had studied Scholtz's score in detail: "The music contains several correspondences to that of Glinka's opera *Ruslan*; the rhythm of both Ruslan themes resemble each other, as do the ossification and temptation scenes, Chernomor's marches, furthermore, both works feature a violin solo as Lyudmila's *Leittimbre*. All these similarities allow us to assume that Glinka had attentively studied the score of his German colleague, and overtook several music-dramatic solutions." Ibid.: 83.

32   For the nationalist reception of Glinka's *Ruslan* see Taruskin 1977 and 1997, Frolova-Walker 1997, and Maes 2002.

33   Taruskin, lemma 'Ruslan and Lyudmila (Ruslan i Lyudmila), from *oxfordmusiconline.com*, Consulted on 19 February 2014.

octatonic and whole-tone scales which the composer employed were indeed unheard of. But the differentiation of diatonic and chromatic idioms to articulate a dramaturgy of opposing "human" and "supernatural" spheres arguably stems chiefly from German Romantic opera, and was first brought to prominence in the *Wolfsschluchtszene* of Weber's *Der Freischütz* (1821).[34]

The immense success of Weber's *Freischütz* was not lost on the Russian music world. During 1824, the opera was performed 25 times at the German theater of St. Petersburg, and also drew audiences into the Russian theater after its translation into *Volshebnïy Strelok* (*The Magic Marksman*). In 1825, the Russian version was first performed in the recently opened *Bolshoi Theater* in Moscow, under the supervision of inspector of music[35] Aleksey Verstovsky. This composer had previously written some comic, folksy dialogue operas, but, as Edward Garden writes, "*Der Freischütz* was the catalyst for Verstovsky's eventual move from opera-vaudeville to what may be called Russian opera-*Singspiel*."[36] In the same year, Verstovsky wrote an article named *Fragments from the History of Dramatic Music*, in which he stated "that the age of music would be over, and all its beauty exhausted – if Weber had not written his *Freischütz*."[37]

Verstovsky's most successful work was *Askol'dova mogila* (*Askold's Grave*), premiered in 1835 at the Moscow *Bolshoi Theater*. Besides the rather conventional folksy numbers, the work contains a baritone part with a complex and impressive musical characterization. This is the part of the Unknown, who acts as an evil genius, claiming to be a comrade of the romantic tenor Vseslav, whereas in fact he frustrates the latter's fortune with his beloved Nadezhda. This Unknown is closely modeled after Weber's Caspar. Moreover, the opera contains a melodramatic witch scene in the fourth act that resembles the sensational *Schauerromantik* of the *Wolfsschluchtszene*.[38] Verstovsky's work was by far the most often performed Russian opera during the nineteenth

---

34   This observation does not imply that Glinka's *Ruslan* is chiefly based on German opera models. Considering its huge five-act structure and the prominence of ballet and ceremony, the model of French grand opéra definitely contributed more to Glinka's style than the "magic" elements that were arguably inspired by German forerunners.

35   The exact function of Verstovsky is mentioned by Abraham. See Abraham 1984: 327.

36   Garden, lemma 'Aleksey Nikolayevich Verstovsky' from oxfordmusiconline.com, consulted at 25 february 2014.

37   Quoted after Abraham 1984: 327.

38   In all these respects, Meyerbeer's *Robert le diable* (1831) may also have been an inspiration, but Verstovsky's fascination for Weber and *Der Freischütz* is clearly more outspoken. Moreover, Meyerbeer and his librettist Scribe also derived many elements of *Robert* from *Der Freischütz*. See 4.2.

century,[39] but regardless of his popularity, Verstovsky severely suffered from the iconical status attributed to Glinka as the founding father of the Russian operatic canon. This process started already after the St. Petersburg premiere of Glinka's *Zhizn' za tsarya* (*A Life for the Tsar*) in 1836,[40] and continued until it fully eclipsed Verstovsky and his contribution to Russian opera.

Why did Verstovsky's *Askold* ultimately not fit into the discourse of Russia's opera history? On the one hand, the folksy remnants of *Singspiel* may have appeared to be outdated, not state-of-the-art enough in 1835. On the other, the overt Weberian influences in *Askold* may have made the work "not Russian enough"[41] in the eyes of those who established the Russian operatic canon. But the matter is more complicated than that, considering the extent to which Glinka actually incorporated foreign, particularly Italian, styles and techniques in his *Life for the Tsar*, an opera that was nonetheless received as a genuinely Russian masterpiece in the years after its premiere.[42]

In the discourse that was employed to present Glinka's "cosmopolitan" work as a "national" treasure, a Russian adaption of German Romantic notions of national culture is clearly discernable, resulting in rhetoric strategies that are highly similar to the conceptualization of German opera. In many cases, the ties between these Russian critics and a German esthetic education are overt. The diasporic chauvinism of the many local German musicians teaching Russian students sometimes led to hilarious misconceptions. In a report about his travel to St. Petersburg, the French opera and ballet composer Adolphe Adam mentions the following:

> Far from home, German musicians display a degree of chauvinism that you will not find among their countrymen living in the homeland. German professors teach the Russians that German music, especially instrumental music, is superior to the triviality of French music. This has

---

39   Abraham mentions "four hundred performances in Moscow alone during the nineteenth century and some two hundred more at St Petersburg," adding that "it was the first Russian opera to be produced in the United States (New York, 1869)." Ibid.: 329.

40   In that year, he wrote to a friend "that the Dawn of Russian Opera occurred in Moscow and not in Petersburg. I am the first admirer of Glinka's most splendid talent, but I will not and cannot yield the claim of precedence." Quoted after Ibid.: 330.

41   "Not Russian Enough" is the evocative title of Rutger Helmer's dissertation, in which, rather than affirming the "canonized" classics, the author aims to shed light upon those works that have a problematic status within the "negotiation of nationalism in nineteenth-century Russian opera." See Helmers 2014.

42   A thorough discussion of the "Italianisms" of Glinka's *A Life for the Tsar* as well as their reception can be found in the first chapter of Helmers's dissertation.

fueled the misconception that French composers like Auber, Halévy, and me are in fact Germans who came to Paris to compose French operas, like Meyerbeer. One day, a Russian lady even complimented me by saying that I spoke French without a German accent![43]

Although Adam's account certainly involves a degree of exaggeration, the German influence on Russian music esthetics and on local discussions concerning the merits of Russian opera can hardly be overlooked. An important voice in these discussions was Yanuariy Neverov, who had studied briefly in Berlin. Taruskin paraphrases Neverov's judgment on Glinka's work as declaring that "delightful Russian tunes" by themselves would never create a truly national style. For that you needed more than tunes; in fact you needed more than a musical style. You had to achieve the "organic unity" that comes from a "dominating idea."[44] In short, it addresses both the ideology of organic unity and the doctrine of the native composer, internalizing foreign influences to take his art to a next level (Weber's "Aber er greift alles tiefer"). Helmers describes this German influence on Russian music esthetics in the following way:

---

43   "In Petersburg sind fast alle Künstler Teutsche, und in folge dessen zwar ausgezeichnete Musiker, aber sie tragen ihre Vorliebe für Instrumentalmusik, und zwar für teutsche, auch auf ihre Schüler über. Diese Erscheinung ist merkwürdig. Weit entfernt von ihrem Vaterlande, zeigen die Teutschen hier eine nazionale Eigenliebe, ein Nationalgefühl, das man in Teutschland selbst nicht findet. So haben sie den Russen die Ueberlegenheit teutscher Musik über die aller anderen Nazionen beigebracht, und daher geniesst die französische Musik nur sehr wenig Achtung; und jedoch in diesem Punkte nicht gar zu sehr gegen die vorliegenden Thatsachen zu verstossen, habe sie den Ausweg erdacht, unsere französischen Komponisten in Teutsche zu verwandeln. Kaum wird man glauben, dass es in Russland eine sehr weit verbreitete Meinung ist, Auber, Halevy und ich seien Teutsche, welche in Paris Opern schreiben, wie Meyerbeer, Rossini und andere Tondichter des Auslandes. Eines Tages machte mir eine Dame Komplimente über meine treffliche Aussprache des Französischen und meinte, ich hätte doch gar keinen deutschen Akzent." Originally published in *La France Musicale*, it was translated and included in the AMZ, accompanied by a conciliatory footnote from the editor that "it is obvious that Adam does not know the Germans well (Man sieht, dass Herr Adam die Teutschen nicht kennt)." AMZ XLII/36, 2 September 1840: 747.

44   Taruskin 2010: 237. We must add, however, that Neverov's ideas cannot be explained as chiefly Herderian. Perhaps the gained interest in folk music is, but notions about "organic unity" and a "dominating idea" arguably came from Schelling rather than Herder. The influence of Schelling on Russian Romantic thought is emphasized by Helmers (2014: 5) as well as Lowe (1982: 307), and summarized by Thaden, pointing out that "in Schelling many young Russian intellectuals believed they had found what they wanted: a philosophy that would provide them with a metaphysical basis for their own ideas on Russian nationality, and for the evolving of a new cultural synthesis that was peculiarly Russian and universal." Thaden 1954: 515–516.

It is a familiar irony that many features of nineteenth-century Russian nationalism were based on the imported work of German thinkers such as Herder, Schelling, and Hegel. In their attempts to cope with their own sense of backwardness of the German-speaking lands compared to France, these authors had offered valuable moral and philosophical support to the Russians.[45]

The fact that Glinka had mastered a cosmopolitan opera style of composing did not compromise the Russian "spirit" of his work, but rather underscored the fact that Russian opera was now becoming a power to be reckoned with on an international level. Or, in the words of Taruskin: "Glinka's *narodnost'* [national significance] was thus paradoxically proved by his cosmopolitan eclecticism. [...] It affirmed the universality of Russian culture, hence its superiority to all other cultures."[46]

Another Russian agent bringing in German music esthetics[47] was the critic Vladimir Odoevsky, who was involved in the creation of Glinka's *A Life* and is often referred to as the "Russian Faust"[48] or "Russian Hoffman."[49] Compared to the latter's often cryptic and ambiguous music criticism, Odoevsky's was rather straightforward and one-dimensional. Lowe states that "there is a remarkable coherence to Odoevskii's opera criticism," adding that "what emerges from Odoevskii's writings on Mozart, Weber, and Wagner is what has been suggested earlier: for Odoevskii there are no bad German opera composers and no good

---

45   Helmers 2014: 5. In the case of Russian opera, as with the discourse surrounding its German counterpart, the "backwardness" of having to rely on foreign influences in order to create something prestigious, was generally turned upside down into a positive force.

46   Taruskin 2010: 239.

47   Odoevsky's predilection for German music and culture was, like Neverov's, indirectly related to an education on German soil, as he received his musical education at Moscow University from D.I. Shprevich, "a graduate of the University of Erfurt whose doctoral dissertation was on the subject *How much music helps to form a sense of good and grace.*" Campbell 1989: 2.

48   His contemporary colleague-critic Vissarion Belinsky characterized Odoevsky in 1839 as "a kind and simple man, but worn down by the cares of life and therefore colourless like a worn-out handkerchief. Nowadays he is mostly interested in mysticism and magnetism." This image of a gray professor dedicating his life to occult science, together with his clear partisanship for German culture, makes the designation of a "Russian Faust" understandable. Quoted after Campbell 1989: 8.

49   See Taruskin 2010: 239. The nickname "Hoffmann" seems appropriate because, like E.T.A. Hoffmann, he was famous for music criticism as well as for his prose fiction, in which he also focused on the "flimsy boundary between sanity and madness, [and] both writers dealt in the fantastic, magic, supernatural, art and the antithesis of the ideal and the real." Quote from Campbell 1989: 19.

Italian ones."[50] Odoevsky's Germanophile leaning did not hinder his chauvinism for Russian opera, but rather resulted in a spiritual alliance against the "venereal disease"[51] of Italian opera. In an 1823 article, Odoevsky argued that "the audience's enthusiasm for Rossini's music [...] epitomizes all that is rotten in the beau monde," a statement that just as well could have been written down by a German commentator in the *AMZ*.[52] But Taruskin points out that "Russians drew an even sharper distinction than the Germans themselves between the 'spirituality' of German romanticism and the 'sensuality' of Italian opera."[53]

In 1836, when *A Life for the Tsar* was created, a reconciliation of this German-Italian antithesis in the Russian music of Glinka was still an aspiring ideal.[54] But when Nicholas I installed a prestigious Italian opera troupe for the 1843–1844 season, Russian opera life was monopolized, leaving little room for non-Italian operatic initiatives. Other companies suddenly faced a severe lack of funding, and Russian composers rarely got the opportunity to stage their works with sufficient means. Little wonder that in this changed climate, hostility towards the Italians increased considerably. There is some irony in the fact that Nicholas's Italian troupe was presented as a contribution to the cosmopolitan status of St Petersburg, since, as a contemporary said, "without an Italian troupe it would always seem as if something was lacking in the capital of the foremost empire of the world!"[55] At the same time, this "cosmopolitan" gesture put an end to the impressive cultural diversity of theater performances in the city. In 1831, an anonymous reporter in the *AMZ* observed that "in the past three years, Petersburg was certainly the only place in the world where four public theaters

---

50   Lowe 1984: 313–314.

51   Lowe quotes a fragment from Odoevsky's *Russian and Italian Opera* (1839), in which he writes that "to try to infect our healthy musical sense with Italian cachexia is truly almost a crime." Ibid.: 309.

52   Quoted after Ibid.: 309.

53   Taruskin 2010: 239.

54   Taruskin writes, for example, that "German music in Russian eyes was all *dukh*, brains without beauty; Italian music was all *chuvstvennost,*' beauty without brains. Glinka resolved that his music, Russian music, would uniquely have both brains and beauty." Ibid.: 239.

55   Quoted after Helmers 2014: 8. This phenomenon can be linked to the tension between patriotism and nationalism in nineteenth-century Russian culture. In his lemma on 'Nationalism' on *Grove Music Online* Taruskin, for example, points out that: "Russian patriotism, as long as it was defined by the aristocracy, was not necessarily interested in fostering indigenous artistic productivity. It could be satisfied by foreign imports that enhanced Russia's self-esteem and prestige in the world." *oxfordmusiconline.com*. Consulted on 9 November 2015.

of four different nationalities could be found, a Russian, a German, a French and an Italian one. If each national company would have presented only national operas, this could have been highly interesting for lovers of art."[56]

The sense of lost opportunities that emerges from this comment is probably still modest compared to the disappointment that Russians felt after the cultural erosion of 1843. In 1844, the German theater terminated their opera branch.[57] In previous decades, the opera repertoire of the company had already consisted chiefly of foreign works in German translation, a development that Lomtev links to an increasingly international orientation of German Russians,[58] but one that is not exclusive to Russia. After the "roaring twenties," in which German opera burst upon the international opera scene with works in the wake of *Der Freischütz*, the development of a national tradition stagnated in the thirties and international interest shifted towards the extremely successful French *grand opéras*. Only a few German works performed at the German theaters of Russia significantly brought about a response in the coming of age of Russian opera: Kauer's *Donauweibchen*, Weber's *Freischütz* and *Oberon*, and arguably Mozart's *Zauberflöte*.[59] In the end, Russian composers

---

56   "In den drey letztverflossenen Jahren war Petersburg unstreitig der einzige Ort, der vier bestehende öffentliche Theater von vier verschiedenen Nationen aufzuweisen hatte, nämlich ein russisches, ein deutsches, ein französisches und ein italienisches. Hätte man nun auf jeder dieser National-Bühnen auch nur National-Opern gegeben, so hätte dies für den Kunstfreund das grösste Interesse haben müssen." *AMZ* XXXIII/41, 12 October 1831: 675.

57   Lomtev 2003: 118.

58   Lomtev compares the share of original German-language operas in the high days of Knipper's company (1776–1779) with the situation between 1838 and 1842. In the time of Knipper, German operas constituted 80 to 90 percent of the repertoire, whereas around 1840, their share lay between 10 to 30 percent, with French operas in translation clearly in the lead. (diagrams can be found in Ibid.: 35 + 52. Lomtev argues that "these changes in the repertoire are directly related to audience taste. In the first quarter of the nineteenth century, the theater aimed to attract those German immigrants visiting the performances in order to establish their cultural ties with the homeland, a relation that was no longer obligatory for the next generation. They inherited the appreciation for German culture from their parents but this did not hinder their general interest in French and Italian opera." Ibid.: 52.

59   Taruskin discerns remnants of *Die Zauberflöte* in Glinka's *Ruslan*, stating: "That the models for his [Glinka's] second opera included Mozart, *Die Zauberflöte* in particular, can be readily seen not only from the gaudy glockenspiel and glass-harmonica colors in the magic music but also from the act 3 finale, in which the good sorcerer Finn first intervenes like a Sarastro to break the spell woven by the evil sorceress Naína (=Queen of the Night), then stands in as a tenor to complete the vocal complement for a concluding quartet [...] that reflects something of the serene radiance of 'Bald prangt, den Morgen zu verkünden.'" Taruskin 1997: 66.

and critics profited more from German discourse on opera than from the example of German operas themselves.

After 1850, the alliance of Russian opera and German esthetics would become more problematic. This is partly the result of a gradual shift from idealist to conservative, ethnic forms of nationalism, of which Slavophile thought is a clear manifestation.[60] In this cultural climate, ethnic solidarity with Russian forefathers, and to a lesser extent with other Slavic peoples, became more important than sympathy for a Western music culture that was rapidly taking over the hegemony that Italian opera had long executed. In 1862, Anton Rubinstein opened the St. Petersburg conservatory, modeled after the Leipzig conservatory that Mendelssohn had founded in 1843. Rubinstein, a Russian composer with German-Jewish roots who had studied in Germany, soon became the object of derision for the dilettante composers of The Mighty Handful[61] and their house critic Vladimir Stasov. From an institutional point of view, German music on Russian soil became a symbol of rigid academism, no longer an allied force in a liberation process, but a foreign oppressor itself.[62]

2   German Opera in Paris

In an 1870 *Dictionnaire musico-dramatique*, the Paris *Opéra* was wryly characterized as a "Grand French theater consecrated by the French taxpayers to the glory of foreign composers."[63] Although this mock definition specifically refers to the operatic situation in Paris in the 1850's and 60's – a time when the *Opéra* had turned into a bastion of conservatism unassailable for native composers – the prominence of and openness towards foreign composers typifies Parisian

---

60   See for example Rabow-Edling 2006.
61   The Mighty Handful, Mighty Five or *moguchaya kuchka* were a group of composers, led by Balakirev, including Mussorgsky, Rimsky-Korsakov, Borodin and Cui, who, during the sixties and seventies of the nineteenth century, created a highly characteristic Russian national opera esthetic and shaped the image of Russian music for years to come.
62   Of course, the image of German music in Russian music culture was not uniform, since after 1850 the German musical world itself was split in partisans of a *Neudeutsche Schule* advocating opera and program music on the one hand and supporters of instrumental genres on the other. In fact, Taruskin even sees both Rubinstein's conservatory and the esthetic horizon of the Mighty Handful as signs of a "thoroughgoing Germanification" of Russian musical life (Taruskin 1997: 67), but Maes lays bare to what an extent Balakirev and other nationalist musicians greeted Rubinstein's initiative with anti-Semitic, anti-German xenophobia. Maes 2002: 39–40.
63   "Théâtre français solennel consacré, par les contriables français, à la gloire des composit-eurs étrangers." Quoted after Lacombe 1997: 19.

opera life in all its historical stages. More than in any other culture, non-native musicians left their mark on the development of French, or rather Parisian, opera: the founding father of French opera during the seventeenth century was the Italian Lully; the reform of eighteenth-century *tragédie lyrique* was carried out by the Bohemian Gluck; in the following decades, the *opéra comique* benefitted from the work of the Walloon Grétry and the Italian Cherubini; and grand opera was dominated by the Italian Spontini and German Meyerbeer during the first half of the nineteenth century.

But opposition to this embrace of foreign talent could already be found in 1801, as shows from a plea for a *patriotisme lyrique*, penned down by the French composer Michael Woldemar in *Le Courrier des spectacles*:

> It is because I am convinced that Paris is the home of the most distinguished talents that I am surprised that [...] foreigners are deified, whereas it would not have been so difficult for us to mount *Les Bardes*, *Adam* [both operas by François Le Sueur], and *Sémiramis* [by Charles-Simon Catel], masterpieces of which the nation can be proud, or *Adrien* [by Etienne Méhul] and other justly celebrated works. But when will we have a *patriotisme lyrique* !!![64]

The foreign work that mainly incited Woldemar's frustration was *Les mystères d'Isis*, composed by the Bohemian Ludwig Wenzel Lachnith on a libretto by Etienne Morel de Chédeville. This reworking of Mozart's *Die Zauberflöte* was premiered at the Paris *Opéra* in August 1801. It marks the first large-scale success of a German opera on French soil.[65] Although this performance remained a rather isolated event, – it would take until the 1820s until German culture and German operas gained a more substantial hold on French audiences – its reception contains in embryonic form many of the dynamics that we will also find in later cultural transfers between German and French opera.

It is clear that around 1800, Mozart's music was considered to be an exotic and progressive refreshment for the Parisian music scene. Mongrédien, for example, writes that "his name served as a catchword for a large group of people who saw themselves as being modern and fashionable, and who more or less

---

64   "C'est au contraire parce-que je suis persuade que Paris renferme les plus distingués, que je suis surpris [...] que l'on y divinize les étrangers pendant qu'il n'en auroit pas tant coûté pour nouys donner les *Bardes*, *Adam* et *Sémiramis*, chefs-d'œuvre dont la nation peut s'énorgueillir, comme d'*Adrien* et autres si justement célèbres. Mais quand aurons-nous un patriotisme lyrique !!!" Quoted after Cannone 1991: 166.

65   Mozart's *Entführung* had already been given at the *Lycée des Arts* in 1798 as *L'Enlèvement au serail*, but had a far more limited effect on the musical world of Paris than *Les Mystères*.

despised contemporary French music," regardless of the fact that "his music was in reality still very unfamiliar to Parisians."[66] Because of this, it hardly mattered to them that Lachnith and Morel adapted Mozart's *Singspiel* to the principles of French *grand opéra*, creating a far more serious action, adding a ballet and changing the spoken dialogues into recitatives, while simultaneously reshuffling and eliminating parts of the music and inserting numbers from other works.[67]

Moreover, those who knew the original in some cases greeted Lachnith and Morel's alterations as a welcome and creditable improvement of an opera that suffered from Schikaneder's poor libretto. For example, a critic of the *Mercure de France* wrote that Morel's libretto "is much less ridiculous than the German narrative," praising that "in the chaos of violent and barbarous scenes that make up *La Flûte enchantée*, [Morel] has discovered a principle of action and the knot of a bearable intrigue for the Parisian theater."[68] These Frenchmen were joined by the German Carl-Friedrich Cramer, who in his *Anecdotes sur W.G. [Gottlieb] Mozart* (1801) admitted that Morel had introduced "that link between scenes, those transitions missing in the German original, which was of course composed for a secondary Viennese theater."[69]

This moderate tone could not be found among most other German inhabitants of the French capital. In 'Nachrichten eines deutschen Künstlers in Paris über die Aufführung der Zauberflöte daselbst', published in the AMZ in October 1801, the anonymous author wrote:

> It is actually a lie that Mozart's *Zauberflöte* was performed here, it was really only a mixture, containing fragments of it, combined with numbers from *Don Juan*, *La Clemenza di Tito*, and *Figaro*, along with contributions of Lachnith himself. Anyone familiar with Mozart's opera is embittered,

66   Ibid.: 196. Until 1800, it was Haydn rather than Mozart whose works were regularly performed in Paris, partly thanks to his *Paris Symphonies* (1785–1786). H.C. Robbins Landon writes for example that "during the early 1780's Haydn's symphonies were performed at the various Parisian concerts with unvarying success, and numerous publishing houses [...] issued every new symphonic work by Haydn as soon as they could lay hands on a copy." Robbins Landon 1963: xiv. Mozart's 1778 *Paris Symphony* had made considerably less waves in the French capital.

67   An elaborate comparison of the German original and the French adaption can be found in Angermüller 1983: 32–56.

68   Quoted after Mongrédien 1985: 204.

69   "Ajoutez que n'ayant eté composé que pour un theater secondaire de Vienne, il manque dans l'original teuton de cette liaison de scènes, de ces transitions, etc." Cramer 1801: 21. Cramer's publication was actually a translation of anecdotes about Mozart written by Rochlitz, which had previously been included in the *Allgemeine Musikalische Zeitung*, but this quotation is a personal addition of Cramer.

and *bonmots* rain down upon Mr. Lachn.: The "opera" is called an "operation [surgery]," "les mystères d'isis" is rephrased into "les misères d'ici" etc.[70]

Cynical *bonmots* from German commentators would continue to rain upon Lachnith's work: Reichardt spoke of "unsere verhunzte [butchered] Zauberflöte" in 1802,[71] an 1803 dictum 'Pariser Zauberflöte' was published in the *AMZ* saying: "Nehmt unsern Dank; ihr halft Sankt Mozart aus den Nöthen! / Der Zauber ist nun weg, habt ihr doch noch die Flöten!,"[72] and the trope of disenchantment was reinforced in the same periodical in 1805, where Lachnith's adaptation was dismissed as "der entzauberten Zauberflöte."[73]

These reports self-evidently fueled animosity towards the French opera world in the homeland, but some German Parisians directly addressed their French fellow-citizens to voice their contempt. A German woman calling herself Wilhelmine wrote an extensive critique of *Les mystères* in *Le Publiciste*, which Stendhal later included in his *Vie de Mozart* (1815):

> How is it possible that no one saw that transforming this work into a grand opera was to distort its nature? [...] The musical unity is disturbed, the general aim is effaced, the enchantment disappears [...]. Constantly, an interesting situation, the developments of which are quite natural, is replaced by one of those terribly cold contrivances told over and over again and upon which the French theater lives.[74]

Dismissals such as this one seem not really to have affected those Frenchmen who adored *Les mystères* as a delightful introduction to Mozart's music. And although German commentators specifically deplored the disappearance of

---

70   "Es ist eigentlich nicht wahr, dass man Mozarts *Zauberflöte* gegeben habe; es war eine Oper aus dieser, aus D. Juan, der Clemenza di Tito, und Figaro von Mozart, nebst eigenen Zusätzen des Herrn Lachnith zusammengebracht. Alle, die M. Oper vorher schon genauer kannten, sind darüber erbittert, und lassen Bonmots auf Herr Lachn. regnen. Die 'Opéra' nennen sie seine 'Opération', die 'les mystères d'isis', 'les misères d'ici' u. dgl." *AMZ* IV/5, 28 October 1801: 69–70.

71   Quoted after Mongrédien 1985: 207.

72   *AMZ* V/46, 10 August 1803: 768.

73   "You rescued the saintly Mozart, Receive our gratitude! / the magic now has vanished, but you retained the flute!" *AMZ* VIII/3, 16 October 1805: 35.

74   "Comment n'a-t-on pas vu que c'était dénaturer cet ouvrage que de le transformer en grand opera? [...] l'unité musicale est troublée, l'intention génerale est efface, l'enchantement disparaît. [...] On voit que, constamment, une situation intéressante, et dont les développements sont pleins de naturel, est remplacée par une de ses combinaisons si ribattues et si froides qui font vivre le théâtre français." Stendhal 1817: 348–352.

elements of the work that they considered to be genuinely "German" – its musical unity, its enchantment and its characteristic blend of the comical and solemn – the adaptation did not hinder French critics to embrace Lachnith's version as an undeniably German artwork. For example, in 1801 Julien-Louis Geoffroy, one of the most influential French opera critics of the early nineteenth century,[75] stated in the *Journal des Débats* that "it seems that Mozart was called upon to reform this beautiful art, disfigured in Italy and suffocating under false brilliance. It is a German who brings us back to nature, to good taste, to truth. What purity of melody. What simplicity! What religious character, somber and melancholy in the marches and in the priests' ceremonies!"[76]

Regardless of the fact that it took until the 1820s until a more substantial vogue for German operas would arise in the French capital, the esthetic positions taken in the case of *Les Mystères d'Isis* were to be revisited over and over again during the nineteenth century. In general, we find a genuine interest in German opera among the French, on the condition that the work concerned will be adapted to the formal prerequisites of French genres, which in its turn appalls German musicians and critics while simultaneously reinforcing feelings of superiority in esthetic matters. One can easily imagine how this animosity would be intensified after the Napoleonic Wars, when a work such as Weber's *Freischütz* was emphatically received as a glorification of German national culture in the homeland. The conflict hardened even further during the years surrounding the Franco-German War (1870–1871).

The unequivocal dismissive tone of many contemporary German commentaries on French operatic practices tends to overshadow the fact that the French did indeed develop a strong interest in and appreciation for German Romantic culture during the first decades of the nineteenth century. A first milestone in this development was Madame de Staël's *De l'Allemagne* (1813), which created an idyllic image of Germany as a decentralized, rural country of *Dichter und Denker*, a foil designed foremost to criticize the character of Napoleonic France.[77] De Staël stirred interest in German literature in the 1820s, resulting in the famous 1828 translations of Goethe's *Faust* (Part I) by Gérard de Nerval and the twenty volumes of E.T.A. Hoffmann tales translated by the German émigré Loève-Veimars, published between 1829 and 1833. According

---

75   For a detailed account of his critical output and esthetic position, see Ellis 1995: 8–14.

76   "Il semble que Mozart ait appelé pour reformer ce bel art, défiguré en Italie, éttoufé par de faux brillans. C'est un allemand qui nous ramène à la nature, au bon goût, à la verité. Quelle pureté de mélodie ! quelle simplicité ! quel caractère religieux, sombre et mélancolique, dans les marches et les cérémonies des prêtres." Quoted after Cannone 1991: 152.

77   Heinrich Heine would comment that "the good lady saw in our country only those things she wanted to see (Die gute Dame sah bei uns nur was sie sehen wollte)." Quoted after Werner 1998: 191.

to Lacombe, Loève-Veimar's adaptions "wilfully stray from their German originals."[78] Indeed there is something peculiar about French translation practice in the Romantic era, which generally entails a far more creative and liberal interpretation of original sources than a fairly literal rendition in French would require. John R. Whittaker, for example, argues that "translation is an inescapable feature of French Romanticism," and adds that "it may [...] be argued that the position of translation is at the core of Romanticism and that, by contrast with the writers of previous centuries, the Romantics turn to it as part of their main creative activity."[79]

We find the same in the Parisian opera scene, where composer-critic François-Henri-Joseph Blaze, better known as Castil-Blaze, devoted his creative talent to "translations" of foreign works rather than to original composition. He was mainly active at the *Théâtre de l'Odéon*. In a rigidly regulated Parisian opera infrastructure in which companies held monopolies concerning the performance of certain genres, *l'Odéon* had to find its niche. The *Opéra*, for example, had exclusive rights to operas with recitative, while a newly-created *opéra comique* could only be given at the eponymous company, and Italian operas were restricted to the *Théâtre italien*. Therefore, *l'Odéon* had to content itself with the music-theatrical leftovers. These consisted of old *opéras comiques* with an expired copyright on the one hand, pasticcios composed of fragments of famous operas and non-Italian foreign operas on the other.

Since newly composed French and Italian operas were exclusively given by the three other companies mentioned above, producing German operas was the best strategy for the administration of *l'Odéon* to attract attention of Parisian audiences. Of course, this was an attempt to capitalize on the vogue for German culture and more specifically on the sudden boom of Weber mania after the premiere of *Der Freischütz*. But although Weber's piece, premiered in 1824, would indeed turn out to be the biggest box-office hit during the 1820s at the *Odéon*, the first German opera success was in fact Peter von Winter's *Das unterbrochene Opferfest*, premiered six weeks earlier in a French version called *La sacrifice interrompue*.[80] On the one hand, these two German operas were not easily digestible for Parisian audiences; Everist, for example, sums up various contemporary newspaper reports stating that these works were "difficult to grasp and required multiple hearings to assimilate."[81] But in December 1824, a critic from *Le Corsaire* praised the two German works performed at the *Odéon*

---

78   Lacombe 2001: 29.
79   Whittaker 2010: 79.
80   Mark Everist argues that this work "had blazed the trail so successfully followed by *Robin des Bois* [an adaptation of Weber's *Freischütz*] with no less than thirty-one performances in 1824 and 1825." Everist 2001: 73.
81   Ibid.: 251.

as not only a welcome alternative to the degenerate nature of contemporary Italian opera, but even comparing German musicians to Orpheus, the "patron saint"[82] of the genre:

> The triumph at the Odéon of operas belonging to the German school will strike a devastating blow to fanaticism for things from south of the Alps. [...] The Rhine will no longer be a barrier to our operatic enthusiasm; and just as we once sought our idols in the villages of degenerate Italy, we shall henceforth forge a glorious alliance with the Orpheuses of a land that was the birthplace of Gluck and Mozart.[83]

In order to sustain the success achieved with the performances of Von Winter and Weber, more German works in French translation were given at the *Odéon*; *Der Augenarzt* (by Adolph Gyrowetz, presented as *La jeune aveugle* in 1826), *Die Schweizerfamilie* (by Joseph Weigl, given as *Emmeline ou La famille suisse* in 1827) and *Adele von Budoy* (by Conradin Kreutzer, in a French version called *La folle de Glaris* in 1827).[84] Even if the five German works performed at the *Odéon* form a rather random selection, they did provide Parisians an impression of what was going on in the German opera world.

But the main attraction of the *Odéon* was clearly Castil-Blaze's version of Weber's *Freischütz*, rechristened into *Robin des bois*. The chief reason for the new title was the fact that *Le chausseur noir*, a name that is more in line with the original work, was already frequently in use for other pieces performed in Paris theaters, and was therefore not distinctive enough.[85] Castil-Blaze and theater director Thomas-Marie-François Sauvage seem to have been inspired by the Europe-wide Walter Scott craze of the 1820s when they chose to rename Samiel into Robin Hood.[86] This change makes little sense though, because the

---

82 Although the status of Orpheus as the essence of opera – think of Adorno's "All opera is Orpheus" in *Bürgerliche Oper* (Adorno 1959: 24) – is probably a twentieth-century invention, the notion of reform, of returning to the roots of the genre is implicitly present in this quote through the reference to Gluck.

83 "Le triomphe à l'Odéon des opéras empruntés à l'école allemande, portera un coup terrible au fanatisme ultramontain. [...] Le Rhin ne sera plus une barrière à notre enthousiasme lyrique, et si nous avons été chercher des idoles dans les hameaux de l'Italie degénerée, nous formerons dorénavant une brillante alliance avec les Orphées d'un pays qui a vu naître Gluck et Mozart." *Le Corsaire*, 8 December 1824. Quoted after Lacombe 1997: 301.

84 Titles derived from Everist 2002: 290–297.

85 See Heidlberger 1994: 316.

86 Rossini's Scott-based *La donna del lago* (1819) was the first important opera on a tale by the British writer, and in 1825, Adrien Boieldieu was incredibly successful with his *La dame blanche*, an opéra comique with a libretto by Eugène Scribe based on Scott's novels *Guy Mannering*, *The Monastery* and *The Abbot*. A year later Castil-Blaze created a Rossini pasticcio called *Ivanhoé*, also performed at the *Odéon* and even attended by the Scott

Robin Hood/Locksley of Walter Scott's *Ivanhoe* (1820) has nothing in common with Weber's satanic ghost. Less problematic is the decision to move the action to England, and to transfer the *Wolfsschluchtszene* to the ruins of St. Dunstan, since Kind's libretto was obviously rooted in the British tradition of Gothic literature.[87] We may witness in it a shift from a specifically German blend of Romanticism to a more general, transnational type.

On top of these changes in locale, Castil-Blaze and Sauvage altered the storyline and reshuffled the music, albeit to a far lesser extent than Lachnith and Morel had done in the case of *Les Mystères*. In an open letter to the editor of the *Journal des Débats*, published on 25 January 1826, Castil-Blaze articulated two motives for his reworking, one concerning the general nature of French opera life, the other related to the nature of Weber's *Freischütz* itself:

> It is well-known that a foreign opera cannot be successful in a French theater if it is not reshaped according to our dramatic rules. Therefore, you have to eliminate and adjust the music and the *mise en scène*, in order to compose a French opera with elements derived from the foreign score. [Concerning the premiere of *Der Freischütz*] I initially decided not to change any of the music. [...] And guess what happened? Everybody knows; the piece was hissed at over and over. After realizing that this opera could not stand on its own two feet, I considered mutilating it, and I succeeded in doing, because since then it has been marching on at such a pace that one wonders if it will ever stop; after 125 performances, the adapter's operation must be regarded a successful one.[88]

---

himself, see Ibid.: 186–187. For a more detailed account of the fascination for Walter Scott in France in this period, see Massmann 1972.

87   Annegret Fauser argues that the move to England did not change the fact that French audiences generally perceived *Der Freischütz* as a genuinely German story, and shows that some commentators criticized the transplantation of the action as senseless and unnecessary. She cites, for example, the *Drapeau blanc* reviewer A. Martainville, who stated on 9 December 1824 that "we do not understand why the *arrangeur* has decided to transport the scene from Germany to England. He should have let this thoroughly German product remain on its soil (Nous ignorons pourquoi *l'arrangeur* a jugé à propos de transporter le lieu de la scène d'Allemagne en Angleterre. Il fallait laisser dans son terroir cette production toute germanique)." Fauser 2001: 262–263.

88   "Il est reconnu qu'un opéra étranger ne sauroit réussir chez nous, sur un theater français, s'il n'est dispose d'après notre système dramatique. Il faut donc couper et adjuster la musique, la mettre en scène, et composer un opéra français avec des elements pris dans les partitions étrangères. [...] Je résolus de ne rien changer à la musique [...]. Qu'arriva-t-il? Tout le monde le sait; la pièce fut sifflé et resifflé. Voyant que cet opéra ne pouvoit se tenir sur ses jambes, j'imaginai de l'*estropier*, et je le fis avec tant de bonheur que depuis lors il a marché d'un tel pas, qu'on ne sait point s'il doit s'arrêter un jour; et cent cinquante representations viennent justifier l'opération de l'arrangeur." Complete letter published in Heidlberger 1994: 483–484. This statement was obviously a slap in the face of Weber.

Castil-Blaze's publication was actually a response to an open letter that Weber had written to several Parisian newspapers to protest against Castil-Blaze's
working method. Before taking this drastic measure, he had approached his
French colleague with two personal letters, which, however, remained unan-
swered. Notwithstanding the fact that Weber was most probably quite upset
about the way in which Castil-Blaze had shaken up a work that had been
meticulously put together with a clear purpose,[89] his main concern seems to
have been to question alleged copyright violations.[90] In the years following
the premiere of *Der Freischütz*, Weber and his publisher Maurice Schlesinger, a
Paris-based descendant of the famous Schlesinger music publishers family in
Berlin, had hoped for an opera success in Paris.[91] Their campaign was frustrated

---

Whether Castil-Blaze was telling the truth about his use of Weber's original music during the flawed premiere and his glorious reconfiguration for the second performance,
only nine days later, has been a matter of debate for centuries. In 1913, Georges Servières
criticized the "falsity of Castil-Blaze's legend [la fausseté de la légende]" (Servières 1913:
37), and in 1942, Hans Schnoor spoke of "Castil-Blaze's attempt to sweep his guilt under
the carpet [....] with persistent insolence" and "cynical mystification (Wie Castil-Blaze
seine Schuld vertuschte) [....] mit hartnäckiger Unverfrorenheit [und] zynischer Mysti-
fikation)." (Schnoor 1985: 191) Heidlberger acknowledges that it seems improbable that
Castil-Blaze could have carried out all those changes in such a short period of time
(Heidlberger 1994: 319). Castil-Blaze's thesis is, however, supported by Adolphe Jullien,
who wrote in 1877 in the *Revue et Gazette musicale de Paris* that "apart from the character
of the hermit, prohibited by the censors, the premiere version was a complete and literal
translation of the German piece (Sauf le personnage de l'ermite, que la censure avait fait
disparaître, c'était une traduction littérale et complets de l'ouvrage allemande)." *Revue
et Gazette musicale de Paris* XLIV/3, 21 January 1877: 19. Although, apart from Servières,
all commentators obviously seem to stick to their national allegiance, a real answer is
impossible to find. The insolubility of the problem has led Mark Everist to conclude that
"Castil-Blaze's account of the premiere of *Robin des bois* is as accurate as can be determined." Everist 2002: 269.

89   Hector Berlioz put it like that in his *Memoires* (1870), writing: "Weber, when discovering
     what Castil-Blaze, that surgeon of music, had done to his *Freischütz*, could hardly have felt
     a deeper indignation and he voiced his rightful grievance in a letter (Weber, en voyant ce
     que Castilblaze, ce musicien vétérinaire, avait fait de son *Freischütz*, ne put que ressentir
     profondément un si indigne outrage, et ses justes plaintes s'exhalèrent dans une lettre)."
     Berlioz 1870: 59.

90   Everist writes that Weber's "complaint lay largely with the fact that he had missed the
     chance to exploit the financial possibilities of *Der Freischütz* and *Euryanthe* in Paris [...].
     The origin of this problem lay quite simply in the fact that French law did not protect
     foreign authors' interests; Weber's claim [...] was therefore futile." Everist 2002: 252.

91   Between 1823 and 1825, Weber and Schlesinger were even corresponding with the Paris
     Opéra about setting a *tragédie lyrique*, called *La colère d'Achille*, to music. On 7 March
     1825, Weber did, however, conclude in his diary that the text "had considerable beauty
     [sehr viel Schönes]," but in the end was too "monotonous [monoton]." See Heidlberger
     1994: 298.

by Castil-Blaze's enterprise, although the Frenchman would have probably retorted that he had actually facilitated Weber's popularity. Weber briefly visited Paris on his way to London in 1826, with the hope of spending a longer period on his way home to Germany after his sojourn in the British capital. Unfortunately, he died in London that summer at the age of 40.

Weber was not the only German musician who had hoped to capitalize on the vogue for German music in Paris. As early as 1802, in the heyday of *Les Mystères*, an *AMZ* correspondent mentions an initiative by the German Haselmayer to found a *Théâtre Mozart, Salle de la cité, opéra comique allemande* in Paris. On 16 November 1801, the theater opened with a performance of *Die Entführung aus dem Serail* that was a big event in the Parisian opera scene. However, due to poor management, a relatively untalented troupe of singers and the programming of second-rate Viennese *Singspiele*, enthusiasm soon waned and the theater was closed.[92]

It would take until 1829 before a more substantial and successful German-language opera company would settle in Paris. This company mainly consisted of members of the Aachen opera house, one of the smaller, less prestigious ensembles of Germany,[93] but was nevertheless received warmly in the French

---

92   In his *Fortsetzung der Briefe eines deutschen Künstlers in Paris*, the anonymous correspondent writes the following about Haselmayer and his company: "Only a man like him, without theater or musical knowledge, without taste, only such a person would dare to suggest to the Parisian public that the German nation is so uncultured as to tolerate his company. [...] Now imagine such a bunch, coming to our city to present Mozart's masterworks tot he Parisians [...]. At the same time, one can imagine the Parisians enthusiasm to finally hear Mozart's operas as he has actually written them, untainted. [After the premiere of *Die Entführung*] people applauded, although no one liked the performance. No one attended the second and third performance. And then? Two performances of *Der Tyroler Wastel* [another *Singspiel* of Emanuel Schikaneder with music of Jakob Haibl (1798)], *Der Wastel* over here! The desecration of Mozart's name through this rubbish deeply offended the public; [...] After that, the director took a French leave(Nur ein Mann, wie dieser, ganz ohne Kenntnisse von Theater und Musik, ohne Geschmack [...]; nur ein solcher konnte es wagen, dem pariser Publikum vorzuspiegeln, die deutsche Nation sey so ungebildet, seine Gesellschaft erträglich zu finden. [...] Nun stellen sie sich ein solches Häuflein vor, welches hierher kommt, um die Pariser Mozarts Meisterstücke kennen zu lehren [...]. Denken sie sich von andrer Seite den Enthusiasmus der Pariser, Mozarts Kompositionen, wie Er sie schrieb, und unverpfuscht, einmal hören zu können. [Bei der *Entführung*-Premiere] applaudirte man am Ende, obgleich niemand mit dieser Vorstellung zufrieden war. Die zweyte und dritte Wiederholung dieser Oper zog niemand mehr im Haus. Und man gab darauf [...] zwey Vorstellungen – wovon? [...] Vom – Tyroler Wastel – Tyroler hier! Vom Wastel und Praterwirth hier! Die Entweihung des Namens Mozart durch solches Zeug war dem Publikum ein Greuel; [...] welches denn den Direktor bewog, sich nachts aus dem Staube zu machen)." *AMZ* IV/20, 10 February 1820: 320–322.

93   On 15 July 1829, after the first series of performances, an anonymous commentator in the *Allgemeine Musikalische Zeitung* wrote that the Aachen company's success was all

capital. This phenomenon of visiting foreign theater troupes was relatively new and arguably the result of the increasing interest in non-French art that accompanied the rise of French Romanticism. A direct example may have been the English Season at the *Odéon* of 1827, providing Shakespeare shows in the original language.[94] The German opera company was led by Joseph August Röckel, and played at the *Théâtre italien* during its summer interval. For the first season, Röckel chose a small but secure repertoire of three operas by German "master composers." First of all, he programmed Weber's *Freischütz* and Mozart's *Zauberflöte,* which both had already proved to be hits in French adaptions. The third crowd puller was Beethoven's *Fidelio,* which had not yet been given in Paris,[95] but benefitted from the Beethoven craze incited by the symphony series at the Paris *Société des Concerts du Conservatoire,* initiated and conducted by François Anton Habeneck from 1828 onwards. A peculiar single performance entailed a German-language version of Auber's *La dame blanche,* combined with *Die Wiener in Berlin,* a *Liederspiel* on a libretto by Karl Eduard von Holtei (no composer is mentioned).[96]

After the success of the first year, Röckel expanded the repertoire with works from Peter von Winter, Louis Spohr, and less famous composers such as Conradin Kreutzer, Johann Peter Pixis, Joseph Weigl, and Ferdinand Ries. In 1831, the company returned with six works composed by the 1829 trinity of well-known composers.[97] The total numbers of performances per season

---

the more remarkable since it was only a fifth-rate troupe in the German theater system, and therefore underlined an increasingly positive climate for German music theater: "Considering the fact that the troupe from Aachen, to which most artists belong, is a fifth-rate opera company, it is all the more remarkable that, despite all warnings and scorn among compatriots, who believed it was a presumptuous enterprise, it is a great success: the reputation of German companies will certainly benefit from this (Nimmt man an, dass die Aachner Truppe, aus welcher meist das hiesige teutsche Theater besteht, zur 5ten Klasse teutscher Bühnen gehört und diese, bey allen Unglücksprophezeiungen und selbst Schmähungen ihrer hier anwesenden Landsleute, die das Unternehmen vermessen fanden, doch so ausnehmendes Glück macht: so kann es den teutschen Bühnen nur zur Ehre gereichen)." *AMZ* XXXI/28, 15 July 1829: 466.

94   See Everist 2002: 5. Willem Schrickx has shown that a first similar English "Shakespeare" Season on the continent had taken place in Brussels and Amsterdam in 1814; Schrickx 1977.

95   Mark Everist has shown that a French-language performance of *Fidelio* had been planned at the *Théâtre de l'Odéon* in 1825 and 1826, but was later dropped because the French origins of the libretto created copyright problems. See Everist 2002: 275–276.

96   The *Liederspiel* was a light genre in which dialogue is alternated with several, often well-known, already existing songs. Von Holtei was one of the most prominent Liederspiel poets, although the term had been coined by Johann Friedrich Reichardt in the article 'Etwas über den Liederspiel,' published in the *AMZ* III/43, 22 July 1801: 709–717.

97   The interest for German operas by lesser gods was apparently limited, especially if it concerned older titles, as is voiced by an anonymous critique of *Das unterbrochene Opferfest*

varied from fourteen in the first season, at least 34 in the all too ambitious 1830 series, and 28 in the more precautiously programmed third year:

Year	Piece	Number of performances
1829	*Der Freischütz* (Weber)	7
	Die Zauberflöte (Mozart)	2
	Fidelio (Beethoven)	4
	Die weisse Dame (Auber)/*Die Wiener in Berlin* (v. Holtei)	1
1830	*Der Freischütz* (Weber)	9
	Faust (Spohr)	3
	Das unterbrochene Opferfest (Winter)	1
	Bibiani (Pixis)	2
	Fidelio (Beethoven)	6
	Oberon (Weber)	7
	Die Schweizerfamilie (Weigl)	2
	Cordelia (Kreutzer)	1
	Die Entführung aus dem Serail (Mozart)	2
	Die Räuberbraut (Ries)	(unknown)
1831	*Der Freischütz* (Weber)	3
	Fidelio (Beethoven)	11
	Die Entführung aus dem Serail (Mozart)	1
	Oberon (Weber)	2
	Don Juan (Mozart)	6
	Euryanthe (Weber)	5

Note: These data have been derived from Everist 2001: 72–74, but extended in some cases. A few performances that have been reported in contemporary criticism are missing in Everist's list. For the seasons 1830 and 1831, Lesure 1983: 61–64 provides the most detailed information.

---

in the *Revue musicale*: "In Germany, the piece is played in the majority of theaters, and enjoys the reputation of a customary element; but in France, where people want to hear new things, where one does not settle for less than Mozart's genius, a composition like *Das unterbrochene Opferfest* is not likely to achieve success (En Allemagne, il se joue encore sur la plupart des théâtres, et jouit d'une réputation qu'on peut appeler *d'habitude* ; mais en France, où l'on veut surtout du nouveau, où il ne faut pas moins que le génie de Mozart pour résister à l'engouement des formes de mode, une composition telle que le *Sacrifice Interrompu* n'est point de nature à obtenir de succès)." *Revue musicale* 7/13, 1 May 1830: 397.

The German performances aroused a lot of media attention, and brought about some interesting cross-cultural confrontations. In preparation of the 1829 opening performance of *Der Freischütz*, some Parisian commentators had clearly become acquainted with German opera esthetics, and judged the performances with this ideological framework in mind, whereas the German troupe tried to adjust their shows to French expectations. For example, an extraneous show aria, included by star tenor Anton Haitzinger, was generally considered to be a severe mistake by the Parisian press. Concerning this choice, the critic Albert Sowinsky[98] wrote that "we cannot terminate our review without correcting an unforgivable error of Mr. Haitzinger; this singer did not find enough room to display his talent in the inconvenient lines of Weber's *Freischütz*, and therefore inserted a florid aria in Italian style into the third act."[99] Concerning the return of the original ending of the piece, which had been altered in Castil-Blaze's version, Sowinsky was moderately positive: "The judgment and absolution of the king at the ending of the piece have been reinstated, and it has been done well. The finale is not very strong, but pleasant, and it gives the work an understandable morality which is lacking in Castil-Blaze's version."[100] Whether Sowinsky's conviction was shared by other attendants is, however, questionable; according to a commentator in the *AMZ*, after the premiere *Der Freischütz* was played in the altered shape familiar to French audiences.[101]

Critical responses to the second season also show that the works performed did not always live up to the expectations of the Parisian public, particularly because the repertoire often lacked the Romantic profundity that French intellectuals expected from German art. François-Joseph Fétis, for example, criticized the Romantic pretensions of many German artists and the deflation of "Romantic" as a label in his review of Pixis's *Bibiana* in the *Revue musicale*:

---

98   The article was signed with A.S., but Peter A. Bloom has identified these initials as referring to Sowinsky. See Bloom 1972: 73–74.

99   "Nous ne terminerons pas sans réparer un oubli qui serait impardonnable, à l'égard de M. Haitzinger : ce chanteur, qui ne trouve pas, dit-on, assez à developer son talent dans les chants incommodes du *Freyschütz*, a intercalé au troisième acte un air fort gracieux, parodié de l'italien, qui lui permet le point d'orgue et la roulade." *Revue Musicale* V/17, Mai 1829: 403.

100   "On a rétabli au dénouement le jugement et le pardon du roi, et l'on a bien fait. Ce finale n'est pas très-fort, mais il fait plaisir, et donne l'ouvrage une moralité intelligible qui lui manquait." Ibid.: 204.

101   "Mit dem Freyschütz wurden die Operndarstellungen eröffnet, nicht nach der französischen Abänderung dieser Oper (Robin des bois genannt), sondern nach der in Teutschland bekannten Ordnung. Doch hat man in der zweiten Aufführung es für gut befunden, der hier beliebten Umänderung zu folgen." *AMZ* XXXI/28, 15 July 1829: 466.

I suppose that those German writers who call their work a *Romantic trag-edy* or a *Romantic opera* do not know what they're doing, because they do not realize how recklessly they use such an ambitious title. If I am not mistaken, the Romantic genre in all arts is the realm in which the author does not limit his imagination and considers all thinkable means to re-alize certain effects. [...] But the poor libretto fabricator who wrote the text of *Bibiana*, who obviously has no imagination whatsoever, should have steered clear from calling one of the most stupid conceptions ever to come out of a sick mind a *Romantic* opera.[102]

A similarly critical view on the alleged profoundness of German opera was voiced by Fétis with regard to Spohr's *Faust*. By 1830, Spohr had quite a reputa-tion as an acclaimed, serious composer in France,[103] and the performance took place at a moment when Goethe mania in Paris was at an absolute peak. Fétis was highly disappointed to encounter a work that, in the end, had so little to do with Goethe's masterpiece:

Faust! A great subject, worthy of inspiring a Germanic muse. But *Faust*, in the eyes of the *French*, is the work of Goethe, with all its beauties, its flaws, the vagueness of its style and the exaggeration of its ideas. [...] Unfortunately, nothing of all this can be retrieved in the *libretto*

---

102   "Je suppose que les auteurs allemands, qui mettent en tête de leurs pièces : *tragédie romantique, opéra romantique*, etc., n'en savent pas davantage ; car il y aurait bien de la témérité de leur part à se servir de ces titres ambitieux. Si je ne me tromme, le genre qu'on désigne dans tous les arts par le nom de *romantique*, est celui dans lequel l'ariste n'assigne point de bornes à son imagination, et considère tous les moyens comme bons, pourvu qu'ils produisent des effects quelconques. [...] Par exemple, le pauvre faiseur de libretti qui a arrangé celui de *Bibiana*, et qui n'a rien à démêler avec l'imagination, se serait bien gardé d'appeler *romantique* l'une des conceptions les plus stupides qui soient sorties d'un cerveau malade." *Revue musicale* 8/1, 8 May 1830 : 8–9. Obviously Fétis's definition of Romanticism is not identical to that of, for example, E.T.A. Hoffmann in *Der Dichter und der Komponist*, but closer to Victor Hugo's notion in the preface to *Cromwell* (1827). This French branch of Romanticism is less concerned with ghosts and fairies, but more with expanding traditional forms of expression and structure, and with "revolting against the still dominant classicistic esthetics in France." Werner 1998: 192.

103   Fétis writes that "the majority of French musicians keenly attended the performance last Tuesday, eager to finally get to know the dramatic composer who now holds the first rank in Germany after Weber's demise (la plupart des musiciens français s'étaient-ils rendus avec empressement à la représentation de mardi dernier (20 avril), desireux de connaître enfin le compositeur dramatique qui tient en Allemagne le premier rang, depuis la mort de Ch. M. de Weber)." *Revue musicale* 7/12, 24 April 1830: 368.

that Spohr set to music. One understands that it is impossible to adapt Goethe's dramatic novel to the lyric stage, as it is the author's intellectual property. [...] Therefore, the ground structure of Spohr's opera was based on an older rendition of the *Faust* legend. [...] But the clumsiness of the librettist lies in the fact that this older tradition is hardly comprehensible in this piece, if we can even call it *a piece*. The stories of Italian operas are often ridiculed, but the stupidity of this *Faust* is unsurpassed. There is no cohesion between the individual scenes, no motivation to the action. [...] Only a highly powerful music can counter the disadvantages of such a bad narrative; unfortunately, I must confess that Spohr did not succeed in doing so: there is nothing in this music that justifies the high reputation of its creator.[104]

In the light of future developments, it is intriguing to see a French critic condemning the lack of fidelity to Goethe and frivolity of a German *Faust* opera, as this would be exactly the critique the French *Faust* renditions of Hector Berlioz and Charles Gounod would be confronted with in German music criticism.[105]

---

104   "*Faust!* Grand sujet, digne d'inspirer une muse germanique. Mais *Faust*, pour les *Français*, c'est l'ouvrage de Goethe, avec ses beautés, ses défauts, le vague de son style et l'exagération de ses idées. [...] Malheureusement rien de tout cela ne se trouve dans l'informe *libretto* sur lequel Spohr a écrit sa musique. En y réfléchissant, on comprend qu'il était impossible qu'on arrangeât en Allemagne le roman dramatique de Goethe pour la scène lyrique. Cet ouvrage est la propriété de son auteur. [...] Il a donc fallu, pour écrire le canevas de l'opéra de Spohr, avoir recours à la traduction d'un ancien *Faust*, [...] mais telle a été la maladresse de l'arrangeur du libretto nouveau, que cette tradition est à peine intelligible dans sa pièce, si toutefois cela peut s'appeler *une piece*. On s'est moqué souvent des canevas d'opéras italiens ; j'avoue que je n'en connais aucun qui puisse lutter de stupidité avec celui de *Faust*. Aucune liaison n'existe entre les scènes ; celles-ci se succèdent sans motif [...] Une musique très-forte pouvait seule lutter contre les désavantages d'une canevas semblable; malheureusement je suis forcé d'avouer que celle de *Faust* n'est pas ce qu'il fallait : elle n'a point justifié la haute réputation de son auteur."*Revue musicale* 7/12, 24 April 1830: 368–369.

105   It is even probable that Faust's infernal ride at the end of Berlioz's *Damnation de Faust* (1846), diverging from the salvation in Goethe's drama, was taken over from Spohr's opera, and actually the result of Berlioz's attendance of the *Saisons Allemands* in Paris in 1830. Berlioz's interest in German opera, particularly that of Weber, was already conceivable from his frequent visits to the *Théâtre de l'Odéon* from 1824 onwards (see Everist 2002: 123). Moreover, in 1829 Berlioz considered translating his opera *Les franc-juges* into German in order to have it performed in Kassel, where Spohr was *Kapellmeister*. A year later, he tried his luck by asking Haitzinger, leading tenor of the German company, for help in gaining access to the German opera world (see Heidlberger 1994: 86–87). During this period, Faust was clearly on his mind, as he completed his *Huit scènes de Faust* in 1829. Although most of these scene were taken over in *La Damnation de Faust* of 1846, the infernal ride was not yet a part of it, and it seems convincing that the attendance of Spohr's *Faust* at the

Apart from individual cases, the German seasons seems to have surpassed the expectations of Parisian audiences.[106] Although the qualities of individual singers were sometimes moderate at best,[107] and regardless of the strange sensation "to hear sophisticated musical phrases sung in a harsh Teutonic tongue," the public was generally receptive.[108] This attitude was more than just a sign of hospitality. The striking novelty of the German company for French spectators could be found foremost in its dedication to the artwork and *esprit de corps*. Sowinsky, for example, wrote in the *Revue musicale* in 1829 about a:

> Zeal, warmth and musical sentiment that is completely new to us, for whom love for art is not yet an inspiring force, to us who are accustomed to hearing cold, indifferent artists; these are the qualities which we have recognized from the start with these German singers, and these qualities have brought about the public favor of Parisian audiences.[109]

The German company did have its star soloists in Haitzinger and particularly in Wilhelmine Schröder-Devrient, who joined in at the start of the second season and created a sensation with her magnetizing combination of vocal skill and acting qualities.[110] These two certainly compensated the less talented rest

---

Parisian German opera during the summer of 1830 spurred him to create this frivolous closing scene.

106 Sowinsky, for example, pointed out that "the hopes have been fulfilled, and, according to many, even surpassed (Les espérances ont eté remplies, et, sous plusieurs rapports, dépassées)." *Revue musicale* V/17, May 1829: 400.

107 Sowinksy remarks that voice has not been considered in German opera production until now: "D'ailleurs, jusqu'à ce jour la voix n'a été considerée, dans la système allemande." Ibid.: 401.

108 "Nous voyions le prejuge contre la dureté de la langue teutonique etabli au balcon avec nos Beau fils, et nous entendions déjà les éclats de rire que provoquerait l'alliance de certaines consonnes plus qu'énergiques, avec la grâce de la phrase musicale. [Mais] le public français en a fait généreusement le sacrifice, et s'est montré plus indulgent, plus attentif et plus patient qu'on ne pouvait le demander. Nous doutons que nos hôtes aient jamais trouvé un auditoire qui sût aussi bien écouter." Sowinsky, *Revue musicale* V/20, June 1829: 469.

109 "zèle, chaleur et sentiment musical tout nouveaux pour nous, chez qui l'amour de l'art n'anime encore que les superiorités, et qui sommes accoutumés à n'entendre que trop souvent des artistes subalternes, froids et indifférens ; telles sont les qualités qu'on a reconnues de prime abord chez les chanteurs allemands, et qui devaient leur concilier la faveur du public parisien." Ibid.: 469–470.

110 In his 1863 biography of the famous soprano, Alfred Freiherr von Wolzogen quotes Schröder-Devrient about the strong responsibility she felt to represent German music in Paris when the contract with Röckel's company was signed: "Not only did I have to safeguard my own reputation, in fact I represented German music; if people did not like me, this would also affect Mozart, Beethoven, and Weber. This sense of duty created such an anxiety that more than once I considered to resign (Ich hatte [...] nicht allein meinen

of the troupe.[111] But these shortcomings in individual quality were, according to Sowinsky, just as much overcome by the power of the ensemble: "It must be said, one will generally not hear artists who are more than mediocre; but this is compensated by the effect of a good ensemble."[112] This ensemble spirit was most obviously present in the handling and performance of the choir, which "displays a remarkable musical intelligence and sentiment."[113] The house orchestra, accompanying Italian operas during the regular season, unfortunately lagged behind in this relatively new and challenging repertoire.[114]

The positive reception of German opera in the French capital fueled chauvinism in the homeland. Especially the *Berliner allgemeine musikalische Zeitung* reported euphorically about the company's successes. In June 1829, at the end of the first season, an anonymous reporter stated that "the success

---

eigenen Ruf, ich hatte die deutsche Musik zu vertreten; wenn die Künstlerin nicht gefiel, so mußten Mozart, Beethoven, Weber, darunter leiden. Bei diesem Gedanken überfiel mich eine solche Angst, daß ich mehr als einmal im Begriff war, alles daranzusetzen, um den Contract wieder rückgängig zu machen)." Wolzogen 1863: 145.

111   An anonymous critic of the *Revue musicale* for example wrote in 1830 that "the united talents of Mme Schroeder-Devrient and Haitzinger have proved to be sufficient attractions to draw in all true lovers of music during more than two months (Les talens réunis de Mme Schroeder-Devrient et d'Haitzinger ont eu assez d'attrait pour attirer, pendant plus de deux mois, tous les vrais amateurs de musique)." *Revue musicale*, 8/9, 3 July 1830: 277.

112   "Il faut le dire, on s'attendait à n'entendre que des artistes médiocres, et aucun chanteur saillant; mais l'on se résignait à s'en dédommager par l'effet d'un bon ensemble." *Revue musicale* V/17, May 1829: 400.

113   "Les choeurs font preuve d'une intelligence et d'un sentiment musical remarquables." Ibid.: 402. Regarding a performance of *Euryanthe* in 1831, the reviewer of *Le Globe* voices a similar judgment: "the members of the choir possess one spirit and one intelligence; their expressive physiognomies, their animated gestures show us men and women that understand and symphatize with their roles ("[les choristes] possèdent une âme et une intelligence; ces physiognomies expressives, ces gestes animés nous montrent des hommes et des femmes qui comprennent, qui symphatisent avec leurs rôles")." Quoted after Everist 2001: 101.

114   With regard to the premiere of *Der Freischütz* in 1829, Sowinsky, for example, writes that "the orchestra has been the least satisfying part. The energy and brilliance were fully missing. One must admit that the orchestra of the *Odéon* has understood far better the savagery of this music (L'orchestre [...] a été jusqu'à present la partie la moins satisfaisante [...] L'énergie et l'éclat ont manqué totalement. [...] On doit avouer que l'orchestre de l'Odéon [...] avait bien mieux compris la sauvagerie de cette musique)." *Revue musicale* V/17, May 1829: 403. The poor quality of the orchestra remained a concern throughout the three years the German opera company ran in Paris. At the end of the 1830 season, an anonymous critic of the *Revue musicale* still called the orchestra "the feeblest element (Il est vrai que [...] l'orchestra etais de la plus grand faiblesse)," and expected that the company would move to the better equipped *Théâtre des Nouveautés*, but that never happened: "enfin les représentations devant avoir lieu au Théâtre des Nouveautés, ou a l'assurance que l'orchestre sera beaucoup meilleur." *Revue musicale*, 8/9, 3 July 1830: 277–278.

pleads for the Parisians; the acclaim that the German genius received, certainly secures the progress of music, and the support for the actors displays a sympathetic attitude."[115] The *BAMZ* was eager to include pro-German statements by native Frenchmen, such as the following anonymous comment, published in July of the same year:

> Highly regretted by all true art lovers did the German singers troupe terminate their performances on the 11th of July. Only a few operas were presented, but these convinced us that, regardless of many shortcomings of the orchestra and singers, German music and the dedication with which German singers perform it have displayed a degree of beauty of which we had not yet been aware. [...] We sincerely hope that this first attempt will result in the foundation of a proficient German opera house, we aspire to it for the sake of art and artists, in the hope that this musical genre, which is certainly more elevated than ours, will find access to us and will expand our musical knowledge.[116]

However, after three summer seasons, the company terminated. In the next twenty years, projects to refill this gap in the Parisian opera world all came to nothing. In July 1834, an initiative to open a permanent German opera institute at the *Théâtre Ventadour/Nautique* was announced in both the *Gazette musicale de Paris* and the *Neue Zeitschrift für Musik*.[117] In April 1835, however, the *Neue Zeitschrift* reported that the project had eventually collapsed because investors had withdrawn their funds.[118] The vanity of launching a permanent German opera theater had been foreseen by a perceptive Frenchman who, in an 1830 *BAMZ* article, had already issued the following warning:

---

115   "Der Erfolg macht den Parisern Ehre; der Beifall, den er für deutsches Genie erntete, bürgt für Fortschreiten der Musik, und die Begünstigungen, welche den Schauspielern gewährt worden sind Beweise guter Gesinnung." *BAMZ* VI/26, 27 June 1829: 207.
116   "Zum grössten Bedauern aller wahren Kunstfreunde beendete am 11. d. die deutsche Sängergesellschaft ihre Vorstellungen. Weinige Opern [...] sahen wir darstellen, doch überzeugten wir uns, dass ungeachtet so mancher Mangelhaftigkeit des Orchesters und Sängerpersonals, deutsche Musik und die Auffassung derselben durch deutsche Sänger uns Schönheiten zeige, die wir bisher darin kaum geahndet hatten. [...]Wir wünschen herzlich, dass dieser Versuch Veranlassung werde zur Gründung einer tüchtigen deutschen Oper, wir wünschen es zum Wohl der Kunst und vieler Künstler, damit diese gewiss höhere Gattung der Musik bei uns Eingang finde und die musikalischen Kenntnisse bei uns erweitere." *BAMZ* VI/28, 11 July 1829: 224.
117   *Gazette musicale de Paris* 1/27, 6 July 1834 : 213, *NZfM* I: 1 / 31, 17 July 1834: 124.
118   *NZfM* II: 2 / 30, 14 April 1835: 121.

the Parisians are courteous, even enthusiastic, towards anything that comes from afar – and leaves soon afterwards. If the German singers would consider to stay with us for an entire year, they would seriously put our reliability to the test. But a visit of a few weeks, followed by an absence of ten months: that's the best strategy to stay *en vogue*, to re-encounter the same amount of credit, goodwill and honor.[119]

The return to Paris of a German troupe in 1842 to perform works of Weber, Beethoven, Spohr and Kreuzer at the Théâtre Ventadour may be illustrative of German opera's vicissitudes in the French capital. After relatively successful performances of *Der Freischütz, Jessonda* and *Das Nachtlager von Granada*,[120] the staff suddenly was confronted with legal prosecution, because the administration had failed to secure a permit to work in France.[121] Penniless and not able to return home, the German singers were treated pitiful by Parisian high circles. After a massively attended performance of *Fidelio*,[122] patricians organized a benefit evening, hosted by Franz Liszt, to raise funds for the Germans' repatriation.[123] As with all earlier German seasons, the well-intended performances were answered with sympathy, this time even with charity, but a lasting success or residence proved to be unattainable.

In the end, the most remarkable "breakthrough" of German opera in the Parisian opera scene was not brought about by the German-language performances, but rather by the epochal success of Giacomo Meyerbeer, the German innovator of French *grand opéra*. Meyerbeer's first operatic activities in Paris concerned a pasticcio rendition of *Das Donauweibchen* (*La nymphe du Danube*), designed in 1826 for the *Odéon* but never staged.[124] After this aborted project, he started a collaboration with poet Eugène Scribe for an *opéra comique* on the legend of Robert le Diable. This project was also frustrated, because the *Opéra comique* administration suffered from an organizational and financial crisis

---

119 "Die Pariser sind gar ein höfliches, sogar ein enthusiastisches Völkchen für alles, was weit her kommt und – bald wieder geht. Liessen die deutschen Sänger sich beikommen, nur einmal ein ganzes Jahr bei uns zu bleiben, wir möchten ihnen für unsre Beständigkeit nicht gut sagen. Aber ein Besuch von wenigen Wochen, danach eine Abwesenheit von zehn Monden: das ist das wahre Mittel, in der Mode zu bleiben, jedes Jahr dasselbe Zutrauen, Gunst und Ehrenbezeugung wieder zu finden." *BAMZ* VII/27, 3 July 1830: 215.

120 See *La Revue et Gazette musicale de Paris* 9/18, 1 May 1842 and *La Revue et Gazette musicale de Paris* 9/19, 8 May 1842 : 202–204.

121 See *La Revue et Gazette musicale de Paris* 9/21, 22 May 1842: 223.

122 See *La Revue et Gazette musicale de Paris* 9/22, 29 May 1842: 231.

123 See *La Revue et Gazette musicale de Paris* 9/26, 26 June 1842 : 269.

124 See Everist 2002: 175–177.

between 1827 and 1832.[125] Thereupon, Meyerbeer and Scribe reworked the piece for the *Opéra*, where *Robert le Diable* was premiered in November 1831.

A proper evaluation of Meyerbeer's contribution to German opera has been tainted severely by the questionable historiography to which he has been subjected,[126] but it is important to realize that, despite his recent successes in Italian opera,[127] many Parisians regarded him as a prototypical German composer on his arrival in the late 1820s. Everist for example writes:

> Before the advent of Meyerbeer's *Robert le Diable*, his operas were frequently described with the aid of vocabulary reserved for German composers, despite the fact that the works known in Paris before 1831 were exclusively Italian. His music was described as *savant*, and of a type that needed to be listened to several times before it could be understood. In this period, he was closely associated in Parisian minds with his erstwhile colleague, Carl-Maria von Weber.[128]

It is insightful to reconsider this German aspect of Meyerbeer's compositional persona, as Everist also points out that "the role of German romanticism has received much less attention in historiography of *grand opéra* than might be thought due."[129] In its initial *opéra comique* form, *Robert* had striking similarities with Weber's *Freischütz*, as Hugh Macdonald indicates: "What Scribe offered Meyerbeer in 1827 was an ingeniously similar opera, with spoken dialogue, a spooky Wolf's Glen scene, a group of characters similar to Agathe, Ännchen, and Caspar."[130] But the similarities were even further reinforced when Scribe and Meyerbeer reworked *Robert* into a *grand opéra*. The part of Bertram, formerly a tenor part, mainly consisting of spoken dialogue,[131] was now turned into a prominent bass-baritone role. This created a perfect analogy between *Der Freischütz* and *Robert* in terms of character and voice type: a triangle consisting of a faltering tenor who uses black magic to pursue his love (Max/Robert), a demonic bass-baritone who tries to sacrifice this tenor to his deity by having him sign a pact (Caspar/Bertram), and an angelic soprano who saves the tenor from evil (Agathe/Alice).

---

125   Henze-Döhring and Döhring 2013: 35.
126   I will reflect on this historiographical tradition in relation to Wagner in Chapter 5.
127   Meyerbeer's *Il crociato in egitto* (Venice, 1824) was an enormous success and soon spread to all parts of Europe, reaching Paris in 1825.
128   Everist 2001: 68–69.
129   Ibid.: 68.
130   Macdonald 1987: 459.
131   Brzoska 2003: 190.

Besides this Faustian scheme[132] which *Robert le Diable* shares with *Der Freis-chütz*, other characteristic elements of German opera were added to the potent stew of the work. A first aspect was the stage appearance of the devil, which by 1830 was considered to be a cliché of German operas in the eyes of some Parisian spectators.[133] Secondly, the cosmic battle over the protagonist's soul between good and bad, represented by parental figures,[134] was an element that went back at least to *Die Zauberflöte*.[135] And the finale of Meyerbeer's opera, in which time runs out for Bertram to win Robert's soul by having him sign the pact, and which shows the title-hero eventually "saved by the bell," seems close-ly modelled after Heinrich Marschner's opera *Der Vampyr* (1828).[136] Although the literary sources for *Robert* were varied and came from different cultures – in addition to the 13th-century Normandic legend of Robert le Diable, Letellier lists the novels *Das Petermännchen* by Christian Heinrich Spiess (1791), and *The Monk* by Matthew Gregory Lewis (1796), besides the play *Bertram* by Charles

---

132   Goethe's *Faust* plays an intriguing role in the background of Meyerbeer's opera career. In a private conversation in February 1829, the famous poet had confided to Johann Peter Eckermann that "if my *Faust* were to be adapted into an opera, the music should have the character of *Don Juan*, Mozart should have composed *Faust*. Meyerbeer could per-haps be capable of it, but he would probably not take up this task ('Die Musik [einer *Faust*-Oper] müßte im Charakter des ›Don Juan‹ sein; Mozart hätte den ›Faust‹ kompo-nieren müssen. Meyerbeer wäre vielleicht dazu fähig, allein der wird sich auf so etwas nicht einlassen.')." Derived from Walwei-Wiegelmann 1985: 185. (Eckermann published his *Gespräche mit Goethe* in 1836) A recently discovered sketchbook, however, shows that Meyerbeer was in fact secretly working on a *Faust* opera during the 1820s. Letellier argues that some of the *Faust* fragments were integrated into *Robert le diable*. Letellier 2013: 46. Another testimony of Meyerbeer's fascination for the Faust legend is Spohr's account in his *Lebenserinnerungen* that Meyerbeer showed a vivid interest in his Faust opera dur-ing a collective sojourn in Vienna in 1813. Spohr adds to this recollection that Meyerbeer retained his interest until 1843, when Meyerbeer produced Spohr's opera with great care at the Berlin Court Opera. See Spohr 1968: 172.

133   The *Berliner allgemeine musikalische Zeitung* mentions a response during the *Blockber-gscene* of Spohr's *Faust* by a Parisian lady, complaining that "all current German operas apparently must have diabolical elements [il y a de la diablerie en tout ceci]." See *BAMZ* VII/35, 28 August 1830: 275. This cliché image was not restricted to France, as an 1824 Eng-lish *Freischütz* commentary in the *Examiner* shows: "The story of the piece [...] is founded on one of these traditional instances of diablerie of which the German imagination has so great a predilection." Quoted after Fauser 2001: 250.

134   The symbolism of this paternal battle in *Robert le Diable* is addressed extensively in Letellier 2013: 43–46.

135   Henze-Döhring 2013: 48.

136   Another common element between Meyerbeer and Scribe's *Robert* and the many vam-pire stories that were written during the 1820s is the motive of the sinister fellow traveler, which is not that prominent in the libretto that Wohlbrück wrote for Marschner's *roman-tische Oper*, but which is indeed an important aspect of the initial short story *The Vampyre* by John Polidori (1819).

Robert Mathurin (1816) as most important influences[137] – the musical dramaturgy of the work was chiefly derived from German operatic examples.[138]

Prior to and in the shadow of *Robert's* glorious but costly premiere in November 1831, the *Opéra* had mounted a humbler performance of Weber's *Euryanthe* in French translation in April of the same year. The version performed was, again, a "translation" by Castil-Blaze, one that "wilfully strayed" from Weber's original even more than had been the case with *Der Freischütz/Robin des bois*.[139] Without going into too much detail regarding this production, it is noteworthy that *Euriante* – as Castil-Blaze had rechristened it – formed the first opera to kickstart the tenure of Louis Véron, the director who took over the *Opéra* in 1831, after the July revolution, and was partly responsible for the house's immense successes during the 1830s and 40s.[140]

It is remarkable that the success of *Robert*, a French work by a German composer, was anticipated by a French translation of Weber's German opera as the programmatic start of Verón's reign. The symbolism of this choice was established and approved by some Parisian commentators, for example by Jules Janin, who concluded in the *Journal des Débats* of 11 April 1831 that "it was a good beginning of the new administration of the *Opéra* to start with an opera of Weber. This 'naturalization' of foreign music presents a brilliant sign for the future of our leading theater."[141] On the one hand, the fact that the "naturalized" foreign work in question was a German work can be seen as a demonstration of the increasingly transnational nature of opera production around 1830 in general. On the other, we may interpret the 1831 upbeat to *Grand opéra's* heyday with a performance of Weber as a remarkable, programmatic reversal of

---

137   Letellier 2013: 16.

138   Of course, the Gothic fancy also affected French opera, but as we see in Scribe's libretto for Boïeldieu's *La dame blanche* (1825), for example, ghostly apparations were generally explained rationally in French operas before *Robert*. The same goes for Scribe's comedy *Le Vampire* of 1820.

139   Castil-Blaze cleverly countered the accusation of inauthenticity by pointing to the French literary origins of the story, which had been neglected by Helmina von Chézy, but reinstated by himself. See Everist 2001: 78–79. Interestingly, surrounding the creation of *Les Mystères d'Isis* we find similarly mitigating arguments about the Frenchification of *Die Zauberflöte*, when contemporary French critics pointed out that "one of the sources for the German libretto by Schikaneder was the French novel *Sethos* by the Abbé Terrasson, first published in 1731." Mongrédien 1985: 202.

140   Despite leaving his directorship already after four years in 1835, he can be seen as the initiator of the Paris *Opéra's* golden era and the dominance of *Grand opéra* as a genre.

141   "C'était bien commencer pour la nouvelle administration de l'Académie royale de musique que de commencer par un opéra de Weber. Ce droit de naturalisation, conservé à la musique étrangère, est d'un brilliant augure pour l'avenir de notre premier théâtre." Quoted after Heidlberger 1994: 344.

Weber's Dresden kick-off with Méhul's *Joseph* in 1817, a reversal that clearly underlines the heightened prestige of German opera in Paris.[142]

3   German Opera in London

In approximately the same period in which German opera spread to Paris, it also got on the British radar, in a highly similar series of events. As in Paris, access to this foreign realm was gained through the success of Weber's *Freischütz* in naturalized form, after which a thirst for German works in translation was quenched by staging operas by other German composers. And the next stage of this campaign was a German company performing in native tongue that first came to the British capital in 1832, – in fact largely the same company that had visited Paris between 1829 and 1831 – followed up by other troupes that were at times successful but ultimately unable to make headway in the long term.

In many respects, opera life was quite similar in London and Paris, two capitals of powerful, highly centralized countries with a dense concentration of competing theaters.[143] An important difference, however, lay in the esteem for native operatic products. The London counterpart of the prestigious Parisian *Opéra* was not an institute where English-language works were performed, but rather the *Italian Opera*, residing in *The King's/Majesty's Theatre*. This made the British situation remarkably similar to that in Germany until the 1820s. As in Russia, German music and music drama could form an ally in the battle against the hegemony of Italian opera, but it simultaneously presented a threat to the native product. More than in Paris, where the arrival of German

---

142   Another cultural transfer from German Romantic opera to French music theater which took place in Paris around 1830 is the beginning of the French Romantic ballet tradition. The first important Romantic French ballet was *La Sylphide*, premiered at the Paris *Opéra* in 1832. The piece was designed for the famous ballerina Maria Taglioni, who had also starred in the ballet of deceased nuns of Meyerbeer's *Robert* a year earlier. The scenario that Adolphe Nourrit, star tenor and the first Robert le diable, sketched out for *La Sylphide* takes over many elements of the quintessentially Romantic opera as E.T.A. Hoffmann had formulated it in *Der Dichter und der Komponist* (1813). The opposition of a human and a supernatural sphere, often both granted a separate act, and the *Undine*-type impossible love between a knight and a fairy play a central role. The basic Romantic constellation, in which the breakthrough of the spirit realm is the nucleus of the dramaturgy, not only governs *La Sylphide*, but was also revisited in other French Romantic ballets such as the *Donauweibchen*-inspired *La fille du Danube* (1836), and *Giselle* (1842), both with music composed by Adolphe Adam.

143   With the significant difference, however, that Paris theaters were dependent on State funding to balance the books, while London was a pure market economy, implying a different relationship to the public.

opera companies was generally received in terms of an evaluation of burgeoning Romantic esthetics, similar troupes triggered discussion on the necessity of a native national opera in London.

The British relation to music at the beginning of the nineteenth century was peculiar. Both in contemporary sources and in historiography, we again and again revisit the trope that music was considered essentially "effeminate," "alien to the British spirit" and chiefly a "foreign product to be imported."[144] Another leitmotif in writings about British music is the notion of a "country without music," a designation that was probably invented in the German-speaking world.[145] As a result, opera was generally restricted to imported, Italian works in their original, "effeminate" language.[146] English music theater existed solely in spectacular forms of melodrama and in *ballad operas*; spoken plays inserted with simple, undemanding songs. In general, the subordinate part of music in British music theater was a result of the common conviction that, as Fuhrmann writes: "on the English stage, dramatic importance equalled [*sic*] speech."[147]

Between the aristocratic taste for Italian opera and the common taste for low forms of spectacle, an emerging middle class was developing a predilection for instrumental, chiefly German, music. The most significant achievement of this movement was the foundation of the *Philharmonic Society* in 1813, organizing concerts "to promote the performance, in the most perfect manner possible, of the best and most approved instrumental music."[148] From this moment onward, an uneven companionship with German music culture gained ground, providing as much inspiration as it brought frustration to advocates of the national musical cause. As Hughes and Stradling formulate it: "painful ambiguities of relationship with the Teutonic tradition is a thread which runs through the whole era of the [British] Musical Renaissance," it was simply

---

144   Hughes and Stradling, for example, state that "for Carlyle, music was not only potentially subversive, but actually quasi-effeminate. [....] Moreover, music was seen as essentially alien: to the English mind, foreigners composed music, and had a monopoly on its performance." Hughes 2001: 4. Christina Fuhrmann reaches a similar conclusion when she argues that "entrenched English stereotypes marked music as frivolous and effeminate, antithetical to the supposedly rational, masculine national character," a discourse that goes back as far as Early Modern England (see Austern 1993).

145   See, for instance, Tim Carter's article *Mozart in a "Land without Music,"* about Henry Bishop's 1819 translation of Mozart's *Nozze di Figaro*. (Carter 2000) Fauser tentatively supposes that this expression might have originated at the end of the eighteenth century. See Fauser 2001: 260.

146   The alleged "effeminacy" of Italian opera is also a returning element in North-Western-European esthetics, see for example Chapter 1.

147   Fuhrmann 2004: 121.

148   Initial mission statement, quoted after Weber 2006: 522.

"always Germany, the obsessive point of comparison, and the object of so much competitive envy in the discourse of English Music."[149] This "steadily increasing [...] interest in serious German music" made it a "propitious time" for, amongst others, Spohr, who visited the British capital in 1820 and became one of London's dearest German composers.[150]

The musical situation seemed unfavorable for the emancipation of native opera, as the aristocracy generally privileged Italian works, the lower classes clung unto their simple fare, and instrumental music was surpassing the prestige of opera in the eyes of many middle-class music lovers.[151] When the news of Weber's phenomenal success with *Der Freischütz* in Germany had spread to the British isles and companies considered performing it, it fell into a comparable lacuna, although more from an institutional point of view. As Fuhrmann formulates it:

> *Der Freischütz* uneasily straddled English theatrical conventions. The complexities of its score seemed to require the operatic resources of the King's Theatre, but its folk-like numbers and spoken dialogue approximated English opera at the major theatres. Its libretto further complicated matters, for it resonated with a genre stigmatized as a minor-theatre staple: melodrama. [...] Too German for the King's Theatre, too melodramatic for the major theatres and too operatic for the minors, *Der Freischütz* languished on London's theatrical drawing board.[152]

Turning the argument around, *Der Freischütz* simultaneously presented a potent stew of attractive elements; as a serious, German composer, Weber appealed to the instrumental music faction, the melodramatic and folk-like

---

149   Hughes 2001: 123 and Ibid.: 29. Hughes and Stradling present several sources that reinforce this perspective. As late as 1911, the British composer Cecil Forsyth pointed out that "musical England was a German colony" (Ibid.: 119.), whereas three years earlier, his female contemporary colleague Ethel Smyth proudly remarked that her latest opera was "in my latter manner – i.e. absolutely out of the German wood." (Ibid.: 129.)

150   Brown 1984: 127. As an opera composer, Spohr obviously receives more attention within this study than Mendelssohn, who was, however, clearly the most popular German composer in Britain during the first half of the nineteenth century. The 1846 world premiere of his *Elijah* in Birmingham was a milestone in British music history, and made Mendelssohn the true heir of Händel, the other favorite German oratorio composer who had lived in London during the eighteenth century.

151   Weber argues that to many "music reformers" during this period, "Romantic and utopian [...] notions about music [...] ultimately applied more to concerts than to opera," increasingly seen as "crudely commercial and simplistic 'salon music'." Weber 2006: 512.

152   Fuhrmann 2004: 119–120.

qualities of *Der Freischütz* could entice the masses and on top of that, Weber had proved to be the first "native" composer to outshine Italian opera composers in his country, thereby forming an inspiring example to those who wanted to advance the situation of national opera in England. This "inspirational" aspect was clearly one of the trump cards of the *English Opera House*, where the work was first presented to the London public on 22 July 1824,[153] as shows from the preface of the English libretto that the company brought out:

> The production of this opera in England will, there is little doubt, be considered hereafter as an epoch in the musical history of this country, and tend, not only to free us from the opprobrium of not being a musical people, but, in the end, bestow upon our composers that confidence which is absolutely necessary for the production of everything great in either art or science.[154]

Whereas in Paris, rigid genre regulations restricted *Der Freischütz* to be given anywhere else than in the *Odéon*, in London a competition of adaptations arose,[155] in which "an unprecedented string of seven additional productions of *Der Freischütz* appeared at seven London theaters within the next four months."[156] The sensational success of the *English Opera House* premiere was partly explained by the huge number of German Londoners in the building,[157] but the extent to which *Der Freischütz* "went viral" in the British capital signals its appeal to the British majority as well.

---

153   In fact, a music theater performance based on the story of *Der Freischütz* had been given at the *Royal Coburg Theatre* as early as February 1824, but "apparently attracted little notice" (Ibid.: 117.) The true "*Freischütz* frenzy," therefore, started after the July performances.

154   Quoted after Fauser 1994: 260.

155   Concerning competition between different London theaters presenting the same works, Tim Carter writes that "it is unlikely that London theatres were under quite the same pressures as those in, say, Paris in terms of the influence of officially sanctioned house-styles for given theatres or of a politicized fear of foreign encroachment upon national idioms. The issue in London may have been much more one of free-market taste." Carter 2000: 203.

156   Fuhrmann 2004: 116.

157   The singer Henry Phillips, singing Rollo (Caspar) at the *English Opera House* premiere, later stated that "The house on that eventful night was thronged with Germans." See Reynolds 1976: 7. This was probably the result of a careful campaign carried out by musical director Hawes, as the *Quarterly Musical Magazine & Review* wrote that "we have it from unquestionable authority, that almost every German in London was invited to attend the first night of its representation, as a matter of honour to his country, by the active interposition of Mr. Hawes." *Quarterly Musical Magazine & Review* VII/26, June 1825: 196.

As was often the case with "translated" works, far-reaching alterations were made in the different versions given at rivaling theaters. The most important changes were the frequent split of Caspar into a speaking and a singing character,[158] the reduction of ensembles by substituting these for "ballads[159]" – the typical simple strophic songs of British music theater –, and the insertion of extra ballads, newly-composed by the British *arrangeurs*. This "simplification" of Weber's musical language did not hinder the *Observer* critic reviewing the *English Opera House* production to point out that the opera's music was "better fitted to instruct than to please,"[160] thereby employing the common accusation of complexity and "learnedness" with regard to German music. Considering the instant success of the work, it must, however, indeed have pleased audiences, and positive press judgments far outnumbered skeptical ones. *The Chronicle*, for example, praised Weber's accuracy in musical characterization: "In the *Freischütz*, the lively, the tender, the solemn, and the mysterious, all are expressed in the most appropriate tones and harmonies."[161] The most eloquent evaluation came perhaps from the *London* reviewer, who countered conservative criticism on Weber's compositional audacity with the following statement:

> It remains to speak of the music [...]. Some of the critics have said it is not so sweet or so good as Mozart's: – Pshaw! It was never intended to be sweet! It is appalling, terrific, sublime! [...] There is a depth, a wildness, which frightens the mind while it charms the ear; and we will confidently say that no music, not even Mozart's was ever heard with such breathless attention and earnestness as this extraordinary production of Weber. It is a great work![162]

---

158   Christina Fuhrmann argues that this split was not only the result of incidental casting problems – as the relatively young but vocally superb Henry Phillips was deemed not yet ripe for such a dramatically demanding part at the English Opera House – but also displays the primacy attributed to the drama. See Ibid.: 121.

159   In his study of the 1819 English adaptation of Mozart's *Le Nozze*, Tim Carter points out that "many contemporary Londoners may have found such ensembles too complicated," (Carter 2000: 200) whereas Christina Fuhrmann relates this to the British abstinence to blur the division between the primary dramatic sphere and the music: "[Weber's] extended ensembles posed a challenge to the careful separation of drama and music in English opera." Fuhrmann 2004: 122.

160   Quoted after Fenner 1994: 504. Theodore Fenner's collection of music criticism in London between 1785 and 1830 has been a highly useful source for this study.

161   Quoted after Ibid.: 504.

162   Quoed after Ibid.: 505.

Nevertheless, even a great work will exhaust audiences in case of continuous reprises. By November 1824, the *European Magazine* called *Der Freischütz* "stale as mackerel a month old,"[163] whereas the first Drury Lane performance was greeted with the *London* critic's comment that "we are beginning to get very sick of this very good music."[164] Fuhrmann mentions a parody called *Dr. Freischütz and the Seven Pancakes*, presented at the *Olympic Theatre* in October of the same year, in which Cuno is renamed into Dr. Freischütz, a doctor-turned-baker who has come to London. Fuhrmann argues:

> This character [...] anthropomorphized the opera itself. [...] Dr. Freischütz embodies the opera's influence and popularity in London. Marked as stereotypically German by both his thick accent and his new name – resonant of another demonic character, Dr. Faustus – Dr. Freischütz also points to underlying resentment at this Teutonic takeover of the English stage.[165]

Whether London audiences were really fed up with Weber and German culture in general is debatable, but it is clear that even *Der Freischütz* inevitably had an expiration date. Theater companies were aware of this, and during 1825 tried to retain the appetite for Weber by offering new fare; Drury Lane gave a "mediocre," yet "quite successful" production of *Abu Hassan* (originally premiered in Munich in 1811) and Covent Garden produced a flawed version of Pius Alexander Wolff's *Preziosa* (Berlin, 1821), for which Weber had written some stage music. The latter was rejected by the *Literary Chronicle* as one of the most "absurd" or "contemptible" productions ever offered.[166] But behind the scenes, a bigger dish was being prepared. Following the success of *Der Freischütz* in 1824, member of the Covent Garden administration Charles Kemble had approached Weber to compose an original English opera to be premiered in London and to be conducted by the composer himself. Weber accepted the challenge.[167]

---

163   Quoted after Fuhrmann 2004: 132.

164   Quoted after Fenner: 506. This production did, however, contain a considerable degree of novelty, as arranger Henry Bishop reinstated many of the original features of Weber's work.

165   Fuhrmann 2004: 130.

166   Fenner 1994: 507.

167   Although Weber was obviously flattered by the invitation from London and proved to be quite congenial to the British culture – in a letter of 6 March 1826 to his wife during his London sojourn he pointed out that "the whole way of English life is very sympathetic to my nature (Die ganze englische Weise ist meiner Natur sehr verwandt)" (see http://www.weber-gesamtausgabe.de/de/A002068/Korrespondenz/A042707) – there was another urgent reason to accept the offer. In a letter to his friend Heinrich von Lichtenstein

From the subjects proposed by Kemble, Weber chose *Oberon*.[168] More than *Der Freischütz*, which was received as a genuinely German work regardless of its "naturalization,"[169] *Oberon* occupies a peculiar "in-between" cultural space, as a work by a German composer created for an English audience. The subject seemed suitable for such an intercultural product, as it provided a comfortable common ground between Weber's German cultural background and his British audience. The libretto's most direct source had been Christoph Martin Wieland's German poem *Oberon* (1780), which was in its turn a combination of the thirteenth-century French *Huon de Bordeaux* story and elements from Shakespeare's *A Midsummer Night's Dream* (1590–1596).[170] Weber displayed a remarkable eagerness to meet expectations of British audiences. Not only did he rapidly learn English, but he also accepted the peculiar form of the libretto that James Planché had created, despite the fact that, as he wrote in a letter to Planché on 6 January 1825, "the cut of the whole is very foreign to my maxims." Weber also stated that "the intermixing of so many principal actors who do not sing, the omission of the music in the most important moments – all deprive our *Oberon* of the title of an opera, and will make it unfit for all other theatres in Europe, which is a very bad thing for me, but – *passons là dessus* [let us move beyond that]."[171] Planché himself later explained:

------

of 6 September 1824, Weber wrote that he hoped to make a "neat fortune" with a few visits to London: "Auf jeden Fall bin ich entschlossen, wenn es angeht, einige Jahre hintereinander vier bis fünf Monate in London zuzubringen, und mir hoffentlich dadurch ein hübsch Vermögen zu machen." (http://www.webergesamtausgabe.de/de/A002068/ Korrespondenz/A042348).

It is probable that this hunger for financial benefits was motivated by his private realization that, considering his physical condition, there was no time to waste before securing his family's prosperity. As Tusa writes: "Recognizing that his days were numbered and believing that the potential rewards offered by London would provide a measure of financial security for his family [...], Weber wrote to Kemble on 7 October [1824] to agree to compose an opera." (*Oxfordmusiconline.com*, attended on 18 August 2014).

168   *Faust* was Kemble's other suggestion, see Chapter 3.

169   In relation to the 1824 London premiere of *Der Freischütz*, Annegret Fauser mentions that, despite its performance language, it was perceived as a German opera from the start, see Fauser 2001: 247.

170   Heidlberger proposes that Weber might have had a similar intercultural strategy when in 1823 he considered a campaign to stage *Euryanthe* in Paris, a work that due to its literary source and formal outlook could also have appealed to local audiences. See Heidlberger 1994: 294.

171   Letter included in Planché 1872: 52. That Planché's text was not just an advance to common taste, but in fact an ingenious, refined libretto in the eyes of some British commentators becomes evident in the judgment of theater critic Horace Foote, who argued that "the poetry of *Oberon*, by Mr. Planché, [...] aspires higher than any recent composition." Quoted after Reynolds 1976: 25.

ballads, duets, choruses, and glees, provided they occupied no more than the fewest number of minutes possible, were all that the playgoing public of that day would endure. [...] Nothing but the Huntsmen's Chorus and the diablerie in "Der Freischütz" had saved that fine work from immediate condemnation in England. [...] An immense responsibility was placed upon my shoulders. The fortunes of the season were staked upon the success of the piece. Had I constructed it in the form which would have been most agreeable to me and acceptable to Weber, it could not have been performed by the Company at Covent Garden, and if attempted must have proved a complete fiasco.[172]

In a similar fashion, and obviously as a result of diverging esthetic horizons, Weber's music stylistically has an "in-between" quality as well, at times showing the composer of *Der Freischütz* and *Euryanthe* exploring new territory, as in the pre-Wagnerian orchestration of the aria 'Ocean! Thou mighty monster,'[173] whereas the Storm Music recalls late eighteenth-century magic fairy-tale operas,[174] as does the story itself.[175]

The premiere of *Oberon* in April 1826 was a big event in British music history, mainly because, as Temperley points out, "never before had a great composer, already famous on the Continent, written an opera to an English text for performance on the English stage."[176] Paraphrasing the *Morning Chronicle* and

---

172   Ibid.: 55.

173   Jürgen Maehder, for example, argues that the first step towards Wagner's technique of the all-encompassing *Mischklang*, as signaled by Adorno in his *Versuch über Wagner* (1952), was actually taken by Weber in *Oberon*. (Maehder 1988: 193) Weber's musical staging of the breakthrough of sunlight with majestic C-major chords is often seen as one of the inspirations for Wagner's similar procedure in the first scene of *Das Rheingold* or the moment in the first act of *Die Walküre* when Siegmund pulls Nothung out of the ash. In a diary note of Cosima Wagner on 3 October 1878, it is mentioned how the old Wagner is still moved to tears when hearing the 'Ocean-aria' from *Oberon*: "R. [...] gedenkt [...] eines Konzertes in Basel, wo die Ozean-Arie aus »Oberon« gesungen wurde, wobei er in Schluchzen ausbrach. So ergriffen ihn diese rührenden Klänge, diese ideale Natürlichkeit bei Weber." wwsb, *Cosimas Tagebücher Band II*: 189. One may, however, contend that these techniques are also of eighteenth-century origin, as the most famous C-major sunlight effect had already been created by Haydn in *Die Schöpfung* (1798).

174   The Storm Music in Gluck's *Iphigénie en Tauride* (1779) appears to be one of Weber's inspirations here.

175   Dahlhaus relates the eclecticism of *Oberon* as not only being the result of or even an attempt to overcome the divergent horizons of Weber and Planché, but also to *Oberon's* status as a "late work," comprising Weber's esthetic and stylistic development. See Dahlhaus 1986: 81.

176   Temperley 1966: 297. *The Quarterly Musical Magazine & Review* also concluded that "the novelty of a foreigner conducting his own operas in an English orchestra [...] contributed to cast around him a halo of glory." *QMMR* VII/30, August 1826: 140. In the field of oratorio,

Literary Chronicle, Fenner states that "on opening night 'all orders were suspend-
ed,' the house was packed, and 'many hundreds' were turned away."[177] As had
been the case with the *Euryanthe* premiere in Vienna, the feverish reception of
Oberon at its first performance had to a considerable extent been the result
of a general sensation that the composer of *Der Freischütz* was physically
present in the Covent Garden theater. But more than in Vienna, the work
succeeded to conquer the audience in the long term, even though its initial
success was, according to Warrack, mainly caused by the splendid scenery,[178]
and perhaps less by the music itself, which, according to *The Harmonicon*, was
"more calculated for the scientific judge than for the multitude."[179]

This variation on the common theme that German music was deemed more
suitable to "instruct than to please" leads to the question whether Weber's
English opera was considered to have an educational value for native composers. A first card pulled by a native composer was that of antagonism, as
Henry Bishop, who had previously arranged the relatively faithful Drury Lane
Freischütz, composed an opera called *Aladdin* – also an Arabic, fairylike subject – which was premiered two weeks after Covent Garden had premiered
Weber's work. In fact, this was the second attempt of Drury Lane to profit from
the *Oberon* rage by putting on a competing show, after an unsuccessful *Oberon*
pasticcio with music by, amongst others, Cherubini and Von Winter. However, these native competitors to Weber's *Oberon* operated more on financial
than on ideological grounds. Indeed, Weber's opera apparently did not spur
any debate on the merits of German opera and its relation to the future of
English opera, probably because a sense of urgency concerning the need of
a native opera was not yet fully established in 1826.[180] But when the native

---

Händel had already figured as a foreign master composing English-language works for
London audiences, but in the realm of opera, this was clearly something novel.

177   Fenner 1994: 509.
178   Warrack 1976: 356.
179   *The Harmonicon* IV/41, May 1826: 108.
180   A rather isolated article concerning the future of native opera had been included in *The
Quarterly Musical Magazine & Review* in 1821, written by Common Sense, who was obviously a partisan of Italian opera. Common Sense wrote: "I quite agree [...] that our own
opera is an insult to common sense as well as good taste, and that until the entire performance be moulded into one consistent *musical* whole, the English nation will still remain
under the disgrace of possessing little or nothing beyond melo-dramatic plays or farces –
certainly nothing like genuine opera. [...] I should therefore incline to think that the selection and adaptation of the fascinating and most perfect dramas of Italy [...] would at
the outset be more likely to super-induce the understanding of and taste for opera than
any thing of our own. [...] It only remains to overcome the absurdity of the connecting
dialogue, and to [...] train the mind and the ear to the enjoyment of recitative." QMMR
III/10, 1821: 157–161.

opera movement got underway during the 1830s, Weber's opera clearly formed a source of inspiration, as Temperley emphasizes:

> It is no coincidence that several of the most successful English operas after 1830 were about fairies or nymphs, notably Barnett's *The Mountain Sylph*, Loder's *The Night Dancers*, Balfe's *Keolanthe*, and Wallace's *Lurline*. In all these the fairy music pays an obvious debt to *Oberon*; and generally, in most English romantic operas the rich, warm glow which distinguishes them from their predecessors comes from Weber more than any other single influence.[181]

Weber's death at the peak of his popularity in London was obviously a stroke to the British Weber mania. According to Percival M. Kirby, "with his death, interest in his music seems to have ceased abruptly," an impression supported by the fact that it took until 1840 before *Euryanthe* was performed in English.[182] Rather than digging out the rest of Weber's oeuvre,[183] which had been done between 1824 and 1826, London theaters now turned their attention to operas by other German composers.[184]

In December 1824, at the peak of London *Freischütz* fever, the London reporter of the *Allgemeine musikalische Zeitung* had already suggested that the British operatic climate was highly favorable to German composers, given that they combined the right ingredients: bright, gay music, a tinge of the wondrous and diabolic, and ample visual splendor.[185] This gentle climate is also perceiv-

---

181 Temperley 1966: 297–298.
182 Kirby 1946: 353.
183 Apart from a production of *Silvana*, translated into *Sylvania*, at the *Surrey Theatre* in 1828, which seems to have failed due to the poor performance. See Fenner 1994: 508.
184 The general search for new operas after the premiere of Weber's *Oberon* did not exclusively focus on German works. Christina Fuhrmann points out that after *Der Freischütz*, "a flood of operatic importation followed in its wake" (Fuhrmann 2004: 136), whereas Kirby concludes that after Weber's death, "the fickle audiences, which had never really understood the genius of Weber, had turned their attention to light operas of the French School" (Kirby 1946: 353). Indeed, the success of *Der Freischütz* also smoothened French opera's path to the British capital, but in this study, focus naturally lies on the situation of German opera.
185 "Demnach wird die Oper [*Der Freischütz*] für deutsche Musik [...] in diesem Lande nicht ohne gute Folgen seyn; und gewiss würde hier eine neue deutsche Oper, von ähnlichem Charakter bey der jetzigen Stimmung des Volkes, großes Glück machen. Die Musik müsste aber durchaus heiter seyn, denn der Engländer hat genug den langen Tag über die Stirne in Falten zu ziehen, abends überlässt er sich seiner frohen Laune; und der Text etwas von dem wunderlichen Wesen im *Freyschütz* enthalten. Vor allen Dingen müsste für das Auge mehr gesorgt seyn als für das Ohr, denn hier ist der Ort zu erwähnen, das hundert und

able from the space devoted to reports of German operas and composers in British music periodicals of the time from 1824 onwards. A generous review of the 1825 Cassel premiere of Spohr's *Der Berggeist* in *The Harmonicon* mentioned that "it is delightful to see how rapidly many of the later compositions of the German school are making their way through Europe, and dividing the attention that was before too exclusively directed to the lighter compositions of the Italian school."[186] In the same period, British music periodicals seemed to make an inventory of "new" German operas worth importing.[187] For example, in June 1825 a memoir of Joseph Weigl was published in *The Harmonicon*, quoting Weber's judgments of Weigl's gracious but trivial style at length.[188] Although most of Weigl's works lack the dark shades of Weber's *Freischütz*, his merry *Singspiel* esthetic seemed quite congenial to the English taste as had been pinned down by the *AMZ* reporter. This predilection for unpretentious music can also be found in a negative review of Spohr's arias in *Faust* by a *Repository of Arts* critic, who stated in 1826:

> there is everywhere abundance of thought and musical science, and no lack of strong modulation; all is very good music: but we are not ashamed to confess it, the pleasing tunes of even Kauer and Dittersdorf, countrymen of Mr. S. much inferior to him in the scale of compositorial gradation, possess more attractions for us according to our *present* relish. What changes time may effect in our taste we will not answer for.[189]

Considering the frequent accusation of "learnedness" and outspoken preference for the musically undemanding, it is all the more remarkable that the first successful imported and translated German opera not written by Weber would be Peter von Winter's *Das unterbrochene Opferfest*, premiered in August 1826 at the *English Opera House* as *The Oracle; or The Interrupted Sacrifice*, a work far removed from a ballad opera esthetic. As *The Quarterly Musical Magazine & Review* pointed out, the opera was:

---

aber hunderte zum *Freyschütz* gingen, lediglich um die Wolfsschlucht und nebenher auch wohl den T.f.l zu sehen."*AMZ* XXVI/51, 16 December 1824: 830.

186 *The Harmonicon* III/33, September 1825: 151.

187 This marks a notable difference with the contemporary situation in French music periodicals, where evaluations of German operas were generally published only when these works were actually presented to the Parisian public – either in performance or in print – whereas British music journalism played a far more active role in the process of selecting works worth to be imported.

188 *The Harmonicon* III/30, June 1825: 91–92.

189 Quoted after Brown 1984: 247.

very successful *on account of the music*, which was not so entirely made up of simple melodies, hitherto supposed to be the most congenial to national taste. Concerted pieces, and those of no slight science, were the principal ingredients, and the pleasure with which they were heard and the frequency of the *encores*, prove in no slight degree the progress of musical knowledge.[190]

The *Harmonicon* hailed the performance of Von Winter's opera as a significant step forward in the process of increasing fidelity towards the score, a process that arguably had been primed by the 1824 Drury Lane *Freischütz*:

> In no opera has so much respect been shown to the original music, which, with some very trifling exceptions, is given without any omission, and what is still better, without the addition of any foreign matter, or any violent transposition of the parts, liberties which, we are sorry to say, are becoming more and more glaring in that school of music, the Opera, which ought to show a better example. It is by this conscientious respect of the score of a master, and by this alone, that the beauties of his compositions can appear in their true light; it is thus only that they can be recognised as a consistent whole, and be seen in their proper and natural proportion.[191]

Whether a work like Von Winter's *Opferfest*, with its episodic and at times "absurd" plot,[192] really thrives on a complete performance is a question worth asking, but from most responses to the work and the audience enthusiasm, it becomes clear that the production was a triumph.[193]

---

190 *QMMR* IX/33, 1827: 60.

191 *The Harmonicon* IV/45, Sept 1826: 176.

192 Fenner mentions that the *Literary Chronicle* found many of the incidents "unnaturally absurd," whereas the *Gazette* pointed out that "never did people sing [...] at more improbable moments" (Fenner 1994: 498). *The Quarterly Musical Magazine & Review* generally stated that the recently performed *The Oracle*, *La dame blanche* and *Il turco in Italia* "have in so far taught our countrymen that good music may be patched in with flippant, poor, or absurd dialogue." *QMMR* IX/33, 1827: 62.

193 Both the enthusiasm for the music and the indulgence to step over plot absurdities may be caused by the fact that Von Winter's style was essentially close to popular Italian opera models, where absurd plots were standard fare. Moreover, the relative datedness of the work, composed in 1796, may have been an advantage for those who found Weber's *Freischütz* too audacious, such as Thomas Talfourd, who characterized the opera's impression in the *New Monthly Magazine* as "more direct and harmonious than that which is left by the 'Freischütz' or the 'Oberon'; there seem to be less violent and startling combinations, and more melody in the concerted pieces." Quoted after Fenner 1994: 499.

Whereas Von Winter was, like Weber, an already deceased composer, Heinrich Marschner was a relatively new appearance on the German opera scene with a promising future. To a considerable extent, Marschner's first hit opera *Der Vampyr* – premiered in Leipzig in 1828 – continued the line of Weber's *Freischütz*, with a mix of comic, *Biedermeier* and Gothic elements within a *Singspiel* constellation, albeit tending more towards a through-composed style. Together with the fact that the story was of British origin, being an adaptation of John Polidori's *The Vampyre* (1819)[194] – initially attributed to Lord Byron – it seemed to have great potential to succeed in London. But the stylistic vicinity to London's deceased idol would prove to be a stumbling block for Marschner's British reception, at least in the press. An enthusiastic report of the opera's success at the Leipzig premiere in *The Harmonicon* in June 1828[195] was followed up by an extensive negative review of the vocal score in *The Quarterly Musical Magazine & Review*, in which the opera was dismissed as being tasteless, excessively orchestrated and little more than a Weber plagiarism.[196]

Despite this scathing judgment, the *English Opera House* dauntlessly put on Marschner's opera in August 1829, in an English translation by James Planché, who transplanted the superstitious action from the homeland to the more "backward" Wallachia.[197] The opera had some of a false start, because, as *The Harmonicon* mentioned, after a few performances, "the illness of a principal actor" laid the piece aside for the rest of the season."[198] It was reprised in 1830

---

194   For a more detailed account of the sources for Wilhelm August Wohlbrück's libretto of *Der Vampyr*, see Palmer 1980: 77–88 and White 1987: 23–26. For a general view of the post-1819 vampire rage in Europe, see Frayling 1991 and Montaclair 1998.

195   *The Harmonicon* VI/6, June 1828: 139.

196   "The story of *Der Vampyr* [...] excites in our minds, we must own, nothing short of disgust. [...] We consider *Der Vampyr*, though possessing much that is excellent in parts, scarcely above mediocrity as a whole. The first objection lies in so unfortunate a choice of subject, and further, the composer has in some degree fallen into the common error of imitating his forerunner [Weber] too closely. [...] Nearly every modern opera we look at forces us more and more to regret the abuse, rather than the use, that is now made of the orchestra in accompaniment. [...] Mr. Marschner is inclined to yield to the prevailing passion of the day – noise." QMMR X/40, 1828: 508–514.

197   In his *Recollections*, Planché recounted that he "laid the scene of action in Hungary, where the superstition exists to this day." Planché 1872: 104.

198   *The Harmonicon* VII/10, October 1829: 261. It would not be the last time in Marschner's career that foreign success with *Der Vampyr* would be tainted by vocal indisposition. The *Revue Musicale* reported in 1833 that a planned performance of *Der Vampyr* by the German company in Paris in the summer of 1830 was cancelled because the proposed title-hero had made such a poor impression singing Mephistopheles in Spohr's *Faust* that the ensemble was reluctant to put the fortunes of Marschner's opera in his hands: "Cet opéra [*Le Vampire*] devait être représenté à Paris en 1830 par les chanteurs allemands; mais l'acteur qui devait remplir le principal rôle avait déjà tellement déplu dans *Faust* qu'on n'osa pas l'en charger." See *Revue musicale* VII/41, 9 November 1833: 333.

and appears to have created quite a sensation.[199] Although some reviews were similarly hostile as *The Quarterly*'s had been,[200] the majority of critics seemed more sympathetic to Marschner's work.[201]

In the wake of the London *Vampyre*, some mistily-reported events suggest that, as had been the case with Weber, Marschner was to present another opera in London, a work partly, or maybe even specifically designed for London. His next opera, *Der Templer und die Jüdin* (premiered December 1829 in Leipzig), also drew on English literature, this time on Walter Scott's *Ivanhoe*. It is likely that Marschner and his librettist Wohlbrück chose this subject in the hope of capitalizing on their previous British success with *Der Vampyr*. In his biography of Marschner, Palmer mentions that the composer had dedicated his score to the King of England, which the latter had accepted, but that "legal bickering" between English Opera House music director William Hawes and a music publisher frustrated the operation.[202]

This "legal bickering" may have been caused by the fact that Hawes had other plans with Marschner. Palmer claims that immediately after the London premiere of *The Vampyre*, Marschner had received a letter from Hawes reporting its triumph and promising to send the composer a new libretto by Planché for an opera to be premiered in London.[203] The exact train of events is hard to

---

199 Palmer mentions 60 performances of it in 1829 alone, which seems improbable. First of all, this may be incorrectly taken over from a highly speculative biography by Ludwig Bischoff, published in *The Musical World* in 1857, in which the German writer maintains that already in the summer of 1828, 60 performances were given in London. Secondly, considering the reports of illness shortly after the 1829 premiere, it seems more likely that the majority of performances took place in 1830. In general, the *Musical World* editor challenged Bischoff's overly victorious depiction of Marschner's London success. See Palmer 1980: 91–92 and *The Musical World* XXXV/8, 21 February 1857: 116–117 and *The Musical World* XXXV/12, 21 March 1857: 182.

200 *The Harmonicon* concluded that "there are very few things in it that we could not trace to some model which appears to have occupied his thoughts; and to the *Freischütz* and *Euryanthe* he has continually made himself a debtor" while simultaneously rejecting the "unremitting fullness of accompaniment." *The Harmonicon* VII/10, October 1829: 261.

201 Holmes, critic of *The Atlas*, was the most enthusiastic judge, countering the skeptics by stating that "we have not heard any modern opera with greater pleasure. [...] No one was tired at the end, and many were longing for more. Can a higher compliment be paid to a composer? [...] Of melody there is abundance, and the musical thoughts are no less original in themselves than in the manner of their expression. [...] we see little that reminds us of Weber; the style is different, and so is the instrumentation." Quoted after Fenner 1994: 501–502.

202 Palmer 1980: 100.

203 This rumor can also be found in the *AMZ* (VI/46, 14 November 1829: 368), as well as in the *Revue Musicale* (VII/41, 9 November 1833: 336), where a detailed account of the proposed but never finalized business agreement was listed. In 1830, the *AMZ* mentioned that Marschner had been invited to London to conduct his *Der Templer und die Jüdin* there,

trace, mainly because the chief source, Ludwig Bischoff's 1857 Marschner biography, obscures rather than clarifies what happened due to a series of factual errors.[204] In the end, if there was a deal in the making concerning a new English opera specifically composed for London, it was prematurely broken off. It seems probable, however, that the plan of a new English work on a libretto by Planché conflicted with Marschner's objectives, since by August 1829, he had already finished *Der Templer* and hoped to bring it to England. Hawes presumably did not approve of this plan because an original work would be more lucrative for him, as well as for Planché, who in his *Recollections*, however, does not mention any considered collaboration with Marschner whatsoever, making the story all the more cloudy.[205] In the end, the apparent clashing of interests nullified Marschner's chances in Britain, and regardless of *Der Templer und die Jüdin*'s enormous success at German theaters, Marschner had to wait until 1840 before its London premiere took place, and by then the momentum for his music had largely vanished.[206]

Two other German composers, already quite famous as masters of serious instrumental music, had their operas presented in London in English translations; Ferdinand Ries and Louis Spohr. Both had strong ties to London. Ries had lived in the British capital between 1813 until 1824 and had connections to the *Philharmonic Society*, where Spohr had been gently received during his London sojourn in 1820.

Ries, a piano virtuoso chiefly composing instrumental music, had long refrained from writing operas, but at the end of his life tried his luck with the genre. The opera *Die Räuberbraut*, on a libretto by Georg Döhring, was warmly received at its Frankfurt premiere in October 1828, and Ries's British connection immediately sparked rumors that the work was to be transported

---

which implies that an original English work was no longer at stake. However, as all this accounts were derived from hearsay, it is hard to draw a conclusion.

204   Palmer maintains that this letter was sent at the End of August 1829 (Palmer 1980: 91), whereas Ludwig Bischoff situates this event even earlier, in November 1828, which is unlikely (*The Musical World* XXXV/12, 21 March 1857: 182). In general, Bischoff's chronology fits quite well if transposed a year later and to another theater. He argues that Marschner and Hawes had already signed a contract when a sudden fire burnt down parts of the theater in 1829. Although Bisschof presents Hawes as working for the Adelphi Theater, the company concerned was in fact the *Lyceum*, or *English Opera House*, which burnt down in 1830 indeed.

205   Planché simply uttered his surprise "that Marschner's most dramatic and melodious works, "Der Vampyr" "Die Judin," &c., have not been introduced to our more advanced musical audiences at one or other of our great operatic establishments." Planché 1872: 105.

206   Palmer 1980: 100.

to London.[207] And indeed, the *English Opera House* produced the work as *The Robber's Bride* in 1829, but it did not create the hit the company had hoped for. Although *The Harmonicon* opened its premiere review with the general remark about German opera that "whatever now comes from that land, a land overflowing with melody and harmony, is sure of a friendly reception, a patient hearing, and if not a favourable, at least a lenient, judgment,"[208] a few weeks later after a re-hearing of the work, the same journal could do nothing but conclude that "the greater portion of the music is uninteresting, and the dramatic part affords the composer no support whatever; it is exceedingly commonplace. [...] *The Robber's Bride* has proved a failure, [...] and is on the point of being withdrawn. "[209] Regardless of *The Robber's Bride*'s failure, Ries got another chance in London, this time to create an original work for the *English Opera House* in 1831. The work concerned, *The Sorceress*, was actually written in a rush during a brief London sojourn, and seems not to have fared much better than its predecessor.[210]

A few months before *The Sorceress* was mounted, *Covent Garden* produced an English version of Spohr's *Zemire und Azor*, re-named as *Azor and Zemira*. Clive Brown argues that the theater's choice to stage Spohr's opera was plausibly caused by the success of Spohr's oratorio *Die letzten Dinge*, given as *The Last Judgment* in 1830 at a festival in Norwich.[211] Judging from the press, the premiere of *Azor and Zemira* was quite an event in London musical life, attended by the majority of prominent musicians.[212] In spite of the fact that

---

207   An anonymous *AMZ* reporter wrote: "This opera, which outshines nearly all new operatic meteors, will certainly gain ground on all stages. It is said that an English translation is already in the making (Gewiss wird diese Oper, welche fast alle neue Opernmeteore weit überglänzt, bald auf allen Bühnen einheimisch seyn. Schon soll man sich mit einer Übertraging in's Englische beschäftigen)." *AMZ* XXX/44, 29 October 1828: 744.

208   *The Harmonicon* VII/8, August 1829: 205.

209   *The Harmonicon* VII/9, September 1829: 233. J.P. Collier from the *Morning Chronicle* voiced a similar contempt: "More common-place stuff we have seldom seen." Quoted after Fenner 1994: 499.

210   *The Harmonicon* concluded that "the music is of that solid, well-constructed kind, which was to be expected from Ferdinand Ries, and proclaims at once its German parentage. As a whole it is rather heavy, for the melodies are not striking, and there are but few effects of combination that immediately seize attention." *The Harmonicon* IX/9, September 1831: 229.

211   Brown 1984: 251.

212   *The Harmonicon* writes that "the number of dilettanti and professors present showed how great were the expectations formed of the piece" (*The Harmonicon* IX/5, May 1831: 117), whereas the *Morning Chronicle* wrote that "we saw in the house many musical professors

The Harmonicon prospect had called the music of the opera "as beautiful and of a more popular character than either the *Jessonda* or *Faust*, promising 'long and lasting popularity'."[213] Brown discerns a 'certain degree of ambivalence towards the opera' in press responses, because 'to many, the seriousness of Spohr's style was less acceptable in opera than in oratorio.'[214] The performance was apparently quite good,[215] but not spectacular, and considering the fact that *Zemire* was already an elder work, it appears that public attention soon shifted to Ries's upcoming *Sorceress*.[216]

Altogether, the German operas performed in London during the five years after Weber's demise display a heightened interest in German music drama in the British capital, but none of the above-mentioned composers could create a sensation anywhere close to what Weber had caused in 1824 and 1826. And although a gradually growing tendency towards fidelity in the way these works were given is discernible, original-language performances still seemed out of the question. This changed when Thomas Monck Mason, at that moment managing the *King's Theatre*, invited a German company in 1832. As was mentioned earlier, the troupe partly consisted of the same members as Röckel's company that had visited Paris from 1829 to 1831, with Anton Haitzinger and Wilhelmine Schröder-Devrient as main attractions. Besides the regular Italian ensemble and the travelling German company, Monck Mason also installed a French troupe. As *The Harmonicon* concluded, this sudden cosmopolitization of London opera life was a treat to the audiences from the viewpoint of variety, but running three, moreover mutually competing companies by one management proved to be impossible in an already flooded market where only the fittest survived.[217]

---

of eminence, both native and foreign, all interested for the success of imported Spohr." Quoted after Brown 1984: 251.

213   *The Harmonicon* IX/4, April 1831: 102.

214   Brown draws this conclusion partly from the *Morning Chronicle* critic, who compared Spohr to Rossini and preferred the latter. Brown 1984: 251. A similar comment can be found in the *Revue musicale*, where the London reporter concluded: "La musique de cet ouvrage est d'un genre trop sérieux pour le public anglais." *Revue musicale* V/23, 9 July 1831: 184.

215   *The Harmonicon* wrote that "it was really admirably got up" (*The Harmonicon* IX/5, May 1831: 117), whereas the *Morning Chronicle* pointed out that the opera was given "without any expression of dissent, and with very warm applause" (quoted after Brown 1984: 251).

216   See for example *The Harmonicon* IX/8, August 1831: 206.

217   In June 1832, *The Harmonicon* wrote that "the present Lord Chamberlain is less rigorous than the last, and permits Mr. Mason to load his shoulders with three companies – for there is now also a French *troupe* – though the latter finds it an arduous if not an insurmountable labor to manage one. While it is utterly impossible that, as a speculation, all three should succeed under the same roof, without a very strong head to conduct the machinery, the public are nevertheless gainers by the attempt, inasmuch as they may now

Nevertheless, the German company appears to have won the competition during their first London season, as the influential critic Henry Chorley concluded in his *Musical Recollections* (1862) that "the most noticeable feature of the year 1832 was the introduction to England of German Opera in its original form," moreover stating that "the Italians, that year not very strong in muster, were fairly beaten out of the field by the Germans."[218] The equally authoritative critic Lord Edgcumbe came to a similar conclusion, stating in his *Musical Reminiscences* (1834) that "the experiment of procuring a German company of singers [...] succeeded beyond expectation: the German opera became the rage, and the Italian sunk into insignificance."[219] The company brought *Der Freischütz* and *Fidelio*, – guarantees of success as much as Haitzinger and Schröder-Devrient were – as well as Weigl's *Schweizerfamilie*, and German-language performances of Mozart's *Don Giovanni* and the originally-French opera *Macbeth* by Hippolyte Chélard, who also functioned as conductor. The biggest hit turned out to be *Fidelio*, for three reasons mainly; the fact that it was the first ever performance of this work in London, Schröder-Devrient's musical and histrionic achievements, and the quality and spirit of the choir.[220]

---

hear some good music well performed, and are not obliged to listen to the trash of *Pacini, Donizetti* and the herd of Italian composers." *The Harmonicon* x/6, June 1832: 145.

218   Chorley 1862: 50 + 55.

219   Edgcumbe 1834: 210.

220   Chorley argued that "Fidelio," as given by artists "to the manner born," amounted to a revelation," and although disapproving of Schröder-Devrient's un-Italian technique, was willing to concede that "as an actress, the devouring suspense of the disquieted wife, throughout the first half of the tale, enabled the German *Leonora* to exhibit all her passion of by-play, in judicious interpretation of the situation.– Her eyes, quickened by the yearnings of her heart, were everywhere." (Chorley 1862: 51 + 57) We may interpret Chorley's criticism of Schröder-Devrient's vocal capabilities as a polemic reaction to the frequent laudations in the press, for example of *The Harmonicon*, writing that she is "a lady of high vocal reputation in Germany, [...] which her performance now will assist in maintaining. [...] She relies on her knowledge of music, correct taste, and sensible manner for success, and has always met with the approbation of judicious critics." (*The Harmonicon* x/6, June 1832: 146) Rather than the acting and singing skills of Schröder-Devrient, Chorley argued that "the principal feature of the German performance of 'Fidelio' which marked an epoch in London, was the spirit and reality of the stage chorus – things till then totally unknown here. The rueful, shabby people who used to shout their easy Italian tunes out of tune, in meagre, motionless semi-circle – so many scarecrows, instead of singers – were in these German Operas replaced by a company of earnest folk, with stout voices (and those of the women fresh), who showed that they took pride in their work by rendering the music, and all its lights and shades, with instant steadiness- and that they understood the scene, by the assistance their appropriate action afforded to every situation in which they took part." (Chorley 1862: 58–59) Lord Edgcumbe also praises the choir as the outstanding feature, and relates this to the common belief that the excellent choral singing is the result of a thoroughly musical nature and education: "It was in the chorusses especially, that the excellence of the German singers was most displayed. These were performed

The latter two qualities had similarly impressed Paris audiences before. Despite individual successes, *The Harmonicon* reached a severe verdict on the 1832 German season in its entirety:

> The German company realized the hopes held out, so far as the *Frieschütz* (sic.) and *Fidelio* are concerned. *Macbeth* did not succeed, – the *Schweitzerfamilie* counted for nothing, and *Don Juan* proved a most decided failure. Instead, therefore, of hearing at least half-a-dozen of the finest works of the best school in Europe, [...] we were, in point of effect, limited to two.[221]

In the two consecutive seasons, the German company could not shake off the ghost of mediocrity. In March 1833, a new season was launched, containing *Der Freischütz*, *Fidelio* and Ferdinand Herold's *Zampa*, a French work translated into German. Due to the apparently poor conducting by Johann Nepomuk Hummel, the high entrance fees,[222] and the absence of Haitzinger and Schröder-Devrient, the German season was quickly turning into a fiasco.[223] In May, the company started up again with a performance of *Die Zauberflöte* with the two star singers in leading parts, but audience attendance remained low.[224] In August, a last attempt at success was made with a performance of *Euryanthe*, but the insufficient number of rehearsals[225] deprived this complicated work of turning into a victory. The downward spiral of the German company was continued in 1834; Chorley concludes that the enterprise went from "being

---

in a manner quite new to an English audience. [...] The cause of this greater excellence is the very superior knowledge of music possessed by the Germans, who study it more scientifically than any other nation. Nobody who has not heard the chorusses of Weber, Beethoven and other great composers, sung by native performers, can have an idea of their perfection." Edgcumbe 1834: 212–213.

221   *The Harmonicon* X/9, September 1832: 214.

222   *The Harmonicon* pointed out that "M. Hummel is the conductor of this corps; but seated at the piano-forte, he appears to greater advantage than when flourishing the baton. [...] M. Laporte's terms of admission have increased. [...] Up to the present moment the speculation has proved a very losing one." *The Harmonicon* XI/4, April 1833: 91.

223   In May 1833, *The Harmonicon* wrote that "*Fidelio* has been performed, but Mad. Pirscher is not to be named with Mad. Devrient; and as the weight of the opera falls on the female character, the difference between the two cannot be made up by any merit that the others may possess." *The Harmonicon* XI/5, May 1833: 115.

224   See *The Harmonicon* XI/7, July 1833: 160: "Their first performance was Mozart's *Zauberflöte*, M. Haitzinger as Tamino, who sung the airs with great feeling, [...] Madame Schroeder Devrient as Pamina, who did the most ample justice to the part." The reporter nevertheless concluded that "The *Zauberflöte* has not drawn, in spite of its many beauties, and the German opera is not in a much better condition."

225   Noted in *The Harmonicon* XI/8, August 1833: 183–184.

made up out of mediocrities" in 1833 to a level "beneath mediocrity" in 1834,[226] and the *Neue Zeitschrift für Musik* also concluded in July 1834 that the "German opera was hardly attended evening after evening."[227] As had already been the case in Paris between 1829 and 1831, the expiration date of a visiting German opera company turned out to be three years.

In his biography of Schröder-Devrient, Alfred Freiherr von Wolzogen argues that the German opera companies in Paris and London generally collapsed because, from the start, they were set up so lavishly that even genuine popular success could not make up for the expenses.[228] To that explanation one might add that these companies thrived to a considerable extent on novelty, or perhaps even fashion,[229] which wears out fast.

But apart from these general remarks, the termination of London's German opera company may also be explained by tectonic shifts in the local musical life unfavorable to the Teutonic muse. The year 1834 marks a decisive moment in the emancipation of native composers and native opera in Britain. First of all, this year saw the foundation of the *Society of British Musicians*.[230]

---

226 Chorley 1862: 61 + 76. Edgcumbe also characterized the 1834 troupe as "being below mediocrity." Edgcumbe 1834: 214.

227 *NZfM* I: 1 / 29, 10 July 1834: 116.

228 "Mr. Bunn aber hatte 1832, ebenso wie Monck Mason 1831 [sic.: dates should be transposed one year later], mit seiner Speculation auf die Anziehungskraft deutscher Musik in London schlechte Geschäfte gemacht; beide waren sie dem Schiksale Röckel's in Paris treulich gefolgt, nicht weil das fremdländische Publikum unsere Componisten und Sänger etwa nicht gebührend zu schätzen gewußt hätte, sondern vielmehr lediglich aus dem Grunde, weil [...] das Unternehmen von Anfang an so ungemein kostspielig eingerichtet war, daß es selbst bei allezeit vollen Häusern unmöglich hätte rentiren können. Rechnet man dazu noch die Mißgriffe, die bei einzelnen Engagements geschahen, welche sich dann nur durch bedeutende Geldopfer wieder rückgängig machen ließen, so ist das Räthsel, warum die Entrepreneurs selbst mit zum Theil enthusiastisch aufgenommen Werken und Darstellern finanziell nicht reussiren konnten, vollständig gelöst." Wolzogen 1863: 216.

229 See the earlier-mentioned French commentator who wrote in the *Berliner Allgemeine Musikalische Zeitung* in 1830 that Parisian audiences warm up for "anything that comes from afar and leaves soon afterwards." Schröder-Devrient similarly complained that her sudden rise to fame in London was merely the result of fashion, and not of a thorough understanding of her art: "To society life I was merely a toy, something which was accidentally en vogue, but should be prepared to be brushed aside at any moment ("für die Gesellschaft war ich eben nur ein Spielzeug, für das sich zufällig die Mode entschieden hatte, das aber gewärtig sein mußte, im nächsten Moment beiseite geschoben zu werden")." Ibid.: 208–209.

230 Simon Mcveigh emphatically relates the foundation of the Society to the rise of a British cultural nationalism that until recently had barely been recorded: "the Society of British Musicians represented a revolution in London musical life. For one should not underestimate the subversiveness of its position nor the vehemence of its appeal to national feelings. The date of its foundation is surely indicative: these were times of increasing

Secondly, the *Lyceum/English Opera House* re-opened, this time more than ever primarily a stage for native music-dramatic talent.[231] Eric Walter White argues that "the year 1834 proved to be something of a milestone. The rebuilt Lyceum was opened that summer for 'the representation of English opera and the encouragement of indigenous musical talent,' and five new English operas were mounted during the first season."[232] Although the theater had been the prime stage for operas by German composers until it had caught fire in 1830, the German-language company was now a business competitor, albeit not as much an adversary as Italian opera and its aristocratic audience. But neverthe-less, for those who felt hostility towards Italian opera in general, the choice between the stylistically similar German and English opera performances was increasingly being decided in the latter's favor.

The return to London of a German company in 1840 again unluck-ily coincided with a powerful press campaign to advance the cause of native opera.[233] Between April and August 1840, a vivid debate on the question how to facilitate a national opera took place in the columns of *The Musical World*, at times interspersed by skeptical remarks from *The Musical Journal*, its short-lived competitor. Returning questions were how to create an audience for native opera, how the genre could be institutionalized, – as the *English Opera*

---

social unrest that intersected directly with a re-evaluation of national identity. Recent debate about British nationalism has generally countered the traditional view that the absence of foreign incursions on British soil minimized the growth of a nationalist ideol-ogy. [...] In the cultural sphere the Other was already here." Mcveigh 2000: 151.

231   Previously, the apparently patriotic name of the theater had not really been suitable, as Fuhrmann concludes concerning the situation in 1824 when *Der Freischütz* was first per-formed there: "The nationalistic agenda explicit in this theatre's name makes it seem an unlikely venue for an important foreign premiere. In reality, however, the name reflected operatic more than patriotic aspirations." Fuhrmann 2004: 120.

232   The status of 1834 as the beginning of a new era for British opera is also underlined by George Biddlecombe, who used it as the starting point for his 1994 study of *English Opera from 1834 to 1864 with Particular Reference to the Works of Michael Balfe*.

233   In the years before, some attempts were made at bringing new German troupes to Lon-don, for example in 1838 when Gaspare Spontini was considered to lead the company, but this came to nothing. On 18 October 1838 *The Musical World* wrote that "the newest report which has reached us for reviving the somewhat dingy lustre of the Drury Lane operas, relates to the appearance of the Chevalier Spontini at the head of the entire corps of the Berlin opera-house, for the purpose of giving in the best and most authentic versions what-ever peculiarly excellent or nationally characteristic the German lyric stage possesses. It would seem by this that the Germans [...] think us still to be instructed in the true mer-its of their stage." (*The Musical World* x/136, 18 October 1838: 93) A month later, the same journal concluded that "this undertaking remains in *status quo*, as Spontini requires a certain subscription to insure his company against loss," a legitimate concern considering the vicissitudes of earlier companies. *The Musical World* x/142, Nov 1838: 202.

House's promising course from 1834 was stagnating – and how collaboration among composers could be enhanced. In the same period, a German company performed in the relatively small *St. James Theatre*, bringing Mozart's *Don Juan,* Weber's *Euryanthe,* Kreutzer's *Nachtlager in Granada,* Gluck's *Iphigenia in Tauris* and Spohr's *Jessonda* and *Faust.* These performances were relatively well-received and well-attended, and within the native opera debate, the company was spared the type of condescendence often directed at the high number of German works on the *Philharmonic Society* program or the status of Italian opera in London musical life.

This quiet coexistence of native and German opera ended when in August 1840, rumors spread that Drury Lane manager Eliason had willfully gridlocked negotiations with English artists in order to install a German opera company.[234] In the article reporting Eliason's betrayal to the national cause, *The Musical Journal* sounded alarm bells about an imminent foreign music-dramatic intrusion of London and called upon the English to revolt against this development:

> Not only is Drury Lane to be converted into a *German Opera,* [...] but the new theatre in Oxford Street is to be tenanted by an *Opera Buffa,* and the St. James Theatre into an *Opera Comique* [...]. We shall shortly expect to hear of the issuing of a proclamation, prohibiting the use of the English language within these realms. Now we call upon the public, if they have one spark of English feeling remaining, to set their faces against these foreign intrusions and intruders, and not allow the French, the German, and Italian opera companies and singers, to drain the sap and destroy the energies of our countrymen.[235]

The public responded ardently to *The Musical Journal*'s appeal. *The Musical World* concluded the following in September 1840:

> If appearances are to be trusted, the metropolis will, during the winter season, exhibit a state of musical affairs the like of which is, we verily believe, not writ down in the artistical records of any city in Europe.

---

234 At the end of August, *The Musical Journal* reported that "it is said, that Eliason having failed in his endeavour to form an English operatic company for the ensuing season at Drury Lane, he intends to engage a German company. [...] That this is a mere *ruse* of the new lessee of Drury Lane we are firm in believing; the terms and conditions were such as he well knew could not be accepted, neither did he intend they ever should be; but knowing that to lower the English professor in the eyes of the public would be to advance his plans of engaging a German company." *The Musical Journal* II/34, 25 August 1840: 113–114.

235 Ibid.: 114.

> London, the largest and wealthiest city of the world [...] is to be abso-
> lutely without a *single* theatre for the performance of native opera.[236]

In the following weeks, public indignation in the press led to new opportunities
for native opera. The sudden boom of partisanship for English opera resulted
not only in the creation of one English opera company, but – hardly astonishing
in the market-governed London of those days – immediately in the formation
of no less than three. *The Musical World,* who had already regretted the lack
of unanimity during the previous debate on native opera, now deplored that
these companies would ruin rather than support each other, and chose the
side of Barnett, a composer willing to take the risk of running an English
troupe.[237] The sudden change of fortune for native opera mitigated animosity
towards German opera, and in December, *The Musical World* included Spohr's
Aufruf an deutschen Komponisten (1823) in translated form, emphasizing the
comparable current state of native opera in England and that in Germany
at the time when Spohr had written it down:

> The following address was published twenty years ago, immediately be-
> fore the production of the author's opera *Jessonda.* [...] It is remarkable
> to observe the analogy between the state of music in Germany in 1820,
> and in England in 1840; and it is deplorable to notice the continuance,
> nay, the exaggeration of the musical abuses which this great composer
> at that time so justly vituperated. Now that the German opera may be
> said to have taken a stand in this country, the opinions on the subject of

---

236   *The Musical World* XIV/233, 10 September 1840: 161.

237   "The cause of English opera seemed, for the present season at least, well nigh hopeless;
      Not a theatre was positively and publicly known to be engaged for the use of our native
      composers, nor seemed there a single breath of effort blowing over the sluggish surface of
      inactivity which entombed their wishes and forces. The aspect of matters is changed how-
      ever: [...] The opening of one operatic theatre in London is now certain, that of another
      almost equally sure, and the establishment of a third in the highest degree possible. [...]
      We do unhesitatingly affirm that London cannot afford to have three little operas. If the
      matter be properly set about, the metropolis *can* undoubtedly support one large operatic
      theatre, but we feel quite certain that it *will* not support three small ones. *That* one of
      the three which produces the best music in the best manner, and is most aristocratically
      patronized, will have the weight of public support, and the others will go to the wall. The
      first case, we rejoice to anticipate, will be Barnett's. As the first, most liberal, and most dis-
      interested of the speculators, he deserves success." *The Musical World* XIV/239, 22 October
      1840: 253–255. *The Musical World* had from the outset maintained that the development
      of an institute for native opera should be led by English composers, and proved loyal
      when one of them accepted the challenge.

Spohr, the greatest living ornament of that classic school, cannot fail to be highly interesting to the musical *dilettante*.[238]

Just as unfeasible as suddenly having three rivalling English opera companies was the plan of the impresario Bunn to move the German company from the modest *St. James Theatre* to the enormous hall of *Drury Lane*, moreover planning no less than a hundred performances.[239] The season started off quite well,[240] but after less than two months, the financial consequences of such a vast repertoire and lavish production style were starting to show,[241] eventually forcing the company to terminate the London season and travel to Liverpool in the hope of making up some of the debts.[242] On 15 July, shortly after the departure of the German company, the *Musical World* published an extensive article by a critic writing under the pseudonym C.,[243] explaining the main causes for the company's failure. C. more than ever before criticized the lack of novelty and quality of the German opera repertoire and its often relatively flawed

---

238   *The Musical World* XIV/248, 24 December 1840: 402–405. The editor errs in dating the text, as well as *Jessonda*, to have originated in 1820, whereas both saw the light in 1823.

239   This number of performances is mentioned in *The Musical World*, XIII/160, 21 January 1841: 47. In the same article, it is told how business partners Bunn and Eliason split up because of an argument, and the former planned to take the company to the *Prince's Theatre*. A month later it was reported that the definitive locale would be *Drury Lane*, see *The Musical World* VIII/165, 25 February 1841: 125. In 1842, *Musical World* critic C. would maintain that the move from the modest St. James Theatre to Drury Lane, and later Covent Garden "seemed to court the odium of having pushed hundreds of talented and industrious natives out of their legitimate market." *The Musical World* XVII/27, 7 July 1842: 210.

240   *The Musical World* stated that "they do things bravely, these Germans; – *Der Freischütz*, *Jessonda*, and *Fidelio*, in one week! Who would not go to see such music so performed [...]?" *The Musical World* VIII/168, 18 March 1841: 161–162.

241   On 6 May, *The Musical World* reported that "the success of the Germans, last year, in Braham's little house, excited high hopes for the present season; but Drury Lane is too vast for the limited circle whence audience to this species of entertainment is to be drawn; and the nonsensical raising of the prices has kept hundreds of the merely curious away. Mr. Andrews should [...] diminish the prices 40 or 50 percent, and produce something of merit which is not known already by heart amongst us (if, indeed, the German opera *Repertoire* can furnish such, which we doubt)." *The Musical World* VIII/175, 6 May 1841: 302.

242   See *The Musical World* IX/185, 15 July 1841: 33.

243   Richard Kitson, responsible for the digitalization of *The Musical World* in the RIPM project, has not identified C. There is a slight chance that the contributor is Henry Chorley, but this author usually signed with his full initials; H.F.C. See Kitson, Richard. 'Introduction to: The Musical World.' *Répertoire international de la presse musicale* (1996): xviii–xix. http://www.ripm.org/pdf/Introductions/MWO1836-1865introEnglish.pdf. Consulted on 9 September 2014.

execution. The significance of his statement as a turning point in the British reception of German opera justifies it to be quoted in length:

> The German opera company has closed its campaign. [...] At the conclu-
> sion of so important a musical career, we feel ourselves called upon to
> review and estimate the proceedings of the enterprise, and to offer an
> opinion of the results [...] The failure of the German Opera this season is
> traceable to various causes [...]. Without recurring to these several errors
> and drawbacks separately, many of which are sufficiently trite and obvi-
> ous, we will go at once to the last and most forcible objection. [...] We
> must be permitted to question the boasted unapproachable superiority
> of the German, so far as they have come within our cognizance. [...] Next,
> let us go through the list of pieces performed during their late sojourn,
> and we shall find that their fruitfulness is by no means more attractive
> than their executive quality. The following, we believe, is a correct list
> – The *Zauberflöte*, *Figaro*, *Clemenza di Tito*, and *Seraglio*, of Mozart; the
> *Fidelio* of Beethoven; the *Freischütz*, *Euryanthe*, and *Oberon*, of Weber;
> the *Jessonda* of Spohr; the *Robert* of Meyerbeer; the *Templar* of Maschner
> [sic.]; the *Masaniello* [*La Muette de Portici*] of Auber; and the *Night in
> Granada* of Kreutzer. If we take from this list the four works of Mozart,
> which assuredly, now-a-days belong to the world, [by the bye, two of
> these were originally composed for the Italian theatre, and set to the Ital-
> ian language,) Weber's *Freischütz* and *Oberon*, the latter owing its birth to
> England and its patronage; Meyerbeer's opera, written for France, and in
> the French style; *Masaniello*, with which they can claim neither "kith nor
> kin," and Beethoven's great work, which has become a household study
> with every thorough musical family in Europe – if we except these nine
> pieces, and remember moreover that *Jessonda* and *Euryanthe* are equally
> familiar to us in private – where, we ask, is the "novelty" upon which the
> German Opera speculation has rested its attractions and pretension?[244]

C. concluded his evaluation by thanking the Germans for their assistance in the campaign against Italian hegemony, while simultaneously stating that their help is no longer necessary to advance the cause of English opera:

> We arrive at the consoling conclusion that if, as a people, we do not yet
> rank in the very highest regions of musical eminence, we have no con-
> temporaries beyond us in the flight; and fully aware that we have talent

---

244   Ibid.: 34.

amongst us at least sufficient for the production of a work like Mas-
chner's or Kreutzer's, we turn hopefully towards the long-coming dawn
of patronage at home, and cordially thank our allies from abroad, who
have helped us to combat our oppressors, and assert (ere long, we trust,
to win) our native rights as artists and as men.[245]

As much as the military metaphor may be congenial to the German discourse
on native opera in the post-Napoleonic period, the fragment underlines the
idea that German opera was now increasingly a force of the past containing no
promise for the future of English opera. But despite the changing sympathies of
English audiences and the lack of success of the previous season, the German
opera company returned in 1842 in *Covent Garden*; it produced the *Freischütz*,
Meyerbeer's *Robert* and *Die Hugenotten*, Spontini's *Vestalin*, Mozart's *Don Juan*
and *Zauberflöte*, Beethoven's *Fidelio*, and Gluck's *Iphigenia in Tauris*. C.'s earlier dismissal of the German company's necessity in London was vehemently
repeated in June 1842 by an anonymous *Musical World* critic, stating:

> If the German company can offer us nothing better than the mutilated
> phantoms of works that have been, and still are, considered great else-
> where, if they can but repeat operas imperfectly which we have long
> naturalized, and revive French and Italian pieces, which are infinitely
> better done elsewhere. In the name of common sense why do they come
> here to win a third and second beggary? In the name of common de-
> cency, why are they patronized at all, to the disparagement and ruin of
> Englishmen, to say the least, *not* their inferiors?[246]

A few weeks later, C. also joined the discussion again, this time slightly more
mildly than before:

> the German company in the small St. James theatre, with the advantage
> of novelty, [...] speculated wisely and profitably – the German company
> at Drury Lane, and Covent Garden, in the first place, seemed to court the
> odium of having pushed some hundreds of talented and industrious na-
> tives out of their legitimate market. [...] If we are to have a German opera
> in this country – and such an establishment might have its advantages
> in contrasting with the Italian opera, and showing us the difference be-
> tween mental and executional music – why then, let us have a company

---

245   Ibid.: 35.
246   *The Musical World* XVII/25, 23 June 1842: 198.

that will be contented to perform German operas alone, and that will be capable to give us perfect examples of their own native commodity; let them establish themselves in some theatre sufficient for their purpose, and no more, where they will be more at home, and more adequately capable – let them no more degrade themselves and their art by acts of charlatanism, and they may rely on the need most desired by merit and virtue – the encouragement and liberal support of discriminating people.[247]

But the damage – if not chiefly self-inflicted – had already been done. As in Paris, after 1842, a German opera company would not return to the British capital. For nearly two decades, German opera had fulfilled a role in London musical life as a powerful opposing force to the hegemony of Italian opera, providing an esthetic discourse more akin to the self-identification of British middle classes. But during the thirties, when the supply of new German operas stopped and the campaign for native opera became louder, it lost its function. Similar to the situation in Russia, after 1840 an increasing urge was felt to finally shake the once inspiring big brother off one's back.

The case studies discussed in this chapter reveal some remarkable similarities between the international dissemination of German opera and the function it fulfilled in different cultural contexts. Despite some early, isolated phenomena, such as the short-lived German companies in St. Petersburg, the European diffusion of Kauer's *Donauweibchen*, and the success of *Les Mystères d'Isis* in Paris, Weber's *Freischütz* clearly marks a turning point. This work was the entrance ticket for German opera performances and original-language companies and launched the vogue for German operas from 1824 onwards. Sometimes, especially in London, this vogue was preceded by an increasing interest in German instrumental music, but German opera proved to be a powerful attraction in its own right.

The popularity of German opera from this moment onwards is clearly related to the European spread of Romanticism in the 1820s, but also to a growing unease about the hegemony of Rossini and Italian opera in general, both incited by an upcoming national conscience and a deliberate bourgeois campaign to counter aristocratic taste. Especially in Britain and Russia, German opera in these years was often perceived to be of use as an ally in the battle against Italian operatic hegemony. German operas presented an inspiring example from the point of compositional technique and subject matter, while simultaneously, German discourse on opera provided ammunition for

---

247   *The Musical World* XVII/27, 7 July 1842: 210.

a domestic national campaign. Around 1840, however, we do witness a shift in attitude, partly caused by the fact that the German opera source had run dry during the 1830s. During this period, no significant new works were composed, consequently no significant new works could be performed, and ultimately the interest and support for the genre vanished. This process was intensified by the fact that German opera companies were now increasingly believed to occupy a space that native opera should have, or at least obtain in the nearby future. German musical culture was now felt to be hegemonic itself, partly due to the dominance of German (chiefly non-operatic) musical culture throughout Europe.

The viability of German-language opera performances was obviously greatly enhanced when the city concerned hosted a German-speaking minority, as was the case in St. Petersburg, Paris, and London. In the latter case, contemporary sources emphasize the attempts made by theater managers to invite German citizens to the premieres. But the share of non-German spectators must have been considerable too, given the extent to which the performances sparked critical responses in the press, and the rapidity with which the German performances came into and went out of fashion within short stretches of time. The attendance of regular, indigenous theatregoers seems to have been absolutely necessary, since less successful performances or a gradual loss of novelty immediately led to financial fiascos. If a company had been chiefly attended by a German minority, one might expect a smaller, but certainly more stable fan base, such as that of the German theater of St. Petersburg in the early decades of the century.

When we look at the pieces performed, the repertoire appears to have been fairly comparable to the common fare on German stages, with the works of Mozart, Beethoven and Weber clearly the most popular, followed by composers such as Spohr, Marschner and Kreutzer. Whereas German companies sometimes tried to adapt to local practices, for example in the case of Haitzinger's "show aria" in his Paris and London *Freischütz*, audiences seem to have longed for the works in their original form, after having become acquainted to them in mutilated versions. In general, German opera and its performance seem to have adumbrated a new, upcoming ideal of fidelity towards the composer's creation and focus on the work rather than the performing singer. Wilhelmine-Schröder Devrient embodied this attitude, as she was arguably the first internationally-acclaimed diva of German opera, but one of whom it was said that she put all her vocal and histrionic skills at the service of the work in question. Moreover, the German opera companies' shows revealed to non-Germans that even an ensemble without stars could be highly impressive if it worked collectively. This unprecedented collective effort turned the choir into the true star of the German stage, as many press reactions confirm.

Apart from the fact that German opera was considered, even expected to have a Romantic character, seriousness was another returning topos. In many reviews of London performances, seriousness was used as a kind of self-evident, gratuitous compliment for music that was, however, often considered hard to digest and not particularly enjoyable. Yet French critics often accused German operas of lacking seriousness, thereby hitting back on the dominant elevated self-image of German composers. For the esteem of German opera in the homeland, the performances abroad presented a clear win-win situation: foreign success affirmed the idea that this national art form was gradually taking over the world, whereas foreign maltreatment – such as the pasticcios of *Die Zauberflöte* (Lachnith's *Les Mystères d'Isis*) and *Der Freischütz* (Castil-Blaze's *Robin des bois*) – or indifference from local audiences towards German-language companies reinforced feelings of cultural superiority. At the same time, as the international focus of this chapter reveals more than a discussion of domestic performances could have done, by 1840 German opera was seriously in need of fresh blood in order to secure its institutionalization in the future.

"Ich bin der deutscheste Mensch, ich bin der deutsche Geist!": Richard Wagner's Role in the Articulation of a German Opera Identity

The title of this chapter is derived from a diary entry of Richard Wagner on 11 September 1864. It reveals the amount to which, at least at that time, Wagner perceived himself as fully embodying German national identity. Considering opera identity, the idea that Wagner's persona and works epitomize what German opera is, forms a frequently-attended topos indeed.[1] How did this common conception gain ground, and what was Wagner's role in this process? This is one of the main questions of this chapter, which deals with the relation between Wagner and the nineteenth-century German national opera tradition.

The debate about Wagner's relation to German nationalism is highly ideology-laden. Some scholars have highlighted nationalist elements of Wagner's art and thought,[2] whereas others prefer to tone down this element as something which unjustly overshadows the more "Enlightened," universal aspects of his worldview and which in itself is unjustly contaminated by the national-socialist appropriation of his cultural heritage.[3] The discussion is blurred because his writings are full of ambivalence on the subject, and because scholarship on this subject often takes the form of either condemning or condoning. A certain amount of consensus based on a more even-handed approach has remained an unattainable desideratum until today.

Rather than to engage in this discussion, I take three assumptions as a point of departure within this chapter, assumptions that are less concerned with Wagner's personal beliefs and intentions, and therefore arguably more productive. The first is that, regardless of the question whether Wagner was a staunch nationalist or not, his persona and works have acquired a huge importance within the German nationalist movement in the second half of the nineteenth and first half of the twentieth century and have shaped the image of German opera. In that sense, I am concerned with Wagner's

---

1 In conversations with colleagues and friends, one frequently attends the conviction that studying German opera simply equals studying Wagner.

2 Chief examples are Josserand's 1981, Salmi 1999, and Hein 2006.

3 Udo Bermbach is arguably the most prominent representative of this position, see Bermbach 1994 and Bermbach 2011.

© KONINKLIJKE BRILL NV, LEIDEN, 2019 | DOI:10.1163/9789004245389_007

image – entailing both his own image-building and his reception – rather than with tracing his "true beliefs." The second is that the rise of German national conscience has catalyzed Wagner's artistic success at crucial moments during his career. An example of this is provided by Martin Gregor-Dellin, who argues that the rejection of Wagner's *Tannhäuser* in Paris in 1861 greatly enhanced sympathetic attitudes towards his work among the Germans,[4] which is clearly related to the fact that German-French animosity was reaching its boiling point during the 1860s. The third is that Wagner's esthetic program deliberately joined in with the German national opera tradition. I argue that in his artistic self-stylization, Wagner appropriated and put to use a great deal of the existing discourse concerning the superiority and sophistication of German opera in relation to its Italian and French sisters.

In the popular current-day discourse surrounding Wagner, interest in German opera esthetics before Wagner is relatively limited, and has arguably been obfuscated by the master himself, who took control of opera history by rewriting it in his theoretical works. Re-establishing the genealogy of Wagner's esthetics may also help to reveal manifestations of national thinking that are hardly discernible without a proper understanding of the peculiar nature of nineteenth-century German opera discourse. National and universal tendencies, for example, may appear to be mutually exclusive at first sight, but often turn out to be intimately intertwined.

Many studies of the relation between Wagner and German nationalism historically approach the subject backwards, taking the late nineteenth-century context and sometimes even the perversions of the Third Reich as a point of departure. Without wishing to tone down the more inconvenient aspects of Wagner's ideology, I hope to complement the scope by taking a different route, interpreting Wagner's esthetic project as a continuation of previous campaigns for the emancipation of German opera. This contextualization of his esthetics will not only contribute to our understanding of Wagner, but also of the specific role that his operas have played in the development of German opera as a genre and as a cultural symbol.

The chapter opens with a discussion of Wagner's troubled relation to German Romantic opera and his more cosmopolitan, at times even anti-German esthetic during the 1830s. The next section about the 1840s discusses a first wave of Germanification within Wagner's cultural and esthetic outlooks around the time of his return from Paris. The third section explores the relation between universalist and German-national tendencies in Wagner's

---

4   Concerning the 1861 *Tannhäuser* scandal in Paris, Gregor-Dellin points out that "For the first time, the German musical public sphere demonstratively supported Wagner. In the Dresden theater, a spontaneous ovation occurred for this traitor who had not yet received amnesty." Gregor Dellin 1983: 469.

theory of music drama and the creation of *Der Ring des Nibelungen*. The final part of this chapter scrutinizes Wagner's artistic and ideological activities in the years preceding the Franco-Prussian War and the eventual German unification (1870–1871), as well as the symbolic significance of the first Bayreuther Festspiele (1876) as a celebration of the political unification of Germany.

1 "Unselige Gelehrtheit, dieser Quell aller deutschen Übel!"

The 1830s clearly belong to Wagner's "dark ages," deliberately obscured in his later self-stylization. He not only preferred to exclude his first three completed operas – *Die Feen* (1834), *Das Liebesverbot oder die Novize von Palermo* (1836) and *Rienzi, der Letzte der Tribunen* (1840) – from his official oeuvre, but also left a few essays penned down in this period out of his collected writings.[5] Wagner himself must have felt that leaving out these "youthful errors"[6] would enhance a proper understanding of his art, and many commentators have respected the composer's will. But in fact, a close examination of what Wagner brushed under the carpet reveals a great deal about the image that he wished to cultivate later on in his career, as it discerns those elements that did no longer fit that image. Wagner's attitude towards German culture and the German operatic heritage can be illuminated by discussing the operas and articles he wrote during this period.

With his first completed opera *Die Feen*, Wagner neatly followed in the tracks of previous German Romantic operas. The libretto is clearly indebted to E.T.A. Hoffmann,[7] as it contains many features of the ideal Romantic opera

---

5 These were posthumously appended to his collected writings, and constitute the twelfth volume.

6 Wagner used the word "Jugendsünde" several times when discussing his earliest operas. In *Eine Mittheilung an meine Freunde* (1851), he recalled how the success of the first Berlin performance of *Rienzi* in 1847 had been tainted by his own statement that he himself by now considered the work to be "a youthful artistic error [eine künstlerische Jugendsünde]" (WWSB, Sämtliche Schriften, Band IV: 303), and he also used the word in the ironic poem written to Ludwig II in 1866 when he handed over the manuscript score of *Das Liebesverbot* to his royal patron: "Ich irrte einst, und möcht es nun verbüßen / Wie mach ich mich der Jugendsünde frei? / Ihr Werk leg ich demütig Dir zu Füssen / dass Deine Gnade ihm Erlöser sei (I once erred, and now wish to atone / how can I make this sin of youth undone? / Its result I hereby lay humbly before you / to be redeemed by thy mercy)." WWSB, Sämtliche Schriften, Band XII: 391.

7 Wagner got acquainted with the work of E.T.A. Hoffmann as a teenager. In his *Autobiographische Skizze* (1842), he mentions how "as a sixteen-year old, reading E.T.A. Hoffmann had sparked the wildest types of mysticism in my mind (Ich war damals in meinem sechszehnten Jahre, und zumal durch die Lektüre E.T.A. Hoffmanns zum tollsten Mystizismus aufgeregt)." WWSB, Sämtliche Schriften, Band I: 6. Thomas S. Grey remarks that Wagner's fascination for E.T.A. Hoffmann was arguably spurred by his uncle Adolf Wagner, who translated Gozzi's works into German and knew Romantics such as Hoffmann and Ludwig Tieck personally. See Grey 2008: 24.

proposed in *Der Dichter und der Komponist* (1813). Its story is concerned with the coexistence of everyday reality and a supernatural spirit world to which the Romantic prince Arindal longs. As in *Undine*, this prince falls in love with a female spirit, Ada in this case. Moreover, the supernatural fairy world is perceived as real, and not merely an illusion, and the libretto is based on the play *La donna serpente* (1763) by Carlo Gozzi, the poet who Hoffmann had lifted out as a viable model for German Romantic opera libretti. Although less prominently than in the *commedia del'arte* style Gozzi play, Wagner also retained the alternation between serious and comic scenes that Hoffmann considered crucial to a truly Romantic opera.

Musically, the work was also a continuation of German, chiefly Romantic models, despite some common-practice operatic elements taken over from Italian and French examples. The through-composed style, type of declamation, and the detailed word-painting in the orchestral accompaniment resemble Weber's *Euryanthe*. Furthermore, most scholars discern the influence from Marschner, Beethoven, and Mozart's *Zauberflöte*, the latter particularly in the comic duet between Gernot and Drolla in the first act and Arindal's third act "Orphic" entrance through a *Schreckenspforte* in order to rescue his ossified beloved.[8]

Altogether, *Die Feen* appears to be a wholehearted embrace and continuation of the German Romantic opera legacy. As such, Michael von Soden finds the work hard to reconcile with the radically anti-Romantic worldview of the burgeoning Young German movement with which Wagner sympathized in these years.[9] Whether or not Wagner believed in the metaphysical Romanticism and alleged "*Biedermeier*" morale[10] of *Die Feen* at the time of composition

---

8   For detailed analyses of the music of *Die Feen*, see for example Finscher 1978, Lippmann 1983: 14–31 and Holtmeier 2003: 33–55.

9   Soden 1983: 283–285.

10 Both Voss and Borchmeyer assume that Arindal and Ada have been married and that their marriage, blessed with two children, is a glorification of "*Biedermeier*" family values, quite unlike Wagner's later problematization of the bourgeois marriage and his depiction of love as a "disruptive force" (Voss 1996: 18 and Borchmeyer 2003:6). This impression is, however, questionable. When Arindal's servant Gernot meets Gunther after having spent eight years in the fairy realm, he mentions the following about Arindal and Ada: "Wer sie getraut, ich weiß es nicht, / doch schon zwei Kinder zeugten sie!." This might as well imply that their relationship is not founded on a conventional agreement such as a marriage, but rather on love and trust; one may think here of Ada's command to Arindal never to ask who she is. This *Lohengrin*-like *Frageverbot* that Arindal ignores sets the drama in motion, after which he has to face terrible ordeals in order to win her back. Arindal's love itself can also be seen as a transgressive rather than a bourgeois force, as it is concerned with overstepping the social/cosmic order and borders on madness during

is hard to decide, but what we do know is that soon after its completion in January 1834, he shifted his esthetic and ideological course dramatically.[11] In June 1834, Wagner published his outlooks, albeit anonymously, in a short, manifest-like text called *Die deutsche Oper* in the *Zeitung für die elegante Welt*. He opens his argument with a dismissal of German provincialism and xenophobia in the realm of opera esthetics because it reminds him of the old-German garments of post-Waterloo chauvinists,[12] and points out that the Germans may have their own domain in instrumental music, but fundamentally lack a domestic opera tradition. The reason for this Wagner finds in the pretentious cultivation of German "learnedness": "a German opera we do not have, on the same ground that we do not have a national drama; we are too cerebral and far too learned to create warm, human characters."[13] The way to enliven these characters he recognizes in Mozart, a German composer who managed to master the vocal beauty of Italian opera in his works.

Wagner establishes that, unfortunately, current German composers have failed or refused to follow in Mozart's trail. He finds Weber and Spohr's[14] vocal writing poor in comparison, and emphatically prefers the melodic beauty of Italian opera over the "eternal allegorizing orchestral bustle [des ewig

---

    his third act phantasmagoria. It is a love that is too all-consuming to be combined with his societal duties as a monarch, and in that sense anything but bourgeois or *Biedermeier*.

11   Two biographical events are often mentioned as catalysts in this shift; both Wagner's frustration concerning the reluctance of the Leipzig theater to produce his work, and the impression that a performance of Bellini's *I Capuleti e i Montechi*, with Wilhelmine Schröder-Devrient as Romeo, had made. Wagner mentioned this performance in his *Autobiographische Skizze* (1843), but in *Mein Leben* (1865) he mentions another performance by Wilhelmine Schröder-Devrient, as Leonore in Beethoven's *Fidelio* in 1829, as a life-changing experience. Thomas S. Grey states that there is no evidence of the *Fidelio* performance, and that this "epiphany" might well have been the result of myth-making (Grey 2008: 19). We may interpret this possible rewriting of his autobiography as an attempt to obscure his earlier sympathies for Italian opera, with this solemn German symphonist replacing the sensuous Bellini.

12   "Wenn wir von deutscher Musik reden, und besonders viel darüber reden hören, so scheint mir in der Meinung über dieselbe noch eine ähnliche Begriffsverirrung zu herrschen, als die, in der sich die Idee der Freiheit bei jenen altdeutsch schwarzgerockten Demagogen befand, die mit ebenso verächtlichem Naserümpfen die Ergebnisse ausländisch-moderner Reformen über die Achsel ansahen, wie jetzt unsere deutschtümelnden Musikkenner." WWSB, Sämtliche Schriften, Band XII: 1.

13   "Eine deutsche Oper aber haben wir nicht, und der Grund dafür ist derselbe, aus dem wir ebenfalls kein Nationaldrama besitzen. Wir sind zu geistig und viel zu gelehrt, um warme menschliche Gestalten zu schaffen." Ibid.: 1.

14   Curiously enough, he never mentions Marschner in this essay.

allegorisirenden Orchestergewühls]"[15] of German opera. His German predecessors also disappoint him from a dramatic point of view, whereas he believes
that dramatic truth is fully achieved in post-Gluckian French opera. To Wagner, the most convincing German opera is still *Der Freischütz*, in which Weber
manages to compose in a lyrical, folksy style, whereas he finds that the unity of
Euryanthe is shattered by all its "pedantic details in the declamation [kleinliche
Klügelei in der Deklamation]," while the underlying emotion could also have
been painted with a single brushstroke.[16] The only reason why Germans can
appreciate such an incomprehensible work is because of the "learned" impression that it makes, but this "learnedness" is exactly the root of all German evil:

> And because all listeners must admit that they have not understood any-
> thing of the piece, they at least find consolation in the fact that it appears
> to be stupendously learned, which in itself commands respect. – O, this
> *unfortunate learnedness, root of all German evil!*[17]

Wagner traces this German cultivation of learnedness back to Bach's time, but
argues that it is as senseless to foster this ideal as it is to still write oratorios.[18]
Rather than to restrict oneself to a "glorious" German past, he pleads German
composers to learn their lessons from international developments as the only
option for future opera success:

> Of course, I do not want the French and Italian to push out our native
> music – which would pave the way to a new evil – but we must acknowl-
> edge the truthful in both traditions, and prevent ourselves from base,
> self-righteous hypocrisy. [...] We must seize the opportunities of our time
> and try to cultivate its new forms; and he will be its master who writes in
> neither an Italian nor a French – nor even in a German style.[19]

---

15   Ibid.: 2.
16   Wagner here takes over many elements from previous dismissive reviews of *Euryanthe*,
      such as Franz Grillparzer's. See Tusa 1991: 63–66, but also Chapter 3.
17   "Und da nun die Leute am Ende zugestehen müssen, daß sie nichts davon verstanden ha-
      ben, finden doch alle wenigstens einen Trost darin, daß sie es für erstaunlich gelehrt halten
      können, und deßhalb großen Respekt haben dürfen. – O, diese unselige Gelehrtheit, –
      dieser Quell aller deutschen Übel!" Ibid.: 2–3.
18   "Die Formen sind freier, freundlicher geworden, wir haben leben gelernt, – und unsere
      Komponisten sind gar nicht mehr gelehrt, und das Lächerlichste ist eben, daß sie sich
      gelehrt stellen wollen. [...] Denn ist es nicht eine offenbare Verkennung der Gegenwart,
      wenn Einer jetzt Oratorien schreibt?" Ibid.: 3–4.
19   "Ich will zwar keineswegs, daß die französische oder italienische Musik die unsrige ver-
      drängen soll; auf der andern Seite wäre diesem als einem neuen Übel eher zu steuern, – aber

One may discern three tendencies in this critical survey of German opera; a self-critical, a developmental, and an ideological one. The criticism concerning the shattered, declamatory style and the allegorizing orchestra is also a coming to terms with the technical flaws of *Die Feen*, whereas his more cosmopolitan orientation would materialize in his next work *Das Liebesverbot*.[20] Regardless of his own compositional experiences, he was simultaneously becoming more aware of the general stagnation of German opera in the early 1830s and the inappropriate complacency of some German music critics concerning their native opera tradition. Even if later in his life Wagner felt a certain unease about his previous fierce dismissal of his German predecessors,[21] it is hard to deny that his more cosmopolitan orientation was fruitful not only to his mature art, but also to the development of German opera in general. But apart from these stylistic issues, *Die deutsche Oper* can best be understood as an expression of – or an attempt to seek alliance with – the Young German ideology, of which the *Zeitung für die elegante Welt* in which the article appeared was the most prominent platform.

Junges Deutschland was a literary movement led by writers such as Heinrich Laube, Heinrich Heine, Karl Gutzkow, Theodor Mundt and Ludwig Wienbarg, formed in the aftermath of the French July Revolution of 1830.[22] The movement fought against reactionary Restoration politics, the prudery and hypocrisy of

---

wir sollen das Wahre in beiden kennen und uns vor jeder selbstsüchtigen Heuchelei hüten. [...] Wir müssen die Zeit packen und ihre neuen Formen gediegen auszubilden suchen; und der wird der Meister sein, der weder italienisch, französisch – noch aber auch deutsch schreibt." Ibid.: 3–4.

20   Holtmeier interprets the text similarly: "This attack at *the* German opera can clearly be read as ruthless self-criticism. All reproaches towards Weber, Marschner and Spohr [...] actually constitute nothing but a critical catalog of *Die Feen*." Holtmeier 2003: 50–51. Inga Mai Groote sees it as a "deliberate course correction on the way to a more expressive musico-dramatic technique." Groote 2014: 99.

21   In *Mein Leben* (1865), Wagner blames the overwhelming impression of Bellini's *I Capuleti e i Montechi* for his ridiculization of Weber's *Euryanthe* in *Die deutsche Oper*: "Welchen Einfluß solche mächtige und ihren Ursachen nach mir unbegreifliche Wirkungen auf mein Urteil übten, zeigte sich in der frivolen Weise, mit welcher es mir möglich ward, über Webers »Euryanthe« eine kurze Rezension für die »Elegante Zeitung« abzugeben [...], in welcher ich die »Euryanthe« geradewegs verhöhnte. – War ich mit meiner Studentenzeit in meine menschlichen Flegeljahre getreten, so beschritt ich nun kühn dieselbe Bahn auch in meiner künstlerischen Geschmacksentwicklung." WWSB, *Mein Leben*: 89–90.

22   This literary movement is often distinguished from the more political secret society *Junges Deutschland* that was founded in 1834 in Switzerland, a spin-off from Giuseppe Mazzini's previously founded *Giovane Italia* and a subgroup of Young Europe, the overarching organization that also featured a Polish department. The literary and secret/political *Junges Deutschland* movements had many similarities – among them a liberal, progressive, anti-Restoration and cosmopolitan orientation – but were led by different people.

Biedermeier society, the naïveté of Romantic metaphysics and mysticism,[23] and narrow-minded German chauvinism. As a positive contrast to the German situation, Italian culture was seen as a paradise of beauty, naturalness and sensuality,[24] whereas Paris embodied the promise of a modern, progressive and liberal world.[25] The Young German movement was a prominent player in the German cultural landscape particularly in the period between 1830 and 1835, the year that the *Bundestag* prohibited their writings, after which some members were arrested, went in exile, or underground.[26]

We find the Young German ideology clearly reflected not only in Wagner's essay *Die deutsche Oper*, but also in *Das Liebesverbot*, Wagner's next opera, premiered in 1836 in Magdeburg. Wagner based the libretto on Shakespeare's play *Measure for Measure* (1623), but modified the action in order to fit more neatly into the Young German worldview. Both Shakespeare's original and Wagner's rendition depict a hypocritical moralist who forbids his people all forms of illicit love, but tries to abuse his power in order to pursue his own erotic desires when he falls for the nun Isabella. His deceit is, however, exposed. Shakespeare's play resolves itself by three "bourgeois" marriages that domesticate erotic passion. Wagner's version deviates from the original, as his opera ends with the transgressive erotic ecstasy of carnival. The subversive tone of Wagner's work is also emphasized by the fact that the moralist is not put to trial by the monarch, but by the people itself.[27]

Another important alteration concerns the locale; whereas Shakespeare's play takes place in Vienna, Wagner transplanted the action to Sicily, while re-christening the hypocritical moralist Angelo into the German viceroy Friedrich. Egon Voss sees the move away from Vienna chiefly as a strategy to make the story less overtly a critique on Metternich's oppressive politics.[28] But

---

23   Ludwig Wienbarg, for example, called for a "poetry of life [Poesie des Lebens]" that, in the words of Norbert Otto Eke, must be "present in the here and now, closely aligned to the reality of the times with all its contradictions and conflicts, which in sum: must be intervening." Eke 2014: 52.

24   We find this fascination, amongst others, in the regained interest in Heinrich Heinse's 1787 novel *Ardinghello und die glückseligen Inseln* as well as Heinrich Laube's epistolary novel *Die Poeten* (1833) from his trilogy *Das junge Europa*.

25   In their biography of Heinrich Heine, who left Germany for Paris in 1831, Jan-Christoph Hauschild and Michael Werner sketch the mythological status attributed to the French capital by German progressives. See Hauschild 1997: 187.

26   See, for example, Kruse 1985.

27   This aspect is often linked to Auber's *La muette de Portici* (1828), which also features a popular insurrection and clearly was an important model for Wagner in composing *Das Liebesverbot*.

28   Voss 1996: 53.

the move to Sicily, with the malicious Friedrich as the only remaining German character within the story, simultaneously lifted out the anti-German tenor of the work far more than a Viennese setting could have done, and was, moreover, fully congenial to the Young German idealization of Italy, creating the following set of antitheses:

Germany (critique)	Italy (ideal)
Police state	Freedom
Bourgeois, Christian morals	Righteousness/beauty
Keeping to the letter of the law	Passion
Cold/rigid	Warm

This imagological scheme is as naïve as it is cliché, but Wagner managed to enliven the system through the use of comedy, such as in the case of Brighella, the Sicilian chief of police who functions as a comic counterpart to the more serious Friedrich. Seduced by the attractive Dorella, he agrees to a masked rendezvous, thereby breaking the law he is supposed to enforce, on the ground that such a "ban on love" may be feasible for a cerebral German, but not for a warm-blooded Sicilian such as himself.[29]

The critical perspective on German culture is also realized in the stylistic orientation of most of the music in *Das Liebesverbot*, which is an amalgam of many Italian and French models. The most obviously discernable influences are that of Bellini in the melodies,[30] and that of Auber's *La Muette* in the animated, forward-pulling rhythms. In an anonymous comment on his own opera, published in a report on the music life of Magdeburg in the *Neue Zeitschrift für Musik*, Wagner stated about these foreign inspirations: "it all sounds well, it contains music and melody, something for which in our current German operas we often search in vain."[31]

---

29   "Und das war nur ein Kuß! / Ein Kuß! Und den will mir der Statthalter verbieten? Den Teufel in sein Liebesverbot! Kann er's aushalten, so ist er Deutscher! Ich bin Sizilianer, und zwar von erstaunlich guter Geburt!"

30   The broad melodies of, for example, the first act duet of Isabella and Mariana display a tendency towards "endless" melodic lines similar to Bellini's procedure in Casta Diva from *Norma*.

31   "Es klingt alles, es ist Musik und Melodie drin, was wir bei unsern deutschen Opern jetzt so ziemlich suchen müssen." *NZfM* IV/36, 3 May 1836: 152. To a certain extent, Wagner hung on to this belief that his cosmopolitan orientation had granted him a "natural" musicality that many of his German colleagues lacked. Cosima's diaries contain the following statement about the positive influence of Bellini's music: "It taught me things that men

Despite the overt Franco-Italian orientation, Wagner's *Liebesverbot* music contains German traits as well. Inga Mai Groote recognizes a dramaturgical differentiation of musical styles, in which the more "learned" German idiom is reserved for the realm of Friedrich and his ban on love, whereas a more direct musical expression is reserved for the warm-blooded Sicilians.[32] On a deeper musical level, Giselher Schubert discerns an even more fundamental "German" handling of the quasi-spontaneous foreign melodies and rhythms, a "tendency to symphonize, which you will not attend in the French opéra comique, and which reveals that Wagner's reception of Mozart and Beethoven is still very much present."[33] In another respect, the Roman lightness and frivolity of the opera is deceptive, as the work expounds a worldview, a serious critique of the society in which Wagner lives. Both in the field of composition as in his pretense that opera is to be far more than entertainment, Wagner ultimately betrays his German roots.[34] In that sense, Giselher Schubert has a case when concluding that "in *Das Liebesverbot*, despite all the French and Italian influences he took up and amalgamated, Wagner still essentially continued to be a 'learned' German opera composer."[35]

What, then, was Wagner trying to escape from when he chose to depart from his German operatic heritage, and what should be the outcome of this process? In a letter to his friend Theodor Apel, written in October 1834, he explains his ideal trajectory when he states about *Das Liebesverbot*:

> This opera shall be my breakthrough, and advance my reputation and wealth; once I've acquired both, I'll use them to travel with you to Italy [...]. In Italy I'll compose an Italian opera, and perhaps even more; once we possess strength and a nice tan, we'll move to Paris, where I will write a French opera, and God knows where I will be by then! But I do know what I will be by then; – no longer a German philistine.[36]

---

like Brahms never learnt, something which has found its way into my melodies (Ich habe davon gelernt, was die Herren Brahms & Cie nicht gelernt haben, und was ich in meiner Melodie habe)." WWSB, *Cosimas Tagebücher*, Band II: 54.

32 Groote 2014: 110.

33 Schubert 2014: 127.

34 This is also observable from the correspondences between *Das Liebesverbot* and Beethoven's *Fidelio*, a work that has a similar revolutionary, anti-tyrannical tenor." See for those correspondences Voss 1996: 48 as well as Lühning 1999: 84–86.

35 Schubert 2014: 136.

36 "Mit dieser Oper muß ich dann durchschlagen, und Ruf u. Geld gewinnen; ist es mir geglückt, beides zu erlangen, so ziehe ich mit Beidem und mit Dir nach Italien [...]. In Italien komponire ich dann eine italienische Oper, u. wie es sich macht, auch mehr; sind wir dann braun u. kräftig, so wenden wir uns nach Frankreich, in Paris komponire ich dann eine französische Oper, und Gott weiß, wo ich dann bin! Wer ich dann bin, das weiß ich; – kein deutscher Philister mehr." WWSB, *Sämtliche Briefe*, Band I: 167.

Wagner's plan is not only an exact copy of Gluck's career, but actually also of the more recent *Werdegang* of Giacomo Meyerbeer, who by that time was enjoying enormous success in Paris.[37] It is well-known that Wagner followed Meyerbeer to Paris in 1839 and hoped to achieve success there with *Rienzi*, a French-style *grand opéra*. What is less known, however, is the extent to which Wagner at that time viewed Meyerbeer's achievement as a cosmopolitan synthesis worked out by a genuinely German composer, creating an art of universal appeal that displayed the superiority of the German spirit. Wagner penned down these thoughts in 1840 in an essay that he never published and later chose to obscure.[38] It was first released after his death as 'Über Meyerbeers "Hugenotten."' Concerning Meyerbeer's accomplishments in French opera Wagner writes:

> What Meyerbeer bred on this [French] ground was not a glorification of a national vanity, but the cultivation of a national manner into a universal sentiment. Meyerbeer wrote world history, history of feelings, he tore down the barriers between national prejudices, destroyed the cramping borders of language idioms, he wrote deeds of music,[39] – music, similar to that composed by Händel, Gluck, and Mozart before him, – and these were German, and so is Meyerbeer. And how did this German steer clear from the pitfall of writing in this or that adopted national manner, how did he avoid becoming a slave of foreign influences? Because he preserved his German heritage, the naïve perception, the chaste invention. [...] the colossal, nearly overpowering expansion of forms has been realized in the most pure and beneficial proportions; yes, this is particularly an aspect that reveals Meyerbeer's mastery; this deliberation [Besonnenheit], even cold-bloodedness in the construction and ordering characterizes Meyerbeer more than anything else.[40]

---

37   The most remarkable achievement during Meyerbeer's Italian sojourn had been *Il crociatto in Egitto* (1824), whereas *Robert le diable* (1831) enraptured Parisian audiences for years, only to be surpassed by his even more successful *Les Huguenots* (1836) five years later.

38   See Döhring 1983: 95–100 for a more detailed account of this article and its publication history.

39   This phrase is all the more remarkable as Wagner would later characterize his own music-dramatic works as "Musical deeds made visible [Ersichtlich gewordene Thaten der Musik]" in *Über die Benennung "Musikdrama"* (1872). *WWSB*, Band IX: 306.

40   "Das, was Meyerbeer nun aber auf diesen Grund baute, war nicht eine Huldigung einer National-Eitelkeit, sondern die Erhebung derselben zum Gefühl der Universalität. Meyerbeer schrieb Weltgeschichte, Geschichte der Herzen und Empfindungen, er zerschlug die Schranken der National-Vorurtheile, vernichtete die beengenden Grenzen der Sprachidiome, er schrieb Thaten der Musik, – Musik, wie sie vor ihm Händel, Gluck und Mozart geschrieben, – und diese waren Deutsche, und Meyerbeer ist ein Deutscher. Und fragen wir, wie war es diesem Deutschen möglich, daß er sich nicht in den Empfindungen

In three respects, Wagner's attitude towards the German musical and operatic heritage within this obscure fragment is remarkable. To begin with, it is a full antithesis of Wagner's eventual Meyerbeer condemnation, which will be addressed later in this chapter. Moreover, Wagner adds Meyerbeer to a list of composers who managed to achieve a universal appeal through a cosmopolitan synthesis, a list consisting *exclusively* of German masters, albeit Germans that composed foreign-language operas. Here we find a reverberation of Carl Maria von Weber's chauvinist dictum that, unlike his complacent Italian and French colleagues, the German composer "takes the most prolific elements from other traditions and takes them to a new level of profundity."⁴¹ And lastly, the idea that, through his "deliberation

---

dieser oder jener angenommenen nationalen Manier festsetzte, sich in ihnen nicht nach einem kurzen Glanz verlor, und daß er somit kein Sklave der fremden Einflüsse ward? Er hat sein deutsches Erbtheil bewahrt, die Naivetät der Empfindung, die Keuschheit der Erfindung. [...] Die riesenhafte, fast schon erdrückende Ausdehnung der Formen hat die reinsten und wohlthuendsten Verhältnisse gewonnen; ja, besonders ist dieß ein Punkt, in dem sich die Meisterschaft Meyerbeer's fast am auffallendsten herausstellt; diese Besonnenheit, ja Kaltblütigkeit in der Anlage und Anordnung charakterisirt Meyerbeer vor Allem." *WWSB*, Sämtliche Schriften, Band XII: 25–27.

41   See Chapter 1. In another 1840 article, "De la musique allemand," published in the *Revue et Gazette musicale*, Wagner almost literally repeats Weber's dictum concerning German composer's ability to cultivate opera into a more elevated, universal genre: "Quite often German musicians were even most successful in this genre, because of their ability to create something universal, even on foreign terrain. [...] It is a characteristic trait of German art to draw from foreign sources in order to compensate for the flaws of its own native tradition, while simultaneously improving the borrowed element by transforming it into something that appeals to the entire world (Il arriva cependant frequemment que la palme du genre fut decernée à des musiciens allemands, car leur aptitude universell pour les beaux arts leur frayait une route facile, même sur ce terrain étranger. [...] C'est en quelque sorte un trait caracteristique de l'art allemand que d'aller puiser aux sources etrangères pour enricher sa patrie de ce qui lui manque, en perfectionnant l'objet de ses emprunts, et le transformant de manière à en faire le point de mire de l'admiration du monde entier)." (*Revue et Gazette musicale de Paris* VII/46, 26 July 1840: 396. The German version included in the *Sämtliche Schriften* makes the reverberation of Weber as well as Wagner's universal pretenses even more obvious: "Nichtsdestoweniger waren es aber oft Deutsche, welche auch in diesem Genre den ersten Preis erhielten; die universelle Richtung, deren der deutsche Genius fähig ist, machte es dem deutschen Künstler leicht, sich selbst auf fremdem Terrain einheimisch zu machen. [...] Der deutsche Genius scheint fast bestimmt zu sein, das, was seinem Mutterlande nicht eingeboren ist, bei seinen Nachbarn aufzusuchen, dieß aber aus seinen engen Gränzen zu erheben und somit etwas Allgemeines für die ganze Welt zu schaffen." *WWSB* Sämtliche Schriften, Band I: 160.

[Besonnenheit]," Meyerbeer realizes perfect musical proportions while colossally expanding the conventional forms is fully in the vein of E.T.A. Hoffmann's 1813 review of the *Fifth Symphony* of Beethoven, that other great German master with universal appeal. Going back to the conclusion of Wagner's letter to Theodor Apel, one may argue that what he hoped to become by following in Meyerbeer's tracks was arguably a "universal German master" rather than a petty, bourgeois German philistine, writing peripheral Romantic operas. Wagner turned his back on the German Romantic opera milieu not because he wanted to do away with German culture altogether, but rather because he aspired to a more "elevated" national stereotype, that of the "universal" genius.

The above discussion of Wagner's little-known writings and operas of the 1830s shows how Wagner distanced himself from the more provincial and bourgeois aspects of German culture, both esthetically and politically, while aspiring to the ideal type of the Great German master with universal appeal. As an opera composer, Wagner desired to enter the world stage,[42] and Paris offered such a stage. But the disillusionment of his Paris campaign drove him back into the arms of those provincial Germans he had previously wished to get away from, and when he finally returned to his fatherland in 1842, the prodigal son had quite a lot to explain.

2   A German Musician Returns from Paris

Was Wagner a musician at all? He was definitely rather something else: namely, an incomparable histrionic, the greatest mime, the most astonishing theatrical genius the Germans ever had. He belongs somewhere else than in the history of music, one should not mistake him for one of the master composers. Wagner *and* Beethoven? Blasphemy!.[43]

NIETZSCHE, *Der Fall Wagner* (1888)

---

42 In his *Autobiographische Skizze* (1842), Wagner writes that around 1834 "Germany had appeared to me to be only a very small part of the world (Deutschland schien mir nur ein sehr kleiner Theil der Welt)." wwsв, Sämtliche Schriften, Band I: 10.

43 "War Wagner überhaupt ein Musiker? Jedenfalls war er etwas anderes *mehr*: nämlich ein unvergleichlicher *histrio*, der größte Mime, das erstaunlichste Theater-Genie, das die Deutschen gehabt haben, unser *Szeniker par excellence*. Er gehört woandershin als in die Geschichte der Musik: mit deren großen Echten soll man ihn nicht verwechseln. Wagner *und* Beethoven – das ist eine Blasphemie!" Nietzsche 1988: 26.

It may seem historically questionable to start a discussion of Wagner's compositional and literary activities in the 1840s with this infamous statement, voiced by Friedrich Nietzsche nearly fifty years later, and five years after Wagner's death.[44] But upon closer consideration, Nietzsche's critique addresses allegations that were widespread within the German music world around 1842, the time when Wagner returned to his fatherland after his three-years Paris sojourn. Allegations, moreover, that Wagner from that moment onward tried to dispute with all his rhetorical strength. Through this violent reckoning of his previous mentor, Nietzsche ridiculed Wagner's artistic pretenses, thereby tearing down the self-stylized image that the composer had developed from the 1840s onward, and attempting to undo a campaign that Nicholas Vazsonyi has compared to "the making of a brand,"[45] and which Sieghart Döhring called "one of the greatest, albeit questionable art-political propaganda successes of our recent European cultural history."[46]

A crucial element of this image – designed and cultivated by Wagner himself, then reinforced by his faithful followership – is Wagner's status as the true heir of Beethoven, realizing the same level of sophistication of Beethoven's symphonies in his operas, or rather music dramas, as he later preferred to distinguish his works from the pre-existing opera tradition. Nietzsche attempted to unmask Wagner as being merely a man of the theater who poses as a German master composer, someone who should be denied a place within the canon of great German works that was taking shape during the second half of the nineteenth century. This accusation of theatricality rather than musical substance is one of the recurring *leitmotifs* within Wagner criticism, and at least from the early 1840s onward, Wagner has been at pains to challenge this view and to gain acceptance as a musical master.[47] Not surprisingly, the beginning of this campaign coincides with his return to Germany after his fruitless sojourn in Paris, the cosmopolitan "capital of the nineteenth-century world," and the bulwark of large-scale operatic spectacle.[48] Considering the

---

44   Before falling out with him, Nietzsche was an admirer and friend of Wagner, to whom he dedicated the preface of *Die Geburt der Tragödie* (1872), a book that can be seen as a vindication of Wagner's art and thought. Nietzsche's later outrage about Wagner is sometimes dismissed as something "all too human" – a philosophical expression of a private conflict – but in his writings against Wagner, he often lays his fingers on his former friend's sore spots.

45   *Richard Wagner. Self-Promotion and the Making of a Brand* (Vazsonyi 2012).

46   Döhring 1999: 145.

47   Music philosopher Lydia Goehr calls Wagner "the composer who so desperately sought his canonic status in the musical Parnassus." Goehr 2002: 308.

48   Walter Benjamin famously granted Paris that title in his essay *Paris. Die Hauptstadt des 19. Jahrhundert*. See Benjamin 1995.

common German self-identification with musicality, Nietzsche's accusation of "theatricality" involved a sense of "Othering." In that sense, one might discern a relation with another question Nietzsche posed elsewhere in his writings, the question whether "Wagner was a German at all?"[49]

In the emphatically nationalist cultural climate of 1888, this could be perceived as a form of blasphemy in itself. But already in the 1840s, a certain affiliation to the German cause in music was necessary for Wagner in order to gain acceptance in the German musical world, especially after his ideologically-questionable Paris campaign. Wagner must have been aware that the national, anti-French sentiment was an increasingly important trump card, as the Rhine Crisis of 1840/41 fouled up relations between France and the German states. During this conflict, the French attempt to take control of lands West of the Rhine triggered unpleasant memories of Napoleonic occupation among many Germans. This not only spurred several artistic expressions of German

---

49 In other instances, Nietzsche is more explicit about the alleged un-German nature of Wagner's histrionic approach to music. In the postscript to *Der Fall Wagner*, Nietzsche asks: "Was Wagner a German at all? [...] It is hard to discern any German trait in him. [...] His being fully *contradicts* the image of what until now has been perceived as German, let alone of what has been perceived as constituting a German musician (War Wagner überhaupt ein Deutscher? [...] Es ist schwer, in ihm irgendeinen deutschen Zug ausfindig zu Machen. Sein Wesen selbst *widerspricht* dem, was bisher als deutsch empfunden wurde; nicht zu reden vom deutschen Musiker)!" (Nietzsche 1988: 37) In *Nietzsche Contra Wagner* (1888), the philosopher emphasizes Wagner's art as being French, or rather Parisian, throughout: "Concerning Richard Wagner, it is quite obvious that Paris is the actual *soil* for his art (Was Endlich Richard Wagner angeht; so greift man mit Händen, nicht vielleicht mit Fäusten, daß Paris der eigentliche *Boden* für Wagner ist)." (Ibid.: 165) In an unpublished fragment written down in the same period, Nietzsche makes the connection between French culture and Wagner's art even more articulate: "People nowadays are completly unwilling to concede how much Wagner owes to France, how much he even belongs in Paris. The artistic ambition of a grand style – even that is French about Wagner... and the grand opera! And the competition with Meyerbeer! A battle fought out even with Meyerbeerian means! What is German about that? Shall we finally mention the decisive character of Wagner's art? It is the histrionism, the act of staging, the art of *étalage*, the desire for effect for the sake of effect [The German original creates ambiguity by writing down only W., wich could refer to effect as well as to Wagner himself] [...]. Does this display a *German* talent in any art discipline (Man will es heute noch am Wenigsten Wort haben, wie viel Wagner Frankreich verdankt, wie sehr er selbst nach Paris gehört. Der Ehrgeiz großen Styls bei einem Künstler – selbst der ist noch französisch an Wagner... und die große Oper! Und der Wettlauf mit Meyerbeer! Und sogar mit Meyerbeerschen Mitteln! Was ist daran deutsch?... Zuletzt erwägen wir doch das Entscheidende: was charakterisirt die Wagnersche Künstlerschaft? Der Histrionismus, das in-Scene-Setzen, die Kunst der étalage, der Wille zur Wirkung um der W.[irkung] Willen [...]. Ist das in irgend einem Genre eine *deutsche* Art Begabung)?" Nietzsche 1972: 202.

nationalism,[50] but can also be seen as the upbeat of this ideology as a mass movement, from which neither political leaders nor artists could distance themselves any longer.[51] The significance of the Rhine as a marker of German culture was certainly not lost upon Wagner in those days, as he concluded his *Autobiographische Skizze* (1843) with the following patriotic statement about his return to the fatherland in April 1842: "For the first time I saw the Rhine, – with tears in my eyes I, poor artist, pledged eternal allegiance to my German fatherland."[52]

The second section of this chapter traces Wagner's campaign to present himself emphatically as a German master composer, started in his unfortunate Paris years, and intensified during his residence in Dresden between 1842 and 1849. The focus lies on the appropriation of Beethoven and Weber's heritage and Wagner's self-stylization as their respective successor, while wiping out the impression of being a Meyerbeer epigone through a ferocious hate campaign. Moreover, it is shown how Wagner during these years returned to German Romantic opera, while simultaneously transforming it into something less "philistine."

Wagner's life appears to be a classic case of what Benedict Anderson has called "long-distance nationalism,"[53] as his sense of German national identity was greatly enhanced during his residence in Paris between 1839 and 1842. This is particularly evident in his literary output of this period, compiled in his collected writings under the title *Ein deutscher Musiker in Paris*. The core of this collection consisted of three short stories, initially published in French translation in the *Revue et gazette musicale de Paris*, entitled: *Une visite à Beethoven, épisode de la vie d'un musicien allemand* (1840), *Un musicien étranger à Paris* (1841) and *Une soirée heureuse* (1841).[54] The former two were included in the *Dresdner Abend-Zeitung* in 1841 in a German version. In the first edition of his collected writings published in 1871, Wagner added a few essays he had written during his Paris years to the collection *Ein deutscher Musiker in Paris*,

---

50   These years saw the creation of both Nikolaus Becker's *Rheinlied* (Sie sollen ihn nicht haben, den freien deutschen Rhein!) in 1840 and August Heinrich Hoffman von Fallersleben's *Lied der Deutschen* (Deutschland, Deutschland über alles) in 1841. See also Vanchena 2000: 239–251.

51   For a discussion of the Rhine Crisis as a catalyst for German nationalism as a mass movement to be reckoned with, see Boterman 2005: 69–70.

52   "Zum ersten Male sah ich den Rhein, – mit hellen Thränen im Auge schwur ich armer Künstler meinem deutschen Vaterlande ewige Treue." *WWSB*, Sämtliche Schriften, Band I: 19.

53   Anderson 1992.

54   Matthias Brzoska mentions that these texts were translated into French by Joseph Duesberg. Brzoska 1995: 174.

presenting them as posthumous texts from the deceased German musician R., the protagonist of the short stories. Besides these texts that Wagner consciously compiled as a work, he wrote many other essays and articles in the same period, in which his viewpoint as a German musician in Paris repeatedly forms the point of departure.

In many of these texts, Wagner appears to present himself as an intermediary, providing German journals and newspapers with information about French cultural and musical life, while explaining the characteristic nature of German culture and music to a French readership.[55] The opportunity to write articles in the *Revue et gazette musicale de Paris* – granted by music publisher Maurice Schlesinger on Meyerbeer's recommendation – offered him the possibility to become better-known in the Parisian music scene, which could enhance his chances to stage his operas. But both his hopes to succeed and his fascination for the French capital vanished when he gradually realized that it was impossible to have his operas performed in a society in which capital and connections appeared to be far more important than genuine talent. Although it is hard to pinpoint a moment when Wagner gave up hope at Parisian success, the summer of 1840 seems to have been a turning point. At that moment, the *Théâtre de la Renaissance*, where a performance of *Das Liebesverbot* had been considered, went bankrupt.[56] From that moment onward, Wagner retained a diplomatic stance towards Paris and the French in some of his articles, but particularly in those addressed to his German compatriots, he started to let loose his frustrations.

The most straightforward tirade against Paris society and its treatment of German fellow citizens was voiced in the 1841 article 'Pariser Fatalitäten für Deutsche,' published in *Europa, Chronik der gebildeten Welt*:

> It is true: nothing is more annoying than to be German in Paris. It is great to be German when at home, where there is Jean Paul, Bavarian beer, where one can discuss Hegelian philosophy or Straussian waltzes, [...] where one can hear or sing an old or new song about the Rhine. Nothing of that in Paris, but many Germans live her nonetheless; how enormous their boredom [*ennui*] must be. [...] Poverty is the greatest shame in

---

55   Examples of this are his texts praising Halévy and his grand opera *La Reine de Chypre* as a useful model for German opera [amongst others 'Bericht über eine neue Pariser Oper ("La Reine de Chypre von Halévy),' *Dresdner Abend-Zeitung*, 26–29 January 1842] on the one hand, and *De la musique allemande* [*Revue et Gazette musicale de Paris* VII/44+46, 12 July and 26 July 1840: 375–378 + 395–398] on the other.

56   See Wagner's 'Autobiographische Skizze,' published in *Die Zeitung für die elegante Welt* in 1843. *WWSB*, Sämtliche Schriften Band I: 15.

Paris, and as Parisians take any German to be poor, he appears to them as stupid, foul and dissolute. [...] But who could imagine what extraordinary individuals live in this city. Haven't you ever experienced that a waiter bringing *eau de vie*, beer or tobacco was actually a student of Hegel, a playwright or a counterpoint pupil of Kirnberger?[57]

According to Wagner, talent is of no use for a Paris success, whereas money is everything, leading to frustration and regained patriotism among German inhabitants:

A banker can do anything in Paris, can even compose operas and have them staged. [...] The most exquisite, genuine Germans are poor. In Paris they learn again to appreciate their native tongue, their weakened patriotic sense is regenerated, and regardless of their fear to return to the homeland, they are homesick. [...] You thirty-thousand national Germans in Paris, may you be granted redemption![58]

Wagner digested the alleged tribulations of being a young, idealist, and talented but prospectless German in Paris in the short stories eventually compiled as *Ein deutscher Musiker in Paris*. In *Un musicien étranger à Paris*, later published as *Ein Ende in Paris*, Wagner paints the vicissitudes of R., a young German

---

57   "Es ist wohl wahr: im ganzen ist es das Ennuyanteste, in Paris Deutscher zu sein. Deutscher
      sein ist herrlich, wenn man zu Haus ist, wo man Gemüth, Jean Paul und bayrisches Bier
      hat, wo man sich über die Hegelsche Philosophie oder die Straußischen Walzer streiten
      kann, [...], wo man endlich ein gutes altes oder neues Lied über den Vater Rhein hören
      oder singen kann. Nichts von alledem trifft man nun in Paris an, und doch lebt eine Un-
      zahl von Deutschen hier; wie groß muß ihr Ennui sein! [...] Armuth [...] ist das größte
      Laster in Paris, und da man jeden Deutschen ausschließlich für arm ansieht, so gilt er in
      gewissen Beziehungen für dumm und schlecht, d.h. lasterhaft, zugleich. [...] Wer kann
      ahnen, welch ausgezeichnete Individuen sich hier und da [...] befinden mögen? Mag es
      nicht schon begegnet sein, daß wir ein Glas Eau-de-vie aus den Händen des verständ-
      nisvollsten Schülers der Hegelschen Philosophie erhielten? Daß uns ein Dichter von
      fünfaktigen Dramen in Versen für zwei Sous Schnupftabak reichte? Daß wir einen Schop-
      pen Straßburger Bier tranken, welches der gefühlvollste Kontrapunktist aus Kirnberger's
      Schule eingeschenkt?" wwsᴮ, Band 12: 45–62.
58   "Ein Bankier kann alles in Paris, selbst Opern komponiren und aufführen lassen. [...]
      Die vortrefflichsten, echtesten Deutschen sind die Armen; sie lernen in Paris ihre Mut-
      tersprache von neuem schätzen, und vergessen darüber, französisch zu lernen. Ihr oft
      schwach gewordener patriotischer Sinn wird hier von neuem gestärkt, und so sehr sie
      gewöhnlich die Rückkehr in die Heimat scheuen, vergehen sie doch vor Heimweh. [...]
      Möge euch, ihr dreißigtausend Nationaldeutschen in Paris, die Erlösung beschieden
      sein!" Ibid.: 58–62.

musician who enters Paris full of ambition, becomes ever more frustrated, gradually turns mad and eventually dies as a martyr for his art in Montmartre. The narrator of the story is another German inhabitant of Paris, who initially infuriates his naïve and idealist compatriot with his practical, if not cynical questions about the reality of the Paris music scene, but is reconciled with R. sitting vigil at the latter's deathbed.

One may discern aspects of Wagner in both characters: R. being the un-compromising, idealist and penniless German composer, whereas the more realist narrator reflects the part of him that has learned by bitter experience that Paris is an impregnable fortress.[59] The story is Hoffmanesque in at least three respects. The esthetic conversation reminds us of *Der Dichter und der Komponist*, whereas the way in which the narrator finds R. in a state of mad-ness in a city park calls the similar beginning of *Ritter Gluck* in Berlin to mind. Moreover, R. is haunted by an Englishman, who resembles the demon figures one often finds in Hoffmann's stories.[60] The wealthy, insincere and utilitarian Englishman presents the absolute antidote to R., functioning as an "other" that helps to establish the German "self."[61] Again it is the poverty, or rather financial disinterestedness of R. that distinguishes him as a genuine German artist.[62]

---

59   There has been quite some scholarly discussion concerning the question whether Wag-ner designed R. as a literary version of himself or not. Vazsonyi concludes that "to read *R* as *R*ichard Wagner makes the most sense, not least because *R*, like Wagner, was born in a 'medium-sized city in the heart of Germany' with first letter 'L.'" [This is mentioned in *Eine Pilgerfahrt zu Beethoven*] Vazsonyi 2010: 35. The identification of R. with Wagner himself was enforced even further when the four Paris essays written by Wagner were included in the edition of *Ein deutscher Musiker in Paris* in Wagner's collected works in 1871. In *Eine Mittheilung an meine Freunde* (1851), Wagner also emphasized the autobio-graphical nature of these Paris writings: "In these stories I painted, in a poetic and slightly humoristic way, my own vicissitudes in Paris, eventually dying from starvation, a fate that I had fortunately managed to escape (Hierin stellte ich, in erdichteten Zügen und mit ziemlichen Humor, meine eigenen Schicksale, namentlich in Paris, bis zum wirklichen Hungertode, dem ich glücklicherweise allerdings entgangen war, dar)." *WWSB*, Sämtliche Schriften, Band IV: 262.

60   Think, for example, of Dapertutto in *Die Abenteuer der Sylvesternacht* (1815) and Coppelius in *Der Sandmann* (1816).

61   In *Richard Wagner and the Anti-Semitic Imagination*, Marc Weiner argues that the Englishman can be seen as a general stereotype for a cosmopolitan, capitalist, and utili-tarian society that Wagner associated as much with the French and Jewish as with the English, and embodies a non-German, morally inferior "other." The choice for an English-man rather than a Frenchman may be explained from the fact that Wagner did not want to upset his initial French readership. See Weiner 1995: 156–157.

62   R. is appalled when the Englishman offers him money to play the violin. Vazsonyi relates this glorification of financial disinterestedness both with age-old national stereotypes about the German people and to the ideals of the European avant-garde around 1840:

The antagonism between R. and the Englishman is even more prominent in *Une visite à Beethoven/Eine Pilgerfahrt zu Beethoven*. Here they both travel to Vienna, with the hope of meeting Beethoven there. The Englishman pops up repeatedly, thereby obstructing R.'s chances to meet Beethoven, the goal of his pilgrimage. Beethoven is annoyed by the many Englishmen who travel to Vienna to meet him, not out of sincere appreciation for his art, but just because he is considered a star composer. Due to R.'s inseparable fellow traveler, Beethoven initially also takes him for an Englishman. Finally, after sending Beethoven a letter to explain the situation, and after Beethoven has dismissed the Englishman from his house, R. can finally enter the sanctuary and join in a conversation with the master. Beethoven confides his esthetic outlooks to R., speaking about the musical drama of the future and explaining the underlying idea of the choral finale of his *Ninth Symphony*. In the context of this study, Beethoven's remarks about opera are of particular relevance:

> I am not an opera composer – that is to say, there isn't a single theater in the world for which I'd willingly write another opera. If I were to write one after my own heart people would run away. All that stuff operas are patched together out of nowadays - arias, duets, terzettos and what have you – I'd get rid of and put in its place what no singer would want to sing and no public to hear. [...] But why shouldn't vocal music be considered as great and serious as instrumental music? [...] The human voice, a far nobler and more beautiful organ than any orchestral instrument, is *there*, a fact of life.[63]

"Tacitus's *Germania* (AD 98) thematizes ignorance of gold and silver amongst Germanic tribes as an indication of their wholesomeness, and as a foil to critique the more decadent, corrupt Romans. These two discursive lines merged with the rediscovery in 1455 of Tacitus's text, and Martin Luther's protest against papal fiscal abuses in 1517. [...] Luther's status as exemplary German seemed to confirm Tacitus's observations about the virtue of the Germanic folk, observations which became crucial in the extended effort to (re-) construct a German national identity during the Eighteenth century. Luther's status as an exemplary author who did not seek profit from his creative work was no less influential. [...] Wagner simply combined existing discourses: one which claimed disinterestedness was a distinctly German trait, with another Europe-wide assertion that genuine art could only be produced in the spirit of disinterestedness." Vazsonyi 2010: 19.

63   English translation derived from Jacobs 1973: 79–80. "Ich bin kein Opernkomponist, wenigstens kenne ich kein Theater in der Welt, für das ich gern wieder eine Oper schreiben möchte! Wenn ich eine Oper machen wollte, die nach meinem Sinne wäre, würden die Leute davon laufen; denn da würde nichts von Arien, Duetten, Terzetten und all dem Zeuge zu finden sein, womit sie heut' zu Tage die Opern zusammenflicken, und was ich dafür machte, würde kein Sänger singen und kein Publikum hören wollen. [...] Warum sollte aber die Vokalmusik nicht ebenso gut als die Instrumentalmusik einen großen,

Anyone familiar with Wagner's later esthetic theories will recognize how Beethoven is used here as a spokesman of Wagner's own artistic convictions,[64] in a curious appropriation which makes Wagner himself appear as "nothing less than the executor of Beethoven's musical will."[65] Wagner takes the prestige of instrumental music – which he, and many contemporaries with him, considers not only the most elevated but also most German genre of his time[66] – as

---

ernsten Genre bilden können [...]? Die menschliche Stimme [...] ist sogar ein bei weitem schöneres und edleres Ton-Organ als jedes Instrument des Orchesters." *WWSB*, Sämtliche Schriften, Band I: 110.

64   Wagner himself repeated Beethoven's dictum "Ich bin kein Opernkomponist" nearly literally in a footnote in *Eine Mittheilung an meine Freunde* (1851), where he writes "Ich schreibe keine *Opern* mehr." (WWSB, Sämtliche Schriften, Band IV: 345) It is often overlooked to what extent Wagner re-used common ideas about Beethoven and about the melting together of instrumental music and other arts into a "total artwork of the future." Brzoszka, for example, has shown that Wagner based his short story on earlier narrations by Ludwig Rellstab and Jules Janin, and argues that many of his views on the "*Gesamt-kunstwerk*" were actually derived from French music esthetics of the 1830s (See Brzoska 1995: 175–177). But the fact that this is often overlooked underlines the extent to which Wagner managed to present this discourse as being his "own" creation, it emphasizes the effectiveness of his press campaign, which arguably started in Paris.

65   Vazsonyi 2010: 39.

66   In 'Über deutsches Musikwesen,' initially published as 'de la musique allemande' in the *Revue et Gazette musicale de Paris* VII/44, 12 July 1840: 377, Wagner writes about the elevated and German nature of instrumental music: "It is in the realm of instrumental music where the artist, free of all alien and restricting influences, is able to attain the ideal of art most immediately. [...] It hardly surprises that it is exactly towards this musical genre that the serious, profound and rapturous German prefers to direct his attention (Hier, im Gebiete der Instrumentalmusik, ist es, wo der Künstler, frei von jedem fremden und beengenden Einflusse, im Stande ist, am unmittelbarsten an das Ideal der Kunst zu reichen; [...] Was Wunder, wenn der ernste, tiefe und schwärmerische Deutsche gerade diesem Genre der Musik sich mit größerer Vorliebe als jedem anderen zuwendet?)." (*WWSB*, Sämtliche Schriften, Band I: 156) Vaszonyi argues that "Wagner wanted to be the 'most German' without foregoing the German Romantic notion of instrumental music's universal appeal and transcendental aspirations" and points out that "the symphony enjoyed a certain aura of esthetic superiority, and, I would add, moral superiority also. So Wagner could take the high ground by claiming the self-sufficient non-commercial symphonic tradition for his music dramas, making his brand of opera conceptually superior to the 'commercial' variety of the French and Italians." Vazsonyi 2010: 65. Carolyn Abbate emphasizes how well Wagner's self-staging as Beethoven's heir has served his admirers as a tool to socially distinguish themselves: "the equation between Wagner and Beethoven and the notion that Wagner's operas are 'symphonic' cannot simply be taken at face value. Both are specious, yet both are widely accepted. Later generations have found them convenient and comfortable: convenient because they provide a neat strand of music-historical continuity through a century of musical dislocations, and comfortable because they place a mantle of absolute-musical respectability – Beethoven's mantle – on Wagner's doubtful theatrical shoulders." Abbate 1989: 93.

well as the sacral aura of its most famous practitioner as a legitimization of his own quest for a more elevated opera of the future.[67] By staging himself as the true heir of Beethoven, Wagner not only presents himself as the future of German opera, but of German music in general, of music per se.

Another deceased composer played an equally important role in Wagner's self-stylization as a German musician in Paris, when in 1841 the Paris *Opéra* produced Carl Maria von Weber's *Freischütz*. Wagner appointed himself as an authority by writing articles in the *Revue et Gazette musicale de Paris* explaining to the French public what made this opera genuinely German. As a chief trait of German life, Wagner lifts out the intimate relationship between nature and the inner life of the characters.[68] He argues that only in Germany, people are still enraptured by the wondrous, and that only in Germany a man of spirit, such as Weber, would decide to set to music such a story.[69] Wagner here seems to emphasize the fact that the story belongs to German folk culture, is enjoyed by a German audience, and is composed by a German musician, creating a sense of collective ownership which enhances its function as a national opera. Wagner also recognizes the national significance of *Der Freischütz* in its ability to unite the shattered and politically divided German-speaking world.[70]

---

67   The fact that Beethoven concluded his *Ninth Symphony* with a chorus in itself serves as a legitimization of Wagner's idea that Beethoven has realized the full potential of the symphony as an instrumental genre, after which a time has come to develop a new genre, combining the "infinite, primal feelings" of instrumental music with the "clear, determined sensation" of the human voice. Or, as Wagner lets Beethoven state it in the short story: "The wild, infinitely-expanding primal emotions that the instruments represent are set against the clear, specific sense of the human heart, represented by the human voice. The involvement of this second element has a soothing and conciliating effect on this battle of the primal emotions, gives their flow a determined, unified direction (Man stelle den wilden, in das Unendliche hinausschweifenden Urgefühlen, repräsentirt von den Instrumenten, die klare, bestimmte Empfindung des menschlichen Herzens entgegen, repräsentirt von der Menschenstimme. Das Hinzutreten dieses zweiten Elements wird wohlthuend und schlichtend auf den Kampf der Urgefühle wirken, wird ihren Strome einen bestimmten, vereinigten Lauf geben.)." *WWSB*, Sämtliche Schriften, Band I: 110.

68   "La tradition du Freischütz porte d'ailleurs profondément l'empreinte de la nationalité allemande. [...] C'est ne que chez les Allemands [...], que la nature extérieure pouvait se confondre aussi intimement avec l'âme de l'homme." *Revue et Gazette musicale de Paris* VIII/34, 23 May 1841: 279.

69   "Ce n'est que chez le people où la tradition du Franc-tireur avait pris naissance, et qui aime encore aujourd'hui à se laisser bercer au charme du merveilleux, qu'un compositeur, home d'esprit, put concevoir l'idée d'asseoir un grand ouvrage musical sur une pareille base." *Revue et Gazette musicale de Paris* VIII/35, 30 May 1841: 285.

70   "Cette fois, tous les divers éléments de la vie politique allemande [...] se réunissaient en un foyer commun: d'un bout de l'Allemagne à l'autre *le Freischütz* était dansé, chanté, ecouté avec transport." Ibid.: 286.

Wagner emphatically relates the emotions that, for example, Max's aria 'Durch die Wälder, durch die Auen' releases among a German audience to the lack of a unified German state,[71] thereby explaining to his French readers the idea of a *Kulturnation.*

Wagner's statement about the unique German character of *Der Freischütz* chiefly served to convince the French that the integrity of its unconventional form should be respected. As had previously been the case with Castil-Blaze's reworking of *Der Freischütz* into *Robin des bois* in 1824, it was a standard procedure that the work had to be adapted in order to fit Parisian audience expectations and the formal requirements of the theater were the piece was to be performed. In the case of the *Opéra*, this included the transformation of the spoken dialogues into recitative – a procedure to be carried out by Hector Berlioz[72] – and the inclusion of a stately ballet scene, both to Wagner's disgust.[73] He particularly feared that presenting the work in a mutilated form

---

71   "Nous sommes un peuple singulier; l'air de *Freischütz: A travers les bois,* fait couler nos larmes, tandis que nos yeux restent secs quand, au lieu d'une patrie commune, nous n'apercevons que trente-quatre principautés." Ibid.: 286.

72   To the composer's defense, one must point out that Berlioz – who had previously detested the *Freischütz* "mutilations" carried out by Castil-Blaze – accepted this task reluctantly, more aiming for damage control by defending the artistic integrity of Weber's piece as much as possible. In his *Memoires* (1870), he wrote the following about his discussions with Léon Pillet, the director of the Paris *Opéra* who gave him the commission: "I don't believe, I told him, that one should add recitatives to *Der Freischütz,* as you ask me; but as this is a necessary requirement to have the work performed at the *Opéra,* and as if I would not do the job, you'd ask someone else most probably less familiar with the work and with Weber, which would make it harder to show the Parisian audience what a masterpiece this is, I accept your offer, be it on the condition that *Der Freischütz* must absolutely be performed as it is, neither changing anything in the libretto nor in the music (Je ne crois pas, lui répondis-je, qu'on doit ajouter au Freyschütz les récitatifs que vous me demandez; cependant puisque c'est la condition sans laquelle il ne peut être représenté à l'Opéra, et comme si je ne les écrivais pas vous en confieriez la composition à un autre moins familier, peut-être, que je ne le suis avec Weber, et certainement moins dévoué que moi à la glorification de son chef-d'œuvre, j'accepte votre offre, à une condition .- le Freyschütz sera joué absolument tel qu'il est, sans rien changer dans le livret ni dans la musique)." Berlioz 1870: 327. The severity of Paris' genre classifications and restrictions have been addressed by Mark Everist in articles such as 'Theatres of Ligitation' (2004) and 'The Music of Power' (2014).

73   In his article for the *Revue et Gazette,* Wagner wrote: "The score of *Der Freischütz* is a coherent whole, its parts are coordinated by a perfect correspondence of form and idea. The attempt to improve this opera by making cuts is actually a kind of mutilation of this masterwork, wouldn't you agree (La partition du *Freischütz* est un tout complet, coordonné dans toutes ses parties sous le double rapport de la pensée et de la forme; y ajouter, en retrancher quelque chose, si peu que cela puisse être, n'est-ce pas en quelque sorte dénaturer, mutiler l'oeuvre du maître)?" *Revue et Gazette musicale de Paris* VIII/35, 30 May

would lead to indifference and a lack of interest to acquaint *Der Freischütz* in its original form.[74] But at the same time, he sadly realized that the French attitude might well be irreconcilable with this German masterpiece anyway.[75]

Wagner's French press campaign had little effect; the opera was indeed given in its Frenchified, "aggrandized" form. But the Paris performance of *Le Freischütz* did provide Wagner the possibility to follow in the footsteps of all those Parisian Germans who had previously complained to their compatriots about the French mutilation of German masterworks, from *Les Mystères d'Isis* (1801) until *Robin des bois* (1824).[76] Wagner seized this opportunity by writing a furious article for the *Dresdner Abend-Zeitung*, published on 20 June 1841, which contributed to both his visibility and his popularity among the German-speaking public, particularly in Dresden. Wagner opens with an exalted declaration of love for the German fatherland, being the cradle of *Der Freischütz* and the place where this opera is cherished, and expresses his pride to be German.[77] After an extensive dismissal of the altered form and the performance of the work, Wagner comes to the conclusion that the promise of

---

1841: 286) In a report called "'Le Freischütz.' Bericht nach Deutschland," published in the *Dresdner Abend-Zeitung*, Wagner underlined the objective of his text for the Parisian audience: "I could not believe that these French, who were incapable of staging our *Freischütz* in its orginal form, would be able to understand this work in a deformed shape. I therefore decided, full of patriotic zeal, to share my opinion concerning this initiative with the Parisian public by writing an article. I did what I felt necessary in order to protect our national heritage from the unavoidable failure of this experiment (Es war mir unmöglich zu glauben, daß dieselben Franzosen, die kein Mittel in der Welt kannten, unserem Freischützen in seiner ursprünglichen Gestalt den Eintritt auf ihrer Bühne zu verschaffen, ihn begreifen und verstehen können würden, wenn er ihnen noch dazu mit entstelltem Äußeren zu Gesicht und zu Gehör käme. Ich entschloß mich daher in meinem patriotischen Eifer, dem Pariser Publikum meine Ansicht über das Vorhaben mitzuteilen, und ließ deshalb einen Aufsatz drucken, in welchem ich mich frei und ohne Scheu aussprach. [...] Ich that somit, was ich für nöthig hielt, um unser National-Eigenthum im Voraus für den fast unausbleiblichen Fall des Misslingens des damit angestellten Experimentes zu rechtfertigen)." WWSB, Sämtliche Schriften: Band I: 224–225.

74   "Peut-être même ce que vous entendrez ne vous inspirera-t-il pas le désir de le voir tel qu'il est dans la naïveté de sa forme primitive." *Revue et Gazette musicale de Paris* VIII/35, 30 May 1841: 287.

75   "Et s'il apparaissait réellement devant vous tel qu'il est, dans toute sa simplicité, dans toute sa candeur; [...] auriez-vous une intelligence plus complète du *Freischütz*? Vous sentiriez-vous disposés à vous laisser aller à cet enthousiasme rêveur qu'il a inspiré à quarante millions d'Allemands? Hélas! j'en doute." Ibid.: 287.

76   See Chapter 4.

77   "O mein herrliches deutsches Vaterland, wie muß ich dich lieben, wie muß ich für dich schwärmen, wär es nur, weil auf deinem Boden der 'Freischütz' entstand! Wie muß ich das deutsche Volk lieben, das den 'Freischütz' liebt, das noch heute, an die Wunder der naivesten Sage glaubt [...]. Wie ist mir wohl, daß ich ein Deutscher bin!" WWSB, Sämtliche Schriften, Band I: 220.

a French-German reconciliation on the operatic plane has proven to be futile,[78] and that a people who has given birth to Mozart and Beethoven can no longer accept to be mocked at by Parisian salons.[79] Fully in line with the rhetoric of the Rhine Crisis, Wagner declares that French-German cultural relations are now in a time of war,[80] and urges his compatriots to return to sender all those French operas so frequently performed in Germany.[81]

Wagner's discussion of the 1841 *Freischütz* production in Paris paved the way for his move to Dresden in 1842, and Weber generally played a prominent role in both Wagner's rise to fame in the Saxon capital and his self-stylization as the future of German opera. As much as with Beethoven, Wagner used Weber as a mythological figure on which his own esthetic ideals could be projected. In the case of Weber, who had actually produced a considerable body of literature concerning the unique nature of German opera, this entailed less manipulation than he had used with the fictive Beethoven figure in *Eine Pilgerfahrt*.[82] In 'Wagner und Weber; Der Vorgang einer Theatralisierung' (1986), Eckart Kröplin states that Wagner repeatedly presented Weber as an exemplification of his artistic outlooks, such as "truthfulness and sincerity, psychological depth, and [...] the rapturous effect of the artwork that effaces the artificiality of its means."[83]

---

78   "[daß] sich seit einiger Zeit bei uns die Idee gebildet hatte, daß zwischen Deutschen und Franzosen, zumal in Kunstgeschmacke, eine Annäherung stattfinde. [...] der 'Freischütz' hat [...] dazu beigetragen, die Franzosen neuerdings von den Deutschen zu entfernen. [...] Hierüber dürfen wir uns keine Illusionen machen; in vielen Punkten werden uns die Franzosen immer fremd bleiben." Ibid.: 237–238. More than any other German, Wagner himself had believed in this possibility, and was frustrated when he found out that this alleged rapprochement did not enhance his chances at Paris success. As is often the case, here Wagner's esthetic and ideological stance is closely related to his personal situation.

79   "Was? – Wir, das begabteste Volk, unter denen Gott einen Mozart und Beethoven entstehen ließ, sollten dazu gemacht sein, das Gespött der Pariser Salons abzugeben?" Ibid.: 239.

80   In a satirical article published on 6 July 1841 in the *Dresdner Abend-Zeitung*, Wagner again employs a similarly martial rhetoric, when he concludes that the French have not managed to kill *Der Freischütz*: "Sie haben ihn nicht todt machen können, unseren lieben herrlichen Freischützen." WWSB, Sämtliche Schriften, Band XII: 94. Significantly, Wagner phrases this sentence in the same structure as Nikolaus Becker's patriotic *Rheinlied* (1840): "Sie sollen ihn nicht haben, den freien deutschen Rhein!"

81   "Wir sind glücklich zu schätzen, daß wir im Stande sind, Alles, was uns das Ausland bietet [...] zu würdigen. [...] Bei alledem ist es aber in der Natur hergebracht, daß es Zeiten des Krieges, wie des Friedens giebt; wollt Ihr daher einmal in Kriegzeiten an den Franzosen Rache nehmen, so könntet Ihr sie nicht empfindlicher bestrafen, als wenn Ihr ihnen die Emissäre ihres heiligen Geistes [...] eines schönen Tages mit Extrapost zurückschicktet." WWSB, Sämtliche Schriften, Band I: 240.

82   Wagner's relationship to Weber was also more concrete in the sense that the latter had been a friend of the Wagner family when the former was a child.

83   Kröplin 1986: 336.

Wagner's most evident public attempt to present himself as the true heir of Weber took place in 1844. A year earlier, Wagner had accepted the position of *königlicher Kapellmeister*, the same position that Weber had occupied until his death in 1826, and which, thanks to Weber's efforts for the German operatic cause, had achieved a national significance. In 1844, the remains of Weber, previously buried in London, were finally repatriated and reburied in Dresden, and this homecoming was celebrated with a monumental funeral service. Wagner played a prominent role, contributing a funeral overture for woodwinds on melodies of *Euryanthe* for the procession, a male chorus, and a speech.[84]

The 1840s saw an immense rise of material commemorations of composers, for example with monuments for Mozart (Salzburg, 1842) and Beethoven (Bonn, 1845). The Dresden ceremony may well have been inspired by the erection of a monument for the Belgian André Grétry, who had initially been buried in Paris in 1813, but whose heart was brought back in an urn to his place of birth Liège in 1842. This ceremony also entailed a repatriation with nationalist overtones, a symbolical return of the composer's heart – a reference to his most famous opera *Richard Coeur-de-lion* – to his homeland which by now had become an independent country.[85] Moreover, part of the celebration consisted of a collective, large-scale performance of Grétry's most famous melody, the romance from *Richard Coeur-de-lion*.[86]

Wagner's funeral overture was just as much linked to the remains of the deceased composer, as it opens and closes with Emma's music from *Euryanthe*. Emma's motif initially wanders in a searching, chromatic idiom, as her soul

---

84   Vazsonyi argues that Wagner himself deliberately magnified his importance in the event, using the ceremony as a means for self-promotion: "neither Wagner nor any other individual is credited either for the idea or for organizing the event as a whole. Nevertheless, today, it is hard to find an account of the Weber translocation that does not in the first place credit Wagner and Wagner alone for the feat. Why the difference between perceptions in 1844 and since? [...] The answer [...] is that Wagner wrote the definitive account of the event; he inscribed himself indelibly into Weber's biographical narrative [...] According to Wagner, 'Wagner' was the prime mover. [...] For Wagner, the event satisfied his general desire for attention while also providing the opportunity to consolidate several elements of his persona: to appear as Weber's successor both in his capacity as Dresden's next world-famous Kapellmeister and, even more, as the next great composer of German opera." Vazsonyi 2010: 51.

85   Another sign of the transnational dynamic at work in these commemorations of national composers is the fact that it was an anonymous article in the *Revue et Gazette musicale de Paris* (VIII/6, 21 January 1841: 45) about the irretrievability of Weber's grave at the Moorfields Church in London that spurred the formation of a committee in Dresden to repatriate the composer's remains. See Warrack 1976: 363.

86   The event was reported in many international music journals. The most elaborate report can be found in *The Musical World* XVII/30: 237–238.

cannot find peace, but at the end of the opera – and of the funeral overture – she finally receives salvation and the motif returns in a solid, diatonic shape.[87] Wagner must have linked this musical procedure to the final homecoming of Weber's spirit now that his remains had returned to his homeland.[88]

In his male chorus, Wagner turned around the perspective, stating that it was the German motherland that could finally find peace after the return of the prodigal son.[89] But Wagner impressed most in his speech, in which he clothed Weber in all the chauvinist rhetoric he had first employed in his Paris writings. He starts by voicing his conviction that Weber would prefer a modest final resting place at home over a mausoleum abroad,[90] emphasizing his German austerity and financial disinterestedness. He mentions that, unlike those cosmopolitan banker-type composers who feel at home wherever they can make profit, Weber constantly yearned for his homeland.[91] In a personal address, he exclaims that "you were the most German musician who ever lived," one who could never abandon his German heritage. "Whereas Britons can do you justice, and Frenchmen can admire you, only Germans can love you. [...] Are we to blame for wanting your ashes to be part of our beloved German soil?"[92]

---

87   In his report of the event, Wagner speaks of a "transfigured restatement of the first motif [verklärte Wiederaufnahme des ersten Motives]." *WWSB,* Sämtliche Schriften, Band 11: 43.

88   The resolution of Emma's motif in *Euryanthe* is an important forerunner to the *Erlösungsschluß* (Redemption Finale) which would dominate Wagner's operas from *Tannhäuser* onwards. In 1860, Wagner adapted the conclusion of *Der fliegende Holländer* in order to conform this earlier work to his musical redemption dramaturgy as well.

89   "Nicht trauert mehr die deutsche Mutter Erde / Um den geliebten, weit entrückten Sohn; / Nicht blickt sie mehr mit sehnender Gebärde / Hin über's Meer zum fernen Albion: – / Aufs'Neu' nahm sie ihn auf in ihren Schooß, Den einst sie aussandt' edel, mild und groß." Ibid.: 49.

90   "Hier sei die prunklose Stätte, die uns Deine theure Hülle bewahre! Und hätte sie dort in Fürstengrüften geprangt, im stolzesten Münster einer stolzen Nation, wir wagten doch zu hoffen, daß Du ein bescheidenes Grab in deutschem Boden Dir lieber zur letzten Ruhestätte erwählt." Ibid.: 46.

91   "Du gehörtest ja nicht jenen kalten Ruhmsüchtigen an, die kein Vaterland haben, denen das Land der Erde das liebste ist, in welchem ihr Ehrgeiz den üppigsten Boden für sein Gedeihen findet. – Zog Dich ein verhängnißvoller Drang dorthin, wo selbst das Genie sich zu Markte bringen muß um zu gelten, so wandtest Du zeitig genug sehnsuchtsvoll Deine Blicke nach dem heimathlichen Herde zurück." Ibid.: 47. One may perceive a clear analogy to Wagner's previous situation in Paris.

92   "Nie hat ein deutscherer Musiker gelebt, als Du! [...] Du bewahrtest sie bis an den Tod, diese höchste Tugend, Du konntest sie nie opfern, dieses schönen Erbmals Deiner deutschen Abkunft Dich nie entäußern, Du konntest uns nie verrathen! [...] Nun läßt der Britte Dir Gerechtigkeit widerfahren, es bewundert Dich der Franzose, aber lieben kann Dich nur der Deutsche; [...] wer will uns tadeln, wenn wir wollten, daß Deine Asche auch ein Theil seiner Erde, der lieben deutschen Erde sein sollte?" Ibid.: 47.

Wagner concludes by emphasizing the transgenerational community[93] of the dead and alive which is celebrated in this ceremony,[94] which clearly has a personal tinge; by vindicating the deceased Weber and attributing him all the qualities of his own artistic persona, Wagner presents himself as the legitimate heir to his German operatic legacy.[95]

Wagner's attempts to present the "most German musician who ever lived" as his progenitor cannot be seen in isolation to his infamous patricide of Giacomo Meyerbeer, the king of Parisian cosmopolitanism. Although Wagner's eventual dissociation from his previous protector is a telling example of both his rude personality and his virulent anti-Semitism, one should not overlook the fact that initially, it was chiefly spurred by his ambition to gain acceptance in the most respectable circles of German music life. In his rich and highly useful collection of nineteenth-century Wagner criticism, Helmut Kirchmeyer, for example, emphasizes how Wagner's early veneration of Meyerbeer was anything but strategic in the dominant German music-journalistic climate of the late 1830s and early 1840s.[96]

Critical attitudes towards Meyerbeer's artistic course go at least as far back as Carl Maria von Weber, who in 1820 voiced the wish that his befriended colleague would return to the fatherland to dedicate his talents to the foundation of a German opera, rather than to achieving success in Italy.[97] Whereas

---

93   "Wo ist nun Tod? Wo ist Leben? Wo beide sich in einem so wunderbar schönen Bund vereinen, da ist des ewigen Lebens Keim! – Laß auch uns, Du theurer Dahingeschiedener, mit in diesen Bund treten! Wir kennen dann nicht Tod, nicht Verwesung mehr, nur Blüthe und Gedeihen." Ibid.: 47. This sense of a transgenerational community or solidarity is one of the prime inventions of nineteenth-century national thought, see for example Leerssen 2006: 113–114.

94   *WWSB*, Sämtliche Schriften, Band II: 48.

95   Wagner's glorification of Weber is, even if not at all devoid of genuine sympathy and admiration for his predecessor, nowadays commonly seen as an attempt to present himself as the new torchbearer of the German operatic cause. See for example Meyer 2003: 172, Vazsonyi 2010: 51, and Ther 2011: 185.

96   See Kirchmeyer 1972: 134.

97   In one of his *Musikalisch-Dramatische Notizen* for the Dresden opera, Weber wrote the following with regard to Meyerbeer's *Emma di Resburgo*: "May the author express one wish, namely that Mr. Meyerbeer, after having studied his art in all its manifold national ramifications, and after having proved the adaptability of his talent, will now return to his fatherland and join the small circle of truly artistic souls who strive for the foundation of a German national opera, one that eagerly learns from foreign examples, but transforms these influences into something truthful and authentic (Darf der Schreiber dieses einen Wunsch aussprechen, so ist es der, daß Herr Meyerbeer nun, nachdem er die Kunst in ihren vielseitigen Abzweigungen nach der Gefühlsweise der sie pflegende Nationen studiert und seine Kraft, sowie die Geschmeidigkeit seines Talents erprobt hat, ins deutsche Vaterland zurückzukehren und mit den wenigen, die Kunst wahrhaft Ehrenden, auch mit

Weber's statement was an encouragement rather than a dismissal, the tone soon hardened, as Meyerbeer was increasingly being seen as an antithesis to the German operatic cause if not the German spirit altogether. In 1831, Felix Mendelssohn-Bartholdy attended a performance of *Robert le Diable* in Paris and felt that the subject was utterly immoral, writing to his father that "if opera nowadays calls for this type of baseness, I will confine myself to church music!"[98] In a letter to his friend Carl Klingemann, written a day later, Mendelssohn also voiced his contempt about the eclecticism of the music:

> The music is very clever; full of effect, well-calculated, well-seasoned. Its melodies are singable and easy to remember, it contains harmony for the learned, instrumentation for the Germans, contredanses for the French; something for everyone. But it has no heart![99]

An 1832 review of *Robert le diable* in the *AMZ* by an author with the pseudonym B. reached a similar conclusion, arguing that Meyerbeer created a "whole, which is in fact a hodgepodge of all artists, a kaleidoscope of all colors and forms, a *rotten pot* of all relishes, in short: *everything*, but no *whole*! In Paris or London this might be effective, but the closer you approach it, the more obvious its lack of coherence, taste and art becomes."[100] Considering the emphasis on organic unity as a trait of genuinely German opera, its alleged absence in *Robert* might be read as implying the un-German nature of Meyerbeer's music. It is noteworthy that Mendelssohn – who was born in a similar milieu of Jewish bankers in Berlin as Meyerbeer and allegedly struggled with his Jewish roots and perceptions thereof in his environment[101] – wrote in 1831 to his father that

---

fortbauen helfen wolle zum Gebäude einer deutschen Nationaloper, die gern von Fremden lernt, aber es in Wahrheit und Eigentümlichkeit gestaltet wiedergibt)." Kaiser 1908: 309.

98　"Es hat Effect gemacht, aber ich habe keine Musik dafür. Denn es ist gemein, und wenn das heut die Zeit verlangte und nothwendig fände, so will ich Kirchenmusik schreiben." Morgenstern 2009: 433.

99　"Die Musik ist ganz vernünftig. An Effect fehlt es nicht, er ist immer wohlberechnet, viel Pikantes ist an den rechten Stellen angebracht, Melodie für das Nachsingen. Harmonie für die Gebildeteren, Instrumentierung für die Deutschen, Contretänze für die Franzosen, etwas für jeden – aber ein Herz ist nicht dabei." Ibid.: 436.

100　"Ein Ganzes, [...] welches ein Stelldichein aller Künstler, ein Kaleidoskop aller Farben und Formen, eine olla potrida aller Genüsse, kurz *Alles* ist, nur – kein *Ganzes*! Je näher man nun einem solchen, in der Entfernung von Paris oder London vielleicht effectuirenden, Werke tritt, je deutlicher erkennt man den Mangel an Zusammenhang, das Geschmacklose, das Kunstwidrige daran." *AMZ* XXXIV/29, 18 July 1832: 486.

101　See for example *The Price of Assimilation* (2006) of Jeffrey Sposato, who argues that Mendelssohn's self-identification as a Jew developed from a relatively neutral attitude in his

as a musician, Meyerbeer no longer had a fatherland, which was dreadful: "He will always be associated with the German school; therefore, he was never truly adopted in Italy. We Germans now do not consider him our own either. It must be disastrous to reside *entre deux*, without a fatherland."[102] Although Mendelssohn does not emphatically relate Meyerbeer's cosmopolitan lack of fatherland to his Jewish descent, this was exactly the consequence that Wagner would later take in writings such as *Das Judenthum in der Musik* (1850) and *Oper und Drama* (1851).

Whereas the AMZ never truly took sides in the debate about Meyerbeer's merits,[103] Robert Schumann's NZfM took the king of Parisian opera as the perfect scapegoat to articulate its esthetic course; as the full antithesis of its German-Protestant vindication of austerity, intimacy, and sincerity. In 1837, Schumann drew a devastating comparison between the virtuous Mendelssohn and his oratorio *Paulus* and the despicable Meyerbeer and his grand opéra *Les Huguenots*.[104] Schumann voices his disgust about the abuse and degradation of *his* Protestant music and history for the sake of commercial entertainment, and his anger about both Meyerbeer's "lack of style and originality" and his "baseness, contortion, hypocrisy, immorality and unmusicality." He resists any comparison between Meyerbeer and Beethoven, scolds the former's tendency towards outward appearance and noise, and dismisses the more

---

youth to a tendency to "demonize the Jews in order to prove the sincerity of his Christian faith" in adolescent years, followed by "an attempt to reconcile his Christian faith and his Jewish heritage" in the construction of the libretti for his oratorios *Elias* (1836) and *Christus* (unfinished). Sposato 2006: 178–179.

102   "die deutsche Schule klebe ihm immerfort an und er habe sie nie recht los werden können; so sey er auch niemals einheimisch in Italien geworden. So sagen wir Deutschen nun auch, und es muß fatal sein, sich so entre deux ohne Vaterland zu finden." Morgenstern 2009: 189–190.

103   The dismissive review quoted above was combined with a more appreciative critique by another author, and accompanied by an editorial comment which took pride in the fact that the journal did not demean itself to partisanship.

104   In the opening statement of the article, Schumann writes: "The reader knows all too well what the ambition of this journal is, so that when we speak of Mendelssohn, we cannot mention Meyerbeer, as their paths are miles apart" and concludes with: "I despise Meyerbeer's fame from the bottom of my heart; his *Huguenots* present a catalog of all shortcomings and the few marginal merits of his time. Mendelssohn's path leads to beatitude, Meyerbeer's to evil. Never did I endorse a conviction as determined as I do now (Der Leser weiß zu gut, welchem Streben sich diese Blätter geweiht, zu gut, daß, wenn von Mendelssohn die Rede ist, keine von Meyerbeer sein kann, so schnurstracks laufen ihre Wege auseinander." [...] "Ich verachte diesen Meyerbeer'schen Ruhm aus dem Grunde meines Herzens; seine Hugenotten sind das Gesammtverzeichniß aller Gebrechen und der einigen wenigen Vorzüge seiner Zeit. [...] Sein [Mendelssohns] Weg führt zum Glück. Jener [Meyerbeers] zum Uebel. Und nie unterschrieb ich Etwas mit so fester Ueberzeugung als heute)." *NZfM* IV: 7 / 19, 5 September 1837: 75.

chamber-musical accompaniment of some of his arias as a sanctimonious concession to the German predilection for intimacy. In the end, everything in Meyerbeer's art is "contrived, deceptive, and hypocritical."[105]

The enormous success of Wagner's *Rienzi* at its Dresden premiere of 1842 greatly depended on its adoption of Meyerbeerian, grand operatic techniques,[106] something that the opera public at large adored, but made the work suspect among the higher echelons of the German music world.[107] Whereas local responses were generally appreciative to *Rienzi*, many papers with a more nationwide appeal emphasized its shortcomings, often referring to these as un-German qualities. A strong dismissal was voiced in the progressive, widely-read *Rheinische Zeitung*.[108] It referred to *Rienzi's* success as relying on "stage effects" rather than "musical quality" and the preferences of the "visually-inclined among the audience." On top of that, it held that Wagner lacked an "artistic education and deliberation [Besonnenheit]," and therefore resorted to the means of French grand opera, creating "noise [Tonlärm], [...]

---

105   The beneath sequence of quotes demonstrates the tenor of Schumann's devastating critique: "Ich bin kein Moralist; aber einen guten Protestanten empört's, sein theuerstes Lied auf den Bretern [sic.] abgeschrieen zu hören, empört es, das blutigste Drama seiner Religionsgeschichte zu einer Jahrmarktsfarce heruntergezogen zu sehen, [...] empört die Oper [...] mit ihrer lächerlich-gemeinen Heiligkeit [...] höchste Nicht-Originalit"at und Styllosigkeit [...] Die Gemeinheit, Verzerrung, Heuchelei, Unsittlichkeit, Un-Musik des Ganzen [...]Hatte doch Ries mit eigener Hand geschrieben, Manches in den Hugenotten sei Beethoven'schem an die Seite zu stellen etc.! [...] Ich müßte denen, die die Hugenotten nur von Weitem etwa dem Fidelio oder Aehnlichen an die Seite zu setzen wagten, unaufhörlich zurufen: daß sie nichts von der Sache verständen, nichts, nichts! [...] Meyerbeer's äußerlichste Tendenz [...]Man soll [...] nicht über Herrlichkeit schreien, wenn ein Dutzend Posaunen, Trompeten, Ophykleiden und hundert im Unisono singende Menschen in einiger Entfernung gehört werden können [...]Ein Meyerbeer'sches Raffinement muß ich hier erwähnen. Er kennt das Publicum zu gut, als daß er nicht einsehen sollte, daß zu viel Lärm abstumpft. Und wie klug arbeitet er dem entgegen? Er setzt nach solchen Prasselstellen gleich ganze Arien mit Begleitung eines einzigen Instrumentes, als ob er sagen wollte: "seht, was ich auch mit Wenigem anfangen kann, seht, Deutsche, seht! [...]Es ist alles gemacht, Alles Schein und Heuchelei." Ibid.: 73–74.

106   Even though stylistically, the example of Spontini seems to have been more important to Wagner than that of his former protector, see Mungen 1999: 129–143.

107   Wagner himself adressed the discrepancy between these two groups in his *de la musique allemande* (1840): "L'allemand, denué de l'ingéniosité qui crée on modifie la mode, accueille toutefois spontanément et sans réserve celles qu'on importe dans sa patrie [...] Mais c'est un reproche qui ne s'adresse qu'à la masse de nos compatriotes; car il arrive au contraire que, révoltés de cette condescendance générale, nos artistes de profession prennent le contre-pied trop direct de l'opinion vulgaire, et, par un excès de patriotisme condamnable, méritent d'être taxés par les étrangers de partialité et d'injustice." *Revue et Gazette musicale de Paris* VII/44, 12 July 1840: 375.

108   The *Rheinische Zeitung* functioned as a platform for leftist Young Hegelians. Both Marx and Engels contributed to the newspaper.

a negation of music in its nobler sense." Just like Schumann had done in the case of Meyerbeer's *Huguenots*, the anonymous critic condemned the analytical competence of those critics who had dared to recognize a "Beethovenian spirit" in this "sea of sound."[109] The lack of originality, beauty and veracity was linked to Wagner's betrayal of his German roots:

> The more we acknowledge the French traits of the composer's talent to *fabricate*[110] an opera, all the more we must lament his inability to retain his German individuality, with which he could have created a dramatic work in which he can believe with all his heart; a work in which human passions and events are depicted in a truthful and beautiful way.[111]

Considering the outspoken anti-Meyerbeerian stance of Schumann and his *Neue Zeitschrift für Musik*, one would have expected a fierce rejection

---

109　"diese hohlen, phrasenvollen und melodiearmen Gedanken [...] leben im Kulisseneffekt. [...] Diese Oper ist hier mit großem Beifall des schaulustigen Publikums gegeben. [...] Er fand die Bahn der großen französischen Oper, die Bahn Meyerbeer's Halevey's (sic.) am lockendsten, [...] da ihm [...] künstlerische Durchbildung und Besonnenheit fehlten. [...] Diese Oper ist eine Negation der Musik in ihrer edlern Bedeutung. [...]Es wird dieß um so nöthiger, als gefällige Kritiker sich so geschäftig erwiesen; betäubte Ohren das Wehen Beethoven'schen Geistes in diesem Tonmeere deutlich verspüren wollten." Kirchmeyer 1967: 75–77. One may recognize a Protestant, iconoclast tendency in this German dismissal of grand opera as a Catholic feast of visual splendor rather than musical and textual substance.

110　The italics at the word *machen* refer to the widespread idea among German thinkers that the composition of a French grand opéra was a matter of cerebral, industrial labor, rather than genuine artistic inspiration. Hence Heinrich Heine's characterization of Eugène Scribe, grand opéra's most influential playwright, as "Librettofabrikator" in *Lutezia* (1844). Quoted after Vazsonyi 2010: 14.

111　"Je mehr wir dem Komponisten diese französischen Attribute des Talents zugestehen müssen, eine Oper zu *machen,* um so mehr ist zu beklagen, daß er nicht die deutsche Individualität festzuhalten wußte, ein dramatisches Werk zu schaffen, woran er selbst mit warmen Herzen glauben kann; ein Werk, wo menschliche Leidenschaften und Zustände auf eine wahrhafte und schöne Weise geschildert werden." Kirchmeyer 1967: 76. Kirchmeyer argues that this image of a "Frenchified" Wagner countered the conviction that *Rienzi* presented a future path for genuine German opera: "He exclusively attributed French traits to Wagner, elements that the composer had arguably appropriated in France [...] It became evident for the first time that the entire argument of these reports was to divest Wagner's pretenses of being German. One hardly needs to explain why: both in Dresden and elsewhere, Wagner's succes was associated with the composer's German nature. He was deemed to be the successor of Weber who brought the German opera style back into blossom. The *Rheinische Zeitung* article convincingly demonstrated that Wagner had actually created French music, a mannerism of second-rate Frenchdom. The *Rheinische Zeitung* excluded Wagner from the ranks of the promotors of German art, and simultaneously of those who advanced German liberty." Kirchmeyer 1972: 173.

of *Rienzi* from the most influential and widely-read music journal of those days. Schumann himself, however, remained tacit, arguably because he felt embarrassed to crucify Wagner, who was doing a lot to win his favor in those years.[112] Rather than to address the esthetic quality of *Rienzi*, Schumann diplomatically decided to mention its success. This resulted in a first report[113] – arguably written by a close connection to Wagner[114] – which was highly appreciative, whereas a second by Albert Schiffner was moderately positive, while regretting "the superfluous noise which threatened to overshadow the beauty of this highly interesting new German opera."[115] Only in 1844, in Theodor Hagen's review of a performance in Hamburg, did *Rienzi* receive the treatment you might expect from a *NZfM* critic. Hagen opened by mentioning a private conversation with Heinrich Heine, in which the latter had argued that "Wagner's talent is suspect, because Meyerbeer serves as its protector."[116] Hagen's most important objection to the opera was that Wagner "had followed the modern-day French convention to write chiefly for the masses."[117]

There is tragic irony in the fact that Wagner eventually had its breakthrough as an opera composer with a work that revealed his debt to spectacular French music theater, at a time when in his esthetic orientation, he was moving in another direction. The image of a Frenchified, sensation-seeking Meyerbeer epigone proved persistent. In letters to Robert Schumann, Wagner mentioned that his next opera to be given in Dresden, *Der fliegende Holländer* (1843), "belonged to an entirely different – namely Romantic – genre,"[118] and pointed out that "the triumph of the premiere of this work fills me with more pride than that of *Rienzi*, because in *Der fliegende Holländer*, I have departed from all

---

112 Wagner undertook a charm offensive to assure the highly influential Schumann that he endorsed the viewpoints of the *NZfM*. Schumann, in his turn, never really trusted Wagner's apparent departure from Meyerbeer's esthetic ideals, but must have felt that he should at least remain collegial to his dedicated young colleague. Wagner's repeated attempts to have the Leipzig-based Schumann visit a Dresden *Rienzi* performances were in vain. See Konrad 1987 and Bischoff 1995.

113 Published in *NZfM* IX: 17 / 36, 1 November 1842: 148–150.

114 See Kirchmeyer 1972: 183.

115 "Verdeckte nicht leider der überflüssige Lärm so manche Schönheit: gewiß, man müßte den Rienzi die interessanteste neue deutsche Oper nennen." *NZfM* IX: 17 / 41, 18 November 1842: 169.

116 "Wissen Sie, was mir an dem Talente verdächtig ist? Das es von Meyerbeer in Schutz genommen wird." *NZfM* XI: 20 / 32, 18. April 1844: 125.

117 "Wagner hat mit den modernen, französischen Operncomponisten begriffen, daß man sich die Masse des Publicums, als diejenige, die die tüchtigsten Hände zum Applaudiren hat, zu Freunden halten müsse." Ibid.: 125.

118 "da sie einem ganz anderen Genre (- dem rein romantischen -) angehört." Letter from Wagner to Schumann of 3 November 1842, quoted from Konrad 1987: 302.

FIGURE 5.1 Wagner caricature made in 1841 by Ernst Benedikt Kietz, when Wagner was living in Paris. Although Kietz, a close friend of Wagner, chiefly appears to highlight the all-encompassing, intense, and revolutionary tenor of his art, it could simultaneously be read as emphasizing the loud, messy, and excessive nature that many critics would discern in *Rienzi*.

conventions to which our opera audiences have grown accustomed."[119] After having studied the score, Schumann, however, wrote to Wagner that he still

119　"Da ich weiß, daß Sie an mir Theil haben, melde ich Ihnen in der Freude meines Herzen's, daß ich gestern durch den Erfolg meiner neuen Oper 'der fliegende Holländer' einen Triumph davon getragen habe, auf den ich stolzer bin, als auf den Erfolg meines 'Rienzi,'

discerned a "Meyerbeerian tone," which the latter interpreted as "a death sentence to my compositional powers."[120]

To many commentators, Wagner always remained a noisy, melodramatic sensationalist. Wagner responded to this by directing a similar judgment towards Meyerbeer and dismissing his own *Rienzi* as "my squaller [mein Schreihals],"[121] in order to distinguish his artistic output from *Der fliegende Holländer* onward as something elevated and completely different. Meyerbeer came to embody elements of Wagner's own artistic method which he tried so hard to conceal, and this – more than anything else – explains his vehemence.[122] In that sense, it hardly surprises that Wagner's most scathing Meyerbeer judgment, the accusation of creating "effects without causes,"[123] actually took its cue from critic Ludwig Rellstab's 1847 dismissal of *Rienzi* as being "a bunch of effects without the cause."[124] After *Rienzi*, Wagner continued to use melodramatic means in order to immerse his audience, but he aimed for greater dramatic unity and intimacy,[125] qualities that were associated with the ideal-typical German opera during the 1840s. In order to realize this, Wagner returned to the relatively stale genre of Romantic opera, from which he had previously distanced himself.

---

eben weil ich mich in dieser neuen Oper scharf von allem absondere, was heutzutage unser Publikum zu hören u. sehen gewöhnt ist." Letter from Wagner to Schumann of 3 January 1843, quoted from Ibid.: 304.

120   "Das eine hat mich erschreckt, u. [...] erbittert: daß Sie mir in aller Ruhe hin sagen, manches schmecke oft nach – Meyerbeer. Vor allem weiß ich gar nicht, was überhaupt auf dieser weiten Welt 'Meyerbeerisch' sein sollte, außer vielleicht raffinirtes Streben nach seichter Popularität. [...] Müßte es ein wunderbares Spiel der Natur sein, wenn ich aus dem Quelle geschöpft hätte, dessen bloßer Geruch aus weiter Ferne mir zuwider ist; es wäre dieß ein Todesurtheil über meine Produktions-Kraft."Letter from Wagner to Schumann of 25 February 1843, quoted from Ibid.: 311.

121   In a letter to a Berlin friend, written on 27 December 1845. WWSB, Sämtliche Briefe, Band II: 470.

122   Helmuth Weinland draws a similar conclusion, see Weinland 1988: 31.

123   "Wirkung ohne Ursache," voiced in *Oper und Drama* (1851). WWSB, Sämtliche Schriften, Band III: 301.

124   "Eine Menge Wirkungen ohne die Ursach." Published in the Berlin *Vossische Zeitung* of 28 October 1847. Quoted after Kirchmeyer 1968: 306.

125   Matthias Spohr, for example, writes that "his continuous incantation of the folklike can also be seen in relation to the melodrama: Wagner gladly compliments himself with his ability to move spectators to tears, and his festival idea idealizes the melodramatic interplay between performers and the audience for the sake of social cohesion. With his unifying tendency and focus on the nucleus of the drama, Wagner attempts to push the by now contemptibly-mainstream phenomenon of melodrama in a new, personal direction. He stabilizes the permanently oscillating musicalization of gesture and declamation, and manages to create a new, 'pure' music-dramatic genre." Spohr 1999: 77–78.

In his Romantic operas *Der fliegende Holländer* (1843), *Tannhäuser* (1845), and *Lohengrin* (1850), Wagner managed, more than any German opera composer before him, to use compositional techniques derived from French and Italian opera in works that nonetheless displayed several carriers of German nationhood and opera identity, and conformed to many of the demands of German opera discourse despite moving beyond the *Singspiel* constellation. Wagner's incessant emphasis on his identity as a sincere and serious *German* opera composer certainly aided in obfuscating the foreign roots of his music-dramatic style.

Wagner's interest in the tale of the Flying Dutchman, who seeks a faithful wife in order to be redeemed and to have his immortality terminated, was awakened by a fragment from Heinrich Heine's *Memoiren des Herrn von Schnabelewopski* (1834). Characteristic for Heine's Young German disdain for Romanticism was the satirical tone in which he discussed this exalted subject matter. He concluded, for example, his narration with the following statement: "The moral of the story is that women must look out not to marry a Flying Dutchman; and we, men, can learn from this piece that women at best will bring about our destruction."[126] In his *Autobiographische Skizze*, Wagner acknowledged his debt to Heine's short-story about the "redemption of this Ahasuerus[127] of the ocean." The tone of Wagner's rendition is, however, everything but satirical. Redemption is not something to make fun of, but becomes the central theme of *Der fliegende Holländer*, the chief goal of its protagonist, and in fact the central concept of Wagner's entire "mature" oeuvre,[128] up until the closing lines

126   "Die Moral des Stückes ist für die Frauen, daß sie sich in acht nehmen müssen, keinen Fliegenden Holländer zu heuraten; und wir Männer ersehen aus diesem Stücke, wie wir durch die Weiber, im günstigsten Falle, zugrunde gehn." Heine 1867: 137. Heine ironizes the plot even further by the fact that, during the performance of the Flying Dutchman play in Amsterdam, he is more interested in a beautiful young lady, leaves the auditorium and only returns to his seat during the final scene.

127   "Besonders die von Heine erfundene, echt dramatische Behandlung der Erlösung dieses Ahasverus des Ozeans gab mir alles in die Hand, diese Sage zu einem Opernsujet zu benützen." *WWSB*, Sämtliche Schriften, Band I: 17. Ahasuerus is the legendary, Wandering Jew, "one of those recurrent representatives of the mood of *Weltschmerz*," according to Dieter Borchmeyer, who also mentions the frequent occurrence of this figure in 1830s literature, such as in poems by Pierre-Jean de Béranger's (*Le juif errant*, 1831) and Nikolaus Lenau (*Ahasver, der ewige Jude*, 1833), and in Georg Büchner's play *Dantons Tod* (1835). Borchmeyer 2003: 82–85. It may well be one of the greatest ironies of Wagner's persona that, being one of the most outspoken anti-Semites of the nineteenth century, he employed the trope of Ahasuerus's demise as a symbol of the future collapse of Judaism in the closing lines of *Das Judenthum in der Musik* (1850), but simultaneously identified himself with the "Wandering Jew-like" Dutchman figure.

128   The so-called *Bayreuth Canon* of works that until today have been performed at the Bayreuth Festival. Even if the decision to perform *Holländer, Tannhäuser, Lohengrin,*

of his last music drama *Parsifal* (1882): "Erlösung dem Erlöser [Redemption to the Redeemer]."

Wagner's unremitting emphasis on redemption as a universal world-changing force[129] is quite unique, but the notion was already a common theme in both "high" and "low" manifestations of German Romanticism. The elevated nature that Wagner ascribed to it is based on the role of redemption in Goethe's *Faust* – perceived as the summit of German culture – but at the same time, Wagner's *Erlösungsdrama* forms a continuation of earlier Romantic operas, where redemption figures in a more trivial sphere of *Biedermeier* culture and melodrama.[130]

The dramatic constellation of both Weber's *Freischütz* (1821) and Marschner's *Der Vampyr* (1828) reflect this *Biedermeier* fascination with redemption. In both cases, there is a homogenous society threatened by a malicious outcast who is looking for victims (Caspar or the vampire Lord Ruthven), generally sung by a bass-baritone. These villains can be superhuman beings or men who have fallen from grace for committing an unforgivable sin. Central to the drama is a character who belongs to the community, but is somehow drawn into the hands of evil, and whose salvation is therefore at stake. This person can be a man, often a tenor (as in the case of Max in *Der Freischütz*), or a young girl, a soprano, who is erotically attracted to the villain (as Janthe and Emmy in *Der Vampyr*). In the case of *Der Vampyr*, evil is seen as contagious, as a vampire will make new victims who will turn into victims as well; it poses a threat to the prosperity and sanity of the community.[131] Luckily, there is a determined person (Agathe in *Der Freischütz*, Aubry in *Der Vampyr*), who defeats evil by his/her trust in God, and thereby saves the endangered soul of his/her lover.

Tristan and *Die Meistersinger* was taken by his widow Cosima in 1886, three years after his death, the canon mirrors Wagner's own understanding of his oeuvre and respects his later renunciation of the three youth operas.

129 The all-encompassing scope of Wagner's redemption theory is evident in the *Ring*, in which Brünnhilde's return of the Ring to the Rhine redeems the entire world.

130 Norbert Miller mentions to what extent curse and redemption were characteristic of Gothic literature and silly *Schicksalsdramatik* of the early nineteenth century. Miller 2007: 549.

131 In Emmy's *Romanze*, which is often seen as a direct model for Senta's *Ballade* about the Flying Dutchman in Wagner's opera, this danger of infection is addressed and related to sexual attraction, which one could read as a warning for syphilis: "Das Mägdlein folgt dem bleichen Mann, / Es lockte sie sein Blick; / Hört nicht der Mutter Warnen an, / Und bald war es um sie getan, / Nie kehrte sie zurück! / Ein Opfer ward sie seiner Lust, / Mit blut'ger Spur an Hals und Brust / Fand man den Leichnam wieder; / Sie fuhr zur Hölle nieder! / Nun geht sie selber, glaubt es mir, / Umher als grausiger Vampyr! / Bewahr' uns Gott auf Erden, / Ihr jemals gleich zu werden!"

Wagner took over many of these stereotypes in *Der fliegende Holländer* (1843) and *Tannhäuser* (1845). The Dutchman embodies the grim outsider type,[132] Tannhäuser is the tragic Faustian hero torn between good and evil, whereas Elisabeth presents the Agathe-like Romantic heroine who overcomes not through action but through believing in Providence.

There are, however, some significant differences, for example between Wagner's Dutchman and his ancestors Caspar and Ruthven. Whereas the latter two seek a victim in order to extend their existence, Wagner's eponymous hero yearns for a woman in order to terminate his eternal life, to fulfill his *Erlösungssehnsucht*.[133] Another important departure from previous models is the fact that Wagner's "villain" actually succeeds, which is highly discomforting for the *Biedermeier* society that is left behind. One of the characteristic traits of the *Schauerromantik* of *Der Freischütz* and *Der Vampyr* had been the fact that the audience was allowed to enjoy the transgressive behavior of its villains, whereas at the end, the social order would be reinstated. Wagner achieved quite the contrary; in the eyes of Joachim Reiber, his *Holländer* "demolishes the chains of Restoration."[134] This sympathy for the transgressive individual rather than the restrictive, philistine collective – which we also find in *Tannhäuser* – seems

---

132 In *Tannhäuser*, Wagner grants this antagonist role to a female in the form of Venus.

133 There is, however, one previous Romantic opera in which the woman-abductor is consumed by a similar death-drive as the Dutchman's. This is Franz Danzi's opera *Der Berggeist* (1813), based on Karl August Musäus's *Rübezahl* stories in his *Volksmärchen der Deutschen* (1782–1787). Soon after the overture, the mountain spirit sings a monologue in which he expresses sentiments that foreshadow the Dutchman's soliloquy 'Der Frist ist um': "Beneidenswertes Glück der Sterblichkeit! / Dein sanfter Fittig kühlt des Leidens Glut. / Und **jede Sehnsucht endet in der Gruft,** / **Nur meine nimmer!** – / Unter deinen Tritten, / O Zeit! Erblüht mir keines Trostes Blume, / mir öffnet sich **kein Grab;** / **hohnlachend geht an mir vorüber die Vernichtung!** / Sonnen verlöschen und Äonen schwinden hin; / Doch endlos dehnt sich fort mein Lebenstage, / Und ewig nie veraltet **meine Qual** [words in bold reveal (nearly) literal correspondences to the Dutchman's lines]." However, unlike the Dutchman's death-wish, Rübezahl's frustration about his immortality is temporary, caused by the fact that he has been separated from his wife. It is questionable whether Wagner knew Danzi's rarely-performed opera, but the similarities between the plots of *Der Berggeist* and *Der fliegende Holländer* are striking: at the start of both operas we encounter a monologue about the agony of eternal existence, in both works the female prey sings a folksong about the sinister spirit who is about to attack her, and in both cases, the villain gains access to the girl by offering treasures to her father. Even if it is impossible to prove Wagner's familiarity with Danzi's opera, – *Der Vampyr*, which has some formal resemblances but a different content in the monologue, may have served as an intermediary – the formal, textual and narrative correspondences between *Der Berggeist* and the *Holländer* underscore to what extent Wagner's opera was rooted in early nineteenth-century Romantic traditions.

134 Reiber 2002: 70. Reiber goes on to conclude that through this reversal, Wagner actually redeemed German opera from the shadow of Weber's *Freischütz*, see Ibid.: 76.

to have been a precondition for Wagner's return to a genre he had previously rejected.

At the same time, the return to a slightly petty Romantic world, think for example of the deliberately petty-sounding triviality of the Spinning Chorus[135] of *Der Fliegende Holländer*, appealed to a considerable part of the German public, as it presented a return to the Romanticism of the 'Jungfernkranz' in *Der Freischütz*. We find something similar with Wagner's use of the Middle Ages in his next two Romantic operas *Tannhäuser* (1845) and *Lohengrin* (1850). This estheticized depiction of the Middle Ages clearly appealed to the contemporary German nostalgia for the Middle Ages as an idyllic bygone age of perfect harmony, a projection that at least partly reflected the desire for a future German unity in political terms.[136] Wagner fueled this idyll more than any other opera composer.[137] But behind the ceremonial beauty of *Lohengrin* and the Catholic lure of the pilgrims' choruses in *Tannhäuser*, a highly critical attitude is present, as it paints a world full of philistine morality. The *Tannhäuser* Wartburg society presents a prudish collective full of fear of life, whereas in *Lohengrin*, the masses are docile and opportunistic.

In *Die Kunst und die Revolution* (1849), written at a time when Wagner had decided to leave the Christian Middle Ages and move further back to a pagan, prehistoric past, he voiced his contempt for the Middle Ages. Here he branded it as a period in which the counter-natural, hypocritical Christian spirit – the absolute antithesis of his idealized Greek mentality – gained ascendancy, a regrettable hegemony which he still perceived in his own day.[138] A closer look at

---

135   It seems that the trivial appearance of such musical numbers in *Der fliegende Holländer* is deliberate, creating a strong contrast to the sinister and advanced sound world of the Dutchman.

136   This idyllic image of the Middle Ages as a utopia of German unity was chiefly introduced by the Roman Catholic August Wilhelm Schlegel, whereas a Protestant thinker such as Jacob Grimm considered the Roman Catholic Church to have been an oppressive force, whereas medieval folk culture presented a portal to a more authentic, pagan German culture. See for example Williamson 2004: 73–74. Wagner's relation to this idealization of the Middle Ages as an example of German unity is discussed by Mertens 1986: 20, Spencer 1992: 165, and Vazsonyi 2010: 18.

137   Mertens, for example, argues that "Wagner may not have been the first to have presented the Middle Ages as an escapist dream, but he is definitely the one who actually opened it up to a broad, cultured audience." Mertens 1986: 56.

138   "Das Christenthum rechtfertigt eine ehrlose, unnütze und jämmerliche Existenz des Menschen auf Erden. [...] die Heuchelei ist überhaupt der hervorstechendste Zug, die eigentliche Physiognomie der ganzen christlichen Jahrhunderte bis auf unsere Tage. [...] Wie in der ganzen Geschichte des Mittelalters wir aber immer nur auf den Kampf der weltlichen Gewalt gegen den Despotismus der römischen Kirche als den hervorstechendsten Zug treffen, so konnte auch da, wo er sich auszusprechen suchte, der künstlerische Ausdruck dieser neuen Welt immer nur im Gegensatze, im Kampfe gegen den Geist des

the plots of *Tannhäuser* and *Lohengrin* reveals that the dissatisfaction with the Middle Ages that Wagner expressed in 1849 was not a just a matter of progressive insight, but a long-held conviction.[139] By situating his Romantic operas in the Middle Ages, Wagner could simultaneously appeal to and problematize the utopian significance of that past. In a way, he managed to enthuse those who projected their national hopes on the image of a past idyll, while also staying true to his Young German conviction.[140]

In a similar vein, Wagner managed to appeal to nationalist sentiments in *Tannhäuser* and *Lohengrin* without writing a one-dimensional opera with an all-too-overt political message. By situating *Tannhäuser* in the halls of the Wartburg, Wagner chose a setting that was imbued with national significance.[141] Not only had Luther – previously vindicated as a national symbol[142] –taken

Christenthums sich geltend machen: als der Ausdruck einer vollkommen harmonisch gestimmten Einheit der Welt, wie es die Kunst der griechischen Welt war, konnte sich die Kunst der christlich-europäischen Welt nicht kundgeben, eben weil sie in ihrem tiefsten Innern, zwischen Gewissen und Lebenstrieb, zwischen Einbildung und Wirklichkeit, unheilbar und unversöhnbar gespalten war." WWSB, Sämtliche Schriften, Band III: 14–16.

139   This impression is reinforced by the fact that, despite the prominence of Christian mysticism in *Tannhäuser*, throughout the 1840s Wagner was actually fascinated by Ludwig Feuerbach's glorification of the divine nature of man, and the latter's idea of God being merely a human fiction. Feuerbach's *Das Wesen des Christenthums* was brought out in 1841 and Wagner himself recalled that he was introduced to it in 1843 (WWSB, Mein Leben: 442), exactly at a time when he was working on *Tannhäuser*. It is, however, clear that Wagner's appreciation for Feuerbach became more outspoken in the late 1840s, for example through dedicating *Das Kunstwerk der Zukunft* (1850) to the philosopher.

140   More than anyone else, the Young German Heinrich Heine was skeptical about his compatriots' obsession with the Middle Ages, – writing in *Die romantische Schule* (1836) that "the German Middle Ages are not dead in the grave, in fact they are frequently reanimated by some evil spirit, entering into our midst in broad daylight to suck the lifeblood from our breasts (Das deutsche Mittelalter liegt nicht vermodert im Grabe, es wird vielmehr manchmal von einem bösen Gespenste belebt und tritt am hellen, lichten Tage in unsere Mitte und saugt uns das rote Leben aus der Brust)" (Heine 2002: 154–155) – while simultaneously basing some of his writings on medieval stories, for example his poem *Tannhäuser; eine Legende*, which functioned as one of Wagner's sources. Wagner deviates, however, from Heine in both his tragic rather than ironic orientation and the fact that, unlike Heine's hero, Wagner's Tannhäuser returns to the Christian Elisabeth instead of the pagan Venus. Williamson argues that "if Heine's poem suggested a certain anti-Catholic paganism, *Tannhäuser* retained the framework of Romantic medievalism associated with A.W. Schlegel or Friedrich de la Motte Fouqué." Williamson 2004: 184.

141   Wagner acknowledges this in *Eine Mittheilung an meine Freunde* (1851) when he talks about "this singing contest, which, together with its historical backdrop, appeared so endlessly native to me ([dieser] Sängerkriege, der mich mit seiner ganzen Umgebung so unendlich heimathlich anwehte.")" WWSB, Sämtliche Schriften, Band IV: 269. For more information concerning the national-symbolical function of the Wartburg in German culture, see Schieder 2001.

142   Amongst others by Herder, Hegel, Fichte, Jahn and Arndt. See for more information Herfried Münkler's chapter on Luther in *Die deutschen und ihre Mythen* (Münkler 2009:

refuge behind its walls in 1521–1522, but the patriotic *Wartburgfest* of 1817 had also taken place there. Tannhäuser's return to the Wartburg can be read as a metaphor for Wagner's return to his fatherland,[143] whereas the outburst during the *Sängerkrieg* reflects the upheaval among the German musical world about Wagner's sensual and transgressive operas. Just as in Wagner's case, the majority of Tannhäuser's colleagues are hostile to his unconventional art.[144] By situating this esthetic battle inside the Wartburg, Wagner emphasized the national significance of his artistic mission.

The appeal to national sentiments appears even greater in *Lohengrin*, as it deals with politics and features several calls for unity among the German people.[145] Lohengrin's final prophecy of a leader who will lead his people to a glorious future – "Seht da den Herzog von Brabant! Zum Führer sei er euch ernannt!" – chiefly underlines Wagner's hope that a determined leader would accept the task to unify Germany, a goal that was actually pursued, to no avail, at the Frankfurt Parliament that was founded in 1848, the year Wagner finished the opera.[146]

To twentieth- and twenty-first-century readers, however, this phrase has an unpleasant ring, for which the nineteenth-century Wagner can hardly be blamed. Perhaps this partly explains why many scholars have tried to play down the allusions to national politics in *Lohengrin*, or neglect them altogether.

181–196) as well as the fifth chapter of the anthology *Die Deutschen und Luther* (Müller 1983: 159–193).

143   At the beginning of the second act, Elisabeth asks the returned Tannhäuser "Wo weiltet Ihr so lange [Where did thou dwell so long]?," to which the title hero responds: "Fern von hier, in weiten, weiten Landen; dichtes Vergessen hat zwischen heut und gestern sich gesenkt [Far away in distant lands; Oblivion has filled the space between today and yesterday]." This alleged oblivion, actually employed in order to conceal his sinful residence in Venus's realm, can be read as an analogy to Wagner's autobiographical attempt to obliterate his initial, "un-German" ambitions in Paris. George S. Williamson also relates the Venusberg to Paris: "The seductions of the Goddess are enticing but insincere, suggesting the outward spectacle characteristic of Paris." Wiliamson 2004: 183.

144   Wagner worked out this theme in a more systematic, and moreover far more patriotic way in *Die Meistersinger von Nürnberg*, which was premiered only in 1868, but initially planned in 1845 as a "satyr play"-like sequel to the tragedy of *Tannhäuser*, as Wagner explained in *Eine Mittheilung an meine Freunde* (1851), see WWSB, Sämtliche Schriften, Band IV: 284–285.

145   To give just a few examples, see König Heinrich's speeches. First Act: "Nun ist es Zeit, des Reiches Ehr zu wahren;/ ob Ost, ob West, das gelte allen gleich! / Was deutsches Land heißt, stelle Kampfesscharen, dann schmäht wohl niemand mehr das Deutsche Reich!"; Third Act: "Wie fühl ich stolz mein Herz entbrannt, / find ich in jedem deutschen Land / so kräftig reichen Heerverband! / Nun soll des Reiches Feind sich nahn, / wir wollen tapfer ihn empfahn: / aus seinem öden Ost daher / soll er sich nimmer wagen mehr! / Für deutsches Land das deutsche Schwert! / So sei des Reiches Kraft bewährt!"

146   The Prussian King Friedrich Wilhelm IV refused to accept the office of emperor.

Carl Dahlhaus, for example, dismisses the political setting of *Lohengrin* as utterly redundant:

> the political event that turns the opera into a historical tableau, the preparation of the armed battle against the Hungarians, is superfluous from a dramaturgical point of view. [...] *Lohengrin* is actually a temporally unspecific mythological drama rather than a dateable, historical work.[147]

In a similar vein, Wulf Konold denies *Lohengrin* the status of a national opera from the viewpoint of form and content, and speaks of a national reception that has no ground in the work itself: "even a piece that does not display any 'national' character at its first appearance can become a national opera in a different political situation, such as *Lohengrin* during the Wilhelmine period."[148] Kurt Overhoff does acknowledge the presence of verses with an outspoken nationalist tenor in *Lohengrin*, but concludes that the shallow, bombast musical style in which Wagner set these lines actually embodies an over-the-top critique of militant patriotism.[149]

Philipp Ther has recently countered this general denial of the national-political importance of *Lohengrin* by a previous generation of scholars, stating:

> He [Wagner] set the plot of [...] *Lohengrin* in a crucial era of Saxon and German history. The opera opens with King Henry the Fowler assembling the German tribes to fight a "threat from the East" and to expel the Hungarians from his dominions in the tenth century.[150] [...] In *Lohengrin* the main actor plays a very political and national role. [...] The opera features numerous crowd scenes, in which the German nation appeared on stage as a collective unit. Moreover, national politics serves as a framework for the plot. When Lohengrin leaves the stage in the famous swan boat, he predicts a great future for the German empire.[151]

---

147   Dahlhaus 2007: 287.
148   Konold 1992: 127–128.
149   Overhoff 1967: 104.
150   Isabella Kreim also emphasizes the analogy of the tenth-century setting and the contemporary situation: "The time that is portrayed reveals concrete references to the time of creation. The time of Henry I, the succesful establishment of a unified, greater, relatively peaceful Germany can be seen as a paradigm for contemporary hopes, for the dream of a German empire (Die dargestellte Zeit weist konkrete Bezüge zur Entstehungszeit auf, die Zeitenwende unter Heinrich I., die erfolgreiche Begründung eines geeinten, größeren, relativ friedenssicheren Deutschland kann als Paradigma für die Hoffnung der Gegenwart, als Traum von einem deutschen Reich gelten)." Kreim 1983: 31–32.
151   Ther 2011: 191.

Even if we concede Dahlhaus's thesis that *Lohengrin* has universal, mythological elements and is much more than a national opera in the narrow sense of the word, it is nonetheless hard to deny that Wagner appealed to German national sentiments in this opera, created in the revolutionary year of 1848, when a German political unity appeared to be in the making. Rather than to decide whether certain passages in *Lohengrin* display Wagner's national or anti-national sympathies, one may assume that Wagner was conscious of the fact that they could be perceived as articulating a national agenda. In that sense, he himself paved the way for the nationalist appropriation which Konold all too easily considers to be extraneous to and not justified by the opera itself.

3   The "Universally German" in the *Zürich Writings* and the
      Conception of *Der Ring des Nibelungen*

The insistence on the non- or even anti-national stance of *Lohengrin* by many scholars may partly be motivated by Wagner's attitude in the famous *Zürich Writings*, created in the years around 1850.[152] In these texts, it appears that with his forced departure from German soil – a result of his involvement in the flawed 1849 revolution in Dresden – he also departed from the German national cause. His political orientation now became increasingly international, dominated by socialist and anarchist concerns that transgress national borders, and often undermine rather than affirm the formation of a state.[153] The most outspoken critique of nationalism in these days can be found in *Die Kunst und die Revolution* (1849), where Wagner criticizes the national orientation of ancient Greek art, which must be overcome in the artwork of the future, designed "for all free humans, regardless of national borders."[154]

Apart from this incidental objection, Wagner generally vindicates ancient Greek culture within his "Zürich" esthetic program, at the expense of the more overt markers of German national identity of his former operas. Nearly all his

---

152 *Die Kunst und die Revolution* (1849), *Das Kunstwerk der Zukunft* (1850), *Eine Mittheilung an meine Freunde* (1851), and *Oper und Drama* (1851) are the most important and influential works within Wagner's theoretical output in this period.

153 The most detailed study of Wagner's political outlooks in this period is Udo Bermbach's *Der Wahn des Gesamtkunstwerks. Richard Wagners politisch-ästhetische Utopie* (1994).

154 "Umfaßte das griechische Kunstwerk den Geist einer schönen Nation, so soll das Kunstwerk der Zukunft den Geist der freien Menschen über alle Schranken der Nationalitäten hinaus umfassen; das nationale Wesen in ihm darf nur ein Schmuck, ein Reiz individueller Mannigfaltigkeit, nicht eine hemmende Schranke sein." wwsʙ, Sämtliche Schriften, Band III: 29–30.

changes of direction discern a shift from the nationally-specific German to the universal: from Romantic opera to music drama, and from the historically specific (the medieval German) to the "universally-human [reinmenschliche]" character of myth. But the move away from overt markers of German national identity is deceptive, as Wagner substitutes these for covert carriers of a less obvious, but similarly potent chauvinism. This covert chauvinism is based on the notion of what I would like to call the "universally-German": the prominent idea among German artists and thinkers that they possessed the exclusive capacity to address the core of human existence. I argue that Wagner actually continued a German-national orientation through his employment of "universally-German" tropes in his *Zürich Writings*[155] and the artwork around which these texts revolve: *Der Ring des Nibelungen*.

From an esthetic point of view, *Oper und Drama* (1851) is arguably the most important and ambitious among the *Zürich Writings*. In it, Wagner deals with the state of opera and spoken theater, discusses their relation to contemporary society and proposes his doctrine of the music drama[156] as the "artwork of the future." As most of his contemporaries did, Wagner makes frequent use of national stereotypes concerning opera styles, particularly in the first part of *Oper und Drama*. Here Wagner takes in an apparently impartial position, presenting himself as overcoming the flaws of each national tradition. This would make him appear to be beyond the chauvinism of many of his German predecessors, but this image is deceptive. To start with, this reasoning is fully in line with the "aber er greift alles tiefer" doctrine that implies that it is the German musician's exclusive privilege to synthesize international developments into a higher degree of profundity. Not only in this respect, but also in many other instances, one may discern continuities rather than breaks with the esthetic discourse considering the merits of German opera that gained prominence in the first decades of the nineteenth century. What appears to be transnational or universal often actually dovetails with existing German values about opera. Wolfgang Michael Wagner, for example, states the following:

> the music drama not only provided the optimal form to lift out German values such as seriousness, "profundity," and the inclination towards sentimentality, but the primacy of the dramatic and characteristic also

---

155   Hannu Salmi also concludes that the *Zürich Writings* already contain the sense of a national mission in the pursuit of universal causes, an idea that would become more explicit in the 1860s and after. See Salmi 1993: 121.

156   This term is slightly problematic, because Wagner himself did not use the term and was even quite skeptical about it in the short essay *Über die Benennung "Musikdrama"* (1872), but until today "music drama" has been the most widely-used and adequate term to refer to Wagner's music-dramatic beliefs as penned down in the *Zürich Writings*.

served to break with musical conventions [...], and to dismiss exactly those qualities traditionally perceived to be specifically Italian.[157]

Throughout *Oper und Drama*, Wagner revisits familiar tropes, for example with regard to Rossini. Wagner presents him as a wicked magician creating "artificial flowers"[158] with his arias; melodies ripped off their lifeblood and completely unrelated to the texts sung on them. Thereby he digs out a completely stale opinion – once put forward by German writers in the 1820s – about a composer who had not written an opera for twenty years. Wagner's crusade against the cosmopolitanism and theatricality of Meyerbeer, which he works out most systematically in *Oper und Drama*, is also hardly original, as I demonstrated earlier in this chapter. Throughout *Oper und Drama*, Carl Maria von Weber is emphatically presented as a positive antithesis to Rossini and Meyerbeer, reviving the lifeless opera melody by reinstating the meaningful union of text and sound of folksong.[159] Wagner considers Weber's *Euryanthe* as the most daring attempt at an integration of music and drama and the most perceptive exploration of the fundamental problem of opera, although the melody suffered from Weber's sincere attempt at writing a truly dramatic opera.[160]

---

157   Wagner 1994: 196.

158   Wagner talks about "arias, which means folk melodies rid of their truthfulness and naïveté, randomly kitted together with verses that fulfill the need for an apparent dramatic coherence. The most apt fabricator of these artificial flowers was Rossini (*"Arien*, d.h. ihrer Wahrheit und Naivetät entkleidete Volksweisen, [...] denen man willkürliche, und aus Not zu einem Anscheine von dramatischem Zusammenhang verbundene, Verstexte unterlegte. [...] der ungemein geschickte Verfertiger *künstlicher* Blumen [...] war *Joachimo Rossini*.")." *WWSB*, Sämtliche Schriften, Band III: 231 + 250. It is intriguing to ask whether Wagner had Rossini in mind when creating the character of Klingsor in *Parsifal* (1882), another wicked magician that creates artificial flower maidens that appear to be real women of flesh and blood.

159   "Es mußte solchen Musikern die künstlerische Aufgabe sich darstellen, der unstreitig allmächtigen Melodie den ganzen vollen Ausdruck schöner menschlicher Empfindung zu geben, der ihr ureigen ist [...], *bis zur Restauration der ursprünglichen Tonweise des Volksliedes*. Von einem *deutschen* Musiker ward diese Umwandelung der Melodie zuerst und mit außerordentlichem Erfolge in das Leben gerufen. *Karl Maria von Weber* gelangte zu seiner künstlerischen Reife." Ibid.: 258–259.

160   "Die 'Euryanthe' ist von der Kritik nicht in dem Maße beachtet worden, als sie es ihres ungemein lehrreichen Inhaltes wegen verdient. [...] Nie ist aber, solange es Opern gibt, ein Werk verfaßt worden, in welchem die inneren Widersprüche des ganzen Genres von einem gleich begabten, tief empfindenden und wahrheitliebenden Tonsetzer [...] konsequenter durchgeführt und offener dargelegt worden sind. Diese Widersprüche sind: *absolute, ganz für sich allein genügende Melodie, und – durchgehends wahrer dramatischer Ausdruck*. Hier mußte notwendig eines geopfert werden [...]. Rossini opferte das Drama, der edle Weber wollte es durch die Kraft seiner sinnigeren Melodie wieder herstellen. Er mußte erfahren, daß dieß unmöglich sei." Ibid.: 292–293.

It is in the reconciliation of dramatic characterization and organic melody, in the solution to the fundamental problem of opera, that Wagner recognizes his own task.

The function of Weber as a model and guide is also perceivable in the closing section of the first part of *Oper und Drama*. Here Wagner compares the national operas to women, calling the Italian a prostitute looking for easy profit,[161] the French a coquette who is cold, vain, and exclusively seeking admiration,[162] and concluding that German opera resembles a prudish young girl.[163] The correspondence to Weber's illustration of national operas as women in *Tonkünstlers Leben* is striking. What Wagner shares with Weber's illustrations is the idea that Italian opera may have a beautiful appearance but is actually soul- and characterless, that French opera is dominated by ostentation and artificiality, and that German opera is still immature, creating room for improvement to be carried out by the writer himself. The emphasis that Wagner lays on unifying formal coherence, not only within individual numbers but overarching the entire music drama, and which he exemplified by his use of "leitmotifs,"[164] is also a variation of Weber's stress on the ideal German opera as a unified whole.[165] The next step in this striving for unity is the integration

---

161   "Man hat die *italienische* Opernmusik sehr treffend eine *Lustdirne* genannt. [...] sie gerät nie außer sich, sie opfert sich nie, außer wenn sie selbst Lust oder einen Vorteil gewinnen will, und für diesen Fall bietet sie nur den Teil ihres Wesens fremdem Genusse dar, über den sie mit Leichtigkeit verfügen kann." Ibid.: 317.

162   "Die *französische* Opernmusik gilt mit Recht als *Kokette*. Die Kokette reizt es, bewundert, ja gar geliebt zu werden. [...] Der Gewinn, den sie sucht, ist die Freude über sich selbst, die Befriedigung der Eitelkeit; daß sie bewundert und geliebt wird, ist der Genuß ihres Lebens." Ibid.: 318.

163   "Aber noch einen Typus entarteter Frauen gibt es, der uns gar mit widerwärtigem Grauen erfüllt: das ist die *Prüde*, als welche uns die sogenannte 'deutsche' Opernmusik gelten muß." Ibid: 319. Wagner explains in a footnote that he is not referring to Weber, but rather to less gifted contemporaries.

164   A slightly problematic term, as Wagner did not use this term in *Oper und Drama*, but rather referred to "melodische Momente," "Grundmotive" or "Gefühlsmomente." As with the term "music drama," "leitmotif" has obtained general currency, and is therefore the most suiting designation.

165   Wagner writes that "transformed into melodic moments, the key motifs of the dramatic action constitute – by means of their referentiality and recurrence – a unified artistic form, one that creates coherence not only in smaller parts of the drama but actually integrates the entire whole. This coherence not only realizes the ideal of a fully unified form, but also the truthful expression of a unified dramatic content (Die [...] melodischen Momenten gewordenen Hauptmotive der dramatischen Handlung bilden sich in ihrer beziehungsvollen, stets wohlbedingten – dem Reime ähnlichen – Wiederkehr zu einer einheitlichen künstlerischen Form, die sich nicht nur über engere Teile des Dramas, sondern über das ganze Drama selbst als ein bindender Zusammenhang erstreckt. [...]

of all art forms into the *Gesamtkunstwerk* (total work of art), an ideal that was already put forward by Weber as well.

The main idea of Wagner's *Oper und Drama* appears to be the over-throwing of the entire genre of opera, despite differences between national traditions.[166] Yet Wagner constantly gives German opera a softer treatment, or at least recognizes in German culture a fertile soil for the development of a new music-theatrical art. In the final section of *Oper und Drama*, Wagner for example argues that German is the only "natural" language among the three opera languages, and concludes that this makes German "the exclusive language in which the perfect (music-)dramatic artwork can be conceived."[167] Wagner, however, counterbalances this rather bold statement by admitting that German opera hitherto has not realized this potential.[168] Just as other branches of the outdated opera genre, German opera has to make way for the music drama of the future, but more than any other national school, it serves as Wagner's stepping stone.

Oper und Drama thus reveals, in spite of its universal pretense of over-throwing the entire opera genre along with the society that accompanies it, a

---

In diesem Zusammenhange ist die Verwirklichung der vollendeten einheitlichen Form erreicht und durch diese Form die Kundgebung eines einheitlichen Inhaltes, somit dieser Inhalt selbst in Wahrheit erst ermöglicht)." wwsB, Sämtliche Schriften, Band IV: 202–203.

166   In the introduction to *Oper und Drama*, Wagner argues that opera is intricately tied to the wicked contemporary society, and therefore has to die, along with its milieu: "Die Wirksamkeit der modernen Oper, in ihrer Stellung zur Öffentlichkeit, ist ehrliebenden *Künstler* bereits seit lange ein Gegenstand des tiefsten und heftigsten Widerwillens geworden; sie klagten aber nur die Verderbtheit des Geschmackes und die Frivolität derjenigen Künstlern, die sie ausbeuteten, an, ohne darauf zu verfallen, daß jene Verderbtheit eine ganz natürliche, und diese Frivolität demnach eine ganz notwendige Erscheinung war. [...] Der Weg aus dem Irrthume [...] heißt hier: der *offenkundige Tod der Oper.*" wwsB, Sämtliche Schriften, Band III: 226.

167   "Überblicken wir nun die Sprachen der europäischen Nationen, die bisher einen selbsttätigen Anteil an der Entwicklung des musikalischen Dramas, der Oper, genommen haben – und diese sind nur Italiener, Franzosen und Deutsche –, so finden wir, daß von diesen drei Nationen nur die *deutsche* eine Sprache besitzt, die im gewöhnlichen Gebrauche noch unmittelbar und kenntlich mit ihren Wurzeln zusammenhängt. [...] Das über alles wichtige Grundmoment der Sprache also ist es, daß uns für den Versuch eines vollkommenen zu rechtfertigenden, höchsten künstlerischen Ausdruckes im Drama auf die deutsche Nation hinweiset; und wäre es dem künstlerischen Willen allein möglich, das vollendete dramatische Kunstwerk zutage zu fördern, so könnte dies jetzt nur in deutscher Sprache geschehen." Ibid.: 412.

168   Wagner offers two reasons for this: the fact that German operas have been harmed by an unnatural prosody inherited from the many incompetent translations of foreign works (Ibid.: 212–215), and the philistine disinterest and lust for mere entertainment of opera audiences in general, which also applies to the German public (221–226).

staunch German chauvinism. At the same time, Wagner repeatedly underlines his artwork of the future as a reinstatement of the unity of arts of Greek tragedy and the harmonizing function of art in the ancient Greek *polis* for the sake of all humanity.[169] Through the years, Wagner's Greek orientation has been a popular trope amongst scholars, often serving to mitigate the dominant image of him being an anti-Semite chauvinist. For example, it was one of the most important trump cards of Wieland and Wolfgang Wagner's attempt to denazify Bayreuth in the postwar years.[170] The dichotomy of Hellenist universalism versus German nationalism and its implicit good-bad value scheme that modern-day observers often wish to establish is, however, less black and white than it appears.

In the nineteenth century, many Germans perceived a cultural affinity with the Greeks clothed in feelings of national superiority.[171] This Philhellenism served as an analogy to the animosity between the politically impotent but culturally superior Germans and the French, who were considered to be modern-day Romans. The peculiar nature of nineteenth-century Graecophilia among German intellectuals lay in its combination of a belief in a Graeco-German *Sonderweg* and its embrace of universal cosmopolitanism. Alexander von Humboldt, for example, stated in *Geschichte des Verfalls und Unterganges der Griechischen Freistaaten* (1807) that "the Germans have the undisputed merit of being the first to have truly grasped and to have deeply understood Greek culture."[172] Intriguingly, many German intellectuals transferred their

---

169　This idea is put forward most explicitly in *Die Kunst und die Revolution* (1849): "Bei den Griechen war das vollendete, das dramatische Kunstwerk, der Inbegriff alles aus dem griechischen Wesen Darstellbaren; es war, im innigen Zusammenhangs mit ihrer Geschichte, die Nation selbst, [...] die große *Menschheitsrevolution* [...] kann uns jenes höchste Kunstwerk wiedergeben." WWSB, Sämtliche Schriften, Band III: 28–30.

170　Jason Geary mentions that "Wieland Wagner's self-conscious decision to play up the Greek influence of his grandfather's operas [...] can be seen as an attempt to impose a more sanitized and universal character upon the traditionally Germanic – or at least Northern European – nature of the work." Geary 2014: 198. Wieland Wagner realized this not only through his timeless stagings cleansed of Germanic iconography, but also by organizing a lecture series by classicist Wolfgang Schadewaldt on Wagner's relationship to the Greeks in the early 1960s.

171　In contrast to the watered-down version of Greek antiquity within many Roman countries, for example that of the "artificial" French *tragédies*, many German intellectuals felt that they understood the *true* nature of ancient Greek culture. The first scholar to devote an integral study to this subject was E.M. Butler with *The Tyranny of Greece over Germany* (1935). In music scholarship, the connection between German Romanticism and utopian visions of Ancient Greece have mainly been scrutinized in the field of song, for example by Marjorie Wing Hirsch's *Romantic Lieder and the Search for a Lost Paradise* (2007).

172　Quoted after Geary 2014: 20.

sense of a German *Sonderweg* to a belief in Greek "cultural autochthony," as George Williamson calls it.[173] Geary also recognizes how "German scholars downplayed indications that the Greeks had been influenced by these more 'barbaric' [neighboring] cultures," and argued that "to the extent that the Greeks *had* appropriated foreign elements, they had succeeded in transforming the source material into something uniquely Greek, thereby affirming their cultural autonomy and, ultimately, superiority."[174]

This sense of Greeks taking foreign elements to a new level of refinement clearly resonates with the by now familiar "aber er greift alles tiefer!" trope of German nineteenth-century esthetics. This capability to take foreign influences to a new level of profundity, exclusively inherited from the ancient Greeks, justified German intellectuals' sense of being the most universal modern culture. This idea was put forward by Georg Friedrich Wilhelm Hegel, when in his *Vorlesungen zur Philosophie der Geschichte* (1817), he presented the Germans as the chosen champions of Western thought.[175] The Left-Hegelian philosopher Moses Hess echoed this idea when he declared in *Die europäische Triarchie* (1841) that "we Germans are the most universal, the most *European* people in Europe."[176] Richard Wagner dwelled in a similar intellectual habitat in the late 1840s and early 1850s. His embrace of universalism, clothed in Philhellenism, cannot be separated from the feelings of German cultural superiority so typical of his age. His turn towards ancient Greece should therefore be seen as a shift towards a perhaps more elevated or subtle form of German chauvinism, but not as a break with this ideology.[177]

---

173   Williamson 2004: 14.

174   Geary 2014: 25.

175   "Wir [Deutschen] haben den höheren Beruf erhalten, die Bewahrer dieses heiligen Feuers zu sein." Quoted after Riethmüller 2002: 291.

176   Quoted after Berry 2006: 18.

177   Jason Geary, for example, writes that "Wagner's use of Greek tragedy as an esthetic construct upon which to build his operatic reforms stems from the [...] German tradition of appropriating Greek antiquity in the name of cultural and artistic regeneration. [...] Wagner understood the power of this trope to give legitimacy to artistic endeavors of an experimental sort." Geary 2014: 7. Whereas Wagner's Graecophilia of the 1840s and 1850s can be seen as a covert manifestation of German chauvinism, he was more explicit about this from the 1860s onwards. In a diary entry of of 20 September 1865, later inserted in *Was ist deutsch?* (1878), he states that "only the German recognized antiquity in all its purely-human originality and as something that enjoyed a significance which, totally remote from utilitarian concerns, was uniquely suited to reproducing the purely human (Nur der deutsche erkannte sie [die Antike] in ihrer reinmenschliche Originalität und der Nützlichkeit gänzlich abgewandten, dafür aber der Wiedergebung des Reinmenschlichen einzig förderlichen Bedeutung)." *wwsb*, Sämtliche Schriften, Band x: 41.

Another important shift in Wagner's thinking around 1850 is his turn to myth. In *Oper und Drama* (1851), he explained that "the unique quality of myth is that its truth is timeless, and its content, in all its conciseness, inexhaustible."[178] This made myth the ultimate vehicle for articulating his societal critique, which both concerns the timeless essence of human nature and the current state of affairs in Europe in the years around 1848. Wagner considered several subjects from divergent cultural backgrounds – the mythical Hohenstaufen Emperor Friedrich Barbarossa, the Greek hero Achilles, the Biblical figure of Jesus Christ, and the Nordic saga of *Wieland der Schmied* – eventually to arrive at his tetralogy *Der Ring des Nibelungen*. What all these stories share is the notion of a corrupt existing order, defeated by an anarchic hero who liberates the oppressed and deprived, and overthrows the previous order to create a better future.

Wagner's eventual choice for the *Nibelungen* myth was arguably motivated by the fact that this material offered the best possibility to voice his critique on contemporary society. But we should not overlook the fact that, by writing a music-dramatical work on the *Nibelungen* story, Wagner chose a subject that in the course of the nineteenth century had grown out to be the German national epic[179] par excellence.[180] The thirteenth-century *Nibelungenlied* had been discovered in the late eighteenth century, but acquired a more widespread national significance during the years of Napoleonic occupation. Friedrich von der Hagen, who published a popular edition in 1807, argued in the foreword that the *Nibelungenlied* was "fully bred from German life and sense," and could "strengthen the patriotic heart" by providing "hope for the return of German glory and world domination."[181] Both Johann August Zeune (in 1812) and

---

178   "Das Unvergleichliche des Mythos ist, daß er jederzeit wahr und sein Inhalt, bei dichtester Gedrängtheit, für alle Zeiten unerschöpflich ist." WWSB *Sämtliche Schriften*, Band IV: 64.

179   In a review of Friedrich von der Hagen's 1807 edition of the *Nibelungenlied*, published in the Heidelberg *Neue literarische Anzeiger*, Jacob Grimm mentioned "the excellence of this national epic, which is unparalleled in the entire modern literature (von der Vortrefflichkeit dieses Nationalepos, das in der ganzen modernen Literatur ohne Beispiel ist)." Quoted after Ehrismann 2005: 98. Joep Leerssen points out that by calling the *Nibelungenlied* a national epic, Grimm coined a term that would become highly influential in nineteenth-century Romantic nationalism. See Leerssen 2014A: 127.

180   The same applies to the myth of Friedrich Barbarossa's return to life to change the world for the better. During the Middle Ages this had chiefly been an eschatological, proto-socialist and proto-Reformist story, but after the fall of the Holy Roman Empire in 1806 it obtained emphatic nationalist overtones, promising a reinstatement of the German empire and its reign over Europe. See for example Borst 1979, Williamson 2004: 108–109, and Kaul 2007.

181   "Das Lied der Nibelungen, unbedenklich eins der größten und wunderwürdigsten Werke aller Zeiten und Völker, durchaus aus deutschem Leben und Sinne erwachsen und zur

August Wilhelm Schlegel (in 1813) hailed the work as an indispensable element of a German national education.[182]

During the 1840s, the patriotic enthusiasm concerning the *Nibelungen* story intensified when various writers recognized in it the perfect basis for a German national opera. Friedrich Theodor Vischer was the first to propose this in his *Vorschlag zu einer Oper* (1844). He argued that "the German yet has to hear his own history in mighty sounds," and recommended "the *Nibelungen* saga as a text for a grand, heroic opera."[183] Visscher established that "the appropriate music for this type of subject had not yet been developed, and that such a subject had not yet been set to music in Germany, just as there had not yet arrived a great national, purely-historical painter."[184] The "national character" of the *Nibelungen* subject was "its prime merit," because Visscher believed that "every nation required pieces that embody its native traits."[185] He also argued that the remoteness and archaic quality of the story made it perfect for a music-dramatic rendition, rather than a spoken play.[186] Vischer concluded with the statement that the *Nibelungenlied* seemed "custom-made

---

eigenthümlichen Vollendung gediehen, und als das erhabenste und vollkommenste Denkmal einer so lange verdunkelten Nationalpoesie. [...] Kein anderes Lied mag ein vaterländisches Herz so rühren und ergreifen, so ergötzen und stärken, als dieses [...], und uns, zwar trauernd und klagend, doch auch getröstet und gestärkt zurücklaßen, uns mit Ergebung in das Unabwendliche, doch zugleich mit Muth zu Wort und That, mit Stolz und Vertrauen auf Vaterland und Volk, mit Hoffnung auf dereinstige Wiederkehr Deutscher Glorie und Weltherrlichkeit erfüllen." Quoted after Wunderlich 1977: 18.

182   See Williamson 2004: 86 (for Zeune) and Leerssen 2014A: 128 (for Schlegel).

183   "Ich möchte die Nibelungensage als Text zu einer großen heroischen Oper empfehlen. [...] Der Deutsche soll noch seine eigene große Geschichte in mächtigen Tönen sich entgegenwogen hören." Vischer 1844: 399–400.

184   "Mit Einem Worte: wir haben die Musik noch nicht gehabt, welche ein solcher Stoff fordert, und wir haben einen solchen Stoff in unserer Musik noch nicht gehabt [...], so wie wir noch keinen großen, nationalen, rein geschichtlichen Maler gehabt haben." Ibid.: 403.

185   "Dieser Stoff ist national, das ist das erste, was von ihm zu rühmen ist. [...] Neben solchen Stoffen, die jetzt aus allen Zonen herbeigetragen werden, soll jedes Volk auch einige nationale Hauptstücke besitzen, worin der heimische Charakter aus dem heimischen Stoffe zu ihm spricht. Die Nibelungen-Helden sind ächt deutsche Charaktertypen." Ibid.: 404.

186   "So viel ist gewiß, daß durch diese große Entfremdung der Stoff der Nibelungensage ganz untauglich geworden ist zum reinen, nicht musikalischen Drama. [...] So wahr dies ist, so ist aber doch sehr zu wünschen, daß es eine Form gebe, in welcher dieser Stoff dem modernen Gefühle genießbar würde, ohne seinen Charakter zu opfern. [...] Wenn es nun aber nicht zu läugnen ist, daß wir die Nibelungen weder mit Haut und Haaren unserem Publikum vorführen, noch diejenige Umbildung auf diesen Stoff anwenden können, welche das Drama fordert, so bietet sich dagegen das musikalische Drama, die Oper, als eine Form dar, worin das Rohe und allzu Schroffe sich mildert, die einfache Gefühlswelt dieser wortlos rauhen Helden und Heldinnen sich bereichern und erweitern läßt." Ibid.: 405–409.

for an opera rendition, but awaits the arrival of a composer capable to realize its potential."[187]

A year later, Louise Otto[188] took a next step by sharing Vischer's ideas in the *Neue Zeitschrift für Musik*, adding her own convictions to the proposal[189] and actually creating a libretto for a two evening-filling *Nibelungen* opera.[190] Otto's plea was more politically outspoken than Vischer's. She first discerned "a lack of ideological engagement with the national cause and insufficient awareness of the times among German musicians,"[191] and incited them "to turn opera into a relevant carrier of contemporary ideas by setting the *Nibelungen* saga to music."[192] Otto went on to stress the importance of a national opera for the eventual creation of a unified German state,[193] and concluded with the

187   "Das Nibelungenlied ist für die Oper wie gemacht, quillt und sprudelt von herrlichen musikalischen Motiven, wartet schon lange auf seinen Componisten, fordert ihn gebieterisch." (Ibid.: 410) "Hätten wir nur erst die Hauptsache, den Componisten." Ibid.: 436.

188   More famous under the name Louise Otto-Peters.

189   She refers to Vischer's *Vorschlag zu einer **nationalen** Oper* rather than the more neutral *Vorschlag zu einer Oper*, emphasizing the national significance even more than Vischer had done. *NZfM* XII: 23 / 13, 12 August 1845: 50.

190   Otto mentions Richard Wagner, in the sense that she foresees that the entire work will be even longer than his *Rienzi* (Ibid.: 51), and even offered the libretto to him, but Wagner turned it down. In a letter of 20 June 1845 to Gustav Klemm, who had acted as an intermediary, Wagner explained that he preferred to set his own texts, and already had plenty of subjects still to set to music: "Ich habe die innige Ueberzeugung gewonnen, daß wenn dem »Opernmachen« unserer Zeit gegenüber dieser Gattung der Kunst noch etwas Bedeutendes und für die Geschichte der Kunst Gültiges erwachsen soll, dies nur durch die Vereinigung des Dichters und Musikers in einer Person geschehen kann. Sie werden auf dem alten Wege im günstigsten Falle immer nur eine gute Dichtung und eine gute Musik erhalten, nie aber ein echtes musikalisches Drama, wie ich denn überhaupt nicht begreifen kann, wie zwei Künstler ein Kunstwerk produciren sollten. [...] Zudem bin ich stets so reichlich mit Entwürfen für die Zukunft versehen, daß ich bei der zeitraubenden Umständlichkeit, die die Vollendung einer Oper kostet, zu fürchten habe, dereinst manchen unausgeführten Entwurf mit in das Grab nehmen zu müssen." *WWSB*, Sämtliche Briefe, Band II: 437–438.

191   "Unsere Dichter ringen danach, der deutschen Bühne endlich ein Nationaldrama zu geben – aber wo sind die Bestrebungen der Componisten, ihr eine Nationaloper zu verschaffen?" Ibid.: 50.

192   "Gebt uns zuerst die Nibelungen als Oper, das ist zugleich auch der erste Schritt, die Oper aus ihrer jetzigen Gesunkenheit wieder auf ihren Höhepunct zu bringen, auf welchem auch sie das neue Zeitbewußtsein in sich aufnehmen und vorzugsweise eine Trägerin der neuen Zeitideen werden wird." Ibid.: 51.

193   "A people must be national, before it can rise to political greatness, from the development of its nationality comes its political development. Therefore, we need a national opera at the moment, because she is capable to contribute to the resurrection of Germany's great art temple of the future. A first step would have been taken if someone would adapt the subject of the Nibelungen into an opera. It often fills me with horror when I look at the

conviction that opera could function as a place where German national identity can collectively be experienced:

> We want to come together in the opera – there we feel the closest kinship. Not only experts go to the opera, but also the masses. Give those masses what they want and require: national music on a national subject – give them a *Nibelungen* opera, and the first step towards unification has been taken.[194]

The *Nibelungen* craze spurred many German composers, also ones without opera experience, to try their luck with this subject. Felix Mendelssohn-Bartholdy and Robert Schumann, for example, designed plans to set the *Nibelungenlied* to music,[195] whereas Heinrich Dorn completed an opera called *Die Nibelungen*, which was premiered in Weimar in 1854 under the baton of Franz Liszt.

---

present, and see all arts fully engaged to advance a great and holy matter, to unification – music, on the contrary, is at a standstill, and directs its dreaming eyes to the past or to the inner life of the soul. The other arts look forward to a future where the national banner flies, and in which they will join determinedly and victoriously in a holy battle, to reach and conquer the promised land of a new, free future, and build altars in the solid temple of the nation – but the musical muse stands still, dreams, and is unwilling to join (Ein Volk muß national sein, eh' es politisch groß sein kann, aus seiner entwickelten Nationalität muß die politische Entwicklung kommen. So brauchen wir auch vorerst eine nationale Oper, denn auch sie ist berufen, mitbauen zu helfen an Deutschlands großem Zukunftstempel [...]. Der erste Schritt dazu wäre gethan, wenn man den Stoff der Nibelungen zu einer Oper bearbeitete. [...] Oft kommt es wie ein eignes Grauen über mich, wenn ich die Gegenwart betrachte, und mit wahrem Jubel sehe, wie alle Künste sich regen im Hinstreben zu einem großen und heiligen Ziele, zu einem einigen Ganzen – [...] doch der Muse der Musik still steht, die träumenden Blicke rückwärts oder in sich hineingekehrt. [...] Fröhlich dareinschauend in die Welt blicken sie vorwärts, wo ihnen voraus das nationale Banner weht, mit dem sie siegesbewußt in den heiligen Kampf ziehen, um das gelobte Land der neuen, freien Zukunft zu erreichen und zu erobern, und dort neue Altäre zu bauen im festen Tempel der Nation – aber der Muse der Musik steht still und träumt und will nicht mitgehen)." Ibid.: 50–51. In 1846, chief editor of the *NZfM* Franz Brendel echoed the idea that German opera will only enter a new phase in its development if it embraces the national cause, stating "that the opera will reach another level, when the national in its elevated and all-encompassing sense, when in general the spirit of our times will finally manifest itself in this genre (Daß sie [die Oper] noch eine Steigerung erwarten muß, indem das Nationale im hohen und umfassenden Sinne, überhaupt der Geist der Neuzeit in ihr noch nicht zur Erscheinung gekommen ist)." *NZfM* XIII: 24 / 15, 19 February 1846.

194 "So wollen wir denn in der Oper einander begegnen – da stehen wir uns am nächsten. In der Oper versammeln sich nicht nur Kunstkenner – da herrscht die Menge. [...] – gebt Ihr was sie will und was sie bedarf: nationale Musik zu einem nationalen Stoff – gebt Ihr die Nibelungen als Oper, und der erste Schritt zur Vereinigung ist gethan." Ibid.: 52.

195 See Jacobs 2009: 179.

What Wagner must have fascinated about Vischer and Otto's pleas for a *Nibelungen* opera was not only its assumed national significance, but also the future-oriented nature of their argument; the idea that an opera on this subject would turn the genre into a relevant carrier of contemporary ideas, and the notion that its composer and music-dramatic style was still to be found. Wagner enhanced the societal relevance of his *Ring des Nibelungen* by combining the action of the *Nibelungenlied* with a prehistory derived from the Islandic Edda and other Nordic myths,[196] something which Friedrich de la Motte-Fouqué had already done in his *Der Held des Nordens* (1810).[197] Through this extension of the action, Wagner added a socialist critique in *Das Rheingold*, a vindication of anarchy in *Die Walküre* and *Siegfried*,[198] and the destruction of the old order in *Götterdämmerung*.[199] In line with this critique of contemporary society and his dreams about a new utopia of freedom and naturalness, he designed his musical *Nibelungen* drama emphatically as the "artwork of the future," an alternative to traditional opera and its milieu. Paradoxically, it was Wagner's turn back towards Nordic prehistory that not only brought him closer to the timeless quality of the purely human,[200] but also facilitated a new, state-of-the-art form

---

196   It may be tempting to recognize in Wagner's use of Nordic myths a move away from the more outspokenly patriotic subject of the *Nibelungenlied*, and therefore a sign of his universal or even anti-national sympathies. This thesis is, however, hardly tenable, as German intellectuals from Herder onward had discerned in Scandinavia an "armory of the German spirit" or a "*Germania Germanicissima*," as Klaus von See calls it (Compare See 2003: 27 + 44, but also Freyberger 2011: 32–33 and Schulz 2009: 10). Moreover, the centrality of the Rhine within the *Ring* - not only as the scenery of the *Nibelungenlied*-inspired *Götterdämmerung*, but also as the opening backdrop of *Das Rheingold* – reinforced the German national significance. Compare Leerssen 2014A: 130.

197   Williamson discusses the close affinity between both works' plots. See Williamson 2004: 87.

198   This anarchy is present in the siblings Siegmund and Sieglinde's transgressive love, Brünnhilde's decision to choose their side rather than to carry out Wotan's command, and in Siegfried, – the fruit of Siegmund and Sieglinde's incestuous bond – who more than anyone else within the *Ring* embodies the values of anarchism.

199   Whereas the *Nibelungenlied* closes with the destruction of the House of Burgundy in a war with the Huns, Wagner only used the first half of the *Lied* and connects the death of Siegfried to the inevitable *Ragnarök* of Nordic mythology: the end of the gods.

200   In *Eine Mittheilung an meine Freunde* (1851), Wagner explains how, by peeling of historical layers, he gradually arrived at the purely-human character of myth: "My studies carried me backwards through the Medieval poems until I arrived at the root of ancient primordial German myth; stripping off all disguising garments of later poetic renditions, I eventually found the arch-myth in its chaste beauty. What I finally witnessed was no longer the historical, conventional figure, but man in his realest, naked form: man as he truly is (Meine Studien trugen mich so durch die Dichtungen des Mittelalters hindurch bis auf den Grund des alten urdeutschen Mythos; ein Gewand nach dem anderen, das ihm die

of music theater that departed from the Romantic medievalism of the first half of the nineteenth century.

Despite the socialist, anarchist and esthetic agenda of his *Nibelungen* project, Wagner was aware of its status as a national treasure, and he held on to its intellectual ownership like a Nibelung. This becomes particularly clear from Wagner's competition with the Viennese playwright Friedrich Hebbel, whose highly successful drama *Die Nibelungen* premiered in 1863. Hugh Ridley points out that "Wagner had the disadvantage that, although he started his Nibelungen much earlier [...], the project took thirty years to finish." Therefore he "had to watch Hebbel pick up the theme, write his drama text, and then enjoy a great success with it, not only on the Viennese stage but also closer to home." In order not to be overshadowed, "Wagner deliberately published the text of the *Ring* [in 1863,] long before the music was ready as a desperate strategy to keep himself in the public eye at a time when Hebbel was milking his success."[201] It is striking how Wagner, in the epilogue of the 1863 publication of the *Ring* text, fully appropriates the *Nibelungen* text as his own "good move," fully disregarding the well-known publications by Vischer and Otto.[202]

The necessity to claim his intellectual ownership of the *Nibelungen* myth in 1863 was all the more pressing for Wagner, as political developments were starting to make German unification more probable than ever. Around that time, Wagner was living in a miserable state, travelling alone to escape his creditors, and had aborted his *Ring* project as an unrealizable enterprise.[203]

---

spätere Dichtung entstellend umgeworfen hatte, vermochte ich von ihm abzulösen, um ihn so endlich in seiner keuschesten Schönheit zu erblicken. Was ich hier ersah, war nicht mehr die historisch konventionelle Figur, an der uns das Gewand mehr als die wirkliche Gestalt interessiren muß; sondern der wirkliche, nackte Mensch [...]: der wahre Mensch überhaupt)." WWSB Sämtliche Schriften, Band IV: 311–312.

201   Ridley 2012: 29. In *Über Schauspieler und Sänger* (1869), Wagner likened Hebbel's play to a "parody of the *Nibelungenlied.*" WWSB, Sämtliche Schriften, Band IX: 167.

202   "Bald zeigte es sich nun, daß ich mit der Wahl meines Stoffes einen besonders 'glücklichen Griff' gethan zu haben schien, welchen Andere um so eher nachzugreifen sich veranlaßt fühlen konnten, als mein Unternehmen jedenfalls für ein chimärisches und gänzlich unausführbares angesehen [...] werden durfte." WWSB, Sämtliche Schriften, Band VI: 261.

203   On 28 June 1857 Wagner had written to Liszt that he had terminated the *Ring* project, had left his Siegfried under the lime tree and would not resume work on it, unless his situation would change in such a degree that he could truly present it to the world: "Mit [Breitkopf &] Härtels werde ich nun keine Noth mehr haben, da ich mich endlich dazu entschlossen habe, das obstinate Unternehmen der Vollendung meiner Niebelungen aufzugeben. Ich habe meinen jungen Siegfried noch in die schöne Waldeinsamkeit geleitet; dort hab' ich ihn unter der Linde gelassen und mit herzlichen Thränen Abschied genommen: – er ist dort besser dran als anders wo. – Soll ich das Werk wieder einmal aufnehmen, so müsste mir diess entweder sehr leicht gemacht werden, oder ich selbst müsste es mir bis dahin

But in the new political climate, Wagner's dream of having his *Ring* performed in a theater specifically designed for this task became more plausible, if he managed to outdo his competitors and gain his *Ring* the status of *the* Nibelungen rendition par excellence. The last section of this chapter deals with the question how Wagner used the nationalism and unification enthusiasm of his contemporaries to make his dream of the Bayreuth Festival come true.

4 "Vollendet das ewige Werk!"[204] Bayreuth as a Unification Festival

In the 1863 preface to the published *Ring* poem, Wagner called for either an association of wealthy citizens or a German monarch to provide the necessary funding to fulfill his dream of presenting the entire *Ring des Nibelungen* in a festival setting.[205] The latter seemed preferable to him, as every monarch could simply use the budget now spent on a court opera to make possible Wagner's music-dramatic festival, which would immediately make this monarch an influential and admirable advancer of the German national cause.[206] A year later, Wagner was actually approached by a minister of Ludwig II, the new king of Bavaria, with the promise of royal protection for his artistic endeavors. The adolescent monarch was an ardent admirer of Wagner, and did not hesitate to reach out to him after having ascended the throne.

This exceptional gesture fully turned Wagner's world around. From now on, he was not only able to carry out his artistic ambitions, but also became a confident, and at times even a prompter, of the king of the second most powerful state of Germany.[207] Wagner's German chauvinism by now had become far more outspoken than it had ever been before, which shows from the following

---

möglich machen können, das Werk im vollsten Sinne des Wortes der Welt zu schenken." *WWSB*, Sämtliche Briefe, Band VIII: 354.

204 This euphoric, but slightly premature outcry of Wotan at the delivery of his celestial palace in *Das Rheingold* clearly resembles the triumphant tone of the 1870s, in which Germany was finally unified, and Wagner saw his dream of an exclusive festival for his art become true.

205 *WWSB*, Sämtliche Schriften, Band VI: 279–281.

206 "Würde er von seinem jährlichen Budget nur die auf Unterhaltung der Oper in seiner Residenz verwandte Summe bei Seite legen, und sie, wenn ausreichend, zu alljährlichen, wenn nicht, sie kombinirend, zu zwei- oder dreijährig sich wiederholenden Festaufführungen der bezeichneten Art bestimmen, und somit eine Stiftung gründen, die ihm einen unberechenbaren Einfluß auf den deutschen Kunstgeschmack, auf die Entwickelung des deutschen Kunstgenie's, auf die Bildung eines wahrhaften, nicht dünkelhaften nationalen Geistes, seinem Namen aber unvergänglichen Ruhm gewinnen müßte." Ibid.: 221.

207 Prussia being the most powerful and influential, of course.

diary entry of 11 September 1864 where he presents himself as the prophet of *Deutschtum*:

> Now nobody understands me: I am the most German human being, I am the German spirit. What else constitutes the magic of my works than their *German* character? But what is this *German*? It must be something marvelous, because it is more human and beautiful than anything else. O heavens! If only I could find my people. What a splendid people this would be! Only to this people could I belong.[208]

This private confession shows to what extent the German national cause and a narcissistic cult merged in Wagner's imagination, a combination that would offend many supporters of the national cause. But Ludwig was intoxicated by Wagner's theories, and fully endorsed the artist's vision, even calling the completion of *Der Ring des Nibelungen* "a joint venture to be offered as a present to the German nation."[209] However, Wagner and Ludwig's intimate collaboration[210] did not last long, because Ludwig's government was worried about Wagner's allowance and his attempts to influence Bavarian politics. This resulted in Wagner's banishment from Munich in December 1865, after which their relation cooled. With the ascendancy of Prussia after winning the Austro-Prussian War in 1866, Wagner realized that the future of Germany would not lie in Bavarian hands.[211] Ludwig, in his turn, lost sympathy with Wagner's exalted theories about the German spirit, and even terminated a series of polemics in the *Süddeutsche Presse* in December 1867, which Wagner would later compile

---

208   "Jetzt begreift mich kein Mensch: Ich bin der deutscheste Mensch, ich bin der deutsche Geist. Fragt den unvergleichlichen Zauber *meiner* Werke, haltet sie mit allem übrigen zusammen: Ihr könnt für jetzt nichts anderes sagen, als – es ist *deutsch*. Aber was ist dieses *Deutsche*? Es muss doch etwas wunderbares sein, denn es ist menschlich schöner als alles Übrige? – O Himmel! Sollte ich mein Volk finden können! Welch herrliches Volk müßte das werden? Nur diesem Volke könnte ich aber angehören." *WWSB*, Briefwechsel Ludwig II, Band I: 64–65.

209   "Dies wundervolle Werk wollen wir der deutschen Nation zum Geschenk Machen und ihr sowie den anderen Nationen zeigen, was ,deutsche Kunst' vermag!" Letter from Ludwig II to Wagner, 7 October 1864. Ibid.: 27.

210   Intimate also in the sense that Wagner deliberately played upon Ludwig's homo-erotic fantasies in their correspondences.

211   In Hannu Salmi's words, "he had now come to believe that the waves of international pseudo-civilization which originated in France and which were pouring all over Germany were a greater threat to the German people than the threat posed by the Prussian authorities," whereas previously, he had considered "Berlin as a perennial nexus of French-Jewish degeneration in Germany." Salmi 1999: 134 + 107.

in *Deutsche Kunst und deutsche Politik* (1868).[212] Despite Ludwig's waning engagement with Wagner's ideas, he nonetheless continued to support him financially.

Even though Wagner quickly lost royal favor, he nonetheless had the prestigious Munich court opera at his disposal for the premieres of *Tristan und Isolde* (1865) and *Die Meistersinger von Nürnberg* (1868). Particularly the latter of these two functioned as a vehicle for Wagner's national-cultural agenda, and turned out to be an enormous success throughout the German-speaking world, putting Wagner at the center of the national movement.[213] The setting of the opera is governed by three markers of national culture: middle-class culture, Protestantism,[214] and the German musical past, presented by the sixteenth-century tradition of *Minnesänger*. More than ever before, Wagner alluded to historical forms of German music, such as Bach polyphony and Lutheran chorales, in order to emphasize the relation of his "artwork of the future" to the national past.

As in *Tannhäuser*, the action revolves around a singing contest with a desirable young woman as its prize, in which the popular song of Hans Sachs and the slightly anarchic but highly lyrical style of Walther von Stolzing – both representants of Wagner's own music – struggle against a Philistine, dogmatic esthetic. Sachs's rhetorical question if it is fair to judge art with a set of rules that is alien to the work in question presents a *cri de coeur* from Wagner himself,[215] who incessantly had to defend his music drama against the claim that it did not observe conventional musical and dramatic regulations, and was therefore formless if not monstrous.

In this respect, *Die Meistersinger* forms a declaration of war against critics, who Wagner sees as a useless, alienated caste obstructing a direct relation between the artist and the people. The quintessential critic is embodied in Sixtus

---

212   An elaborate account of the relation between Wagner and Ludwig is offered by Hannu Salmi. Ibid.: 87–144.

213   *Tristan und Isolde*, completed in 1859, was inspired by a personal love affair and the discovery of Schopenhauer's philosophy rather than by chauvinist sentiments. At the same time, the work does display traits of a German music-dramatic esthetic, such as austerity of plot and scenery, prominence of the orchestra, and concentration on the psychology of the characters.

214   In a letter to Hans von Bülow of 20 February 1866, Wagner remarked how significant it was that Nuremberg, despite the fact that it belonged to Catholic Bavaria, was a Protestant town. (*WWSB*, Briefe an Hans v. Bülow: 244) In this period after his banishment from Munich, the Lutheran Wagner must have enjoyed the Protestant character of this city at the outskirts of the Bavarian territory as a pleasant vehicle for disobedience. With the eventual settlement in Bayreuth, he also chose a Protestant city at the margins of Bavaria.

215   "Wollt ihr nach Regeln messen, was nicht nach eurer Regeln Lauf,'" (First Act).

Beckmesser,[216] who is a rigid rule-keeper and a mere copycat, making him a pseudo-French, if not Jewish *Fremdkörper* in the homogenous German society of Nuremberg.[217] The singing contest exposes him as a fraud, who steals Walther's poem but cannot create a proper melody.[218] Through Beckmesser's *demasqué*, followed by the celestial melody of Walther's *Preislied*, society can experience its unity.[219] The work concludes with Sachs's final monolog, in which he praises the German *Kulturnation*, and warns for the dangers of cosmopolitan alienation:

> Habt Acht! Uns dräuen üble Streich': / zerfällt erst deutsches Volk und Reich,
> in falscher wälscher Majestät / kein Fürst bald mehr sein Volk versteht,
> und wälschen Dunst mit wälschem Tand / sie pflanzen uns in deutsches Land;
> was deutsch und echt, wüsst' keiner mehr, / lebt's nicht in deutscher Meister Ehr'.
> Drum sag' ich euch: / ehrt eure deutschen Meister!
> Dann bannt ihr gute Geister; / und gebt ihr ihrem Wirken Gunst,
> zerging' in Dunst / das heil'ge röm'sche Reich,
> uns bliebe gleich / die heil'ge deutsche Kunst!

---

216 Wagner modelled Beckmesser after Eduard Hanslick, his most vehement opponent, and for a time even considered calling the dramatic character Veit Hanslich, an idea that he later abandoned.

217 The ideology of *Die Meistersinger* combines the tenor of Constantin Frantz's *Untersuchungen über das europäische Gleichgewicht* (1859), in which the author discerns a hegemony of French civilization among European nations, and particularly the Germans, with Wagner's own ideas that Jewish can merely copy, but cannot be original. This belief was put forward in *Das Judenthum in der Musik* (1850), an essay that Wagner re-issued in 1869, not coincidently a year after the *Meistersinger* premiere. The idea that Beckmesser's character and musical physiognomy embody anti-Semitic stereotypes is frequently addressed, for example by Millington 1991, Weiner 1995, and Levin 1996. During the 1860s, Wagner became acquainted with the patriotic thinker Constantin Frantz, and dedicated the second edition of *Oper und Drama* (1868) to him, thereby highlighting the chauvinism that the work already contained in a covert form.

218 Here Wagner revisits the idea put forward in *Oper und Drama* that the organic unity between melody and text that characterizes folksong, as well as his music drama in which poet and musician are one and the same person, can never be achieved with artificial means.

219 Wagner's open air singing festival in *Die Meistersinger* resembles the large-scale communal oratorio performances so popular among the nineteenth-century patriotic German bourgeoisie, with the crucial difference that here it is not a dated relict of the past that is celebrated – as Wagner perceived it – but actually the "music of the future."

[Beware! Evil tricks threaten us: / if the German people and kingdom should decay,
under a false, foreign rule / soon no prince would understand his people;
and foreign mists with foreign vanities / they would plant in our German land;
what is German and true none would know, / did not it live in the honor of German Masters.

Therefore, I say to you: / honor your German Masters,
then you will conjure up good spirits! /And if you favor their endeavors,
even if the Holy Roman Empire / should dissolve in mist,
for us there would yet remain / holy German Art!]

This statement has various historical dimensions. As a 16th-century German, Sachs was himself a subject to a foreign monarch with no command of the German language, Charles v. His warning simultaneously foresees the alienation between the German people and a Frenchified monarch such as the 18th-century Frederick the Great, and the prominence of culture after the demise of the Holy Roman Empire in 1806. In that sense, Wagner looks back to the past through Sachs's eyes. But in the political context of 1868, it was easy to read into this "call of arms" against French/Romanic civilization an invocation of war enthusiasm; despite the idyllic and light-versed tone of this comedy, the belligerent sentiments of its time of creation are ever present.

We may assume that both aspects appealed to the German public, who immediately embraced *Die Meistersinger*. The Munich premiere was followed up by various performances elsewhere in Germany, and many reviews were ecstatic about this *German* masterpiece. In *Signale für die musikalische Welt*, a reporter from Karlsruhe wrote the following about the national significance of Wagner's new work:

History books will once tell us that, exactly at the moment when our national conscience more than ever awakened, an artist stood up among us who did not appeal to critics but to the people, who rescued our *German National Opera* that was nearly destructed by a Roman spring flood, and created a monument of German spiritual sovereignty.[220]

---

220 "In den Geschichtsbüchern wird einst zu lesen sein, daß gerade zu jener Epoche, in welcher uns das nationale Bewußtsein der Deutschen stärker als je erwachte und rang, ein Künstler uns erstand, der an das Volk und nicht an die Recensenten appelirte und uns den, in den romanischen Springfluthen fast rettungslos schon untergegangen

The review shows how Wagner's art was finally fully acknowledged as a reflection of the German spirit.[221] Wagner himself was obviously thrilled with this final widespread acknowledgement, and equally excited when the Franco-Prussian War broke out in 1870; Paris, the city that had treated him so badly, was now under siege by the German army. Wagner decided to send a poem to the battlefield (*An das deutsche Heer vor Paris*), in which he called the soldiers the real writers of Siegfried's lied, thereby drawing a parallel to his *Ring* and the war.[222]

Wagner was not the only one who at the time associated the battle against France with the heroic deeds of Siegfried in the *Nibelungen Saga*,[223] and he must have understood that this post-War euphoria was the perfect climate to finally realize the dream of performing his *Ring des Nibelungen* under suitable conditions. Although he still received an allowance from Ludwig II, this was by no means sufficient to attain his goals. Therefore, he placed his hope on

---

Begriff einer *deutschen National-Oper* gerettet hat, zum bleibenden Denkmal *deutscher Geistessouveränität.*" *Signale für die musikalische Welt* XXVII/16, 11 February 1869: 242.

221   The reviewer continues by praising his unconventional musical form as creating a higher sense of unity comparable to the splendor of a German dome: "Wagner's *Meistersinger* are comparable to a Gothic building, grand and massive in its design, aspiring and brave, yet inexhaustible in its ornamention and detail. These motifs surround and pervade each other, governed by the unifying fundamental idea, but at the same time infinitely subtle and diverse. When entering such a Dome, we enter a world that exclusively belongs to us, and has nothing to do with the outside world. We feel that we have reached our spiritual fatherland that no foreign power can take away from us, and no one can insult (Die Wagner'schen 'Meistersinger' sind in der That einem gothischen Bauwerk zu vergleichen, groß und gewaltig in der Anlage, hochstrebend im Bau, kühn in den Wölbungen und doch unerschöpflich in der Ornamentik, fast unübersehbar im Detail. Stylvoll umschlingen und durchdringen sich diese Motive, einheitlich in der Grundidee, aber von unendlicher Mannigfaltigkeit in der Ausführung. Treten wir in einen solchen Dom, so fühlen wir uns in einer eigenen Welt, die mit der Außenwelt Nichts mehr gemein hat. Und doch fühlen wir erst recht, daß wir in unserer deutschen Geistesheimath sind, die uns kein Fremder rauben kann und kein Tadler verleiden und verbittern soll)!" Ibid.: 242–243.

222   "So heißt das Lied / vom Siege-Fried, / von deutschen Heeres That gedichtet." (*WWSB*, Sämtliche Schriften, Band IX: 2) In 1870, Wagner moreover wrote the text for a satirical operetta, *Eine Kapitulation*, in which he ridiculed French culture and criticized the passive adoption of French taste among German audiences.

223   Max Jähns, for example, wrote the ceremonial play *Die Heimkehr*, premiered on 17 June 1871 in Berlin, in which the new emperor Wilhelm I is praised as a "Siegfried who has slayed the French dragon and has captured the Nibelungen hoard: Alsace-Lorraine." (see Borst 1979: 46–47) In a poem that was also called *Die Heimkehr* (1872), Julius Rodenberg called Wilhelm "*Sieg-Fried'*des deutschen Volkes! (Wunderlich 1977: 43–44), whereas in *Den Siegestrunknen* (1872), Wagner's friend Georg Herwegh likened Siegfried to the new chancellor Bismarck: "Vorüber ist der harte Strauß / Der welsche Drache liegt bezwungen, / Und Bismarck-Siegfried kehrt nach Haus / Mit seinen Schatz der Nibelungen." (Ibid.: 42).

the Prussia-led government of the new German state. The closest he came to the status of an official state composer was when in May 1871, he was allowed to conduct his *Kaisermarsch* in a Berlin concert attended by the Emperor. Wagner's offer to compose a commemorative symphony for the fallen victims was, however, kindly refused, and spurred a reporter from the *Norddeutsche allgemeine Zeitung* to state that Wagner "shouldn't believe that he exclusively owned the German spirit."[224] That Bismarck may have had similar objections is probable, as, despite an audience and several letters from Wagner demanding financial backing, he never gave a dime for the latter's festival plans.[225]

As public funding seemed unattainable, Wagner decided to seek private sponsors. In April 1871, he published the brochure *Über die Aufführung des Büh-nenfestspiels "Der Ring des Nibelungen,"* in which he characterized his proposed festival as a "truly national enterprise."[226] An association of patrons was founded, as well as several Wagner societies throughout the German-speaking world. In 1872, the Berlin *Academische Wagner-Verein* published a supplement to the *Musikalisches Wochenblatt*, in which the national significance and necessity of financial support was once again underlined:

> Just as in ancient Greece, where the prosperity of the state went hand in hand with the blooming of art, should the ascension of the German Empire be commemorated by a tremendous artwork celebrating the German spirit. For the second time in history did the German mission triumph in the political realm – the spiritual victory must be celebrated in the German Festival in Bayreuth. Richard Wagner, the great poet-composer, whose steadfast reform of art resembles Bismarck's political deeds, Richard Wagner, the bard of German greatness, gave his live for the fatherland. The nation should do its share by making a dignified performance possible.[227]

---

224   "er solle nicht glauben, daß er den deutschen Geist für sich gepachtet habe." Quoted after Großmann-Vendrey 1977: 18.
225   See Salmi 1999: 161–165.
226   *WWSB*, Sämtliche Schriften, Band IX: 317.
227   "Wie in Hellas mit der größten staatlichen Blüthe die der Kunst Hand in Hand ging, so soll auch neben der Auferstehung des deutschen Reiches dem deutschen Geiste durch ein ge-waltiges Kunstwerk ein ewiges Denkmal gesetzt werden. Zum zweiten Male triumphirte in diesen Tagen der welthistorische Beruf des Germanen auf politischem Gebiete – der geistige Sieg soll durch die deutschen Festspiele in Bayreuth gefeiert werden. Richard Wag-ner, der große Dichter-Componist, dessen unbeirrtes reformatorischen Wirken auf dem Gebiete der Kunst mit Bismarck's politischer Thätigkeit verglichen werden kann, Richard Wagner, der Sänger deutscher Größe, weihte das Werk seines Lebens dem Vaterlande.

Even though at the end of 1874, a giant fund by Ludwig II was necessary not to fail at the last hurdle, the Bayreuth Festival was indeed to a considerable extent funded by nationally-conscious middle classes. This it has in common with enterprises such as the erection of the *Hermannsdenkmal* (1838–1875) and the completion of the Dom of Cologne (1248–1880), monumental projects to which many bourgeois citizens subscribed, and that were finally realized after the unification of Germany.[228] At the same time, despite Wagner's national pretensions, it was also the fulfilling of an individual artist's dream, moreover designed for a relatively select followership. Could the first Bayreuth Festival in 1876 actually live up to Wagner's promise of being a "truly national enterprise?"[229] A discussion of the reports of the laying of the foundation

---

Das Volk soll eine ehrwürdige Aufführung ermöglichen." *Musikalisches Wochenblatt* III/18, 26 April 1872: 272.

228   The unfinished Dom of Cologne was sometimes considered to be a symbol of the fractured state of Germany. Klaus von See interprets the financial support of these nearly unfinishable projects as a clear expression of patriotism: "At the middle of the nineteenth century, the Dom of Cologne and the *Hermannsdenkmal* were considered to be the two great symbols of the German *Kulturnation*, because both were architectural initiatives that advanced with difficulty and took a long time to be realized, and therefore served as a reminder of the still-not-completed unification of Germany. As a result, financing these projects became a demonstration of patriotism among the middle classes." See 2003: 80.

229   Besides the German answers to this question, the critical evaluation of Victor Tissot, a Swiss-born Paris-based writer who visited the first Bayreuth Festival and reported about it in his *Les Prussiens en Allemagne* (1877), is equally revealing. To him, and to many of his compatriots, the post-Unification chauvinist triumphalism surrounding the festival was illustrative of its artistic insignificance: "After having demonstrated its superiority at the battlefield, Germany must now display its supremacy in the arts; Wagner is the ultimate expression of the German musical genius, like Kaulbach [a painter of monumental historical tableaus] is for German painting. His operas epitomize the battle carried out against French and Italian operas. His theater in Bayreuth has a patriotic significance like the monuments for Arminius and Luther; for future generations, it marks a victory for German culture, as well as a Sedan for French musical art. [The *Ring*] is the 'most surprising and colossal' creation of this poet-musician, destined to efface Aeschylus's *Prometheus* and Goethe's *Faust*; a work with a philosophical impact big enough to establish the worldwide supremacy of German music. This is all nearly as grotesque as those famous frescoes [by Kaulbach] in Berlin (Ápres avoir montré sa superiorité dans les armes, l'Allemagne veut la montrer dans les arts; Wagner est l'expression suprême du génie allemande. Ses opéras sont des batailles livrées aux opéras français et italiens. Le théâtre de Bayreuth a sa signification nationale et patriotique, comme le monument d'Arminius et le monument de Luther; il marquera, pour les générations futures, une victoire de la culture allemande, ce sera le Sedan de l'art musical français. [...] Telle [le *Ring*] est la création "la plus surprenante et la plus colossale" du poëte-musicien; l'œuvre destinée à effacer le *Prométhée* d'Eschyle et à enfoncer le *Faust* de Goethe; l'opéra d'une porteé toute philosophique, destiné à establir la suprématie de la musique allemande dans le monde. C'est à peu près aussi grotesque que les fameuses fresques du musée du Berlin)." Tissot 1877: 184–196.

stone and reviews of the first festival provide a fascinating array of answers to this question.[230]

As most ardent supporters of Wagner's esthetic cause also subscribed to his German chauvinism, it hardly surprises that affirmative answers could frequently be heard. It is striking that three critics – Victor K. Schembera,[231] Ludwig Speidel,[232] and Franz Gehring,[233] all writing for Viennese media[234] – state literally the same when they point out that "Wagner's cause can no longer be separated from the German cause."[235] Gehring offers the most elaborate motivation of his statement, signaling an "impressive, highly disciplined collective effort" undertaken by all participants of the festival, comparable to the "courage and perseverance of German soldiers,"[236] and stresses that since the festival is "funded by the people," it presents "the most *Volksthümlich* artistic endeavor of this scale ever achieved."[237] The collective element, giving the

---

230   Many of these reports can be found in *Bayreuth in der deutschen Presse* (1977), a compilation of Wagner criticism by Susanna Großman-Vendrey, which has been of great use for my research.

231   'Das Bühnenfestspiel zu Bayreuth. – Die Schlußbilanz von Bayreuth.' *Neues Wiener Tageblatt*, August 1876, quoted after Großman-Vendrey 1977: 143.

232   'Richard Wagner und die deutsche Sache.' *Deutsche Zeitung* (Wien), May 1872, quoted after Ibid.: 23. Speidel here addresses the laying of the foundation stone ceremony (1872) and not the festival.

233   Das Baireuther Bühnenfestspiel, *Deutsche Zeitung* (Wien), August 1876, Ibid.: 83.

234   Susanne Großman-Vendrey mentions how in the years after the German unification, German chauvinism reached a highpoint in Austria, which explains why many exulted statements about Wagner's German greatness were voiced in Vienna. See Ibid.: 18–19. For a discussion of German chauvinism in Viennese late nineteenth-century music life, see Brodbeck 2014.

235   "daß die Sache Richard Wagner's von der deutschen Sache nicht zu trennen sei."

236   The comparison of Wagner's enterprise with the Franco-Prussian War was also drawn by Wilhelm Mohr in the *Kölnische Zeitung* (August 1876): "Wagner has won the battle. Where many doomsayers had predicted a fiasco comparable to the French' defeat in Sedan, it was actually like Sedan, but then from a German perspective (Wagner hat die Schlacht gewonnen. Was gewissen Unheilspropheten zufolge ein Sedan im französischen Sinne sein sollte, ist wirklich ein Sedan gewesen, aber im deutschen Sinne)." Quoted after Ibid.: 109.

237   "Alle [Mitwirkende] aber haben ihre Pflicht und Schuldigkeit bei der Vorbereitung des Festspieles in einer Weise gethan, wie sie sich mit Gold gar nicht bezahlen läßt, und nur Wagner und seinem Kunstwerke zuliebe haben sie unsägliche Opfer gebracht, [...] Opfer, wie sie bisher nur in einem nationalen Kriege von den Vertheidigern dem Vaterland dargebracht wurden. [...] Der Gehorsam und die Subordination der Mitwirkenden wird man immer als Beispiele echten deutschen Wesens zu preisen und den späteren Zeiten als Muster hinzustellen haben. [...] Daß nur *deutsche* Consequenz und Festigkeit ein solches Riesenwerk vollenden und darstellen konnte. Hiermit ist zum erstenmale, seit von den Deutschen in der Weltgeschichte die Rede ist, diese Haupttugend derselben in das

festival a trans-individual, and therefore national significance was also lifted out by Oscar Berggrün, who compared it to the individualistic cult of Jean Paul pilgrimage that had previously dominated Bayreuth cultural life.[238]

From the four parts of the *Ring*, *Siegfried* was considered to be the most successful, and most nationally appealing work, even by critics how were generally dismissive of Wagner's esthetic and national pretenses.[239] Reasons for the widespread appraisal of *Siegfried* lay in the spiritual affinity with the story, – compared to the relatively alien myths from the Edda[240] – the fairy-tale character and the way in which Wagner revisited elements of German Romantic opera.[241] Franz Gehring, writing for *Im neuen Reich. Wochenschrift*

ästhetische Gebiet übertragen. [...] In diesem Sinne ist es nunmehr wahr geworden, daß Wagner's Sache von der deutschen nicht mehr zu trennen ist. [...]In Einem freilich hat sich die Wechselwirkung zwischen Kunst und menschlicher Gesellschaft radical verändert: [...] das deutsche Volk tritt als Mäcenas auf. Die Beziehungen zwischen der Kunst und dem Volke sind, dem Zuge unseres Zeitalters entsprechend, demokratisirt. Präciser ist der Stempel der Volksthümlichkeit noch niemals einem künstlerischen Unternehmen aufgedrückt worden als diesem." Ibid.: 81–84.

238   "Der durchaus individuelle, in einzelne Besuche aus den 'empfindsamen Kreisen' aufgelöste Cultus, der für Jean Paul gleichwie für andere Dichter, noch vor fünfzig Jahren in Deutschland sich entfaltete [...] ist heutzutage der gemeinsamen Feier nationaler Ideen, der gemeinsamen Unterstützung nationaler Unternehmungen gewichen. Auch diesmal war es allein die Idee, die nationale, wie die künstlerische, welche Besucher aus allen Gegenden Deutschlands, aus allen Kreisen und Ständen nach Bayreuth führte; das persönliche Element hingegen trat so ganz in den Hintergrund." 'Der Wiener Nibelungen Fahrt. – *Deutsche Zeitung* (Wien), May/June 1872, quoted after Ibid.: 24. As was also the case with Speidel's remarks, this article concerns the laying of the foundation stone ceremony in 1872, and again, the national affirmation comes from Vienna.

239   Eduard Hanslick, for example, recognized in the first act of *Siegfried* a certain "freshness [Frische]," a "nature boy-like quality [Naturburschenhaftes]." *Neue Freie Presse* (Wien), August 1876. Quoted after Ibid.: 210.

240   Ludwig Speidel, for example, wrote "that the greater success of *Siegfried* stems already from the subject. Finally one leaves the nebulous atmosphere of the *Edda*, [...] and breathes the fresh air of the folk tale of the horned Siegfried and the lovely fairy-tales of the boy who wanted to be taught how to fear and the sleeping beauty ('Der günstigere Erfolg des 'Siegfried' liegt schon im Stoff, denn endlich kommt man durch ihn heraus aus der nebelhaften Atmosphäre der 'Edda' [...] und athmet die frischere Luft des Volksbuches vom gehörnten Siegfried und der reizenden Märchen von Einem, der das Fürchten lernen wollte, und vom Dornröschen.')." *Fremden-Blatt* (Wien), August 1876. Quoted after Ibid.: 225.

241   Karl Frenzel, for example, writes: "When Wagner approaches the nature and beauty of the old saga; when he tries to musically evoke the life of elementary powers, when, in sum, he emerges as a Romantic and follows in the footsteps of Tieck, Novalis, and Weber, then he manages to create magical moments (Wo Wagner sich der Natur und der Schönheit der alten Sage anschließt; wo er es versucht, das Weben und Walten der elementaren Kräfte musikalisch anzudeuten, wo er mit einem Worte Romantiker ist, auf den Pfaden Tieck's

für das Leben des deutschen Volkes in Staat, Wissenschaft und Kunst, comprises all of these elements in the following passage, in which he also recognizes a perfect spiritual merging between artist, work and public, an aspect that Wagner himself had previously lifted out as constituting the national significance of *Der Freischütz* in his Parisian writings:

> *Siegfried* has undisputably received the warmest sympathy among German listeners. It is easy to see why. Every German has experienced an idealized version of his inner self in it, and realized that our much-acclaimed sensitivity is not an illusion. Wagner has penetrated into the heart of our character. [...] The fresh breeze that once enchanted an older generation of Germans in *Der Freischütz* has been revived in our age, in which materialism is rampant. *Siegfried* has enraptured us. That a work of our times can invoke this poetic mood in us proves its authenticity, which we can trace in its spontaneity and sincerity. [...] To a certain extent, it becomes irrelevant whether Wagner composed it or someone else, subconsciously we feel identical to the artist and his work.[242]

This impression of the *Ring* as a work for and *quasi* created *by* the German nation was, however, not shared by all attendants. The first frequently-uttered objection to the Bayreuth festival's national significance was that from a social point of view, the audience did not represent the nation at large. Hanslick,

---

und Novalis' und Weber's, da gelingt ihm stets das Schönste)." (*Nationalzeitung* (Berlin), August 1876. Quoted after Ibid.: 211) Ludwig Speidel recognized the spirit of Weber and Marschner in the work, particularly the first two acts: "Die ersten beiden Akte [...] lehnen sich an die Weber-Marschner'sche Romantik an." *Fremden-Blatt* (Wien), August 1876. Quoted after Ibid.: 226.

242   "Unstreitig ist den deutschen Zuhörern 'Siegfried' am meisten sympathisch geworden. Weshalb, das ist leicht zu sagen. Es hat jeder deutsche Zuhörer ein Stück seines eigensten inneren Lebens darin idealisirt wieder gefunden und lebhaft gefühlt, daß unsere vielgerühmte deutsche Gemüthstiefe auch heute noch kein leerer Wahn ist. Wagner hat damit an eine Grundeigenschaft unseres Herzens angeknüpft [...]. Jener frische Hauch, welcher einst, wie erzählt wird, die der heutigen Generation vorangehenden Deutschen aus Webers 'Freischütz' so zauberisch angeweht hatte, ist nunmehr auch zu uns gedrungen, die wir in der als materiell verschrieenen zweiten Hälfte des neunzehnten Jahrhunderts leben: im 'Siegfried' hat er uns entzückt [...]. Durch ein Werk unserer eigenen Zeit ist in uns diese poetische Stimmung erzeugt worden! Darin beruht der kräftige Beweis ihrer Aechtheit, das bekundet am meisten ihre Unbefangenheit und Aufrichtigkeit. [...] gewissermaßen gleichgültig wird uns, ob Wagner es gemacht hat oder ein Anderer, und unbewußt reichen wir dem Künstler die Palme, indem wir unser tiefstes Empfinden mit dem seinigen und mit seinem Kunstwerke identificiren." Quoted after Ibid.: 123.

for example, stated that these "patrons represented anything but the nation,"[243] and Karl Frenzel went into great detail about the elitist one-dimensionality of Wagner's following in the Berlin *Nationalzeitung*. He mentioned the "exclusion of the folk'"and missed the "mixing of classes so fundamental for a theatrical congregation." Moreover, he pointed out that Bayreuth's position in the countryside made it "undemocratic" and "societally-irrelevant" per se. What he found in Bayreuth was not "a solemn, devotional community," but rather "a combination of a conventional opera house's foyer with the promenade of a spa": high society life rather than a social utopia.[244]

The accusation of exclusivity was also uttered in another sense, namely that the sectarian cult of an individual composer was irreconcilable with the national cause that Wagner and his followership pretended to advance. Karl Frenzel (*Nationalzeitung*) and Otto Gumprecht (*Die Gartenlaube*) lifted out this paradox,[245] whereas in the *Schlesische Presse* (Breslau), Paul von Lindau conceded that "Bayreuth was the most powerful individual achievement one could think of," but simultaneously concluded that "this eminent personal nature of the enterprise actually makes it a complete negation of the national."[246] In the *Vossische Zeitung*, Gustav Engel offered another valid reason why Wagner was unsuitable to obtain the status of a national artist, namely the fact that there was so much dissent among the German nation about his person and art:

---

243 "am wenigsten repräsentiren diese 'Patronatsherren' das deutsche Volk." Quoted after Ibid.: 172.

244 "Das Volk in seiner Masse ist völlig ausgeschlossen. [...] Was einem gewöhnlichen Theaterpublikum Reiz und Werth verleiht, die Mischung der Stände [...] ist hier gänzlich ausgeschlossen. [...] Überall tritt uns das Prinzip der geladenen Gesellschaft entgegen. [...] Die dramatische Kunst, ihrer Natur nach demokratisch und an die städtische Bevölkerung gebunden, bedarf zuerst und zuletzt des Publikums. [...] Das Ganze ist eine Mischung aus dem Foyer eines Theaters und der Promenade eines Badeorts. Von Weihe und Nachdenklichkeit keine Spur." Quoted after Ibid.: 204–207.

245 Frenzel mentions the absurdity of "the common argument among Wagnerians that, in order to fully present the master's work to the German nation, they require a theater that exclusively belongs to Wagner (Vor den Aufführungen behaupteten die Wagnerianer, um das Werk des Meisters voll und ganz dem deutschen Volke zu zeigen, sei eben ein Theater nöthig, das ausschließlich Wagner gehöre)." (Quoted after Ibid.: 213) Gumprecht also criticizes the fact that "he [Wagner] guarantees his following that the alleged grand music-dramatic national festival will be exclusively accesible to the private circle of his friends and devotees (Zugleich gewährt er die Bürgschaft, daß der Dichtercomponist das von ihm in Aussicht gestellte große musikalisch-dramatische Nationalfest nur in dem geschlossenen Kreis seiner Freunde und Verehrer feiern wird)." Quoted after Ibid.: 34.

246 "Bayreuth ist zwar kein 'nationales Unternehmen'; es ist in seinem eminent persönlichen Charakter sogar die volle Negirung des Nationalen. Aber unzweifelhaft ist es die stärkste individuelle Leistung, die zu denken ist." Quoted after Ibid.: 69.

Is Wagner to such an extent accepted by the German people that one can consider the world premiere of a musical drama composed by him in a theater built by him to be a national matter? We wish to speak out strongly against this. [...] The opposition to Wagner is exceptionally huge, he is by no means as unanimously celebrated by his people as Mozart and Beethoven were. [...] We Germans therefore perceive the Bayreuth Festival as a bold attempt by a man who has achieved enormous musical successes amongst his contemporaries and is honored by a certain part of the nation, but simultaneously invokes hate and suspicion by another part. Those are the facts.[247]

A frequently-heard objection to Wagner's *Ring* amongst those Germans who did not sympathize with his endeavors was the immoral, "un-German" nature of the tetralogy's characters,[248] at times compared to Friedrich Hebbel's more

---

247   "Ist Wagner eine so anerkannte Größe im deutschen Volk, daß schon darum allein ein von ihm geschaffenes musikalisches Drama, zum ersten Mal in einem eigens dazu erbauten Hause aufgeführt, als eine nationale Sache gelten könnte? Schon dies müssen wir bestreiten. [...] Die Gegenpartei ist bei Wagner ungewöhnlich groß [...], noch ist kein Gedanke daran, daß er von seinem Volke in ähnlicher Weise gefeiert wäre, wie es Mozart und Beethoven waren. [...] Uns Deutschen gilt daher das Bayreuther Bühnenfestspiel als der kühne Wurf eines Mannes, der unter seinen Zeitgenossen die größten musikalischen Erfolge errungen hat und von einem Theil der Nation gefeiert, von einem andern gehaßt oder doch mit mißtrauischen Augen betrachtet wird. Das ist der Thatbestand." Quoted after Ibid.: 163.

248   Particularly the character of Wotan is frequently rejected. Eduard Hanslick, for example, writes about Wotan: "Should this sententious pedant be worshipped as a divine ideal by 'the German people (Dieser salbungsvolle Pedant soll "von dem deutschen Volk" als göttliches Ideal verehrt werden)?' (Quoted after Ibid.: 178) Max Kalbeck (*Schlesische Zeitung*, Breslau) extends this critique to nearly all of the *Ring*'s characters: 'Wagner indeed has some strange perceptions about the "purely-human" he permanently advocates. Should scoundrels and fools, liars and crooks, thieves and murderers, adulterers and the incestuous, in short, should the type of heroes that generally inhabit the world of Wagner's *Ring* serve as examples of truthful and sane humanity and be presented at the stage of a national theater for the sake of elevating the people at large (Wagner hat in der That merkwürdige Vorstellungen von dem so gern bei ihm hervorgerückten "Reinmenschlichen". Sollen Schufte und Thoren, Lügner und Gauner, Diebe und Mörder, Ehebrecher und Blutschänder, wie sie die Helden seines Nibelungendramas mit wenigen Ausnahmen sämmtlich sind, als die Vorbilder ächter und gesunder Menschlichkeit von der Bühne des Nationaltheaters herab veredelnd und bildend auf das grosse Volk wirken)?' (Quoted after Ibid.: 194) Ludwig Speidel draws a similar conclusion: The morality of the main characters' behavior is nothing but repulsive. It is unbelievable that with the God Wotan, Wagner actually wanted to show us the highest possible German ideal (Wenn wir auf den sittlichen Gehalt ihres Handelns sehen, können sie uns nur ab- und zurückstoßen.

dignified rendition in *Die Nibelungen*.[249] Here it becomes clear how difficult the *Ring* poem – conceived during Wagner's revolutionary period and serving both to display the flaws of contemporary society and the moral freedom of post-Revolutionary humanity – could live up to its by now acquired function of an affirmation of supreme German-national values in an increasingly conservative society.

But the most important aspect of the widespread dismissal of Wagner's "immoral" characters was the common idea that the arrogance, narcissism and megalomania of Wotan equaled the character of his creator. In a speech held on 17 August 1876, after the first performance series, Wagner had stated that "now that you have seen what we're capable of, it has become clear that, if you want it, we can have an art."[250] Even if Wagner merely intended to voice his hope that, after all the efforts made, the festival would not turn out to be a once-only event, it immediately became a bone of contention among his opponents, as it seemed to imply that German art had first saw the light with the advent of himself. Ludwig Speidel called it "an unprecedented impudence" that Wagner dared to "renounce the glorious past of the German people and its holiest achievements."[251] Gustav Engel also countered Wagner's presumptuous statement with the words that one could not deny that there had already been "Germans, German composers, and even German opera composers in the past."[252] In the *Neue Evangelische Kirchen-Zeitung* (Berlin), Hermann Messner acknowledged that "Wagner, with serious determination, had fought the triviality of opera," but also concluded that "Mozart, Gluck, and Weber had already

---

In dem Gotte Wotan wollte uns Wagner das höchste deutsche Ideal vor die Augen stellen)." Quoted after Ibid.: 228.

249   Karl Frenzel, for example, writes: "The relationship between Siegfried and Brünnhilde in Wagner's *Ring* disgusts me; how much nobler and magnanimous is Hebbel's Siegfried, the true German hero (Das Verhältniß Siegfrieds zu Brünnhilde bei Wagner widert mich an; um wie viel edler und großherziger ist Hebbel's Siegfried, der wahre deutsche Held)." Quoted after Ibid.: 209.

250   "Sie haben gesehen, was wir können. Wenn Sie wollen, haben wir nun eine Kunst."

251   "Nie ist mit kühlerem Muth eine größere Frechheit ausgesprochen worden. [...] Auf gut Deutsch wollen sie besagen: Hier, in meinen Nibelungen habt ihr das deutsche Normal-kunstwerk; ihr braucht blos Ja zu sagen, um es zu besitzen. Aber wir hoffen und glauben, daß das deutsche Volk dieses Ja und Amen nicht sprechen werde, denn es bedeutete einfach eine Abdankung seiner Vergangenheit, ein Preisgeben seiner heiligsten geistigen Güter." Quoted after Ibid.: 227.

252   "Nein, so schlimm ist es mit uns doch nicht bestellt; es hat auch schon vor Wagner Deutsche, deutsche Componisten und deutsche Operncomponisten gegeben." Quoted after Ibid.: 166.

guided the way through their masterworks, but without the excessive reflection of their successor, and with more respect for the laws of musicality."[253]

Summing up, Engel's conviction that Wagner's art was simply too controversial to function as a symbol of the newly-won unity of the German people seems to be justified. In its embrace of the future, the Bayreuth Festival obviously conflicted with the widespread tendency to canonize and "musealize" artefacts of the national past. But this situation soon changed. Already in 1876, some commentators characterized Wagner's *Ring* as less pioneering than it appears.[254] Ernst Lehmann for example, writing for the *Frankfurter Zeitung*, characterized the *Ring* as the monumental echo of a "bygone Romantic age that strove for total art and hoped to achieve a German art by imitating ancient Greece."[255] In accordance with that, Lehman saw Wagner's musical drama

---

253   "Es wird ihm für alle Zeiten das Verdienst ungeschmälert bleiben müssen, daß er mit ernster Stimme die Oper von ihrer leichtfertigen Bahn zurückgerufen hat. [...] Nur haben Mozart, Gluck, Weber durch ihre Meisterwerke, allerdings ohne die Ueberfülle von Reflexion, schon vorher den rechten Weg gewiesen, aber [...] die Musik musikalischer gelassen." Quoted after Ibid.: 79.

254   Both Eduard Hanslick and Karl Frenzel observed that Wagner's insistence on stage magic recalled the outdated genres of *Zauberoper* and the *Féerie*. Hanslick pointed out that "Wagner's *Ring* indeed has a lot in common with the genre of magic pieces and *Féeries*. There is a curious discrepancy between Wagner's pure, idealist pretenses and these highly material effects (In der That hat Wagner's 'Nibelungenring' am meisten Aehnlichkeit mit dem Genre der Zauberstücke und 'Feerien'. Zu der reinen Idealität, welche Wagner seinem Werke nachrühmt, stehen diese sehr materiellen Effecte in seltsamen Widerspruch)." (Quoted after Ibid.: 179) Frenzel: "The *Zauberoper*, the magic play is finished. The Wolfsschlucht of *Der Freischütz* transforms upward into the Valkyrie's rock and the Walhalla, downward into Nibelheim and the bottom of the Rhine. The philosphical element is accompanied by a Romanticism full of Baroque exaggeration. As a playwright with an accute dramatic instinct, Hebbel had pushed this entire magic sphere into the background. Wagner, on the contrary, a man who has completely different goals and is absolutely incapable of presenting a simple, human action, emphasizes the supernatural elements to such an extent that the neutral spectator no longer feels involved with the vicissitudes of the characters (So ist die Zauberoper, das Zauberspiel fertig. Die Wolfsschlucht des 'Freischütz' dehnt sich nach oben zum Walkürenfelsen und zur Walhalla, nach unten zu Nibelheim und dem Rheingrund aus. Zu dem philosophischen Element [...] gesellt sich in barocker Übertreibung das Romantische. Mit dem Instinkt des geborenen Dramatikers hat Hebbel diese ganze Zauberwelt in den Hintergrund gedrängt [...]. Wagner, der ganz andere Zwecke verfolgte und dem es absolut versagt ist, eine einfache, menschliche Handlung auf die Bühne zu bringen, betonte dagegen das Uebersinnliche und Unirdische in einer Weise, das der Unbefangene zugleich das Urtheil und die Theilnahme gegenüber seinen Figuren verliert)." Quoted after Ibid.: 209.

255   "Man muß sich einen Augenblick die Geisteratmosphäre vergegenwärtigen, in der der Dichterkomponist zum künstlerischen Bewußtsein aufwuchs. Diese Atmosphäre ist die der Romantik. Die Allkunst ist keine Erfindung Wagners und auch der Rückgriff auf den

chiefly as the conclusion of a past artistic development, and as an amalgam of German musical history:

> Wagner, and even more so his supporters, have typified the musical drama as it unfolded in Bayreuth as the art of the future; I'd prefer to recognize in it the grand, monumental conclusion of a past artistic development [...]. Something similar applies to Wagner's music, which I'd rather call a music of the past than a music of the future. I witness in Wagner's *Nibelungen* a cross section of every achievement of German music from its cradle until today.[256]

As a monument to German music in general and nineteenth-century German Romantic opera in particular, Wagner's art could indeed be canonized and musealized. We find this tendency towards canonization and musealization clearly in Bayreuth, where after the master's death in 1882, the performances acquired an extremely prescriptive, fixed and ritualistic character, accompanied by a highly conservative form of German nationalist ideology. Outside Bayreuth, Wagner's oeuvre became a treasure of the German *Bildungsbürgertum*, and arguably the most refined branch of the nineteenth-century German opera canon. Here the national significance of his work, separated from the extremely personal and ideologically radical cult of Bayreuth, could prosper as well.

Wagner also became the greatest musical export product of the Wilhelmine era, spurring music-dramatic explorations of native myths elsewhere in Europe, often with a marked cultural-national imprint.[257] Considering the more progressive elements of Wagner's art, he sometimes became the idol of a Europe-wide counter-culture – be it against normative bourgeois culture or the nationalism of the establishment.[258] At the same time, Wagner's incredible

---

Mythos überhaupt und den deutschen Mythos insbesondere war bereits vor ihm in Aussicht genommen." Quoted after Ibid.: 128.

256 "Wagner und noch mehr seine Anhänger haben das musikalische Drama, wie es dort in Bayreuth vor den erstaunten Augen des Zuschauers sich entfaltete, als die Kunst der Zukunft bezeichnet; ich möchte es vielmehr den gewaltigen und großartigen Abschluß einer vergangenen Kunstentwicklung nennen [...] auch die Wagner'sche Tonkunst viel eher eine Musik der Vergangenheit, als eine Musik der Zukunft zu nennen. Ich finde in Wagner's Nibelungen gleichsam einen Auszug alles dessen, was die deutsche Musik seit ihrem ersten Recitative bis zu dem heutigen Tage geleistet." Quoted after Ibid.: 131–132.

257 This we find, for example, in Scandinavia, but also in the Spanish region Catalunya. See Salmi 2005 and Infiesta 2001.

258 Noteworthy in this respect is the popularity Wagner enjoyed among German nationalists in Vienna who opposed the Habsburg regime. In the *Kölnische Zeitung*, Wilhelm Mohr

influence on the course of European opera and music history became a symbol of the increasing power of the Wilhelmine Empire. As late as 1914, Wagner's continuing influence on French art was the subject of heated discussion about a gradual "German cultural occupation" of France in the run-up to the First World War. The by then already 79-year-old composer Camille Saint-Saëns actually likened the ongoing *Wagnérisme* to the "preparation of the planned conquest of France by way of a peaceful penetration."[259]

The drumbeat of German national politics has never abandoned Wagner and the Bayreuth Festival. As much as this applies to the darkest days of German national history, Wagner's art continues to be associated with positive values of German culture as well, such as the cultivation and preservation of art, the ideal that art must strive for more than merely trivial entertainment, and the idea that opera, in its ultimate merging of music and the other arts, can be a transformative experience. In short, Wagner's operas and the festival he designed for them have institutionalized many of the elements of "the opera that the German wants," the opera to which Carl Maria von Weber, and many other German opera makers and critics with him, have so long aspired. It has clearly granted these ideals a permanent, prominent place in German culture.

---

moreover noticed that within the Romanic world, it were never the capitals, but always provincial towns with a progressive counter-culture that vindicated Wagner: "Not only in London and Paris, also in Italy and Spain there is a battle about the meaning and value of the music of the future. In the chauvinist capitals of these Romanic countries, adversaries are in the majority, but in the progressive provincial cities such as Bologna or Barcelona, there are many devotees of the brave innovator (Wie in London und Paris, so streitet man auch in Italien und Spanien über den Sinn und Werth der Musik der Zukunft. In den nationalstolzen Hauptstädten dieser romanischen Länder überwiegen die Gegner, in den aufstrebenden Provincialstädten, wie in Bologna oder in Barcelona, die Verehrer des kühnen Neuerers)." August 1876, quoted after Großman-Vendrey 1977: 108.

259   "De préparer par la pénétration pacifique la conquête projetée." *L'Écho de Paris*, 21 November 1914. Quoted after Schmid 2008: 90.

Epilogue

This book had two objectives. First, as the surtitle indicates, it has been my goal to demonstrate how a German opera was articulated in the period between 1798 and 1876, tracing the formulation and development of what I call a German opera identity. I have characterized this opera identity as complying with a more general cultural self-image current in Germany while contrasting itself against the perceived opera identities of other nations. The second objective was to explain why this articulation was problematic, and to scrutinize how nineteenth-century advocates of German opera handled the problems concerned.

The articulation of a German opera identity has been approached from the hypothesis that the relation of German opera to the construction of national identity in music and society is essentially problematic, not only in comparison with other fields of German nineteenth-century music life, but also to manifestations of national opera elsewhere in nineteenth-century Europe. I have signaled a *German Opera Problem*, revolving around the question how to formulate a national opera identity in a music culture that, as I have argued, in many cases was articulated in opposition to opera. This question forms a thread throughout this book, which chiefly investigates the answers and solutions formulated by composers, librettists, and opera critics in a vast array of nineteenth-century music journals, as well as in the creation of operas themselves.

In line with common formulations of German national identity, German musical identity has often been defined as serious, all-encompassing or universal, and ascetic, comprising "depth (*Tiefe*), hard work (*Arbeit*), thoroughness (*Gründlichkeit*), intellect (*Geist*), and inwardness (*Innerlichkeit*)." This ascetic ideal was also realized on the level of libretto plotlines, generally idealizing bourgeois morals while criticizing aristocratic manners.

Whereas early nineteenth-century German musicians and critics could boast of impressive achievements in the fields of instrumental and church music, the accomplishments of German opera were modest in comparison. Proponents of German opera used this circumstance to their advantage by pointing out the growth potential of the genre in comparison to the established Italian and French traditions, and contemplated a bright future for German opera by emphasizing the serious and ascetic qualities of German composers. Italian opera in particular was frequently presented as being "over the hill" and decadent, comparable to attacks on French literature and drama in the late eighteenth century. French opera was often depicted as cerebral, formulaic, and lacking true musical qualities due to its focus on the dramatic text.

© KONINKLIJKE BRILL NV, LEIDEN, 2019 | DOI:10.1163/9789004245389_008

One of the remarkable features of early nineteenth-century discourse on German opera is the fact that the conceptualization of the genre often preceded the actual composition of works. Important aspects of this conceptualization were dramatic veracity, symphonic profundity, and – last but not least – organic unity and formal coherence, a notion taken over from German discourse on instrumental music and one of the most important tools to vindicate the German qualities of an opera. The *AMZ* reviews of Beethoven's *Fidelio*, Hoffmann's *Undine* and Weber's *Der Freischütz* show the extent to which opera criticism was used to re-affirm these aspects of a German opera identity. Even if the enormous popularity of *Der Freischütz* demonstrates that the work lived up to the requirements of "the opera that the German wants," as Weber himself defined it, several critics felt that the folksy *Singspiel* esthetic of *Der Freischütz* did not meet the demand of sophistication expected from a national opera.

Agendas to elevate German opera into a more sophisticated, serious, and at the same time distinguishably German genre were addressed in the second and third chapters. The second chapter discussed Romanticism, more specifically Novalis's notion of "Romanticization," as one way to realize a more elevated, genuinely German form of opera. I have explained how Romanticism became one of the most important markers of the identity of early nineteenth-century German opera, and how the discourses of German national and Romantic opera shared ideals such as dramatic veracity, the power of opera to create new worlds, and the common emphasis on organic unity and austerity. At the same time, writers such as Franz Horn and E.T.A. Hoffmann questioned the tendency of many German operas to indulge in trivial Romanticism, and propagated a more thorough Romanticization in which a mysterious, otherworldly realm opens up and transforms everyday reality. *Singspiel*, with its alternation of spoken dialogues and musical numbers, served as a viable structure for displaying the co-existence and oscillation between everyday life and a supernatural world.

At the same time, composers such as Louis Spohr and Carl Maria von Weber felt that, after *Der Freischütz*, German opera should strive to attain a higher level of sophistication and musical unity by discarding spoken dialogues and by becoming through-composed. Their attempts to create all-sung operas with *Jessonda* and *Euryanthe* (both 1823) inevitably obliged them to use forms, styles, and character types derived from foreign, established opera traditions. Particularly in the case of *Euryanthe*, these borrowings – together with Weber's overly "German," learned attempt to musically express every single detail of the text – constrained the opera's popularity among German audiences. Yet despite campaigns for and experiments with all-sung opera in the 1820s, the *Singspiel* constellation of spoken dialogues and musical numbers remained remarkably prominent on the German opera stage. In spite of its trivial or folksy associations, spoken dialogue remained a popular element and a strong marker of a German operatic identity, arguably causing a stylistic stagnation of German opera after the "roaring 1820s."

Although the success of *Der Freischütz* in 1821 did not yet lead to a national opera tradition comparable to that of Italy or France, it did provide German opera with access to the international opera scene. The focus on German opera abroad in the fourth chapter is informative in three respects. It reveals German opera's exemplary function for national opera movements elsewhere in Europe, while simultaneously showing foreign conceptions of German opera and the way in which foreign experiences helped to shape notions of German opera in the homeland.

In Russia and England, German opera and its discourse were initially welcomed as an alternative to the hegemony of Italian opera, but later dismissed as a potential threat to the native product. This decreasing popularity was also related to the fact that, after 1830, German opera production ran dry. In France, interest for German opera was chiefly sparked by the French vogue for Romanticism that started in the 1820s. French critics often deplored the underdeveloped Romanticism and lack of serious character of the German operas brought to Parisian stages, showing that important markers of a German operatic identity had already reached Paris before any substantial acquaintance of German operas through performance attendance. Besides seriousness and Romanticism, commitment and collective effort – for example the achievements of the choir – were often highlighted in reviews of German-language opera companies.

For the esteem of German opera at home, the performances abroad presented a risk-free advantage: foreign success affirmed the idea that this national art form was gradually taking over the world, whereas foreign maltreatment or indifference of local audiences towards German-language companies reinforced feelings of cultural superiority. The contact with foreign opera practices helped to establish the principal of fidelity to the opera score and its protection against *pasticcio* practices, still relatively common outside the German-speaking world but increasingly abhorred within the country. At the same time, foreign performances of German works contributed to the dissemination of the ideal of fidelity to the opera score outside the German-speaking world.

The fifth chapter discussed how Wagner handled the *German Opera Problem* and how he articulated a German operatic identity in his works and writings. At the start of his career, Wagner appears to have been aware of several aspects of the *German Opera Problem*. In his early writings (1834–1840), he questioned German musicians' glorification of seriousness and their misplaced sense of superiority, and pleaded for a cosmopolitan fusion instead. Wagner hoped to realize this cosmopolitan fusion by writing grand opéras for Paris. During a disastrous sojourn in the French capital (1839–1842), Wagner redirected his course and began to cultivate his German identity like no opera composer before him. His anti-French attitude was motivated by personal experiences, but simultaneously rode the wave of increasing Francophobia in the German-speaking world, propelled by the Rhine Crisis of 1840 and ultimately culminating in the Franco-Prussian War of 1870–1871.

Wagner's cultivation of his German identity was all the more necessary because his breakthrough with *Rienzi* (1842) had made him a noisy, French sensualist in the eyes of many German critics. In *Der Fliegende Holländer* (1843), *Tannhäuser* (1845) and *Lohengrin* (1850), Wagner managed to incorporate many state of the art elements of French and Italian opera while branding his art as essentially German. In that sense, he managed to solve one of the crucial aspects of the *German Opera Problem*, even if his self-centered understanding of opera history and demonization of Meyerbeer made him obnoxious to some contemporaries and to many later critics. In these works, he simultaneously resuscitated the relatively stale genre of Romantic opera, and endowed it with a more elevated and social-critical character.

The post-1848 years of Wagner's banishment are frequently interpreted as a period in which he abandoned the national cause. I challenge this idea, because the tenor of most of his *Zürich Writings* – in which Wagner, more than ever before, presents himself as the type of serious German composer he had previously abhorred – is in line with previous campaigns for German opera. Wagner's glorification of the universally-human and his Graecophilia can be understood as a variation on the common trope of the universally-German, the idea that Germans are akin to the ancient Greeks in having an exclusive capacity to address universal issues. In his most all-encompassing artistic project, *Der Ring des Nibelungen* (1848–1876), Wagner also managed to address a universal theme by means of a story imbued with national significance. In *Die Meistersinger von Nürnberg* (1868), the merging of his artistic and societal agenda with the national chauvinism of his day is even more outspoken.

It felt natural to conclude this journey through nineteenth-century opera history with an elaborate chapter on Wagner's role in the formulation of a German opera identity, as I do believe that, more than any other composer before him, Wagner shaped the image of German opera and, arguably, offered the most convincing and successful solution to the supposed *German Opera Problem*. In a scholarly climate in which teleological explanations are suspect, this might sound frightening or utterly simplifying. My point is, however, not that Wagner perfected anything, but rather that his appropriation and rewriting of opera history, while objectionable, was both highly effective and productive. At the same time, his outlooks and achievements are unthinkable without a thorough understanding of the previous campaigns for German opera and of nineteenth-century German identity construction on a more general level. I hope to have contributed to this necessary contextualization.

Wagner simultaneously is a highly problematic figure who affected German opera production and performance practices in severe ways. In that respect, the story certainly does not end with him. As much as Wagner may have left its mark on the nineteenth-century formulation of a German opera identity, his status and oeuvre simultaneously have cast a shadow eclipsing both his successors and, arguably more regrettably, also his forefathers. The predominance of Wagner clearly frustrated future developments in the final decades of the nineteenth century, as most attempts at writing emphatically German operas merely resulted in *Wagner-Epigonalismus*. On the contrary, developments deemed innovative in German opera – such as Richard Strauss's *Salome* (1905) or *Der Rosenkavalier* (1911) – generally departed from the Teutonic *Leitkultur*, preferring a Viennese, sensual, frivolous, and at times operetta-like esthetic instead. In that respect, Wagner's achievements can be seen as a dead end rather than a promising model for the foundation of a German opera tradition in the years after his demise.

Wagner's prominence also had severe consequences for the status of German predecessors who had written operas with spoken dialogues. In a way, operas by composers such as Spohr or Marschner already got slightly out of fashion from the 1840s onwards. But in the late nineteenth century, when national canon formation processes became more important, these could have acquired a more prominent place, given their esthetic quality and cultural-societal significance. In our current conception of more or less canonic repertoire, it appears that there is only room for three or four German operas with spoken dialogue: Mozart's *Zauberflöte* and *Die Entführung*, as well as Beethoven's *Fidelio* due to the master composer status of their respective creators, and Weber's *Freischütz* because of its significance as *Nationaloper*.

Between 1908 and 1922, an interesting project was carried out by Hans Pfitzner. Pfitzner, an outspokenly chauvinist cultural pessimist, attempted to re-animate the German Romantic opera repertoire by creating all-sung versions of three *Singspiel*-inspired works – E.T.A. Hoffmann's *Undine* and Marschner's *Der Vampyr* and *Der Templer und die Jüdin* – in the hope of making them more sustainable for the future. Although Pfitzner's project was certainly intended to salvage a waning cultural heritage, it simultaneously signals an attitude towards early nineteenth-century German opera that has become increasingly strong in recent decades, now that *Biedermeier* Romanticism is more than ever before considered as outdated or ideologically questionable. It presupposes that – performed in their original shape, including spoken dialogue – many of these works are untenable onstage.

Recent revivals of Marschner's *Der Vampyr*, for example, display this mentality. A 2014 outdoor performance from *Oper Halle* cut nearly half of the music while having the dialogues replaced by narrations. The *Komische Oper Berlin* produced the work in 2016, rid of its dialogues and with extensive insertions by contemporary composer Johannes Hoffmann. A 2017 production at the *Theater Koblenz* finally offered the entire premiere score, including spoken dialogue, in a 2009 edition by musicologist Egon Voss. This integral performance reasserted my conviction that revivals of this particular work, and arguably also of other early nineteenth-century German operas, are tenable indeed.

In order to appreciate this repertoire, contextual knowledge and sensibility for early nineteenth-century operatic style is of crucial importance. In the end, I hope that this book not only shows the relevance of early nineteenth-century German opera for our notions of German opera identity, for our understanding of the relation between discourse on music and national culture in general, but also for the development of German opera after 1850. Hopefully it will ultimately also contribute to a renewed engagement with these works in the realm of musical performance.

Bibliography

Quoted Historical Newspapers and Periodicals

Allgemeine musikalische Zeitung, Leipzig: Bärenreiter, 1798–1848.

Berliner allgemeine musikalische Zeitung. Berlin: Schlesinger, 1826–1830.

Berlinische Nachrichten von Staats- und gelehrten Sachen. Berlin: Haude und Spenerschen Buchhandlung, 1812.

Caecilia, eine Zeitschrift für die musikalische Welt. Mainz: Schott, 1825.

Deutsche Zeitung. Wien: 1876.

Die Horen. Stuttgart: Cotta (Schiller), 1796.

Die Muse. Leipzig: Göschen, 1822.

Die Musen; Eine norddeutsche Zeitschrift. Berlin: Hitzig (De la Motte Fouqué / Neumann), 1812.

Dramaturgisches Wochenblatt in nächster Beziehung auf die königlichen Schauspiele zu Berlin. Berlin: 1815–1816.

Dresdner Abend-Zeitung. Dresden: Hell, 1822–1841.

l'Écho de Paris. Paris: Blanc, 1914.

Europa, Chronik der gebildeten Welt. Karlsruhe: Verlag des artistischen Instituts, 1841.

Gazette musicale de Paris. Paris: Schlesinger, 1834.

Im neuen Reich; Wochenschrift für das Leben des deutschen Volkes in Staat, Wissenschaft und Kunst. Leipzig: Hirzel, 1876.

Journal des Débats. Paris: Bertin, 1801–1831.

Kölnische Zeitung. Köln, 1876.

Le Corsaire; journal des spectacles, de la littérature, des arts et des modes. Paris: Viennot, 1824.

Le Courrier des spectacles; Journal des théatres et de litterature. Paris: 1801.

Le Globe. Paris: 1827.

Literarisches Wochenblatt. Leipzig: Kotzebue, 1818.

Mercure de France, litteraire et politique. Paris: l'Imprimerie de Didot Jeune, 1801.

Morgenblatt für gebildete Stände. Stuttgart: Cotta, 1812–1816.

Münchner Theater-Journal. München: Carl, 1814.

Münchner allgemeine musikalische Zeitung. München: Sidler, 1828.

Musikalisches Wochenblatt. Leipzig: E.W. Fritsch, 1872.

Nationalzeitung. Berlin: Wolff, 1876.

Neue evangelische Kirchen-Zeitung. Berlin: 1876.

Neue freie Presse. Wien, 1876.

Neue Zeitschrift für Musik. Leipzig: Robert Schumann / Franz Brendel, 1834–1846.

Neues Wiener Tageblatt. Wien, 1876.

Norddeutsche allgemeine Zeitung. Berlin: Norddeutsche Buchdruckerei und Verlag-sanstalt, 1871.

Quarterly Musical Magazine & Review. London: Baldwin, Cradock & Joy, 1821–1828.

Revue et Gazette musicale de Paris. Paris: Schlesinger, 1835–1877.

Revue musicale. Paris: Fétis, 1827–1835.

Rheinische Zeitung. Köln: 1843.

Schlesische Presse. Breslau: Trewendt, 1876.

Signale für die musikalische Welt. Leipzig: Verlag der Signale: 1869.

The Atlas. London: 1829.

The Chronicle. London: 1824.

The European Magazine. London: Sherwood, Jones and Co., 1824.

The Harmonicon. London: Samuel Leigh, 1824–1833.

The Literary Chronicle. London: Davidson, 1825–1826.

The Morning Chronicle. London: 1826–1831.

The Musical Journal. London: 1840.

The Musical World. London: Novello, 1838–1857.

The New Monthly Magazine and Literary Journal. London: Henry Colburn, 1826.

The Observer. London: 1824.

Vossische Zeitung. Berlin: 1816–1876.

Wiener Zeitschrift für Kunst, Literatur, Theater und Mode. Wien: Gerold, 1823.

Zeitung für die elegante Welt. Berlin: Janke, 1834–1843.

Zeitung für Theater und Musik zur Unterhaltung gebildeter, unbefangener Leser. Berlin, Schlesinger, 1821.

Online Sources

www.deutsche-biographie.de, Bayerische Staatsbibliothek.

www.documentarchiv.de, Riedel, Kai, web master.

www.oxfordonline.com, Root, Deane, editor in chief.

www.ripm.org, Cohen, Robert H., founder and director.

www.spinnet.eu, Study Platform on Interlocking Nationalisms.

www.weber-gesamtausgabe.de, Veit, Joachim, editor in chief.

Literature

Abbate, Carolyn. 'Opera as Symphony, a Wagnerian Myth.' *Analyzing Opera; Verdi and Wagner*, Abbate, Carolyn and Roger Parker, eds. Berkeley: University of California Press, 1989: 92–124.

Abbate, Carolyn and Roger Parker. *A History of Opera; The Last 400 Years.* London: Penguin Books Ltd., 2012.

Abraham, Gerald. 'The Operas of Alexei Verstovsky.' *19ᵗʰ-century Music* 7/3 (1984): 326–335.

Adorno, Theodor W. *Klangfiguren; Musikalische Schriften 1.* Frankfurt am Main: Suhrkamp Verlag, 1959.

Adorno, Theodor W. *Musikalische Schriften IV; Moments Musicaux; Impromptus.* Frankfurt: Suhrkamp Verlag, 2003 [1982].

Amburger, Erik. 'Musikleben in St. Petersburg um 1800.' *Kulturbeziehungen in Mittel- und Osteuropa im 18. und 19. Jahrhundert; Festschrift für Heinz Ischreyt zum 65. Geburtstag.* Kessler, Wolfgang a.o., eds. Berlin: Verlag Ulrich Camen, 1982: 201–210.

Anderson, Benedict. *Imagined Communities; Reflections on the Origins and Spread of Nationalism* (second revised edition). London: Verso, 1991 [1983].

Anderson, Benedict. *Long-Distance Nationalism; World Capitalism and the Rise of Identity Politics* (Wertheim Lecture, Centre for Asian Studies Amsterdam), 1992.

Angermüller, Rudolph. '"Les Mystères d'Isis" (1801) und "Don Juan" (1805, 1834) auf der Bühne der Pariser Oper.' *Mozart-Jahrbuch 1980–83 des Zentralinstituts für Mozartforschung der internationalen Stiftung Mozarteum Salzburg.* Angermüller, Rudolph and Dietrich Berke, eds. Kassel: Bärenreiter, 1983: 32–97.

Apel, Willi. *Harvard Dictionary of Music* (second edition). London: Heinemann Educational, 1970.

Applegate, Celia. *Bach in Berlin; Nation and Culture in Mendelssohn's Revival of the St. Matthew Passion.* Ithaca: Cornell University Press, 2005.

Applegate, Celia. 'How German is it? Nationalism and the Idea of Serious Music in the Early Nineteenth Century.' *Nineteenth-century Music* 21/3 (1998): 274–296.

Applegate, Celia. 'What is German music? Reflections on the role of art in the creation of the nation.' *German Studies Review* 15 (1992): 21–32.

Applegate, Celia and Pamela Potter. *Music and German National Identity.* Chicago: Chicago University Press, 2002.

Arend, Max. *Gluck. Eine Biographie.* Berlin: Schuster & Loeffler, 1921.

Aspden, Suzanne. 'Opera and National Identity.' *The Cambridge Companion to Opera Studies.* Till, Nicholas, ed. Cambridge: Cambridge University Press, 2012: 276–297.

Auhagen, Wolfgang. *Studien zur Tonartencharakteristik in theoretischen Schriften und Kompositionen vom späten 17. bis zum Beginn des 20. Jahrhunderts.* Frankfurt am Main: Peter Lang, 1983.

Austern, Linda Phyllis. '"Alluring the auditorie to effeminacie"; Music and the Idea of the Feminine in Early Modern England.' *Music and Letters* 74 (1993): 343–354.

Barish, Jonas A. *The Antitheatrical Prejudice.* Berkeley: University of California Press, 1981.

Baumgartner, Karin. 'In Search of Literary Mothers Across the Rhine. The Influence of Genlis and Staël on the Writing of Helmina von Chézy.' *Women's Writing* 18/1 (2011): 50–67.

Beck, Ulrich and Edgar Grande. *Cosmopolitan Europe*. Cambridge: Polity, 2007.

Becker, Wolfgang. *Die deutsche Oper in Dresden unter der Leitung von Carl Maria von Weber 1817–1826*. Berlin: Colloquium Verlag, 1962.

Beer, Otto. *Mozart und das Wiener Singspiel*. Wien: unpublished dissertation, 1932.

Behler, Ernst. *Friedrich Schlegel in Selbstzeugnissen und Bilddokumenten*. Reinbek bei Hamburg: Rohwohlt Taschenbuch Verlag GmbH, 1978 [1966].

Behler, Ernst, ed. *Kritische Friedrich-Schlegel-Ausgabe; Erste Abteilung; Kritische Neuausgabe; Zweiter Band; Charakteristiken und Kritiken I*. München: Schöningh, 1967.

Beller, Manfred. 'Perception, Image, Imagology.' *Imagology: The Cultural Construction and Literary Representation of National Characters – A Critical Survey* (Studia Imagologica 13). Beller, Manfred and Joep Leerssen, eds. Amsterdam: Rodopi, 2007: 3–16.

Beller-McKenna, Daniel. *Brahms and the German Spirit*. Cambridge, Massachusetts: Harvard University Press, 2004.

Benjamin, Walter. *Illuminationen; Ausgewählte Schriften 1*. Frankfurt am Main: Suhrkamp Verlag, 1995.

Benz, Richard. *Märchen-Dichtung der Romantiker; Mit einer Vorgeschichte*. Gotha: F.A. Perthes, 1908.

Bergeron, Katherine and Philip V. Bohlman, eds. *Disciplining Music; Musicology and Its Canons*. Chicago: University of Chicago Press, 1992.

Berlioz, Hector. *Memoires de Hector Berlioz, membre de l'Institut de France; Comprenant ses voyages en Italie, en Allemagne, en Russie et en le Angleterre, 1803–1865*. Paris: Michel Levy Frères Éditeurs, 1870.

Berlioz, Hector. *Grand traité de l'instrumentation*. Paris: Schönenberger, 1843.

Bermbach, Udo. *Der Wahn des Gesamtkunstwerks; Richard Wagners politisch-ästhetische Utopie*. Frankfurt am Main: Fischer, 1994.

Bermbach, Udo. *Richard Wagner in Deutschland; Rezeptionen – Verfälschungen*. Stuttgart: J.B. Metzler, 2011.

Berry, Mark. *Treacherous Bonds and Laughing Fire; Politics and Religion in Wagner's Ring*. Aldershot: Ashgate, 2006.

Biddlecombe, George. *English Opera from 1834 to 1864 with Particular Reference to the Works of Michael Balfe*. New York: Garland, 1994.

Bischoff, Bodo. 'Von Teilnamslosigkeit über Skepsis zur Faszination. Robert Schumanns Begegnungen mit Richard Wagner und seinen Dresdner Opern.' *Die Dresdener Oper im 19. Jahrhundert*. Heinemann, Michael and Hans John, eds. Laaber: Laaber Verlag, 1995: 227–241.

Bloom, Peter A. *François-Joseph Fétis and the Revue Musicale (1827–1835)*. Ann Arbor: UMI Press, 1975.

Bonds, Mark Evan. *Music as Thought; Listening to the Symphony in the Age of Beethoven*. Princeton: Princeton University Press, 2006.

Borst, Arno. 'Barbarossas Erwachen; Zur Geschichte der deutschen Identität.' *Identität; Poetik und Hermeneutik*. Marquard, Otto, ed. Paderborn: Fink, 1979: 17–60.

Boterman, Frits. *Moderne Geschiedenis van Duitsland; 1800-heden (tweede, uitgebreide druk)*. Amsterdam: Arbeiderspers, 2005.

Bourdieu, Pierre. *Distinction; critique sociale de jugement*. Paris: Les Éditions de Minuit, 1979.

Brodbeck, David. *Defining Deutschtum; Political Ideology, German Identity, and Music-Critical Discourse in Liberal Vienna*. Oxford: Oxford University Press, 2014.

Bruckmüller, Ernst. *Nation Österreich; Sozialhistorische Aspekte ihrer Entwicklung*. Wien: Hermann Böhlaus Nachf., 1984.

Bruckner-Bigenwald, Martha. *Die Anfänge der Allgemeinen Musikalischen Zeitung*. Hilversum: Frits A.M. Knuf, 1965.

Brzoska, Matthias. *Die Idee des Gesamtkunstwerks in der Musiknovellistik der Julimonarchie* (Thurnauer Schriften zum Musiktheater; Bd. 14). Laaber: Laaber Verlag, 1995.

Brzoska, Matthias. 'Meyerbeer: *Robert le Diable* and *Les Huguenots*.' *The Cambridge Companion to Grand Opera*. Charlton, David, ed. Cambridge: Cambridge University Press, 2003: 189–207.

Burke, Kevin Robert. *Propagating a National Genre; German Writers on German Opera, 1798–1830*. University of Cincinnatti: unpublished dissertation, 2010.

Butler, E.M. *The Tyranny of Greece over Germany; A Study of the Influence Exercised by Greek Art and Poetry over the Great German Writers of the 18th, 19th and 20th Centuries*. Cambridge: Cambridge University Press, 1935.

Campbell, James Stuart. *V.F. Odoyevsky and the Formation of Russian Musical Taste in the Nineteenth Century*. New York: Garland, 1989.

Cannone, Belinda. *La réception des opéras de Mozart dans la presse parisienne (1793–1829)*. Paris: Klincksieck, 1991.

Charlton, David. 'Introduction.' *The Cambridge Companion to Grand Opera*. Charlton, David, ed. Cambridge: Cambridge University Press, 2003: 1–20.

Chorley, Henry. *Thirty Years' Musical Recollections; In Two Volumes: Volume 1*. London: Hurst and Blackett, 1862.

Clayton, Martin, Trevor Herbert, and Richard Middleton, eds. *The Cultural Study of Music; A Critical Introduction*. New York: Routledge, 2003.

Curtis, Benjamin. *Music Makes the Nation; Nationalist Composers and Nation Building in Nineteenth-Century Europe*. Amherst, NY: Cambria Press, 2008.

Cramer, Ch. Fr. *Anecdotes sur W.G. Mozart*. Paris: Cramer, 1801.

Dahlhaus, Carl. 'Das ungeschriebene Finale. Zur musikalischen Dramaturgie von Webers *Oberon*.' *Carl Maria von Weber* (Musik-Konzepte 52) (1986): 79–85.

Dahlhaus, Carl. *Die Idee der absoluten Musik*. Kassel: Bärenreiter, 1994 (1978).

Dahlhaus, Carl. *Die Musik des 19. Jahrhunderts* (Neues Handbuch der Musikwissenschaft, Band 6). Laaber: Laaber Verlag, 1980.

Dahlhaus, Carl. 'Große romantische Oper und *grand opéra*: "Euryanthe", "Robert le Diable", "Genoveva" und "Lohengrin."'*Europäische Romantik in der Musik. Band 2. Oper und symphonischer Stil 1800–1850*. Dahlhaus, Carl and Norbert Miller, eds. Stuttgart: J.B. Metzler Verlag, 2007: 742–756.

Dahlhaus, Carl. *Klassische und romantische Musikästhetik*. Laaber: Laaber Verlag, 1988.

Dahlhaus, Carl. 'Purpurschimmer der Romantik; Die Idee eines musikalischen Dramas aus dem Geiste des symphonischen Stils.' *Europäische Romantik in der Musik. Band 2. Oper und symphonischer Stil 1800–1850*. Dahlhaus, Carl and Norbert Miller, eds. Stuttgart: J.B. Metzler Verlag, 2007: 280–294.

Dahlhaus, Carl. '"Wechsel der Töne"; Webers "Freischütz" und die Ästhetik des Charakteristischen.' *Europäische Romantik in der Musik. Band 2. Oper und symphonischer Stil 1800–1850*. Dahlhaus, Carl and Norbert Miller, eds. Stuttgart: J.B. Metzler Verlag, 2007: 481–488.

Daverio, John. *Nineteenth-Century Music and the German Romantic Ideology*. New York, NY: Schirmer Books, 1993.

Daverio, John J. '"Total Work of Art" or "Nameless Deeds of Music". Some Thoughts on German Romantic Opera.' *Opera Quarterly* 4/4 (1986–87): 61–74.

Dechant, Hermann. *E.T.A. Hoffmanns Oper Aurora*. (Regensburger Beiträge zur Musikgeschichte, Band 2). Regensburg: Gustav Bosse Verlag, 1975.

Dennis, David B. *Beethoven in German Politics 1870–1989*. New Haven: Yale University Press, 1996.

Dent, Edward. *The Rise of Romantic Opera*. Dean, Winton, ed. Cambridge: Cambridge University Press, 1976.

Dieckmann, Liselotte. 'Einleitung.' *Kritische Friedrich-Schlegel-Ausgabe; Band 33: Abt. 3, Editionen, Übersetzungen, Berichte. Sammlung von Memoiren und romantischen Dichtungen des Mittelalters aus altfranzösischen und deutschen Quellen*. Behler, Ernst, ed. Paderborn: Schöning Verlag, 1980: VII–XXIX.

Döhring, Sieghard (sic.). 'Meyerbeers Konzeption der historischen Oper und Wagners Musikdrama.' *Wagnerliteratur – Wagnerforschung; Bericht über das Wagner-Symposium München 1983*. Dalhaus, Carl and Egon Voss, eds. Mainz: Schott, 1983: 95–100.

Döhring, Sieghart and Sabine Henze-Döhring. *Oper und Musikdrama im 19. Jahrhundert* (Handbuch der musikalischen Gattungen, Band 13). Laaber: Laaber Verlag, 1997.

Edgcumbe, the Earl of Mount. *Musical Reminiscences, Containing an Account of the Italian Opera in England. Fourth Edition, Continued to the Present Time, and including the Festival in Westminster Abbey*. London: John Andrews, 1834.

Eggebrecht, Hans Heinrich. *Musik im Abendland; Prozesse und Stationen vom Mittelalter bis zur Gegenwart*. München: Piper Verlag GmbH, 2008 [1996].

Ehrismann, Otfrid. *Das Nibelungenlied*. München: C.H. Beck, 2005.

Eichner, Barbara. *History in Mighty Sounds. Musical Constructions of German National Identity 1848–1914*. Woodbridge: Boydell & Brewer Press, 2012.

Eke, Norbert Otto. '"Besser als die Engländer haben die Deutschen den Shakspear begriffen". Shakespeare im Vormärz und Richard Wagners Oper "Das Liebesverbot oder die Novize von Palermo" (1836).' *Das ungeliebte Frühwerk. Richard Wagners Oper "Das Liebesverbot"* (Wagner in der Diskussion, Band 12). Lütteken, Laurenz, ed. Würzburg: Königshausen & Neumann, 2014: 45–72.

Ellis, Katharine. *Music Criticism in Nineteenth-Century France. La Revue et Gazette musicale de Paris*, 1834–1880. Cambridge: Cambridge University Press, 1995.

Everist, Mark. *Music Drama at the Paris Odéon, 1824–1828*. Berkeley: University of California Press, 2002.

Everist, Mark. 'The Music of Power; Parisian Opera and the Politics of Genre, 1806–1864.' *Journal of the American Musicological Society* 67/3 (2014): 685–734.

Everist, Mark. 'The Name of the Rose; Meyerbeer's *opéra comique, Robert le Diable*.' *Revue de Musicologie* 80/2 (1994): 221–250.

Everist, Mark. 'Theatres of Litigation; Stage Music at the Théâtre de la Renaissance, 1838–1840.' *Cambridge Opera Journal* 16/2 (2004): 133–161.

Everist, Mark. 'Translating Weber's *Euryanthe*; German Romanticism at the Dawn of French Grand Opéra.' *Revue de Musicologie* 87/1 (2001): 67–104.

Fauser, Annegret. 'Phantasmagorie im deutschen Wald? Zur "Freischütz"-Rezeption in London und Paris 1824.' *Deutsche Meister – böse Geister? Nationale Selbstfindung in der Musik*. Dannuser, Hermann and Herfried Münkler, eds. Schliengen: Edition Argus, 2001: 245–273.

Fellinger, Imogen. 'Zeitschriften.' *Musik in Geschichte und Gegenwart, Band 14*. Blume, Friedrich, ed. Kassel: Bärenreiter, 1962: 1041–1188.

Fenner, Theodore. *Music in London; Views of the Press 1785–1830*. Carbondale: Southern Illinois University Press, 1994.

Fetzer, John. 'Ritter Gluck's Unglück; The Crisis of Creativity in the Age of the Epigone.' *The German Quarterly* 44/3 (1971): 317–330.

Finscher, Ludwig. 'Weber's *Freischütz*; Conceptions and Misconceptions.' *Proceedings of the Royal Musical Association* 110 (1983/1984): 79–90.

Finscher, Ludwig. 'Wagner der Opernkomponist; Von den *Feen* zum *Rienzi*.' *Richard Wagner; Von der Oper zum Musikdrama*. ed. Kunze, Stefan. Bern: Francke Verlag, 1978: 25–46.

Flaherty, Gloria. *Opera in the Development of German Critical Thought*. Princeton: Princeton University Press, 1978.

Forkel, Johann Nikolaus. *Über Johann Seb. Bachs Leben, Kunst und Kunstwerke*. Basel: Haldimann Verlag, 1900 [orig. 1802].

Frank, Peter and Karl Pörnbacher, eds. *Franz Grillparzer; Sämtliche Werke; Ausgewählte Briefe, Gespräche, Berichte. Dritter Band. Satiren – Fabeln und Parabeln – Erzählungen und Prosafragmente – Studien und Aufsätze*. München: Carl Hanser, 1964.

Frayling, Christopher. *Vampyres; Lord Byron to Count Dracula*. London: Faber and Faber, 1991.

Freyberger, Regina. 'Esaias Tegnérs "Frithiof"; Nordischer Held in germanischem Reich.' *Eddische Götter und Helden. Milieus und Medien ihrer Rezeption*. Schulz, Katja, ed. Heidelberg: Universitätsverlag Winter, 2011: 31–59.

Frolova-Walker, Marina. 'On *Ruslan* and Russianness.' *Cambridge Opera Journal* 9/1 (1997): 21–45.

Fulcher, Jane F., ed. *Oxford Handbook of the New Cultural History of Music*. Oxford: Oxford University Press, 2011.

Fuhrmann, Christine. 'Continental Opera Englished, English Opera Continentalized: *Der Freischütz* in London, 1824.' *Nineteenth-Century Music Review* 1/1 (2004): 115–142.

Garlington, Aubrey S. Jr. 'August Wilhelm von Schlegel and the German Romantic Opera.' *Journal of the Musicological Society* 30/3 (1977A): 500–506.

Garlington, Aubrey S. Jr. 'E.T.A. Hoffmann's "'Der Dichter und der Komponist" and the Creation of German Romantic Opera.' *The Musical Quarterly* 65/1(1979): 22–47.

Garlington, Aubrey S. Jr. 'German Romantic Opera and the Problem of Origins.' *The Musical Quarterly* 63/2 (1977B): 247–263.

Geary, Jason. *The Politics of Appropriation; German Romantic Music and the Ancient Greek Legacy*. Oxford: Oxford University Press, 2014.

Gerhard, Anselm. *Die Verstädterung der Oper; Paris und das Musiktheater des 19. Jahrhundert*. Metzler: Stuttgart, 1992.

Geyer-Kiefl, Helen. *Die heroisch-komische Oper* (Würzburger Musikhistorische Beiträge, Band 9). Tutzing: Hans Schneider, 1987.

Goehr, Lydia. 'In the Shadow of the Canon.' *The Musical Quarterly* 86/2 (2002): 307–328.

Goehr, Lydia. *The Imaginary Museum of Musical Works; An Essay in the Philosophy of Music*. Oxford: Clarendon Press, 1992.

Goslich, Siegfried. *Beiträge zur Geschichter der deutschen romantischen Oper; Zwischen Spohrs "Faust" und Wagners "Lohengrin"*. Leipzig: F. Kistner und C.F.W. Siegel, 1937.

Goslich, Siegfried. *Die deutsche romantische Oper*. Tutzing: Schneider, 1975.

Gossett, Philip. 'Carl Dahlhaus and the Ideal Type'. *19th-Century Music* 13/1 (1989): 49–56.

Gossett, Philip. 'Giuseppe Verdi and the Italian Risorgimento.' *Proceedings of the American Philosophical Society* 156/3 (2012): 271–282.

Gramit, David. *Cultivating Music; The Aspirations, Interests, and Limits of German Musical Culture, 1770–1848*. Berkeley: University of California Press, 2002.

Gregor-Dellin, Martin. *Richard Wagner; Sein Leben, sein Werk, sein Jahrhundert*. München: Piper Verlag, 1983.

Grey, Thomas S. 'Richard's Apprenticeship: The Early Operas (1833–1840).' *The Cambridge Companion to Wagner*. Grey, Thomas S., ed. Cambridge: Cambridge University Press, 2008: 18–46.

Groote, Inga Mai. '"weder italienisch, französisch – noch aber auch deutsch"; "Das Liebesverbot" zwischen den Gattungstraditionen.' *Das ungeliebte Frühwerk; Richard Wagners Oper "Das Liebesverbot"*. Lütteken, Laurenz, ed. Würzburg: Königshausen & Neumann, 2014: 97–114.

Gruber, Gerold W. *Der Niedergang des Kastratentums; Eine Untersuchung zur bürgerlichen Kritik an der höfischen Musikkultur im 18. Jahrhundert, aufgezeigt am Beispiel der Kritik am Kastratentum – mit einem Versuch einer objektiven Klassifikation der Kastratenstimme*. Wien: Universität Wien, 1982.

Gubkina, Natalia. 'Deutsches Musiktheater in St. Petersburg am Anfang des 19. Jahrhunderts.' *Musikgeschichte in Mittel- und Osteuropa* (Mitteilungen der internationalen Arbeitsgemeinschaft an der Technischen Universität Chemnitz, Heft 4). Chemnitz: Gudrun Schröder Verlag, 1999: 95–116.

Hänggi, Christoph E. *G.L.P. Sievers (1775–1830) und seine Schriften; Eine Geschichte der romantischen Musikästhetik*. Frankfurt am Main: Peter Lang, 1993.

Hardtwig, Wolfgang. *Nationalismus und Bürgerkultur in Deutschland, 1500–1914*. Göttingen: Vandenhoeck & Ruprecht, 1994.

Hauschild, Jan-Christoph and Michael Werner. *"Der Zweck des Lebens ist das Leben selbst"; Heinrich Heine; Eine Biographie*. Köln: Kiepenheuer & Witsch, 1997.

Heidlberger, Frank. *Carl Maria von Weber und Hector Berlioz; Studien zur französischen Weber-Rezeption*. Tutzing: Hans Schneider, 1994.

Hein, Stefanie. *Richard Wagners Kunstprogramm im nationalkulturellen Kontext; Ein Beitrag zur Kulturgeschichte des 19. Jahrhundert*. Würzburg: Königshausen & Neumann, 2006.

Heine, Heinrich. *Der Doktor Faust; Ein Tanzpoem; Nebst kuriosen Berichten über Teufeln, Hexen und Dichtkunst*. Hamburg: Hoffmann und Campe, 1851.

Heine, Heinrich. *Sämmtliche Werke IV; Novellistische Fragmente*. Hamburg: Hoffmann & Campe, 1867.

Heinel, Beate. *Die Zauberoper; Studien zu ihrer Entwicklungsgeschichte anhand ausgewählter Beispiele von den Anfängen bis zum Beginn des 19. Jahrhunderts*. Frankfurt am Main: Peter Lang, 1994.

Heinemann, Gerd. 'Horn, Franz'. *Neue Deutsche Biographie* 9 (1972): 627.

Helmers, Rutger. *Not Russian Enough; Nationalism and Cosmopolitanism in Nineteenth-Century Russian Opera*. Rochester: University of Rochester Press, 2014.

Henderson, Donald G. *The Freischütz Phenomenon; Opera as Cultural Mirror*. Bloomington, IN: Xlibris, 2011.

Hentschel, Frank. *Bürgerliche Ideologie und Musik; Politik der Musikgeschichtsschreibung in Deutschland. 1776–1871*. Frankfurt: Campus Verlag, 2006.

Henze-Döhring, Sabine and Sieghart Döhring. *Giacomo Meyerbeer. Der Meister der Grand Opéra.* München: C.H. Beck, 2013.

Herder, Johann Gottfried. *Kalligone.* Heinz Begenau, ed. Weimar: Arion Verlag, 1955.

Herder, Emil Gottfried von, ed. *Johann Gottfried von Herder's Lebensbild; Sein chronologisch geordneter Briefwechsel, verbunden mit den hierhergehörigen Mittheilungen aus seinem ungedruckten Nachlasse, und mit den nöthigen Belegen aus seinen und seiner Zeitgenossen Schriften; Zweiter Band.* Erlangen: Verlag von Theodor Bläsing, 1846.

Hirsch, Marjorie Wing. *Romantic Lieder and the Search for a Lost Paradise.* Cambridge: Cambridge University Press, 2007.

Hobsbawm, Eric and Terence O. Ranger, eds. *The Invention of Tradition.* Cambridge: Cambridge University Press, 1983.

Hoffmann, E.T.A. *Tagebücher; Nach der Ausgabe Hans von Müllers mit Erläuterungen herausgegeben.* ed. Friedrich Schnapp. München: Winkler-Verlag, 1971.

Hohendahl, Peter Uwe. *Building a National Literature; The Case of Germany, 1830–1870* (translation by Renate Baron Franciscono, initially published as *Literarische Kultur im Zeitalter des Liberalismus, 1830–1870*). Ithaca: Cornell University Press, 1989 [1985].

Holtmeier, Ludwig. 'Von den *Feen* zum *Liebesverbot*; Zur Geschichte eines Dilettanten.' *Richard Wagner und seine Zeit.* Kiem, Eckehard and Ludwig Holtmeier, eds. Laaber: Laaber Verlag, 2003: 33–73.

Höyng, Peter. *Die Sterne, die Zensur und das Vaterland. Geschichte und Theater im späten 18. Jahrhundert.* Köln: Böhlau Verlag, 2003.

Hroch, Miroslav. *Die Vorkämpfer der nationalen Bewegung bei den kleinen Völkern Europas; Eine vergleichende Analyse zur gesellschaftlichen Schichtung der patriotischen Gruppen.* Praha: Universita Karlova, 1968.

Huck, Oliver. *Von der Silvana zum Freischütz; Die Konzertarien, die Einlagen zu Opern und die Schauspielmusik Carl Maria von Webers.* Mainz: Schott Musik International, 1999.

Hughes, Meirion and Robert Stradling. *The English Musical Renaissance; Constructing a National Music, 1840–1940* (2nd edition). Manchester: Manchester University Press, 2001.

Infiesta, Maria. *El Wagnerisme a Catalunya* (Terra Nostra 42). Barcelona: Infiesta Editor, 2001.

Istel, Edgar, ed. *E.T.A. Hoffmanns musikalische Schriften.* Stuttgart: Greiner und Pfeiffer Verlag, 1907.

Jacobs, Rüdiger. 'Die Bedeutung nordischer Mythen in Richard Wagners Dramenkonzept am Beispiel der *Ring*-Konzeption.' *Sang an Aegir; Nordische Mythen um 1900.* Schulz, Katja und Florian Heesch, eds. Heidelberg: Universitätsverlag Winter, 2009: 179–211.

Jacobs, Robert L. and Geoffrey Skelton, eds. *Wagner Writes From Paris; Stories, Essays and Articles by the Young Composer.* London: George Allen & Unwin Ltd, 1973.

Janz, Tobias. *Klangdramaturgie; Studien zur theatralen Orchesterkomposition in Wagners Ring des Nibelungen* (Wagner in der Diskussion, Band 2). Würzburg: Königshausen & Neumann, 2006.

Janz, Tobias, ed. *Wagners Siegfried und die (post-)heroische Moderne* (Wagner in der Diskussion, Band 5). Würzburg: Königshausen & Neumann, 2011.

Josserand, Frank B. *Richard Wagner; Patriot and politician.* Washington D.C.: University Press of America, 1981.

Kaiser, Georg, ed. *Sämtliche Schriften von Carl Maria von Weber.* Berlin: Schuster und & Loeffler, 1908.

Kanz, Roland. *Ästhetik des Charakteristischen; Quellentexte zu Kunstkritik und Streitkultur in Klassik und Romantik.* Bonn: Bonn University Press, 2008.

Kaul, Camilla G. *Friedrich Barbarossa im Kyffhäuser; Bilder eines nationalen Mythos im 19. Jahrhundert.* Köln: Böhlau Verlag, 2007.

Kerman, Joseph. 'How We Got into Analysis, and How to Get Out.' *Critical Inquiry* 7/2 (1980): 311–331.

Kienzle, Ulrike. *Daß wissend würde die Welt; Religion und Philosophie in Richard Wagners Musikdramen* (Wagner in der Diskussion, Band 1). Würzburg: Königshausen & Neumann, 2005.

Kirby, Percival M. 'Weber's Operas in London: 1824–1826.' *The Musical Quarterly* 32/3 (1946): 333–353.

Kirchmeyer, Helmut. *Situationsgeschichte der Musikkritik und des musikalischen Pressewesens in Deutschland IV: 1; Das zeitgenössische Wagner-Bild; Wagner in Dresden.* Regensburg: Gustav Bosse Verlag, 1972.

Kirchmeyer, Helmut. *Situationsgeschichte der Musikkritik und des musikalischen Pressewesens in Deutschland IV: 2; Das zeitgenössische Wagner-Bild; Dokumente 1842–1845.* Regensburg: Gustav Bosse Verlag, 1967.

Kirchmeyer, Helmut. *Situationsgeschichte der Musikkritik und des musikalischen Pressewesens in Deutschland IV: 3; Das zeitgenössische Wagner-Bild; Dokumente 1846–1850.* Regensburg: Gustav Bosse Verlag, 1968.

Kitcher, Philip and Richard Schacht. *Finding an Ending; Reflections on Wagner's Ring.* New York, NY: Oxford University Press USA, 2005.

Kleßman, Eckart. 'Einleitung.' *Undinenzauber; Von Nixen, Nymphen und anderen Wasserfrauen.* Max, Frank Rainer, ed. Stuttgart: Phillip Reclam Verlag, 2003 [1991]: 9–18.

Kohlhase, Thomas. '"Undine" von Fouqué und Hoffmann; Bemerkungen zur Partitur und ihrer Edition.' *Der Text im musikalischen Werk; Editionsprobleme aus musikwissenschaftlicher und literaturwissenschaftlicher Sicht* (Beihefte zur Zeitschrift für

Deutsche Philologie 8). Dürr, Walther a.o., eds. Berlin: Erich Schmidt Verlag, 1998: 247–256.

Konold, Wulf. 'Nationale Bewegungen und Nationalopern im 19. Jahrhundert; Versuch einer Definition, was eine Nationaloper ausmacht.' *Der schöne Abglanz; Stationen der Operngeschichte*. Hamburg: Dietrich Reimer Verlag, 1992: 111–128.

Konrad, Ulrich. 'Robert Schumann und Richard Wagner. Studien und Dokumente.' *Augsburger Jahrbuch für Musikwissenschaft 1987*. Krautwurst, Franz, ed. Tutzing: Hans Schneider, 1987: 211–320.

Kooten, Kasper van. 'Wie Hell grüßt uns heute der Herr! Hexatonic Poles and Mystical Transformation in the Act I Grail Scene of Richard Wagner's *Parsifal*.' *Dutch Journal of Music Theory* 18/1 (2013): 1–12.

Kreim, Isabella. *Richard Wagners "Lohengrin" auf der deutschen Bühne und in der Kritik; Studien zur Aufführungs- und Rezeptionsgeschichte*. München: Ludwig-Maximilians-Universität, 1983.

Kremtz, Eberhard. 'Das "deutsche Departement" des Dresdner Hoftheaters.' *Die Dresdener Oper im 19. Jahrhundert*. Heinemann, Michael and Hans John, eds. Laaber: Laaber Verlag, 1995A: 107–112.

Kremtz, Eberhard. 'Weber – Hoffmann – Spontini: Deutsche Oper – Französische Oper.' *Die Dresdener Oper im 19. Jahrhundert*. Heinemann, Michael and Hans John, eds. Laaber: Laaber Verlag, 1995B: 113–118.

Kretschmar, Hermann. *Geschichte der Oper* (Kleine Handbücher der Musikgeschichte nach Gattungen, Band vi). Leipzig: Breitkopf & Härtel, 1919.

Kron, Wolfgang. *Die angeblichen Freischütz-Kritiken E.T.A. Hoffmanns; Eine Untersuchung*. München: Hueber Verlag, 1957.

Kröplin, Eckart. 'Weber und Wagner. Der Vorgang einer Theatralisierung.' *Carl Maria von Weber und der Gedanke einer Nationaloper*. Stephan, Gunther and Hans John, eds. Dresden: Hochschule für Musik Carl Maria von Weber Dresden, 1986: 336–344.

Kruse, Joseph A. *Verboten! Das Junge Deutschland 1835; Literatur und Zensur im Vormärz*. Düsseldorf: Droste Verlag, 1985.

Lacombe, Hervé. *Les voies de l'opéra français aux XIXe siècle*. Paris: Fayard, 1997.

Lacombe, Hervé. *The Keys to French Opera in the Nineteenth Century*. Berkeley: University of California Press, 2001.

Lajosi, Krisztina. *Opera and Nation-Building in Nineteenth-Century Europe; The (Re) Sounding Voice of Nationalism*. Amsterdam: University of Amsterdam, unpublished dissertation, 2008.

Leerssen, Joep. 'Imagology: History and Method.' *Imagology: The Cultural Construction and Literary Representation of National Characters – A Critical Survey* (Studia Imagologica 13). Beller, Manfred and Joep Leerssen, eds. Amsterdam: Rodopi, 2007: 17–32.

Leerssen, Joep. 'From Bökendorf to Berlin; Private Careers, Public Sphere, and How the Past Changed in Jacob Grimm's Lifetime.' *Free Acces to the Past; Romanticism,*

Cultural Heritage and the Nation. Jensen, Lotte Eilskov, Joseph Theodoor Leerssen and Marita Matthijsen, eds. Brill: Leiden, 2010: 55–70.

Leerssen, Joep. 'Het *Nibelungenlied*, de *Ring* en de Duitse identiteit.' *Conflict en Compassie; 200 jaar Richard Wagner*. Westbroek, Philip en Rutger Helmers, eds. Amsterdam: Nationale Opera en Ballet, 2014A: 125–132.

Leerssen, Joep. *When Was Romantic Nationalism? The Onset, The Long Tail, The Banal*. Antwerpen: NISE, 2014B.

Leerssen, Joep. *National Thought in Europe; A Cultural History*. Amsterdam: Amsterdam University Press, 2006.

Leerssen, Joep. 'Romanticism, Music, Nationalism.' *Nations and Nationalism* 20/4 (2014C): 606–627.

Leerssen, Joep. 'The Cultivation of Culture; Towards a Definition of Romantic Nationalism in Europe.' Amsterdam: Working Papers European Studies 2.

Legband, Paul, ed. *Christiann Heinrich Schmids Chronologie des deutschen Theaters; Neu herausgegeben von Paul Legband*. Berlin: Verlag der Gesellschaft für Theatergeschichte, 1902 [1775].

Lesure, François, ed. *La musique à Paris en 1830–1831*. Paris: Bibliothéque Nationale, 1983.

Levin, David J. 'Reading Beckmesser Reading: Antisemitism and Esthetic Practice in *Die Meistersinger von Nürnberg*.' *New German Critique* 69 (1996): 127–146.

Lindenberger, Herbert. *Opera; The Extravagant Art*. Ithaca, NY: Cornell University Press, 1984.

Lippe, Marcus Chr, ed. *Oper im Aufbruch; Gattungskonzepte des deutschsprachigen Musiktheaters um 1800*. Köln: Gustav Bosse Verlag, 2007.

Lippmann, Friedrich. '*Die Feen* und *Das Liebesverbot*, oder die Wagnerisierung verschiedener Vorbilder.' *Wagnerliteratur – Wagnerforschung*. Dahlhaus, Carl and Egon Voss, eds. Mainz: Schott, 1983: 14–46.

Lomtev, Denis. *Deutsches Musiktheater in Russland*. Bonn: Klaus-Peter Koch, 2003.

Lovejoy, Arthur Oncken. *Essays in the History of Ideas*. Baltimore: The John Hopkins Press, 1948.

Lühning, Helga. 'Spuren des *Fidelio* in Wagners Opern.' *Richard Wagner und seine Lehrmeister*. Mahling, Christoph-Helmut and Kristina Pfarr, eds. Mainz: Are Musik Verlags GmbH, 1999: 81–93.

Macdonald, Hugh. 'Robert le Diable.' *Music in Paris in the Eighteen-Thirties/La Musique à Paris dans les années mil huit cent trente*. Bloom, Peter, ed. Stuyvesant, NY: Pendragon Press, 1987: 457–469.

Maehder, Jürgen. 'Klangpoesie und Fratze. Zur Dramaturgie der Klangfarben in den Opern Carl Maria v. Webers.' *Deutsche Oper Berlin, Beiträge zum Musiktheater* VII. Berlin: Kupijai & Prochnow, 1988: 163–194.

Maehder, Jürgen. 'Verfremdete Instrumentation – Ein Versuch über beschädigten Schönklang.' *Schweizer Beiträge zur Musikwissenschaft* 4 (1980): 103–150.

Maes, Francis. *A History of Russian Music; From Kamarinskaya to Babi Yar.* Berkeley: University of California Press, 2002.

Mähl, Hans-Joachim, ed. *Novalis; Werke, Tagebücher und Briefe Friedrich von Hardenbergs; Band 2.* München: Carl Hanser Verlag, 1978.

Manning, Elizabeth. *The Nationalsingspiel in Vienna from 1778 to 1785.* Durham: Durham University (unpublished dissertation): 1975.

Marchenkov, Vladimir L. *The Orpheus Myth and the Powers of Music.* Pennington: Pendragon Press, 2009.

Markx, Francien. *E.T.A. Hoffmann, Cosmopolitanism, and the Struggle for German Opera* [Internationale Forschungen zur allgemeinen und vergleichenden Literaturwissenschaft 192]. Leiden: Brill Rodopi, 2016.

Massmann, Klaus. *Die Rezeption der historischen Romane Sir Walter Scotts in Frankreich (1816–1832).* Heidelberg: Carl Winter Universitätsverlag, 1972.

McVeigh, Simon. 'The Society of British Musicians (1834–1865) and the Campaign for Native Talent.' *Music and British Culture 1785–1914; Essays in Honour of Cyril Ehrlich.* Bashford, Christina and Leanne Langley, eds. Oxford: Oxford University Press, 2000: 145–168.

Meinecke, Friedrich. *Weltbürgertum und Nationalstaat; Studien zur Genesis des deutschen Nationalstaates.* München: Oldenbourg, 1908.

Mel'nikova, Svetlana I. 'Das deutsche Theater in Sankt Petersburg am Anfang des 19. Jahrhunderts.' *Jahrbücher für Geschichte Osteuropas* 44/4 (1996): 523–536.

Mertens, Volker. 'Richard Wagner und das Mittelalter.' *Wagner Handbuch.* Müller, Ullrich and Peter Wapnewski, eds. Stuttgart: Kröner, 1986: 19–59.

Meyer, Stephen C. *Carl Maria von Weber and the Search for a German Opera.* Bloomington: Indiana University Press, 2003.

Miller, Norbert. 'Carl Maria von Weber in Berlin II; Die drei romantischen Opern.' *Europaïsche Romantik in der Musik; Band 2; Oper und symphonischer Stil 1800–1850.* Dahlhaus, Carl and Norbert Miller, eds. Stuttgart: J.B. Metzler Verlag, 2007: 489–579.

Miller, Norbert. 'E.T.A. Hoffmann und die Musik I; Die Lehrjahre des reisenden Enthusiasten'. *Europaïsche Romantik in der Musik; Band 2; Oper und symphonischer Stil 1800–1850.* Dahlhaus, Carl and Norbert Miller, eds. Stuttgart: J.B. Metzler Verlag, 2007: 55–150.

Miller, Norbert. 'E.T.A. Hoffmann und die Musik II; Zum Verhältnis von Oper und Instrumentalkomposition.' *Europaïsche Romantik in der Musik; Band 2; Oper und symphonischer Stil 1800–1850.* Dahlhaus, Carl and Norbert Miller, eds. Stuttgart: J.B. Metzler Verlag, 2007: 151–279.

Miller, Norbert. 'Für und wider die Wolfsschlucht; E.T.A. Hoffmann, die "Freischütz"-Premiere und das romantische Singspiel.' Herttrich, Ernst and Hans Schneider, eds. *Festschrift Rudolf Elvers zum 60. Geburtstag.* Tutzing: Hans Schneider, 1985: 369–382.

Miller, Norbert. 'Hoffmann und Spontini; Vorüberlegungen zu einer Ästhetik der romantischen opera seria.' *Studien zur Musikgeschichte Berlins im frühen 19. Jahrhundert*. Dahlhaus, Carl, ed. Regensburg: Gustav Bosse Verlag, 1980: 451–468.

Miller, Norbert. 'Topographie der Tonkunst; Carl Maria von Weber in Berlin I.' *Europäische Romantik in der Musik; Band 2; Oper und symphonischer Stil 1800–1850*. Dahlhaus, Carl and Norbert Miller, eds. Stuttgart: J.B. Metzler Verlag, 2007d: 295–386.

Miller, Norbert. 'Zwischen Hofoper und Nationaltheater; Die Berliner Oper unter Friedrich Wilhelm III. und im Schatten seines "General-Musik-Directors" Gaspare Spontini.' *Apollini et Musis; 250 Jahre Opernhaus Unter den Linden*. Quander, Georg, ed. Frankfurt am Main: Propyläen, 1992: 47–91.

Millington, Barry. 'Nuremberg Trial; Is there Anti-Semitism in *Die Meistersinger?*' *Cambridge Opera Journal* 3/3 (1991): 247–260.

Mongrédien, Jean. '*Les Mystères d'Isis* (1801) and Reflections on Mozart from the Parisian Press at the beginning of the Nineteenth Century.' *Music in the Classic Period; Essays in Honor of Barry S. Brook*. ed. Atlas, Allan W. New York: Pendragon Press, 1985: 195–211.

Montaclair, Florent. *Le vampire dans la littérature et au théâtre; du mythe oriental au motif romantique*. Besançon: Presse du Centre Unesco de Besançon, 1998.

Morgenstern, Anja and Uta Wald, eds. *Felix Mendelssohn-Bartholdy, Sämtliche Briefe Band 2: Juli 1830 bis Juli 1832*. Kassel: Bärenreiter, 2009.

Morrow, Mary Sue. *German Music Criticism in the Late Eighteenth Century; Aesthetic Issues in Instrumental Music*. Cambridge: Cambridge University Press, 1997.

Müller, Hans and Friedrich Schnapp, eds. *E.T.A. Hoffmann Briefwechsel Erster Band; Von Königsberg bis Leipzig 1794–1814*. München: Winkler-Verlag, 1967.

Müller, Johann Baptist, ed. *Die Deutschen und Luther; Texte zur Geschichte und Wirkung*. Stuttgart: Reclam, 1983.

Müller, Marius Gregor. *Untersuchungen zu Carl Maria von Webers frühen Bühnenwerken*. Mainz: unpublished dissertation, 1998.

Müller-Dyes, Klaus. *Der Schauerroman und Ludwig Tieck; Über die dichterische Fiktion im "Blonden Eckbert" und "Runenberg"; Ein Beitrag zur Wechselbeziehung von Trivialliteratur und Dichtung*. Göttingen: Phil. Diss, 1965.

Münch, Paul. '"Italiener" – Volkscharakter und Rassetyp.' *Das Bild der italienischen Oper in Deutschland* (Forum Musiktheater, Band 1). Brandenburg, Daniel and Sebastian Werr, eds. Münster: LIT Verlag, 2004: 21–47.

Mungen, Anno. 'Morlacchi, Weber und die Dresdner Oper.' *Die Dresdener Oper im 19. Jahrhundert*. Heinemann, Michael and Hans John, eds. Laaber: Laaber Verlag, 1995: 85–105.

Mungen, Anno. *Musiktheater als Historienbild; Gaspare Spontinis Agnes von Hohenstaufen als Beitrag zur deutschen Oper* (Mainzer Studien zur Musikwissenschaft, Band 38). Tutzing: Hans Schneider Verlag, 1997.

Mungen, Anno. 'Wagner, Spontini und die Grand Opéra.' *Richard Wagner und seine Lehrmeister.* Mahling, Christoph-Helmut and Kristina Pfarr, eds. Mainz: Are Musik Verlags GmbH, 1999: 129–143.

Münkler, Herfried. *Die Deutschen und ihre Mythen.* Reinbek bei Hamburg: Rohwolt Taschenbuch Verlag: 2009.

Nabokov, Vladimir, transl. *Alexander Pushkin; Eugene Onegin; Volume II, Commentary and Index.* Princeton: Princeton University Press, 1975.

Naroditskaya, Inna. 'Russian *Rusalkas* and Nationalism; Water, Power, and Women.' *Music of the Sirens.* Austern, Linda Phyllis and Inna Naroditskaya, eds. Indiana: Indiana University Press, 2006: 216–249.

Neubauer, John. *The Emancipation of Music from Language; Departure from Mimesis in Eighteenth-Century Aesthetics.* New Haven, Conn.: Yale University Press, 1986.

Neubauer, John. *The Persistence of Voice; Instrumental Music and Romantic Orality.* Leiden: Brill, 2017.

Neumann, Alfred R. *The Evolution of the Concept of the Gesamtkunstwerk.* Unpublished dissertation, University of Michigan, 1951.

Nietzsche, Friedrich. *Der Fall Wagner; Götzen-Dämmerung; Nietzsche Contra Wagner.* Pütz, Peter, ed. München: Goldmann Verlag, 1988.

Nietzsche, Friedrich. *Werke; Kritische Gesamtausgabe; Band VIII/3; Nachgelassene Fragmente, Anfang 1888 bis Anfang Januar 1889.* Colli, Giorgio and Mazzino Montinari, eds. Berlin: Walter de Gruyter, 1972.

Overhoff, Kurt. *Die Musikdramen Richard Wagners; Eine thematisch-musikalische Interpretation.* Salzburg: Pustet, 1967.

Palmer, A. Dean. *Heinrich August Marschner 1795–1861; His Life and Stage Works.* Ann Arbor, MI: UMI Research Press, 1980.

Paltridge, Brian. *Discourse Analysis; An Introduction.* London: Continuum, 2006.

Pederson, Sanna. 'A.B. Marx, Berlin Concert Life, and German National Identity.' *19th-Century Music* 18/2 (1994): 87–107.

Pederson, Sanna. *Enlightened and Romantic German Music Criticism: 1800–1850.* Ann Arbor, MI: UMI, 1995.

Pietschmann, Klaus. 'Die deutsche komische Oper um 1830 im Spannungsfeld zwischen Tradition, nationalen Opernschulen und bürgerlichem Musiktheaterkonsum.' *Das ungeliebte Frühwerk; Richard Wagners Oper "Das Liebesverbot".* Lütteken, Laurenz, ed. Würzburg: Königshausen & Neumann, 2014: 9–25.

Planché, James Robinson. *Reflections and Recollections; A Professional Autobiography.* London: Sampson Low, Marston & Company, 1872.

Quantz, Johann Joachim. *Versuch einer Anweisung die Flute traversiere zu spielen; mit verschiedenen, zur Beförderung des guten Geschmackes in der praktischen Musik dienlichen Anmerkungen begleitet, und mit Exempeln erläutert.* Berlin: Johann Friedrich Voss, 1752.

Radow-Edling, Susanna. *Slavophile Thought and the Politics of Cultural Nationalism.* New York: State University of New York: 2006.

Reiber, Joachim. *Bewahrung und Bewährung; Das Libretto zu Carl Maria von Webers "Freischütz" im literarischen Horizont seiner Zeit.* München: W. Ludwig Verlag, 1990.

Renan, Ernest. *Qu'est-ce qu'une nation? et autres essais politiques.* Roman, Joël, ed. Paris: Presse Pockets/Agora, 1992.

Reynolds, David, ed. *Weber in London 1826; Selections from Weber's Letters to His Wife and from the Writings of His Contemporaries London in 1826.* London: Oswald Wolff Limited, 1976.

Ridley, Hugh. *Wagner and the Novel; Wagner's Operas and the European Realist Novel: An Exploration of Genre* (Internationale Forschungen zur allgemeinen und vergleichenden Literaturwissenschaft 156). Rodopi: Amsterdam, 2012.

Riethmüller, Albrecht. "'Is that not something for *Simplicissimus*?!' The belief in musical superiority.' *Music and German National Identity.* Applegate, Celia and Pamela Potter, eds. Chicago: Chicago University Press, 2002: 288–304.

Robbins Landon, H.C. *Joseph Haydn; Critical Edition of the Complete Symphonies.* Vienna: Universal Edition, 1963.

Rumph, Stephen. 'A Kingdom Not of This World; The Political Context of E.T.A. Hoffmann's Beethoven Criticism.' *19th-Century Music* 19/1 (1995): 50–67.

Safranski, Rüdiger. *Romantik; Eine deutsche Affäre.* Frankfurt am Main: Fischer Taschenbuch Verlag, 2009.

Salmen, Walter, ed. *Johann Friedrich Reichardt; Über die deutsche comische Oper.* München: Katzbichler Verlag, 1974 [1774].

Salmi, Hannu. *"Die Herrlichkeit des deutschen Namens..."; Die schriftstellerische und politische Tätigkeit Richard Wagners als Gestalter nationaler Identität während der staatlichen Vereinigung Deutschlands.* Turku: Annales Universitatis Turkuensis, 1993.

Salmi, Hannu. *Imagined Germany; Richard Wagner's National Utopia.* New York: Peter Lang, 1999.

Salmi, Hannu. *Wagner and Wagnerism in Nineteenth-Century Sweden, Finland, and the Baltic Provinces; Reception, Enthusiasm, Cult.* Rochester: University of Rochester Press, 2005.

Samson, Jim. *Music in the Balkans.* Leiden: Brill, 2013.

Schieder, Wolfgang. 'Die Wartburg als politisches Symbol der Deutschen.' *Deutsche Meister – böse Geister? Nationale Selbstfindung in der Musik.* Danuser, Hermann and Herfried Münkler, eds. Schliengen: Edition Argus, 2001: 15–35.

Schiedermair, Ludwig F. *Deutsche Oper in München; Eine 200jährige Geschichte.* München: Langen Müller, 1992.

Schiedermair, Ludwig. *Die deutsche Oper; Grundzüge ihres Werdens und Wesens.* Bonn: Ferd. Dümmlers Verlag, 1940.

Schläder, Jürgen. *Undine auf dem Musiktheater; Zur Entwicklungsgeschichte der deutschen Spieloper.* Bonn: Verlag für systematische Musikwissenschaft, 1979.

Schlechter, Armin. *Die Romantik in Heidelberg; Brentano, Arnim und Görres am Neckar.* Heidelberg: Universitätsverlag Winter, 2007.

Schlegel, August Wilhelm Schlegel. *Vorlesungen über dramatische Kunst und Literatur, Band I.* Giovanni Vittorio Amoretti, ed. Bonn: Kurt Schroeder Verlag, 1923A [1808–09].

Schlegel, August Wilhelm Schlegel. *Vorlesungen über dramatische Kunst und Literatur, Band II.* Giovanni Vittorio Amoretti, ed. Bonn: Kurt Schroeder Verlag, 1923B [1808–1809].

Schmid, Marion. 'À bas Wagner; The French Press Campaign against Wagner during World War 1.' *French Music, Culture, and National Identity, 1870–1939.* Kelly, Barbara L., ed. Rochester: University of Rochester Press: 77–91.

Schmidt, Erich and Bernhard Suphan, eds. *Xenien 1796; Nach den Handschriften des Goethe- und Schiller-Archivs.* Weimar: Hermann Böhlau, 1893.

Schnoor, Hans. *Weber auf dem Welttheater; Ein Freischützbuch.* Hamburg: Deutscher Literatur-Verlag Otto Melchert, 1985 [1942].

Schreiter, Solveig. *Friedrich Kind; Carl Maria von Weber; Der Freischütz; Kritische Textbuch-Edition.* München: Allitera Verlag, 2007.

Schrickx, Willem. 'A Shakespeare Season on the Continent. Brussels 1814 and Its Prelude in Amsterdam.' *Neophilologus* 61/4 (1977): 619–640.

Schubert, Giselher. 'Orchestertechnik und musikalische Dramaturgie. Zu den französischen und italienischen Einflüssen in Wagners "großer komischer Oper Das Liebesverbot".' *Das ungeliebte Frühwerk; Richard Wagners Oper "Das Liebesverbot".* Lütteken, Laurenz, ed. Würzburg: Königshausen & Neumann, 2014: 115–136.

Schulz, Gerhard. *Romantik; Geschichte und Begriff.* München: Verlag C.H. Beck, 1996.

Schulz, Katja. 'Einleitung' *"Sang an Aegir – Nordische Mythen um 1900."* Schulz, Katja and Florian Heesch, eds. Heidelberg: Universitätsverlag Winter, 2009: 8–11.

See, Klaus von. *Texte und Thesen; Streitfragen der deutschen und skandinavischen Geschichte.* Heidelberg: Universitätsverlag Winter, 2003.

Sengle, Friedrich. *Biedermeierzeit; Deutsche Literatur im Spannungsfeld zwischen Restauration und Revolution 1815–1848; Band I: Allgemeine Voraussetzungen, Richtungen, Darstellungsmittel.* Stuttgart: J.B. Metzler Verlag: 1971.

Servières, Georges. *Freischütz; Opéra romantique en 3 Actes; Musique de Carl-Maria von Weber: Traduction du poème de Friedrich Kind; Précédée d'un historique de l'oeuvre et de ses adaptations françaises, illustré de 2 portraits hors texte.* Paris: Librairie Fischbacher / Librairie H. Floury, 1913.

Simon, Dr. Heinrich, ed. *Gesammelte Schriften über Musik und Musiker von Robert Schumann; Vier Bände.* Leipzig: Philipp Reclam, 1888–1889.

Smith, Anthony D. *Nationalism and Modernism; A Critical Survey of Recent Theories of Nations and Nationalism.* London: Routledge, 1998.

Smith, Anthony D. *The Antiquity of Nations*. Cambridge: Polity Press, 2004.

Spencer, Stewart. 'Wagner's Middle Ages.' *The Wagner Compendium; A Guide to Wagner's Life and Music*. Millington, Barry, ed. London: Thames and Hudson, 1992: 164–167.

Spohr, Louis. *Lebenserinnerungen; Erstmals ungekürzt nach den autographen Aufzeichnungen herausgegeben von Folker Göthel*. Tutzing: Hans Schneider, 1968.

Spohr, Matthias. 'Medien, Melodramen und ihr Einfluß auf Richard Wagner.' *Richard Wagner und seine Lehrmeister*. Mahling, Christoph-Helmut and Kristina Pfarr, eds. Mainz: Are Musik Verlags GmbH, 1999: 49–80.

Sposato, Jeffrey S. *The Price of Assimilation; Felix Mendelssohn and the Nineteenth-Century Anti-Semitic Tradition*. Oxford: Oxford University Press, 2006.

Staël, Madame de. *De l'Allemagne*. Paris: Librairie Firmin Didot Frères, 1853 [orig. 1813].

Steblin, Rita. *A History of Key Characteristics in the Eighteenth and Early Nineteenth Centuries* (Second Edition). Rochester: University of Rochester Press, 2002 [1983].

Steinecke, Hartmut. 'Der Dichter und der Komponist. Zur Einführung: Fragen und Thesen.' *Der Text im musikalischen Werk; Editionsprobleme aus musikwissenschaftlicher und literaturwissenschaftlicher Sicht* (Beihefte zur Zeitschrift für Deutsche Philologie 8). Dürr, Walther a.o., eds. Berlin: Erich Schmidt Verlag, 1998: 235–239.

Stendhal. *Vies de Haydn, Mozart et Métastase*. Paris: L'Imprimerie de P. Didot, l'Aîné, 1817.

Streitenberg, Verena. *Der Einfluß Goethes und Calderóns auf E.T.A. Hoffmanns Opernwerk*. Berlin, Inauguraldissertation Freie Universität Berlin, 1989.

Taruskin, Richard. *Defining Russia Musically; Historical and Hermeneutical Essays*. Princeton: Princeton University Press, 1997.

Taruskin, Richard. 'Glinka's Ambiguous Legacy and the Birth Pangs of Russian Opera.' *19th-Century Music* 1/2 (1977): 142–162.

Taruskin, Richard. *Oxford History of Western Music, Volume 3; The Nineteenth Century*. Oxford: Oxford University Press, 2010.

Temperley, Nicholas. 'The English Romantic Opera.' *Victorian Studies* 9/3 (1966): 293–301.

Thaden, Edward C. 'The Beginnings of Romantic Nationalism in Russia.' *American Slavic and East European Review* 13/4 (1954): 500–521.

Ther, Philipp. *In der Mitte der Gesellschaft; Operntheater in Zentraleuropa; 1815–1914*. Wien: Oldenbourg, 2006.

Ther, Philipp. 'The Genre of National Opera in a European Comparative Perspective.' *Oxford Handbook of the New Cultural History of Music*. Fulcher, Jane F, ed. Oxford: Oxford University Press, 2011: 182–208.

Ther, Philipp. 'Wie national war die Oper? Die Opernkultur des 19. Jahrhunderts zwischen nationaler Ideologie und europäischer Praxis.' *Wie europäisch ist die Oper? Die Geschichte des Musiktheaters als Zugang zu einer kulturellen Topographie*

Europas. Stachel, Peter and Philipp Ther, eds. Wien: Oldenbourg Böhlau Verlag, 2009: 89–112.

Thiesse, Anne-Marie. *La création des identités nationales; Europe XVIIIe–XXe siècle.* Paris: Éditions du Seuil, 1999.

Tusa, Michael C. 'Cosmopolitanism and the national opera; Weber's *Der Freischütz.' Journal of Interdisciplinary History* 36/3 (2006): 483–506.

Tusa, Michael C. *Euryanthe and Carl Maria von Weber's Dramaturgy of German Opera.* Oxford: Clarendon Press, 1991.

Tyrrell, John. *Czech Opera.* Cambridge: Cambridge University Press, 1988.

Vanchena, Lorie A. 'The Rhine Crisis of 1840; *Rheinlieder,* German Nationalism, and the Masses.' *Searching for Common Ground; Diskurse zur deutschen Identität 1750–1871.* Vazsonyi, Nicholas, ed. Köln: Böhlau Verlag, 2000: 239–251.

Vazsonyi, Nicholas. *Richard Wagner; Self-Promotion and the Making of a Brand.* Cambridge: Cambridge University Press, 2010.

Veit, Joachim. *Der junge Carl Maria von Weber; Untersuchungen zum Einfluß Franz Danzis und Abbé Georg Joseph Voglers.* Mainz: Schott's Söhne, 1990.

Vischer, Friederich Theodor. *Kritische Gänge, Band II.* Tübingen: Ludwig Friedrich Fues, 1844.

Völker, Klaus. *Faust; Ein Deutscher Mann; Die Geburt einer Legende und ihr Fortleben in den Köpfen.* Berlin: Verlag Klaus Wagenbach, 1975.

Voss, Egon. *"Wagner und kein Ende"; Betrachtungen und Studien.* Zürich: Atlantis Musikbuch-Verlag, 1996.

Wackenroder, Wilhelm Heinrich and Ludwig Tieck. *Phantasien über die Kunst.* Stuttgart: Reclam Verlag, 2005 [1799].

Walker, Alan. *Franz Liszt; Volume II; The Weimar Years 1848–1861.* London: Faber and Faber, 1989.

Wagner, Wolfgang Michael. *Carl Maria von Weber und die deutsche Nationaloper.* Mainz: Schott's Söhne, 1994.

Walwei-Wiegelmann, Hedwig, ed. *Goethes Gedanken über Musik; Eine Sammlung aus seinen Werken, Briefen, Gesprächen und Tagebüchern.* Frankfurt am Main: Insel Verlag, 1985.

Warrack, John. *Carl Maria von Weber* (Second Edition). Cambridge: Cambridge University Press, 1976.

Warrack, John. 'Französische Elemente in Webers Opern.' *Carl Maria von Weber und die Gedanke der Nationaloper.* Günther, Stephan and Hans John, eds. Dresden: Hochschule für Musik "Carl Maria von Weber", 1986: 277–290.

Warrack, John. *German opera from the beginnings to Wagner.* Cambridge: Cambridge University press, 2001.

Warrack, John. 'German Operatic Ambitions at the Beginning of the Nineteenth Century.' *Proceedings of the Royal Musicological Association* 104 (1977–78): 79–88.

Watkins, Holly. *Metaphors of Depth in German Musical Thought; From E.T.A. Hoffmann to Arnold Schoenberg.* Cambridge: Cambridge University Press, 2011.

Weber, Max Maria von. *Carl Maria von Weber; Ein Lebensbild. Erster Band.* Leipzig: Ernst Keil, 1864.

Weber, William. 'Redefining the Status of Opera; London and Leipzig, 1800–1848.' *The Journal of Interdisciplinary History* 36/3 (2006): 507–532.

Weber, William. 'The History of Musical Canon.' *Rethinking Music.* Cook, Nicholas and Mark Everist, eds. Oxford: Oxford University Press, 1999: 336–355.

Weber, William. *The Rise of Musical Classics; A Study in Canon, Ritual and Ideology.* Oxford: Oxford University Press, 1992.

Weiner, Marc. *Richard Wagner and the Anti-Semitic Imagination.* Lincoln, NE: Nebraska University Press, 1995.

Weinland, Helmuth. 'Wagner und Meyerbeer.' *Richard Wagner; Zwischen Beethoven und Schönberg* (Musik-Konzepte 59). München: Edition Text & Kritik, 1988: 31–72.

Werner, Michael. 'Romantik – Ein typisch deutsches Phänomen?' *Wege in die Romantik; Vorträge des europäischen Musikfestes Stuttgart 1997.* Prinz, Ulrich, ed. Kassel: Bärenreiter, 1998: 186–199.

Werr, Sebastian and Daniel Brandenburg, eds. *Das Bild der italienischen Oper in Deutschland* (Forum Musiktheater, Band 1). Münster: LIT Verlag, 2004.

White, Pamela C. 'Two Vampires of 1828.' *Opera Quarterly* 5/1 (1987): 22–57.

Whittaker, John R. 'Translation and French Romanticism; Periphery or Core?' *French Studies Bulletin* 31/117 (2010): 79–81.

Williamson, George S. *The Longing for Myth in Germany.* Chicago: The University of Chicago Press, 2004.

Williamson, George S. 'What killed August von Kotzebue? The Temptations of Virtue and the Political Theology of German Nationalism, 1789–1819.' *The Journal of Modern History* 72/4 (2000): 890–943.

Wimmer, Andreas and Nina Glick Schiller. 'Methodological Nationalism and Beyond; Nation-State Building, Migration and the Social Sciences.' *Global Networks* 2/4 (2002): 301–334.

Wolzogen, Alfred Freiherr von. *Wilhelmine Schröder-Devrient; Ein Beitrag zur Geschichte des musikalischen Dramas.* Leipzig: Brockhaus, 1863.

Wunderlich, Werner. *Der Schatz des Drachentödters; Materialien zur Wirkungsgeschichte des Nibelungenliedes.* Stuttgart: Klet-Cotta, 1977.

Youens, Susan. *Schubert, Müller, and Die schöne Müllerin.* Cambridge: Cambridge University Press, 1997.

Zeidler, Jakob. 'Ein Zensurexemplar von Grillparzer's "König Ottokar's Glück und Ende".' *Ein Wiener Stammbuch, Karl Glossy zum fünfzigsten Geburtstage.* Wien: Konegen, 1898: 287–311.

Žižek, Slavoj. 'Foreword: Why is Wagner Worth Saving?' *In Search of Wagner.* Adorno, Theodor W. [transl. by Rodney Livingstone]. London: Verso, 2005: viii–xxvii.

Index